BLUE SKIES AND BOILER ROOMS

CHRISTOPHER ARMSTRONG

Blue Skies and Boiler Rooms: Buying and Selling Securities in Canada, 1870–1940

UNIVERSITY OF TORONTO PRESS
Toronto   Buffalo   London

© University of Toronto Press Incorporated 1997
Toronto   Buffalo   London
Printed in Canada

ISBN 0-8020-4184-1

Printed on acid-free paper

Canadian Cataloguing in Publication Data

Armstrong, Christopher, 1942–
Blue skies and boiler rooms : buying and selling
securities in Canada, 1870–1940

Includes bibliographical references and index.
ISBN 0-8020-4184-1

1. Securities – Canada – History.   2. Securities industry –
Canada – History.   I. Title.

HG5152.A75 1977   332.63'2'0971   C97-930957-3

This book has been published with the help of a grant from the Humanities and Social
Sciences Federation of Canada, using funds provided by the Social Sciences and
Humanities Research Council of Canada.

University of Toronto Press acknowledges the financial assistance to its publishing
program of the Canada Council for the Arts and the Ontario Arts Council.

For Charles H.W. Cane

Contents

Acknowledgments

Funding for this book came from both the Social Sciences and Humanities Research Council of Canada and the Aid to Scholarly Publications Programme of the Humanities and Social Sciences Federation of Canada. Such support is vital to research in disciplines like history, and I gratefully acknowledge this assistance. While they were members of the Graduate History Program at York University, Penny Bryden, David Kimmel, and Kenneth Sylvester did valuable research work by reading the financial press. Archivists and librarians at various repositories across the country proved helpful and accommodating in permitting access to the collections of which I made use, and at the end in finding and making available historical photographs to illustrate the book. Particular note should be made of the assistance from the Toronto Stock Exchange in allowing me to make use of their records and pictures, and of the fine work by John Dawson, the York University photographer, who clarified the images in a number of the photographs.

On a personal level I owe a number of sizeable debts. The greatest of these is to my friend and frequent collaborator, H.V. Nelles, who not only discussed the project with me as it went along, but also, and most importantly, read the entire manuscript and made many useful suggestions that I have tried to incorporate as far as possible. Another old friend and colleague, John T. Saywell, read the chapters covering the 1930s and also dug about in his basement and supplied me with a number of important sources, which he had collected for his own work, that improved my text. Gerald Hallowell and the staff of the University of Toronto Press efficiently oversaw the production of the book; Elizabeth Hulse did a particularly valuable job of copy-editing. Two members of my family joined enthusiastically in this enterprise: my daughter Emily suggested a design for the dust jacket, and my sister, Julian Armstrong O'Brien, went far beyond the call of familial duty in searching out photographs in Montreal. This book is dedicated to my father-in-law, an ever-confident investor in northern Ontario mining. Any errors and omissions are my fault.

C.A.

1 Watching the prices of Cobalt and Porcupine mining shares on Toronto's Standard Stock and Mining Exchange, c. 1910

2 Toronto Exchange building on Wellington Street East at Leader Lane, c. 1891

3 Members of the Toronto Corn Exchange and Board of Trade, who also traded stocks, in the rotunda of their building, 1885

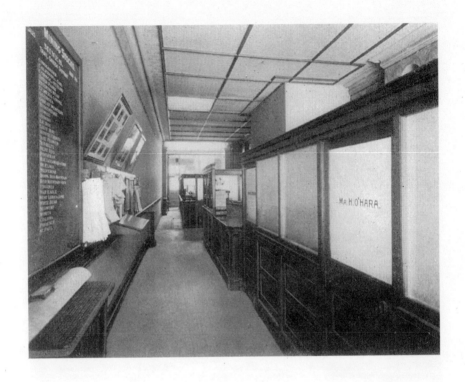

4 Brokerage office of H. O'Hara and Company, Toronto, 1897, with list of mining stocks from the Trail Creek camp in British Columbia

5 Montreal Stock Exchange building on rue Saint-François-Xavier, c. 1904

6 Trading floor of the Montreal Stock Exchange with trading posts for continuous auction market and telephone booths along the far wall, c. 1904

7 Members of the Toronto Stock Exchange in the room where trading took place, with the secretary behind the raised desk, c. 1905

8 Toronto Stock Exchange building on Bay Street during the booming 1920s. It was opened in 1914.

9 Founders of the Vancouver Stock Exchange (from left: E.W. MacLean, J.R. Waghorn, C.D. Rand, C.J. Loewen, and J. Kendall) outside its first premises on West Pender Street, c. 1907

10 Members of the Vancouver Stock Exchange in their West Pender Street trading room (with railing to exclude the public), 1910

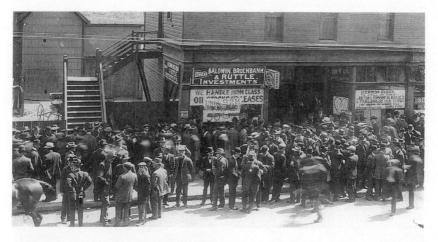

11 Crowd at Alberta Corner, 1st West, in Calgary, with board counters for selling oil shares hidden at left, 1914

12 Offices of Calgary oil-stock brokers Imes, Lake and Pelarske with Wm. A. Imes, seated, 1914

13 H.A. Robson, administrator of Canada's first blue-sky law, passed by Manitoba in 1912 to regulate securities selling, c. 1915

14 Billboard advertising Victory bonds on College Street, Toronto, in November 1917

15 Members of Toronto's Standard Stock and Mining Exchange on a visit to mining country in northern Ontario, 1924

16 Brick of gold from mines of northern Ontario shown to visiting brokers in 1924

17 In 1929 the Vancouver Stock Exchange opened its new building at Howe and Pender streets; quotation boards are at the back.

18 Before the crash of 1929 I.W.C. Solloway ran one of the largest brokerage firms in Canada, but within a year afterwards he was in jail for having defrauded his customers.

19 Frederick H. Deacon with one of the prize cattle from his Glenburn farm, which he
was forced to mortgage to save his brokerage firm during the 1930s

20 Members of the Toronto Stock Exchange on their trading floor in 1935, after the merger with the Standard Stock and Mining Exchange

21 New Toronto Stock Exchange building on Bay Street in 1937, with decorative frieze designed by Charles Comfort

22 Trading opens at 10 a.m. on 30 March 1937 on the new trading floor, with telephone clerks along the wall under Comfort's modernistic murals

BLUE SKIES AND BOILER ROOMS

Introduction

Blue Skies and Boiler Rooms is one of two volumes dealing with the evolution of public securities markets in Canada. This book examines the trading of stocks and bonds from its origins in the mid-nineteenth century through the Great Depression of the 1930s. Buying and selling shares was little known before Confederation, when people usually invested their scarce savings in real estate and other kinds of property. By the late 1920s, however, Canadians from all walks of life were rushing to get in on soaring stock prices, purchasing even the most speculative issues in the hopes of a quick killing. The decade-long depression that followed undercut both the value of shares and the volume of trading, leaving most investors poorer in pocket and spirit. Although the return of palmier days was much desired and often predicted, they saw little reward prior to the outbreak of the Second World War.

A companion volume (to be entitled *Moose Pastures and Mergers: The Ontario Securities Commission and the Evolution of Share Markets in Canada, 1940–1980*) is intended to carry the story forward from that point. Stock prices had begun to revive even before the fighting ended, and the prolonged spurt of growth during the era of the Cold War gave continued life and vitality to securities markets. Canadian mining enterprises, in particular, enjoyed boom times reminiscent of the 1920s as valuable discoveries were revealed under the 'moose pastures' of the North. Many industrial companies also experienced unprecedented growth. One by-product of these prosperous years was a wave of corporate mergers that occurred during the 1970s as takeovers populated the corporate landscape with a new breed of conglomerates. What ties these two books together is their focus on regulation: as stocks and bonds became increasingly important elements of the Canadian financial system, demands grew for new types of controls over their issuing, marketing, and trading.

Why did trading in the securities of public companies gradually become commonplace during the late nineteenth century? Capital-intensive undertakings such as railways, banks, and other financial institutions early understood the advantages of the joint-stock form of enterprise, and the well-to-do were gradually persuaded to put their savings into such stocks and bonds. In the 1890s mineral finds in the Rocky Mountains of British Columbia and later in the Precambrian Shield of northern Ontario spawned a multitude of public mining companies; stockholders who purchased speculative shares for pennies might revel in both handsome dividends and capital gains, particularly if there was a rich strike of gold or silver. As time passed, therefore, an increasing number of Canadians became accustomed to investing in public companies.

The feeling of confidence was enhanced by the growth of the stock exchanges. During the 1870s brokers in both Toronto and Montreal organized such permanent bodies. The existence of these institutions helped to inspire more trust among share buyers because they seemed to guarantee the liquidity of investments. Each day the newspapers carried lists of 'bid' and 'ask' prices for issues traded on the exchanges, so that people could calculate precisely how much their holdings were worth at any given time. If they had to realize these assets, they could do so relatively quickly and easily through the services of the growing number of specialized stockbrokers.

For the brokers themselves the development of the exchanges was beneficial in several ways. Here was a forum where they could gather daily to swap information, rumours, and hunches while filling orders. Dealing with fellow members was advantageous (and not only because it eliminated competition on commission rates) since the purchase of a seat bound brokers to fulfil their financial obligations for agreements struck only by word of mouth. Those who failed to make delivery of stock or to pay their debts could forfeit their seats and see them sold to satisfy their creditors. Not only were customers readier to trust brokers who belonged to an exchange, but brokers could trade among themselves with greater assurance.

Of course, many stocks did not trade on the exchanges. New issues and speculative shares were generally handled through brokerage offices where investors could take delivery of their certificates 'over the counter.' Moreover, many well-established blue-chip companies saw little advantage in having a stock-exchange listing during the nineteenth century: their shares traded directly from hand to hand, as well as in 'street' markets held outside the formal sessions of the exchange or after hours among the brokers themselves. After the turn of the century, however, attitudes gradually changed as the managers of public corporations became more conscious of the role of the exchanges in attracting and maintaining investor interest. In addition, the appearance of new exchanges in Toronto, Vancouver, and Calgary that specialized in the shares of speculative mining and oil companies appealed to a new class of promoters, brokers, and investors whose activities overlapped with the over-the-counter markets.

As share ownership expanded beyond the ranks of the well-to-do, and particularly once the lure of low-priced mining shares drew in those with less business background, the issue of trust assumed greater and greater importance. Some investors were simply well-meaning innocents, so that demands began to be heard for tighter regulation of promoters and brokers to protect the gullible from being duped. At the same time, however, surprising numbers of people proved willing to risk money on highly speculative issues, aiming to use the latest rumour or hot tip to make a quick and easy profit. Such a situation was, of course, rife with possibilities for both deception and self-deception. While the naive might be unable to distinguish truth from falsehood, the cynical and the greedy could on occasion be persuaded to act with equal ease. Over-optimism as much as venality could make converts even out of the tellers of tales. How could protection be provided all at once for the honest and well intentioned, for the innocent and the trusting, and for the greedy or the self-deceived?

Proposals for regulating securities markets had (and still have) a good deal in common with other legislation aimed at controlling conduct such as the sale and consumption of alcohol. Some people simply wanted stock speculation banned as flat-out immoral, since it aimed at effortless profit from the exertions of others. A rival view was that the gambling spirit was ineradicable and should be accommodated, but that the punters merited an honest chance to win. Economic theorists argued that securities trading fulfilled a valuable and necessary function, efficiently linking investors with entrepreneurs who needed funds to bring their productive schemes to fruition. Too tight a clamp upon speculation would only interfere with this process or else drive these dealings underground, where there would be even less protection for the uninformed.

Although no honest person could be found to endorse fraud and misrepresentation as a means of separating investors from their money, arguments for a relatively loose regulatory rein had a particular potency in Canada. Their appeal stemmed from the importance of resource development to economic growth, particularly in the field of mining. Geology held its mysteries: fabulous finds could turn up in the most unexpected and unpromising places. Every prospector had a pet theory about where a mother lode might be located, and the mythology of the mining community strongly reinforced the notion that the independents, rather than the large producers, had been responsible for the most significant discoveries. Investing in an unproven mine was undeniably a speculation without any guaranteed return; but if the rules governing company flotation were made too stringent the flow of capital into this key sector might be choked off. Both mining promoters and investors with an appetite for a risky plunge were determined that their activities should not be legislated out of existence.

Governments, therefore, tended to approach the regulation of the securities business crabwise. Crooks could not be openly tolerated; serious swindles created periodic pressure for action. But how best could the state intervene, especially when the ordinary criminal sanctions against fraud and misrepresentation proved very difficult to apply because so much of the evidence consisted of conflicting accounts of purely verbal dealings? One attractive solution was the self-regulation of securities markets. Why should the exchanges themselves not be made responsible for the soundness of listed issues and for prohibiting trading practices that might artificially inflate or depress the value of a security? Yet the boards of directors of the exchanges found it very difficult to impose or enforce such rules because they ran contrary to the cut and thrust that provided the lifeblood of the trader. Moreover, these were voluntary organizations with fairly narrowly specified powers; the task of enforcement was difficult and unpopular since there were always members who opposed any interference in their affairs.

When it did occur, forceful self-regulation by the exchanges most commonly took the form of a defensive reaction to a crisis. If the fear of war or depression made a disastrous collapse of share prices likely, the instinctive response in many quarters was to close markets altogether. That action, in theory, bought time for investors to calm down and see the unwisdom of a headlong rush to dump their stocks and bonds. Cooler heads should prevail, prices stabilize, panic evaporate, and, in time, trading might resume under more or less strict constraints designed to prevent too rapid price swings. Such a reaction appeared in Canada during the First World War and again in the depths of the Great Depression. The exchanges might close altogether at first, then operate only on limited hours, and minimum prices were imposed for months at a time in hopes of checking a sharp downward slide. The problem, as brokers soon discovered, was that off-the-floor trading soon burgeoned. The stock exchanges never possessed a monopoly on securities dealing, and these restraints only led to thriving 'street' or 'gutter' markets that eventually undermined the restrictions. That outcome did not entirely avert pressure to reinstitute controls when another crisis came along, though by the outbreak of the Second World War most brokers had concluded that such restrictions were largely futile.

Self-regulation thus had its limitations (and, in any event, hardly touched over-the-counter markets at all). By the turn of the century, worthless stock in fly-by-night undertakings was being peddled by smooth-talking con men who, it was said, did not scruple to offer a simpleton shares even in the blue sky above. Public pressure led to the passage of 'blue sky' laws, under which governments created tribunals to oversee all new securities offered to the public in an effort to ensure that they were sound investments. That solution, which was first adopted in the western United States, quickly moved northward, and by 1912 the province of Manitoba became the first jurisdiction in Canada to pass a blue-sky law. The other two prairie provinces quickly followed suit, but many doubters remained unconvinced that such legislation could provide effective protection for investors.

The extent of Canada's financial commitment to the First World War had important consequences for securities markets, since it led to heavy government borrowing in domestic capital markets. For many citizens the purchase of a Victory bond marked their first foray into such an investment. When prosperity returned in the 1920s, Canadians in all walks of life plunged enthusiastically into stock speculation, especially in mining shares. Concern about several well-publicized swindles reinforced doubts about the effectiveness of the blue-sky approach to investor protection. At the same time, moreover, the courts limited the power of the provinces to regulate federally incorporated companies from selling their shares. In 1928, therefore, the province of Ontario, the centre of the mining-share market, adopted a different kind of regulatory legislation. It aimed at controlling fraudulent practices by registering all brokers and salesmen to eliminate the bad eggs and by granting the government wider powers to investigate and prosecute suspected fraudsters. When the stock-market crash occurred the following year, it was nonetheless widely blamed upon misconduct by insiders, and a number of prominent brokers were arrested and convicted of criminal offences. Persistent concern about the recurrence of such scams during the early 1930s also led the provincial government to create the Ontario Securities Commission, Canada's first specialized tribunal for the regulation of securities trading.

By that time, technology was beginning to transform the marketing of speculative shares into a continent-wide operation, the falling cost of long-distance telephone calls being the most important development. Though recovery after the crash was extremely sluggish, there was a brief boom in Canadian mining stocks in 1933–4. That upsurge led to the appearance of numerous 'boiler rooms' where salesmen manned banks of phones to deliver high-pressure pitches to prospective customers all across North America. In the face of these new sales techniques, the Ontario government banned calling upon private residences for the purpose of selling securities. No regulatory measures, however, could do much to overcome slow economic recovery, which kept most stocks selling below pre-crash levels and made for comparatively sluggish trading on the exchanges.

These, then, are the main themes to be treated in this book: the development of the exchanges and their faltering efforts at self-regulation; the increasing demand for government regulation of securities markets, whether by blue-sky laws, anti-fraud statutes, or the creation of specialized tribunals; and the evolution of new sales techniques, in particular the telephone boiler room, that presented special challenges to the authorities. Readers may complain that too much attention is devoted to crooks and shysters. To that charge the plea must be one of 'guilty, but with mitigation.' Using cash to purchase a blue-chip stock to be held as an investment is a significant economic event, but not one that normally requires extensive description or analysis. If every investor was satisfied with a comparatively safe and steady 5 per cent return, then the boiler room would have no function. In search of bigger gains, individuals can display an astonishing combination of cupidity and naivety. Governments had a hard time protecting them from their own stupidity, yet felt some obligation to counter outright dishonesty; hence the impetus for regulation.

Regulation was important in another way. Modern economic theory directs our attention to the margin, and the pedlars and purchasers of dubious stocks operated at (or beyond) the margin. The rules were drawn (and redrawn) to contain their activities, but, of course, these rules then applied to everyone. Regulators continually groped for means that would hobble the fly-by-nighters without constricting the life-giving flow of capital. The provision of funds for sound, productive enterprises had undeniable social and economic significance, but here the focus tends to be upon those who strained or transgressed the boundaries of acceptable behaviour and thus created pressure for the rules to be remade. The good and the grey therefore tend to get short shrift. Indeed, the themes treated may seem better suited to a Victorian novel than to sober nonfiction: trust and innocence assailed by greed and self-deception. The truth is that the bottom feeders usually provide more entertainment than the worthy and the righteous.

1

Beginnings

Stocks and bonds have been traded for centuries, and great commercial cities such as London and Amsterdam developed busy stock exchanges at a very early date.[1] In Britain's North American colonies, joint-stock banks began selling shares by the 1820s, and after mid-century, railways also became important security issuers. Governments, too, began to market bonds and debentures to finance public works schemes.[2] Suspicions about the joint-stock corporation as a form of business organization, which were linked to its association with monopolies, gradually evaporated as North American entrepreneurs and investors came to appreciate the advantages of limited liability.[3] As the ownership of securities, public and private, became more widespread among the wealthy, so did the desire to enhance the liquidity of such investments by providing opportunities to buy, sell, and exchange them. Gradually there developed in the principal cities of British North America groups of brokers who dealt in securities along with other commodities and real estate. By the late nineteenth century the largest centres, Montreal and Toronto, had recognized financial districts where most of those who engaged in such activities located their offices. These districts were customarily referred to by insiders as the 'street,' and its central institution was the local stock exchange, where brokers gathered daily to share information and trade securities.

As prosperity increased, pools of savings accumulated for which investors sought profitable employment. The existence of exchanges theoretically improved the efficiency of financial markets by bringing together buyers and sellers at an auction, which narrowed the margins between 'bid' and 'ask' prices and increased the liquidity of the securities traded. Securities became more attractive to investors as a result of fairer pricing and readier saleability. Not only banks, railways, and governments issued stocks and bonds, but other kinds of financial and industrial undertakings began to seek capital in this way. The well-to-do gradually became more confident about putting funds into securities as well as into real estate or other personal possessions.

Yet the stock exchanges did not escape criticism. Particularly in the United States, a series of financial panics following the Civil War were blamed upon the predations and speculations of market insiders. Certain trading practices were roundly condemned in the business press, and from time to time proposals were made to clean up the securities business, though these were usually criticized as unwarranted interferences with the free play of market forces. Some people looked to the exchanges themselves to curtail the more antisocial activities of speculators, but these bodies were voluntary private associations with relatively limited powers. Moreover, a good deal of securities trading was always done off their floors, and many stocks and bonds were not formally 'listed' on any exchange at all. To the critics a stroll down the 'street' in the late nineteenth or early twentieth century seemed akin to a walk through the jungle.

I

Securities trading in British North America developed slowly during the nineteenth century. By the 1840s brokers had begun to congregate in certain coffee houses and taverns in Montreal and Toronto to transact business. After 1850 there were efforts in both cities to organize formal stock exchanges, but as financial journalist W.R. Houston later noted, for the first twenty-five years or so Montreal brokers had to deal 'in whatever they could, such as pork, flour, butter, mines, stocks, bonds or banking. In fact, anything a commission could be made out of.' In 1872 the Montreal Board of Brokers changed its name to the Montreal Stock Exchange; two years later a charter of incorporation had been secured from the province of Quebec, and seats were sold for between $150 and $200. Silver and copper discoveries in northwestern Ontario led to the organization of a number of joint-stock companies such as the Montreal Mining Company, and shares in these mines and a few chartered banks accounted for most of the trading in the early days of the MSE.[4]

The Toronto Exchange, chartered in 1854, was organized to erect a building that might house a stock exchange and the offices of brokers.[5] At first, trading did take place in the rotunda, but regular meetings soon ceased. Founded in 1861, the Toronto Stock Exchange was a casual association of brokers who met informally to trade. Between 1863 and 1869 sessions were held in the offices of various brokers, but by the end of the decade there appear to have been just six members. In the words of W.R. Houston, 'There were brokers and plenty of them, but each constituted a Board in himself – each making the best bargain he could, obtaining the greatest amount of profit on each transaction. It opened the way for irregular, and if anyone was so disposed, dishonest dealing, where one of the parties in a transaction was not fully posted on the state of the market.' The Toronto Stock and Mining Exchange, incorporated in 1868 as a result of a boom in the shares of gold mines in the Madoc area of Ontario, never seems to have functioned. Not until 1871 was an effort made to organize a new exchange, but the second Toronto Stock Exchange began continuous operation only in 1874. Four years later it secured a charter of incorporation from the province of Ontario, and it was really set on its feet permanently by a boom in bank stocks in the early 1880s which attracted a number of new members (see photos 2 and 3).[6]

The advantages of exchange membership for brokers were obvious. At a time when share issues were comparatively few in number and the volume of trading tiny, more detailed information about prices and the volume of trading in each stock was desirable for investors. The *Monetary Times* welcomed the establishment of a Toronto exchange in 1871 by noting, 'A daily list will be issued showing the quotations of banks and other shares. Such a price current will have the advantage of being quite reliable, since it will be based on all the transactions of the market and not compiled by an individual or a firm. This exchange will be the means of saving much valuable time which is now lost for want of a common place and hour of meeting.'[7]

The invention of the stock ticker machine in 1867 also made it possible for markets to be more closely linked together. A running record of the price and volume of trades could now be transmitted telegraphically onto a narrow paper tape. After an improved ticker was developed in 1881, the TSE was linked to the New York and Montreal stock exchanges the following year, and transatlantic cable service arrived in 1886.[8] Not only did these links ensure that different markets moved roughly in unison, but they also permitted a much larger volume of arbitrage trading, in which investors sought to profit from price differentials on the same stocks in different markets.

Under their charters the Canadian exchanges were managed by annually elected boards, which could make rules binding upon members and possessed the power to fine or suspend delinquents. For brokers the most significant rules were those fixing a uniform schedule of commissions. Trading practices were standardized; of particular importance were regulations about the time for the delivery of certificates and the making of payments. In case a member proved unable to meet his obligations, he could immediately be suspended to protect the others. If the situation was not rectified, his seat was forfeited and resold, the proceeds going to cover his debts to the other members. The committee also received applications from intending members and approved the prices paid for seats, but decisions on admission (including the right to blackball applicants) and on the number of seats issued were left to a vote of the whole membership.

Twice daily, at 12:30 and 3:30 p.m., the thirty-odd members of the Toronto Stock Exchange would gather in their rented premises on King Street for a half-hour session of trading.[9] Hats jammed firmly on their heads, they milled around beforehand, gossiping, making deals, and scanning the out-of-town prices being entered on the boards along the walls by the chalkboys. At the appointed hour each man would take his seat at one of the small desks ranged around three sides of the room. The patriarchally bearded assistant secretary, Lyndhurst Ogden, would bring the 'board meeting' to order and begin to read the alphabetical list of stocks one by one. After each call, shouted bids were exchanged; to ensure orderly trading, orders more than 5 per cent above or below previous prices were prohibited. Finally Ogden would silence the din with his 'sweet little bell' and record the transactions in a particular stock in his ledger before moving on. Anyone engaging in 'unduly loud talking or boisterous conduct' during the call might be reprimanded and, if he continued to behave in this unseemly fashion, fined between 25 cents and $5 by the presiding officer. When the call had been completed, other business such as the reading of notices and election of members was attended to, whereupon members might request the reopening of trading on any issue, and a recall would be made to confirm transactions before the brokers dispersed back to their offices.[10]

Doing business in this way was intensely personal. In 1882 the TSE did permit its members to appoint 'attorneys' to occupy their places at board meetings, but only if the seat holder was away as a result of absence from the city or illness. After 1889 a member's business partner or clerk could be designated a permanent attorney.[11] The assumption remained that a member's place was on the floor during board meetings to sense how the market was moving. Gordon Wills, who started as a floor-trading attorney on the TSE in 1902 at the age of twenty-one, recalled that most of the trading was done by the principals of brokerage firms. A shrewd trader with a large 'buy' order who suspected that an unjustifiable amount was being demanded would often offer to sell a similar block in order to establish a fair price. The danger was that somebody might take up the offer and force him to complete the deal. Companies were under no obligation to release news or financial data, so in that period, as Wills recalls, information and rumours were exchanged on the floor and then disseminated onto the 'street' rather than vice versa.[12] Since the majority of trades then executed by Toronto brokers were for shares traded on the New York Stock Exchange rather than on the TSE or the MSE, ticker service was of great importance to them. Following the ebb and flow of local prices by ticker was not what concerned brokers since they were always represented on the TSE floor during board meetings. As a result, the TSE did not provide ticker service even to local brokerage offices until 1909.[13]

Some of the characters who met 'on 'change' each day were pretty raffish, and tempers could flare in the heat of trading. A.E. Webb once demanded that the TSE board discipline W.J. O'Hara for assaulting him on the floor. Called before the managing committee, O'Hara claimed that he had been offering some General Electric shares when he overheard Webb complaining that he was asking an unduly low amount for the stock, trying to push down its price. He had told Webb to mind his own business, whereupon Webb elbowed his way towards O'Hara in a 'very bullying and aggressive way,' shouting, 'Who cares for you, you dirty old bumhole!' O'Hara then punched Webb. He told the committee that he had not even spoken to Webb during the previous two years, but admitted that he had struck out, thinking himself about to be assaulted. In the end both men were suspended from the floor for one week since Webb's language and threatening demeanour were 'thoroughly disgraceful,' while O'Hara, though severely provoked, had also acted unacceptably in striking the other man.[14] On another occasion N.G. Cassels complained that, when he bought 20 shares of bank stock from the same O'Hara, and immediately resold them at two-thirds of a point (66 cents) higher, the man had charged that he had pulled a 'dirty rotten trick.' Members, said Cassels, should not be allowed to say such things about one another. O'Hara's apology was accepted by the board, though Cassels continued to press for a more severe punishment.[15]

Though the stock exchanges in Montreal and Toronto functioned continuously after the mid-1870s, both remained fragile institutions; their existence depended upon trust, which could only be built up gradually. On the one hand, members had to trust one another to live up to their bargains, to pay their debts, to deliver the shares that they owed. Membership in this type of private 'club' was voluntary, and only those who saw benefit to be gained sought to belong. On the other hand, the investing public had to be convinced to trust the exchange as a place where the best prices could be obtained for their shares and honest dealing was the order of the day. Neither kind of trust could be created overnight but had to be earned, and a market downturn could always cast a dark pall.

Despite its location in Canada's financial capital, the Montreal Stock Exchange's membership remained small and trading volumes comparatively low during the nineteenth century. By the middle of the depressed 1890s the number of listed issues had declined from the original sixty-five to just fifty-one. Seats that had been sold for $800 in 1874 rose to $2,500 two years later and peaked at $4,650 in 1883 before falling sharply in value. By 1897 only 4,000–5,000 shares were changing hands on the MSE floor on an average day.[16] Still, volume in Montreal tended to be much greater than in Toronto. In an effort to exploit this advantage during the depression of the 1890s, the MSE refused to permit the publication of the TSE's quotations on its floor. Toronto broker A.E. Ames suggested to the TSE board that, since the MSE's members 'have generally assumed a very independent position towards us,' the MSE should 'receive no official recognition from the Toronto Stock Exchange' and its quotations should no longer be displayed on their floor. While such retaliation might seem tempting, an aspiring rival such as the TSE could not afford to cut off its nose to spite its face in this way since many customers had orders that might have to be executed in Montreal. Ames's proposal was voted down.[17]

During the 1870s almost all public trading in bank stocks, which were the most widely held, was conducted at the MSE. The TSE did gain some ground in the early 1880s when a boom in the shares of Ontario banks and mortgage loan companies attracted new business. The members sought to capitalize upon this growth by raising seat prices from $500 to $4,000, but in 1882 only a single buyer was found willing to pay this much. Two years later the cost of a seat had slipped to $1,000, and it dropped to a low of $675 in 1892 before starting to rise again. The TSE's annual trading volume for the entire nineteenth century peaked in 1882 at 340,000 shares, as a result of the demand for the shares of banks and loan companies, but in 1888 only 93,000 shares changed hands, a low point equalled again in 1893. Five years later volume had reached 294,000 shares, but it slipped once more to 224,000 in 1900.[18]

These figures, of course, reflected only transactions in the officially 'listed' issues that were reported on the exchange's daily quotation sheets. Any security could obtain a listing provided that two members informed the board that they wished to trade in it. The TSE's 1882 constitution required the managing committee to 'thoroughly investigate' any enterprise proposed for a listing, but its ledgers show that less than half the newly listed companies (or their sponsoring brokers) even bothered to pay the $50 fee between 1881 and 1900. Nor, once listed, was a company required to supply any information concerning its affairs. The listing of a security had no prestige value for a company, so that many blue-chip stocks continued to be traded off the exchanges.[19]

In fact, a great deal of trading clearly took place outside the formal meetings; as well as its 'regular' board, the MSE maintained an 'open' board for the use of non-members. In 1887 the TSE committee defined a 'stock exchange transaction' as any trade between two members in a listed security whether it took place on or off the floor. Members were supposed to report these trades to the assistant secretary, but there was nothing to compel them to do so. Moreover, while the rates of commission were fixed, the TSE never levied any fines on members for splitting commissions with each other or with outsiders in an effort to drum up business.[20]

The exchanges also permitted dealings in 'unlisted' securities among members on the exchange floor both before and after their formal sessions. Information about these trades was not reported on the daily quotation sheets or carried in the press. Beginning in 1895 the TSE tried to confine unlisted dealings to the period between its two daily meetings, but it is clear that this restriction was never effectively enforced.[21] Moreover, members and non-members of exchanges continued to deal directly among themselves (and increasingly by telephone and telegraph) in issues that were not listed at all. These securities eventually came to be referred to as 'over-the-counter' stocks since delivery of the certificates was made to customers through the individual brokers' offices. Thus the exchanges had only minimal control of the quality of the listed securities traded and none at all over unlisted and over-the-counter shares.

Part of the reason for the weakness of the stock exchanges as institutions was rapid fluctuations in membership. A study of the TSE from the 1870s through 1900 uncovered about ninety persons who were members at some time or other, of whom only twenty-three belonged for over sixteen years, nineteen for between seven and fifteen years, and the rest for shorter periods. The typical brokerage firm was a sole proprietorship or partnership, and virtually all firms also handled one or more of commodities, produce, insurance, or real estate. Men such as Henry Pellatt or E.B. Osler were sometimes retained to sell stock in newly launched financial institutions directly to the public on a commission basis. Others played managerial roles in the companies whose stocks they were promoting. In the nineteenth century successful brokers survived by conducting a general financial agency business since stockbroking was not sufficiently lucrative to sustain them through the swings of the business cycle. In his study of the TSE, J.F. Whiteside estimates that the total commission income earned by members on listed trades totalled just $16,300 in the depression year of 1892, though it rose to $43,000 two years later.[22]

Bonds and debentures were not handled on the exchanges in any significant volume.[23] George Stimson, for instance, got into the municipal bond business as bursar of the University of Toronto while placing that institution's surplus funds in local issues. In the 1890s he formed G.A. Stimson and Company to undertake the marketing of such bonds to banks, life insurance companies, and individuals; his firm did not belong even to the Toronto Stock Exchange.[24]

By the late 1890s, with Canada recovering from a serious depression, the stock exchanges in Montreal and Toronto had finally become established on a fairly solid basis, but they were not yet key financial institutions. Whiteside notes that 'the Toronto share market in 1900 was still very small; it operated much the same way it had twenty years before; the market values per share remained very high, thus restricting the number of persons who could afford to invest in shares. Accordingly, the share market in 1900 was such that a few very powerful figures could exert an inordinate amount of influence on the market.'[25] Like its counterpart in Montreal, the TSE could not discipline its members for abusing their privileged positions to profit at the expense of ordinary investors, despite criticism of certain abuses that were arousing increasing public concern.

II

The financial panics of 1873, 1884, and 1893 in the United States were widely blamed upon the antics of stock-market operators. Publicity focused upon the 'bulls' and 'bears'[26] of Wall Street helped to create the perception that small groups of insiders, such as the legendary speculators Cornelius Vanderbilt and Daniel Drew, could manipulate share prices almost at will.[27] Despite New York's increasingly dominant position in the North American financial system, the New York Stock Exchange achieved real organizational stability only in the 1870s. The governors of the NYSE remained reluctant to enforce their own rules, which banned dealing with non-members or splitting commissions with them. After 1886 the NYSE faced competition from the Consolidated Stock Exchange, which waxed and waned as the so-called Big Board tried more or less strenuously to prevent dealings with Consolidated members. As well, in New York securities could be traded on the Mercantile Exchange, the Metal Exchange, and (after 1907) the Produce Exchange.[28]

Even so, the NYSE was a bastion of order compared to New York's 'Curb.' Up to 1921 the Curb operated outdoors at Broad Street and Exchange Place in Manhattan, with traders in the street communicating by hand signals to offices in the surrounding buildings. Any security for which a market could be found was traded, including such blue-chip stocks as Standard Oil and American Tobacco. The Curb kept no records of prices or volume of trades and imposed no rules about payment, delivery of certificates, or hours of trading. Only in 1911 did the New York Curb Market formally organize with an elected governing body and committees on membership and listings, and it remained a voluntary unincorporated association that exercised little control over its members.[29]

Complaints were often heard about a number of stock exchange practices common in both Canada and the United States. Frequently condemned was 'margin' trading, where purchasers were required to put up only a small percentage (margin) of the price of each share of stock, borrowing the remainder of the cost from the broker. The investor thus secured great leverage, having put up as little as 5 per cent of the cost in anticipation of a profit equal to the entire difference between the purchase and final sale prices (less only brokerage commissions and interest charges paid on the borrowed money). Should the shares fall, however, clients would speedily receive calls from their brokers to provide additional funds for 'under-margined' accounts or face having the shares sold out on them. If the price decline were steep and sudden, margin traders might find themselves facing catastrophic losses.[30]

Conservative voices in the business community often preached against margin trading as mere gambling. In the 1880s Canada's leading financial weekly, the *Monetary Times*, grumbled that if such practices continued, the exchanges might have to be closed, since

Gambling in its various forms is illegal. And yet what goes on every day at our Stock Exchanges? There men meet together in person or by proxy and stake large sums upon the contingency of stocks rising or falling in price. The *bulls* and the *bears* are organized bodies of men, who play with loaded dice ... They put their loaded dice against the unloaded dice of the public; the game is not fair; it is even more unfair, and more disreputable than other forms of gambling. Stock gambling, backed by large amounts of borrowed capital, is the scandal of the day. If gambling in other forms, even where there is no 'bank' with the odds in its favour, is put down by the strong arm of the law, is it not then an anomaly that a form of gambling in which the chances are not equal, in which there are loaded dice on one side, should be fostered by respectable financial institutions?

How, asked Montreal's *Journal of Commerce* about the same time, was the economic well-being of the country advanced by the operations of brokers who were 'merely a parcel of speculators, more or less reckless, who hardly have any other means of support, ... and by their manipulations disturb the commerce of the country?'[31]

Twenty years later, when popular interest in stocks in Canada had greatly increased, Edward Trout of the *Times* was still fulminating against margin trading. In 'A Stock Exchange Sermon' he described the financial and moral ruin that it had brought one young man. Feeling his oats after making a $1,000 profit on margin, this individual began smoking cigarettes in the street before lunchtime, taking 'nips' in saloons during business hours when he should have been at work, ordering fancy clothes, and giving expensive presents to his male and female friends. Soon he was frequenting brokerage offices all day long. Fired from his job and loaded with debts from a market slump, this youth failed to understand the extent of his folly, but thought that he had suffered only a temporary run of bad luck; he still dreamt of buying a yacht, like a friend who played the market more successfully, not realizing, said Trout, that the only real route to financial success lay in 'steady diligence and steadfast economy.'[32]

From time to time there were proposals to end margin trading by a legal prohibition on lending money for the purpose of speculating on securities. The brokerage community, however, enthusiastically supported the practice because it raised the volume of trades and commissions. Not only that, but the *Monetary Times* reported in 1896 that brokers made eight to ten times as much on margin accounts as on straight cash deals. Moreover, even critics such as Trout had to admit that it was difficult to see how such legislation could be framed without impeding legitimate trading in stocks and bonds. He reluctantly conceded that the disposition to gamble was deeply rooted in human nature, though he still complained that 'stock speculation on margin is only inferior to horse racing as a means of betting against chance, in that in the latter the victim does at least know how much he is booked to leave on the ground, whereas stocks have a contempt for such mild privileges.'[33]

A particularly controversial stock exchange practice was 'short selling,' where shares were borrowed from their owners and sold by bears anticipating a fall in prices. Short sellers aimed to buy back the stock at a lower cost to repay the original owner, the difference between the selling and buying prices being profit for them. The notion of selling something that one did not really own had long attracted criticism. Many people, country folk in particular, equated short selling with trading in commodity futures – contracts to buy and sell agricultural products at a given price at some future date – which was widely believed to operate to the disadvantage of working farmers.[34]

Since short sellers were looking for a decline in share prices, they were seen as antagonistic to the interests of other investors. The shorts, who typically operated on margin, were also frequently accused of carrying out 'bear raids' on perfectly sound companies in an effort to force down share prices for their own benefit, regardless of the effect on the other shareholders and the business itself. Exchange members either acted as raiders on their own account or earned large commissions on the trading involved in such operations. Yet it was extremely difficult to distinguish between such raids and ordinary trading activity. More-over, short selling had its defenders, who argued that it was perfectly legitimate to 'hedge' against anticipated price declines and that the need for shorts to buy into the market to meet their obligations actually helped to check steep declines and stabilize prices.

Another market practice that was often criticized was 'wash trading,' where promoters and brokers conspired to enter matching buy and sell orders for a particular stock. The increased volume of trading was bound to attract interest, and a skilled trader could impart an upward push to share prices through carefully graduated orders. Outside investors, convinced that the stock must have promising prospects, would be drawn into the bidding, and the insiders would seize the opportunity to dump their low-priced shares at a profit. After the operation was complete, if prices slumped sharply, as often happened when the support of the market for thinly traded issues by the insiders ceased, they might take further profits from short sales. Brokers, of course, had little desire to stamp out wash trading since it also helped to increase their flow of commissions.

The classic stock exchange coup was a successful 'corner,' in which the attempt to acquire all (or almost all) the available 'float' of a given stock forced share prices up dramatically. This was a particularly effective way of punishing short sellers who needed to buy in to meet their obligations.[35] Pulling off a corner allowed a seller to demand almost any price from prospective buyers and often led the stock exchange authorities to intervene and fix a settlement price in order to avert the financial ruin of hard-pressed shorts, among whom their members were usually well represented.[36]

As the market for shares in North America became broader, such speculative operations helped to fuel demands that the stock exchanges themselves ought to regulate their members more closely and force them to police their clients. Eliminating the unfair advantages that these insiders and other large players had would give the growing number of small investors a fairer shake at making a profit and enhance their trust about putting their money into stocks. In truth, however, the stock exchanges were institutions that had weaknesses which made it almost impossible for them to assume a leading role in regulating securities markets. They were, after all, voluntary private associations possessing only narrow disciplinary powers over their own members. Their rules were designed for the benefit of the members, not for the protection of the public. The by-laws merely fixed commissions (thus eliminating price competition among their members) and specified such trading practices as the time allowed for delivery of certificates and the making of payments.

Even if the exchanges had possessed the will to undertake regulation, they were poorly equipped to do so. Much share trading continued to be done off the floors of the exchanges (even by their own members), and too stringent rules would only increase the volume of entirely uncontrolled 'curb' or 'gutter' markets. In addition, there was the ever-present threat of competition from other exchanges, which restrained any one of them from imposing too tight controls.[37] Even the relatively stable and long-established London Stock Exchange was several times threatened with upstart competitors. London members continued to do a considerable volume of their business off the floor, both with each other and with outsiders, especially in American stocks because of the time difference between Britain and the United States.[38]

Public suspicions about the amount of manipulation on the stock exchanges were well founded. Margin trading, short selling, and bear raids could all destabilize the values of thinly traded stocks in short order, while wash trading permitted the manipulation of prices by insiders. Yet those who looked to the exchanges themselves to rectify this situation and guarantee the small investor fair treatment were doomed to disappointment. Even if exchange members had wished to remedy the situation, there was little they could do to compel miscreants to conform. Too harsh punishment only led to defections, and the volume of off-the-floor dealings was such that the value of an exchange membership remained comparatively low.

Still, the importance of the stock exchanges in Canada's two largest cities gradually increased, especially after the depression of the 1890s began to lift. Although some critics were convinced that action was needed to end the worst abuses on the 'street,' as long as investing in shares remained a privilege open only to the comparatively well-to-do, pressure for tighter regulation produced few changes. After 1900, however, as stocks and bonds came to be more widely held and a new class of investors was drawn into securities markets by penny mining stocks, attitudes began to change.

2

Selling Stuff

Between 1896 and 1913 the Canadian economy enjoyed one of the greatest booms in its history as the gross national product increased at an annual average rate of 4.2 per cent.[1] Canadians poured their savings into banks, insurance companies, and other investments at an unprecedented rate. Ian Drummond has estimated that between 1901 and 1914 public issues of corporate securities (excluding mines) totalled $572.7 million, while net purchases of new securities, both public and private, equalled $782.2 million. Since institutional buyers such as banks and trust and life insurance companies absorbed about 43 per cent of these, individual buyers took up about $446.2 million worth of stocks and bonds.[2]

New financial intermediaries quickly emerged to channel flows of funds from savers to borrowers, and the securities business underwent a rapid expansion. Underwriters, promoters, brokers, and their salesmen fanned out across the country in search of people willing to put their money into the shares of joint-stock companies – selling the 'stuff,' as members of the brokerage fraternity referred to it among themselves. By 1900 the buying and selling of securities was becoming familiar to an increasing number of Canadians. On the stock exchanges in Montreal and Toronto, shares in banks, railway, and mortgage loan companies changed hands in sizeable, if fluctuating volume. The prosperous had gradually come to accept such investments as a part of their financial strategy along with mortgage loans, bank deposits, and life insurance. Around the turn of the century, however, shares in new types of undertakings gained broader acceptance with investors. Urban utility companies based upon electrical technology began to attract interest. Industrial undertakings, previously considered too risky for most conservative investors, gained wider popularity. Investment men worked to create markets for all kinds of securities wherever possible.[3]

The discovery of gold and silver in British Columbia in the 1890s and later on in northern Ontario aroused widespread interest. Low-priced, speculative mining shares held out the lure of fortunes to be made with the investment of just a few dollars. As a result, mining stocks were bought by people who previously had not been involved in securities markets. Bank, railway, utility, and industrial shares had been purchased by the relatively well-off, typically businessmen or professionals presumed to have the ability to judge a company's prospects of success. Because such securities commanded relatively high prices, normally having par values of $50 or $100, salaried workers and wage earners were rarely buyers. Taking a flyer on a penny mining stock, however, could have the same appeal for a shop clerk as for the boss. While stock and bond salesmen combed the countryside with increasing diligence, concerns began to be expressed about the kind of claims that promoters, especially mining promoters, were making. How should the unwary, the naïve, even the downright avaricious, be protected? Was public education the answer or would government regulation be required to control the worst abuses of unscrupulous share pushers?

I

As the depression of the early 1890s began to lift, a new generation of stock and bond dealers appeared on the Canadian scene. By the time of the First World War the more adroit and successful of these men had created firms that would dominate the Canadian financial community for the next several generations and had built themselves large personal fortunes in the process. One of the pioneers, George A. Cox, formed Central Canada Loan and Savings in 1884 and watched as its business was gradually transformed from mortgage lending to bond dealing and underwriting. In 1889 Cox backed his son-in-law, A.E. Ames, in founding his own Toronto brokerage house. Dominion Securities Corporation was set up in 1901 as a subsidiary of Central Canada Loan and Savings with E.R. Wood as its president. J.H. Gundy and G.H. Wood left Dominion Securities in 1905 to set up Wood, Gundy and Company. A.E. Ames and Company, Dominion Securities, and Wood, Gundy soon came to dominate the bond underwriting business in Canada.[4]

Ambitious salesmen not only concentrated on a growing clientele in the cities but also began to comb the small towns and back roads in search of prosperous professionals, merchants, and farmers. One young man who spotted the new opportunities was Frederick H. Deacon; he dropped out of university in the mid-1890s and became an itinerant bond salesman in the townships to the west of Toronto. Soon he branched out from loan and trust company debentures to urban utilities, marketing the stocks and bonds of companies being promoted by wealthy fellow Methodists such as Cox, Ames, and Joseph Flavelle. Deacon was a persuasive enough salesman that by 1905 he calculated that he was worth $100,000, and the following year he put up $18,500 to purchase a seat on the Toronto Stock Exchange. Deacon not only retailed securities but also began to take on modest underwritings; he and Ames joined together to promote the Sterling Coal Company in 1909. With J.W. McConnell, Deacon gained control of Morrow Screw and Nut of Ingersoll, Ontario, of which he later became president. By 1914 the Deacon firm employed a staff of fifteen and had a solid reputation on the 'street'; its founder became a millionaire at the age of thirty-nine.[5]

Starting out in Halifax, William Maxwell Aitken (later Lord Beaverbrook) carved out an even more spectacular career as a stockbroker and company promoter. Capitalizing on a chance meeting in 1902 with the prominent Halifax businessman John F. Stairs, the twenty-three-year-old Aitken quickly displayed impressive talent as a salesman. The following year, when Stairs and his associates set up the Royal Securities Corporation to act for them as 'investors, capitalists, financiers, concessionaires, brokers and agents,' Aitken became its manager. The firm's earliest success was the underwriting and promotion of the Trinidad Electric Company, which supplied power, lighting, and transportation to the island's capital; it was followed by a string of other promotions in Cuba and Puerto Rico.[6]

Such utility companies were normally financed by issuing sufficient bonds to raise the money to build a generating station, string wires, and acquire and electrify any existing horse-car lines. The aim was to sell each $100 bond to investors for between 75 and 90 per cent of par. In addition, the company would issue a roughly equal number of shares with a nominal par value of $100, but these were normally given away to the insiders for almost nothing. A portion of this stock was then retained by the syndicate members in order to maintain control of the company, while the rest of it was used as a bonus for those prepared to purchase the bonds. If these ventures were successful (as they frequently were), earnings were sufficient to pay not only the 5 per cent bond interest but also generous dividends on the common stock. As a result, share prices often appreciated rapidly, rewarding the promoters with handsome capital gains.

By the end of 1904 Aitken could boast that $300,000 worth of Trinidad Electric Company bonds had been sold during the year and that in November alone 3,000 common shares had been placed in Atlantic Canada at a price of $77.50. Despite the untimely death of his mentor John Stairs that autumn,

Aitken had made Royal Securities a solid success. He also orchestrated flotations for such important regional industries as Nova Scotia Steel and Coal and the Robb-Mumford Boiler Company.

Porto Rico Railways, set up to modernize the utility services in San Juan, proved the sternest test of Aitken's ability, since a key part of the financing had to be handled in the midst of a severe recession in 1907. He did his utmost to galvanize the staff of Royal Securities to sell Porto Rico Railway bonds.[7] The nature of the Canadian market for stocks and bonds can be discerned from the 376 reports that his salesmen, H.E. Bradford and W.E. Todgham, filed on prospective clients between October 1907 and February 1908.[8] Bradford had the territory stretching from Bridgewater and Liverpool on the Atlantic coast of Nova Scotia around to the Fundy shore, up through Pictou County, and across the Northumberland Strait to include Prince Edward Island. Todgham worked out of Saint John, New Brunswick, and also covered Sussex and Moncton. The character of their clientele was predictable: forty-two merchants, thirty-two doctors, twenty-seven lawyers, a dozen each of sea captains and bank managers, ten clergymen, nine insurance agents, and eight druggists made up two-thirds of the list. Even a village of six hundred like Bear River (near Digby) could hold a dozen clients, one-third of them connected to a single family with a large estate that had funds to invest. Surprisingly large pools of capital existed: one man in Westville, Nova Scotia, was said to be worth $50,000, another had $20,000 saved up, and a third $10,000.

Many of the people whom Bradford and Todgham encountered on their travels preferred to stick to the tried-and-true; a retired farmer told Bradford that he had put all his savings into mortgages and was 'too old to make any changes in his habits.' A wealthy Pictou merchant declared that he was 'not inclined to buy anything but Bank stocks.' Yet resistance to investing in industrial undertakings had begun to decline. One hundred and twelve individuals were persuaded to name fifty different companies in which they owned shares, and the largest group, twenty, were industrials. Important regional firms such as Stanfield's Woollens of Truro and Dominion Iron and Steel and Dominion Coal on Cape Breton Island were popular. Aitken observed, 'There is no use offering Western [Canadian] bonds down here yet. People want local issues nine times out of ten. The tenth time you can give them your own stuff.'[9] Fortunately, utility shares were becoming increasingly popular, and the men from Royal Securities were able to sell many clients on the virtues of promotions such as Trinidad Electric. Helping to save Aitken's bacon in 1907 was the fact that thirty-four individuals were persuaded to buy bonds in Porto Rico Railways at 92.5 per cent of par (often with a bonus of common stock thrown in as a sweetener).

Competition was not lacking. Both J.C. Mackintosh and Company and F.B.

McCurdy and Company of Halifax had representatives, while over in New Brunswick McCurdy and J.M. Robinson and Sons of Saint John were active. McCurdy tried to steal away business in the fall of 1907 by offering Porto Rico bonds at 90 per cent until the frustrated Aitken advised his men, 'I am quite satisfied to have you meet his quotations and would suggest that you continue to do so as long as you are satisfied that his cutting prices is bona fide. I cannot understand where he is getting the securities from and am doing everything possible to purchase his bonds. I cannot get a quotation from him.' Early in 1908, with the Puerto Rican utility still staggering under the weight of unpaid construction bills, Aitken directed his salesmen to 'meet McCurdy's price in every instance except Porto Rico, and that [there] our securities should be marked down to a half point lower than McCurdy's.'

Aitken complained frequently and bitterly that the other Porto Rico under-writers failed to pull their weight. To A.E. Ames he wrote, 'I am very sorry if I was too hard at our meeting in Toronto ... I can assure you that my quarrel with your firm was not half as bad as my quarrels with the Halifax underwriters.' A year and half later Ames still felt aggrieved at his treatment: 'we fell somewhat behind placing our securities, due both to bad money conditions and to its becoming known that Porto Rico securities could be had at better than the ordinary subscription price. Some little concessions were made to us, but later on you dunned us unmercifully by letter and telegram and personally in my office. You arbitrarily witheld for months the bonus stock to which we were entitled.'[10]

In the end, however, the syndicate had to hang together or hang separately. Much attention was lavished by Aitken upon a pamphlet to be attached to the first annual report of Porto Rico Railways, setting forth the work already completed 'in a manner calculated to meet our purposes in the sale of securities.' Eventually it was decided that Ames would send out three thousand copies of this production to all new bondholders as well as to brokers and financial institutions across Ontario. Contrary to his usual practice, Aitken even felt compelled to publish earnings figures for the company in order to attract bond buyers.[11] Gradually sales picked up as the recession began to lift, and by late January 1908 Aitken could see light at the end of the tunnel: 'The market in Porto Rico is opening up. We have sold more bonds during the latter part of December and in the month of January than in the past six months. There is every indication that this market will continue and we hope to see all the underwriters through safely.'[12]

Out on the road the men from Royal Securities still faced plenty of competi-tion. In July 1908 Bradford reported from the village of Pubnico in southwest-ern Nova Scotia on one of his rivals, 'Rossborough was here yesterday and the

Coast has been infested with investment men.' Itinerant salesmen were also about: from Wolfville Bradford noted, 'There is a Baptist parson in town from Toronto pushing Sewer Pipe [shares] and other securities but not doing much, I fancy.'

Aitken had a shrewd eye for promising recruits, some of whom soon made their mark in the Canadian financial world. Of I.W. Killam, who joined Royal Securities at nineteen, Aitken later observed, 'He had a big head, and he was more than intelligent.' After his boss moved to Britain, Killam succeeded him as head of Royal Securities.[13] A.J. Nesbitt, whose job was to persuade Quebec insurance companies to take up the issues that the corporation was promoting, went on to found the successful brokerage and underwriting firm of Nesbitt, Thomson and Company.

Despite the success of Royal Securities, Max Aitken concluded early on that operating in the Maritime regional market was too confining. The number of potential investors was limited, and the lack of scope for raising capital to finance underwritings limited the corporation to smaller promotions. Almost from the first he was eyeing a move to Montreal, the national financial capital, and increasingly he centred his activities there. By 1909 he had persuaded Herbert Holt of the Royal Bank and Sir Edward Clouston of the Bank of Montreal to invest in Royal Securities, and he soon engineered mergers in both the Canadian cement and steel industries. By the time that Aitken departed Canada for good in 1910 he had capitalized upon the rapid growth of the stock and bond market to turn Royal Securities into a 'tremendous money spinner.'[14]

Promoters, underwriters, and brokers such as Max Aitken, A.E. Ames, E.R. Wood, G.H. Wood, J.H. Gundy, and Frederick H. Deacon prospered mightily in the heady times between 1897 and 1913, though they had to get through some heavy weather in the recessions of 1903 and 1907. Canadian buyers proved ready to snap up the 'stuff' – bonds and shares issued by new utilities and industrials. By 1914, 11,000 Canadians owned shares in the nation's two dozen leading public companies.[15] Salesmen in search of investors were not only combing the downtown financial districts of the growing cities but also the small towns and the back concessions.

II

Well-off Canadians took to blue-chip securities with enthusiasm, but it was penny mining stocks that really focused public attention on share markets for the first time. The discovery of precious metals in the interior of British Columbia in the 1890s, followed by the development of a dazzling constellation of northern Ontario mines such as Dome, Hollinger, Wright-Hargreaves, and Lake

Shore in the decade before the First World War, seemed proof positive that Canada was a storehouse of mineral wealth. Prospectors and mining promoters were quick to realize that there were pools of capital waiting to be tapped. Each new discovery set off a wave of mining promotions, with investors lining up for the action. Despite the fact that most companies never found commercial ore bodies or paid any dividends, it was still possible for shareholders who got in on the ground floor to take profits from trading the shares as they moved up and down. And who knew where the next bonanza might be found? Even the relatively conservative clients of a brokerage firm such as F.H. Deacon and Company became keenly interested in mining issues following the discoveries in northern Ontario. Among the many gold and silver stocks on Deacon's books, Beaver Consolidated in the Cobalt camp was a particular favourite. Marketed at between 53 and 65 cents beginning in 1908, Beaver sold for 36 to 52 cents by 1911, but was paying annual dividends of 11 per cent to its shareholders.[16]

The office clerk or shop assistant who picked up a rumour or read a tip in the press was just as eager as any businessman (or his wife) to join in a play. People began to flock to brokerage offices, intently watching the fluctuations in the share price of the hottest prospect of the moment. Most of them knew little and cared less about geology or mineralization, but all were eager to get in on the ground floor and ride a stock for as much profit as they could. Too often, however, their dreams were dashed when no discovery was made and the price of the shares slid away to nothing. Seeing that process repeat itself time after time was enough to convince some investors, businessmen, and financial journalists that there needed to be better regulation of securities markets. Mining exploration by its very nature was highly speculative. Raising money through the sale of penny shares in a public company seemed to open the way for all manner of abuses. After all, what was to prevent promoters from composing over-optimistic, fanciful, or downright false pitches with which to woo unsophisticated investors? Wasn't it all too easy for a stockbroker or company promoter to launch a company with great fanfare based upon nothing more than the rights to an unproved mining claim in a distant location? Did the money raised by the sale of shares even go to the prospectors, or did it mostly end up in the hands of the share-pushing insiders, who dumped their holdings while markets were hot?

True, there were a few companies, such as Temiskaming and Hudson Bay Mining, whose shares rose from 8 cents to $300 in 1903.[17] But in scores of other promotions, stock was marketed for a nickel or a dime and even rose to a quarter or more, before the insiders silently folded their tents and stole away as the bottom dropped out of the market, leaving the shareholders with nothing but finely engraved certificates useful only as wallpaper. Surely something should be done to ensure that investors who put their hard-earned savings into stocks got a fair shake and enjoyed protection against the depredations of insiders and speculators who lied, cheated, and manipulated share prices for their own advantage.

But what? The problem was that one person's speculative gamble was another's shrewd investment. How bad was the situation? Could the operation of securities markets be significantly improved without fatally impairing their efficiency? Could brokers, promoters, and stock exchanges be relied upon to act on their own to clean things up? Would this approach, combined with broader public education, suffice or would government intervention be required? Some people believed that promoters and brokers needed to be hemmed in by tighter legal requirements which would compel them to disclose the information that investors required to make sound decisions. Such restrictions would require both the federal and provincial governments to make major revisions to their companies acts.[18] If there was to be direct intervention in securities marketing, how would it operate and who would oversee it? Debate on such questions periodically swirled through the financial community from the mid-1890s until the time of the First World War.

What started the great Canadian love affair with mining stocks was Rossland. By 1896 that word seemed to be on everybody's lips on the 'street' in Toronto and Montreal. Prospectors swarmed into the camp in the southern interior of British Columbia in search of further strikes of gold, silver, and copper. Stories about the riches of mines such as Le Roi, War Eagle, and Centre Star filled the press. As Canada began to struggle out of the painful depression of the early 1890s, a great wave of enthusiasm mounted.[19] People feverishly sought out the latest tips. Full-page advertisements for new joint-stock mining companies sprouted in the newspapers amid endless columns of 'News from the Mines.' Early in 1897 the fortnightly *Canadian Miner* began to appear in Toronto, its pages crammed with appealing come-ons. The number of mining brokers listed in the Toronto city directory increased from just 4 in 1896 to 29 a year later and 40 by 1898. If the 50 or more stockbrokers already active in the city and the very high rate of turnover among mining promoters are taken into account, there were probably at least 150 firms peddling mining shares by the late 1890s (see photo 4).[20]

Money from eastern Canada poured into British Columbia mining, supplanting investment from the U.S. northwest that had dominated earlier development. In 1898 Toronto interests acquired both the War Eagle and Centre Star mines for $2 million. The Canadian Pacific Railway Company was already planning a branch line through the Crowsnest Pass into southern British Columbia in order to secure the area against competition from northward extensions of American lines. Eventually a deal was struck by the CPR to acquire an American-controlled rail line and an ore smelter at Trail, British Columbia, for $800,000. By the time that Canada's governor general, Lord Aberdeen, visited Rossland in the summer of 1898, the boom had reached its height.

From the very beginning warnings had been heard that the gullible were being taken advantage of. In October 1896 the Toronto Board of Trade noted that only two British Columbia mining companies (Le Roi and War Eagle) were paying dividends, while no more than a dozen in all were actually shipping any ore. Most of the other promotions were mere 'wildcat' prospects on which as little as $200 had been spent. Responsible businessmen were urged to try to stop inexperienced investors from squandering their savings without making careful enquiries. Only those who could afford to lose their money should invest in mining.[21]

Why, asked the *Monetary Times*, were mining promoters being so greedy? Selling shares at inflated prices would only retard development by frightening away real investors, who wanted more than 'a list of the names of directors and the assurances of a glib manager with a ready pen.'[22] Fred Stokes took a more direct tack; in January 1897 he haled fifteen Toronto brokers into the police court for misrepresenting the paid-up capital of the companies that they were promoting in their advertisements. At first the editor of the *Monetary Times* wondered exactly what Stokes was up to. Was he really trying to protect that public or was he 'on the make' for a pay-off like some 'whisky detective'? If he really succeeded in establishing that many well-known brokers were making misleading claims, then he deserved a statue of himself wrought from British Columbia gold in the 'mining hall of fame.' Stokes, however, failed to present proof, and all the charges were quickly dismissed.[23]

The *Monetary Times* reminded its readers that during the 1880s there had been few issues traded on Canadian stock exchanges except bank and loan company shares, and speculation in them had been rife. Then along came railway securities, and now there were all sorts of stocks and bonds to choose from. There was nothing wrong with investing in legitimate mining enterprises, but floating shares on the strength of a six-foot-deep hole in a remote location based upon the guess that something of value lay underneath was another matter.[24] Even some mining men admitted that there were serious problems. At a convention in Montreal in the spring of 1897 several people questioned whether the current system of company promotion was satisfactory. Was it right to sell 5-cent mining shares over the counter to gullible people who would likely get nothing for their investment? Should the capitalization of a company be advertised at $1 million[25] when, in fact, all of its 1 million shares might have been sold for less than $50,000?[26]

The naive and unsophisticated were swiftly caught up by the Rossland boom. The *Monetary Times* claimed that hundreds of young men in Toronto now read the mining pages with as much interest as the sports news. Though such people might talk glibly about 'veins' or 'stopes,' none of them had ever visited mining country or had any real knowledge of geology. As a result they were 'just ignorant enough for the clever western talker,' who could convince them that the shares he was promoting were a sure thing. What seems to have offended the editor was that most of these share buyers were hardly innocents; rather, they were the self-deluded who thought that they could outwit the experts. Perhaps, he concluded, nothing could be done to prevent 'born gamblers' from taking a fling, but was there no means to protect impressionable young men and women, impecunious clerks, and unsuspecting retired folk?[27]

Stories about naïfs victimized by unscrupulous share pushers became commonplace. The *Monetary Times* described how a Kingston clergyman had been induced to part with $50 in cash and a note for $250 for ten shares in a building and loan association. No wonder the minister had been fooled. 'These concerns employ the smartest talkers they can get, supply them with the most alluring literature and authorize them to promise all sorts of unlikely things in the way of profitable results to them who will believe and invest. All this is often done under pretense of promoting habits of thrift among the wage-earning classes. The investor is told to take five or ten of the million shares of the "Do-as-you-would-be done-by-Bucolic-Mutual-Help-and-Accumulation Company."' In this case, however, the sharper had been so delighted at obtaining some cash that he promptly blew it on getting drunk; whereupon the anxious cleric wired the loan company, discovered that the man was not one of their agents at all, and had him arrested for false pretences.[28] The clergy were evidently thought to be particularly gullible; in another of his diatribes against speculation the editor of the *Monetary Times* remarked that stockbrokers were being besieged with orders for speculative shares from (as an English wit had put it) 'all three sexes, men, women and clergymen.'[29]

Clearly many people who ought to have known better did become caught up in mining-share speculation. The manager of the Traders' Bank in Guelph, Ontario, complained to British Columbia's gold commissioner in Rossland that in 1896 he had bought several thousand shares of Ivanhoe Gold Mines at 10 cents apiece, only to discover that the company had failed to comply with the provisions of the Mines Act so that its claims had lapsed. The angry banker bitterly condemned 'the promoters, or rather those in control, [who] evidently decided to swindle those shareholders to whom they had sold stock by letting the Co.'s [sic] license lapse and getting *a stool pigeon to restake the claim for their benefit.*' 'A swindle, pure and simple,' the banker called it, but the official insisted there was nothing that he could do.[30]

The peaking of the Rossland boom in 1898 and the collapse of the gold rush to the Rainy Lake region of northwestern Ontario the following year[31] only reinforced a growing chorus of complaints that people who purchased shares in joint-stock companies required greater protection against unscrupulous promoters. But how could this be provided? Simply counselling prudence seemed doomed to failure, especially in the midst of a speculative frenzy. In 1896 Toronto lawyer J.J. Kingsmill was reported to have sent out a circular letter to investors and brokers warning 'against efforts that are likely to be made by men addicted to sharp practices to float wildcat speculations on the mining market.' He advised making a careful investigation before putting a nickel into any venture.[32] But no more attention was paid to his advice than to the stern editorials in the *Monetary Times.*

Some people argued that tightening up the legal requirements governing company incorporation could compel promoters to disclose their intentions and ensure that they were carried out. Such reforms were already being contemplated in Britain after a series of fraudulent promotions.[33] The British Companies Act of 1900 required promoters to make extensive disclosure and created the framework for the modern company prospectus by specifying its contents. What properties were being conveyed to the company and the number of shares that the promoters intended to award themselves had to be set forth.[34] Disclosure by prospectus was required for any company to make written solicitations inviting investment.

Large losses had occurred in Britain through promoters raising money by the sale of shares and then failing to carry out the planned activities. Shareholders had little recourse against the misapplication of funds already in a company treasury. In order to remedy this situation the new British act banned the allotment of any shares until subscriptions in cash equal to 5 per cent of the nominal value of the shares offered had been received.[35] Compliance was mandatory before companies could legally commence operations; failure to do so within forty days required the return of all subscriptions. This statute was to form the basis of modern British company law, its major weakness being that it did not require the official filing of either financial statements or shareholder lists.

In Canada the federal Joint Stock Companies Act of 1877 was modelled upon an earlier, less-stringent British statute, and the provincial laws concerning company incorporation were similar. Only in 1897 did Ontario require that companies furnish their shareholders with copies of annual financial statements. Despite the new British legislation of 1900, however, neither level of government in Canada moved at that time to overhaul company law to protect investors further.

In the boom times after 1900 new abuses appeared. Critics complained that when existing companies were amalgamated into new ventures, promoters often took advantage of the laxity of company law to 'water' their stock by overpaying for the assets acquired from insiders and by overvaluing the 'goodwill' of the conglomerates. Loaded down with interest payments on bonds and heavy dividends on large issues of common shares, these enterprises sometimes found it hard to earn sufficient profits to meet their obligations. In one notorious instance the Canada Cycle and Motor Company acquired bicycle plants all across the country, but the collapse of the cycling craze put it in deep difficulty. When the insiders at CCM fell out and started suing one another over the promotional profits, the messy details became public knowledge.[36]

By the time that the Rossland boom ended, attention had already switched to the Yukon. There pure 'placer' gold lay in flakes and nuggets in the stream beds and could be extracted by panning or washing away the sand and gravel. Thus rich hauls could be recovered by individuals using only primitive and inexpensive equipment. As a result, not many incorporated companies seem to have been formed, and central Canadian investors were not much involved. In the east, however, conditions were different; hard-rock mining required extremely heavy capital investments. Valuable copper deposits in the Sudbury basin in northern Ontario had been known for some time, but they were combined with nickel, a compound of devilish difficulty to refine, so that only gradually did the International Nickel Company overcome its technical problems. For a while it appeared that the future prosperity of 'New Ontario' might rest upon the agricultural development of its vast Clay Belt. The provincial government was persuaded to finance the construction of the Temiskaming and Northern Ontario Railway to open up the area for farming. By 1903 the rails were creeping towards the western shore of Lake Timiskaming[37] when a fabulously rich lode of silver mixed with cobalt was uncovered. The following year there were four producing mines, and by 1905 hundreds of people were pouring through the T&NO station at Cobalt, under whose townsite lay some of the best claims. The agricultural prospects of northern Ontario were abruptly forgotten.[38]

Was this really the long-anticipated bonanza? Financial journalists such as Edward Trout of the *Monetary Times* hemmed and hawed, wavered and waffled. Yes, he opined in the fall of 1905, the discoveries were real, but who wanted cobalt anyway and how was it to be separated from the silver? In 1904 five mines shipped ore worth only $140,000, but a year later seventeen mines were producing $1.5 million in silver. By 1906 nineteen mines delivered $3.6 million of ore, and the following year there were twenty-nine mines in a twelve-square-mile area shipping 9 million ounces of silver worth $5.5 million. In 1908 twenty-eight mines produced bullion valued at $9.5 million. After three private railway cars carried forty-four New York brokers to Cobalt in the summer of 1906 to see the camp with their own eyes, Trout became a convert at last.[39]

As the rush gained momentum, 99 public mining companies were incorporated in Ontario in 1905 with total authorized capital of $27.5 million. The following year 263 were formed, capitalized at $185 million, and in 1908, 321 with capital of $320 million. Obviously these 683 companies fell far short of raising $530 million, but Cobalt mining shares became very hot properties. Some people got rich through shrewdness or good luck, but as the editor of the *Canadian Annual Review* noted astringently, some benefited from 'the unscrupulous manipulation of public confidence and individual cupidity by means of stock companies; to still more, an actual loss of money had resulted through careless investment in wild-cat concerns or easy submissions to the plans of the financial fakir. The difficulty has been to discriminate between ... the real mine and the mere empty claim, the stock with a future and the stock not worth the paper it was printed on.'[40]

Stephen Leacock captured the popular mood of enthusiasm for taking a flyer on mining stocks perfectly in *Sunshine Sketches of a Little Town* (1912). To the people of the mythical Mariposa, a hundred miles north of Toronto,

it seemed like the finger of Providence. Here was this great silver country spread out north of us where people had thought there was only a wilderness ...

So no wonder the town went wild. All day in the streets you could hear men talk of veins and smelters and dips and deposits and faults – the town hummed with it like a geology class on examination day. And there were men about the hotels with mining outfits and theodolites and dunnage bags, and at Smith's bar they would hand chunks of rocks up and down, some of which would run as high as ten drinks to the pound.[41]

At the beginning of 1907, with the Cobalt boom going full tilt, John B. Maclean brought out his new *Financial Post*. The publisher of the *Canadian Grocer*, the *Dry Goods Review*, and *Hardware and Metal* had concluded that the businessmen who read his other publications needed information and advice on investments. A weekly devoted to financial news would fill a niche that the commercial papers largely ignored. As editor, Maclean chose Stewart Houston, who was determined to pull no punches.[42] The very first issue of the *Post* carried a pointed warning: 'Mining stock should be bought only by men who have made mining a business, or the rich individuals who can afford the hazard a mining

proposition inevitably entails.' 'Consulting Engineer,' the paper's Cobalt correspondent, warned repeatedly against accepting the reports of self-styled 'Mining
Engineers.' Most mining prospects were wildcats whose 'very sharp teeth and
claws were plentiful, and in nine cases out of ten the unscrupulous mining
engineer was largely responsible for them being at large.' Consulting Engineer
also pooh-poohed the push of exploration fifty miles north from Cobalt into the
Larder Lake gold country, predicting that 95 per cent of the claims would be
thrown out when the mining recorder established that the prospectors had not
made the required mineral discovery. To invest without the fullest information
on an ore body was 'blind gambling with the odds always against the shareholder.'[43]

Eventually even the sceptics had to admit the richness of northern Ontario as
one dramatic find succeeded another, like the great gold discoveries at Porcupine near Timmins in 1909 and at Kirkland Lake in 1912.[44] But while the boom
in mining shares raced ahead some people still worried that investors continued
to be swindled left, right, and centre. As early as 1904, before the Cobalt rush
was fully under way, one member of the Ontario legislature had introduced a
private member's bill to revamp the provincial Companies Act along the lines of
the British revisions of 1900, requiring promoters to make extensive disclosure
by prospectus. In the debate a government spokesman claimed that investors
already had more protection in Ontario than elsewhere, and no action was
taken.[45]

By 1907, however, the Ontario cabinet had finally decided that the time had
come to revise the law. Provincial Secretary W.J. Hanna drafted a bill based
upon the British act of 1900. The new legislation not only required all companies with more than ten security holders to make much fuller disclosure by
issuing prospectuses, but it rendered void stock subscriptions solicited verbally
unless a written prospectus was also delivered to the buyer. The *Monetary Times*
warmly applauded the new law and suggested that all other governments should
follow suit to ensure a uniform regimen across the country; but Ottawa and the
other provinces failed to act.[46]

With the Cobalt mining boom in full swing, however, it was clear that new
company legislation alone would not be sufficient to protect the gullible from
themselves. In the fall of 1907 the *Financial Post* began working to educate the
public through a weekly 'Black List' (printed in special bold type), which
described the more outrageous stock-selling operations.[47] Some of the mines on
the list were out-and-out frauds, such as Highland Mary; Toronto broker Frank
Law was shown to have used ore samples sent to him by a completely different
company to bilk the public and was charged with conspiracy to defraud. He was

convicted of swindling share buyers of $235,000 and sent to the pentitentiary for five years.[48]

The *Financial Post* also revealed how easily shady mining promoters could skate round the law. For instance, the backers of the Silver Leaf Mining Company created 5 million $1 par-value shares and struck a deal with a Toronto brokerage to sell them for whatever it could get on a commission of 40 per cent, the balance to go into the company treasury. Some 2 million shares were apparently sold for about $140,000, or just under 15 cents per share. In one community a well-known investor was persuaded to buy shares and was paid a dividend to induce him to recommend the stock to others without his realizing that his neighbours would receive no such dividends. The $85,000 owed to the company treasury was never paid over, but simply kept by the insiders.[49]

In an effort to convince the Toronto financial community that there were plenty of sound mining companies, the town of Cobalt invited a large delegation from the Toronto Stock Exchange to visit in the fall of 1908. The brokers were wined and dined by town officials and miners, who tried to impress upon them that the 'rush' was over and that the stage was now set for more orderly development of the mines. Yet evidence of how common such swindles remained at that time was one Cobalt promotion that attracted great attention from the Toronto mining fraternity because of the unusual approach taken by the sponsoring brokers. Though located near other valuable mineral finds, the company's property was simply represented as a prospect that might or might not turn out. Moreover, the insiders committed themselves to maintaining their interest in the company until the claims had been thoroughly explored. In addition, investors were promised that there would be no 'clean-out' at their expense once share prices had been run up as the insiders abandoned the stock. The comment that this proposition aroused indicates how exceptional these commitments were.[50]

Also in the fall of 1908 Ontario's provincial secretary admitted that the changes in company legislation passed the previous year had failed to correct many of the more serious problems. 'Flagrant disregard of the prospectus clauses of the Ontario Companies Act appears to be as great as ever ... Flotations of the Highland Mary class, and the methods there adopted, seem to prevail unabated.' Nothing could be done to prevent recklessness by investors, but the required prospectuses would at least reveal the number of shares paid out for properties and the names of the recipients, as well as the commissions paid to promoters and the interests of the directors. The provincial secretary threatened legal action 'unless those interested proceed at once to bring themselves within the law.'[51]

Despite such warnings, the market for mining shares in Toronto continued to boom as a result of news of the silver finds at Gowganda. The *Canadian Annual Review* noted that the excitement over the new discoveries had resulted in 'the public being gulled into innumerable sugar-coated investments which could, in the main and in the very nature of things, result in little but disappointment.' In the spring of 1909 the *Financial Post* complained that the advertisements in the daily press for the Bartlett Mine were 'absurd.' Share prices were being propped up by letting out the stock in dribs and drabs and holding back delivery of certificates from purchasers. Once the insiders had disposed of their shares, the paper predicted, these advertisements would cease and the stock would collapse, despite the fact that there was a real possibility of developing a viable mine.[52] The *Post* contended that most Cobalt issues had become 'footballs of speculation,' manipulated for the benefit of their promoters. The problem was that the market for these stocks was so narrow that prudent investors avoided them because of their violent fluctuations. Short-sighted market rigging by insiders was likely to undermine public confidence in the worth of these shares, which would only retard mining development until the bad memories faded away.[53]

Canadian mining stocks also acquired a bad reputation abroad. The backers of Canada Consolidated Cobalt Mines used the names of several prominent men on both sides of the Atlantic without their approval, taking in nearly $40,000 from investors in Britain before being exposed. Other promoters ran advertisements in the British press claiming that the Ontario government would guarantee investments in the mines at Cobalt, a ploy that helped to lure in more of the unwary.[54] Eventually the *Financial Times* of London became so disgusted that it denounced Canadian company law as unduly lax and warned outright against investing there until the rules were tightened up.[55]

Cobalt stocks had initially received an enthusiastic welcome in the United States. In the fall of 1906 the wealthy Guggenheim brothers investigated the Nipissing mine and took an option to buy 400,000 shares at $25. Nipissing stock shot up to over $35 on the strength of this endorsement. When the Guggenheims changed their minds and dropped their option, prices swiftly collapsed, hitting $6 by early 1907.[56] Promoters tried to interest U.S. investors in various other ventures, but allegations of manipulation, combined with memories of Nipissing, gave Canadian mining shares as bad a reputation in New York as they had acquired in London.[57]

Canadians were not the only people pushing dubious shares, of course. As the *Financial Post*'s 'Black List' was quick to point out, a growing number of Americans were trying to peddle their wares in Canada. The Sterling Debenture Corporation of New York sent a flood of mail northward in the autumn of 1907, flogging issues such as American Telegaphone, a scheme to make voice recordings that could be sent by mail. The *Post* approvingly quoted the advice of British capitalist R.M. Horne Payne[58] that any American promotions being advertised in Canada should be avoided 'as one would the pestilence.' The hallmarks of such scams were offerings of penny stocks with promises of advances in stock prices on a particular date or of imminent dividends ranging from 30 to 1,000 per cent of par value, and the failure to state the amount of money to be raised and its planned disposition.[59]

Other come-ons included a promise from A.B. Spencer and Company of New York to repay investors the exact purchase price of any stock regardless of its present market value. Rather than getting their money back, those who responded received an offer to switch to another of the issues that Spencer was currently promoting. A.L. Wisner and Company offered a six-month free subscription to its tipsheet, the *Investment Herald*, and then bombarded those who responded with literature and calls from agents selling stocks such as the Philippine Plantation Company. C.F. King masqueraded as a conservative brokerage house with offices that occupied a full floor in a New York skyscraper and hired well-known authors to prepare the copy for full-page advertisements in the quality newspapers.[60]

Despite all the negative publicity, mining stocks retained their allure for many Canadians. The Porcupine strike of 1909 was an extremely rich one, starting with a rounded quartz formation containing the so-called golden stairway of the Dome mine, followed by the discovery at Hollinger. Demand for mining shares was buoyed by further finds at Kirkland Lake in 1912 which ultimately became the Wright-Hargreaves and Lake Shore mines.[61] In addition there was the excitement created by the gold find at Portland Canal on the northwestern coast of British Columbia in 1909, which sparked renewed interest in western mining shares.

Unfortunately, the operations of the shady side of the brokerage fraternity seemed to become more and more blatant. 'Bucket shops' had been operating in Canada for years. These undertakings preyed upon the less well-to-do, encouraging them to buy stocks listed on the exchanges by putting down only a small percentage of the purchase price. Instead of acquiring the shares, however, these operators simply held onto, or bucketed, the orders. If the share price rose, the buyer could claim a small profit. In the event that a client actually paid the full cost of the stock and demanded delivery of his certificates, the bucketers were confident that they could acquire the shares at a lower price through market manipulation. Meanwhile, the investors were charged interest on the money 'lent' to them, and the bucket shops had the use of the deposits.

Bucket shops had appeared in many towns and cities across Canada during the 1880s as interest in stocks began to increase. The federal government had responded in 1888 by introducing the first Canadian legislation to control the buying and selling of securities directly.[62] In order not to interfere with the activities of legitimate brokers the new law focused, not upon the act of trading itself, but upon the intentions of those who frequented bucket shops, buyers and operators alike. An amendment to the Criminal Code declared it an offence to enter a contract to purchase or sell stocks without the intention of completing the transaction. Those who traded in bucket shops were deemed mere gamblers and the premises 'common gaming houses'; persons 'found in' such dens of iniquity were liable to be prosecuted.[63] Because of the difficulty of establishing the intentions of share traders, however, few charges were ever laid under section 201 of the Criminal Code. In 1904 one dealer in Niagara Falls, Ontario, was charged when he advertised the potential for large profits from putting down a mere 2 per cent of the purchase price of stocks traded on the New York Stock Exchange. Although customers received a contract stating that shares would be purchased, neither they nor the operator were found to have made any effort to see that orders were actually executed, and the operator was convicted of keeping a gaming house.[64]

When complaints were received in 1906 that a number of bucket shops were operating in Hamilton, Ontario, the local Crown attorney was instructed to lay charges. Evidence was presented that some otherwise legitimate brokers in the city were accepting orders for stocks traded in New York which they then failed to execute. Meanwhile, clients were charged up to 5 per cent interest on the borrowed sums supposedly expended to buy shares. The prosecutions were aimed at securing undertakings to desist from these operators rather than punishing them with fines or jail terms.[65] At the same time the police reported that there were at least twenty-five bucket shops in Toronto, but since an undercover detective would be required to spend at least $10 to gather evidence against each of them, nothing seems to have been done about the problem.[66]

The Criminal Code provisions concerning fraud and misrepresentation were of no more use in controlling security dealing. One angry investor wrote to the attorney general of British Columbia in 1911 to complain that an American had sold stock in Vancouver after 'salting' a mine[67] and had then fled to New York, where he was giving interviews in the press puffing his discovery. Why were steps not being taken to extradite the offender? The attorney general replied that it was doubtful if a prosecution would succeed, but in any case the provincial government 'have made it a strict rule not to go the expense of extradition in pure cases of mining gamble[s], because if we were to do that the criminal law might be set in motion every time stockholders were unfortunate enough to invest in a non-paying mine.'[68]

With little fear of prosecution, dubious operators became more and more brazen. Journalist Hector Charlesworth recalled that by 1910 the situation in Toronto and elsewhere was wide open. The existing laws were quite inadequate to combat the more skilful type of shark, adept at 'keeping within the law'. Some had become so impudent that they even did not hesitate to violate the common law against fraud. Regulations against bucketshops and other measures of financial protection were as 'scraps of paper' to most of them ... [O]ne could not go into the King Edward Hotel at Toronto without seeing scores of crooks at work trying to separate victims from their money, flashy fellows and big spenders. This was true also of every large hotel in Canada and in every village and on every countryside 'strong arm' salesmen were at work endeavouring to bamboozle ignorant men and women out of their savings.[69]

The daily press largely ignored these abuses as bucketers such as Patriarche and Company began running full-page advertisements in the Toronto papers on the understanding that all their tips would be covered as straight news. The most vociferous demands for a clean-up, therefore, came from a rather unlikely source, the Toronto social and literary weekly *Saturday Night*. In 1910 editor Frederick Paul recruited an experienced journalist, Norman Harris, to run the financial section. The magazine's 'Gold and Dross' column quickly became a kind of informal tribune dedicated to exposing shady dealings.[70]

Harris vehemently denounced operators such as C.D. Sheldon in Montreal, who solicited deposits in multiples of $500 for a 'blind pool' that he pretended to invest in stocks, taking a small commission and sharing the profits (but not the losses) with investors. As canvassers Sheldon recruited civil servants and men from other financial institutions, who offered special inducements to new depositors, and he soon claimed to have $4 million in the pool. Despite repeated warnings in the *Financial Post* and *Saturday Night*, when Sheldon absconded in the autumn of 1910, several people lost over $50,000 each, and there were many accounts worth between $15,000 and $20,000. Yet the law seemed to provide no remedy for the victims. Harris raged, 'Is there to be no restitution in these cases? Will the law step in and adjust this matter, or will the law allow these men and their "profits" to slip through their fingers as they have the boss of the gang?'[71]

Harris recruited another experienced journalist, W.H.P. Jarvis, who composed a series of articles under the pseudonyms Cobalt and Shepherd. He hammered away so relentlessly at dubious mining promotions that the Cobalt Board of Trade and the Mine Managers Association threatened a boycott of the magazine.[72] *Saturday Night* kept up its campaign, however, and in 1911 Harris added a 'News of the Mines' column to report upon 'Near Mines, Flotations, Developments, Promotions, Dividends,' which he cheekily subtitled 'Pork-U-Pine.' The magazine pointed out that the Porcupine boom was now attracting Americans such as Charles A. Stoneham, who had come to Toronto to peddle shares in a company holding only abandoned claims. 'If Canadian authorities are awake,' wrote Harris, 'they will keep a watchful eye on this modern gang of financial cutthroats and stave off the raid they have planned on the savings of investors and have put into operation.' Apparently Stoneham's activities even offended the local mining promoters, who set a trap to prove that he was running a bucket shop.[73] The barrage of criticism eventually led to a police raid on his premises, and charges were finally laid under the Criminal Code.[74]

Charles Stoneham was far from the only American promoter operating in Canada at that time. In the spring of 1911 *Saturday Night* and the *Financial Post* noted that the notorious Oscar Adams Turner had begun flooding the country with literature. His mailing list was rumoured to include between ten and twenty thousand names, and he thought nothing of sending out so much material each week that it cost him up to 30 cents a head for postage alone. Toronto brokers reported that 'sucker' lists, gleaned from the share registers of mining companies, were being regularly offered for sale at 2 cents per name.[75]

If abuses were so common, what could be done to rectify the situation? As early as 1906 suggestions had begun to be heard that restrictions ought to be imposed upon financial advertising.[76] *Saturday Night* frequently criticized the daily press for running advertisements for bucket shops and shady promoters. In 1911 the *Financial Post* claimed that if newspapers were more careful about the advertisements that they accepted, they could do much to prevent the losses by small investors which might run as high as $10 million annually. Despite concerns in some quarters about freedom of the press and the difficulties of papers ascertaining the truthfulness of advertising, the *Post* applauded the idea and urged the government of Ontario to act.[77]

The use of the mails for fraudulent purposes also attracted attention. The U.S. postal service was said to be becoming much more strict with such fraudsters, which made it all the more likely that they would prey upon Canadians. The *Post* reported that every crook in New York who fell afoul of the post office there simply switched his activities to Toronto and continued business as usual. Why shouldn't Canada require that all mail solicitations include disclosure of the information required under the Ontario Companies Act as to the names of the promoters of companies and their plans for the use of stockholders' funds?[78] The federal government, however, failed to take any action to control the use of the mails.

By 1900 Canadians were becoming accustomed to the idea of investing their money in stocks and bonds. During the first decade of the twentieth century brokers and promoters such as Max Aitken and his hard-driven salesmen from Royal Securities helped to persuade more people to put their money into new kinds of 'stuff,' including shares in industrials and urban utilities, as well as in more traditional bank and railway stocks and municipal bonds. But it was the discovery of precious minerals in British Columbia and Ontario and the rapidly increasing popularity of speculative mining stocks that broadened the clientele of share buyers. The possibility of a huge return from a penny stock if a rich strike was made drew in not only the traditional securities buyers but also less prosperous investors who were willing to take a flyer.

Canadian company law provided stockholders with precious little protection against unscrupulous share pushers; the sanctions in the Criminal Code were both ineffective and easily evaded. The promotion of speculative mining ventures created all too many opportunities for dishonest insiders to fleece the gullible, a fact that aroused increasing concern among financial journalists. Despite the stern warnings to investors in the pages of *Saturday Night* and the *Financial Post*, however, few people seem to have been deterred from acting on the basis of the latest hot tip. By 1910 some reformers were wondering how much longer this situation could be allowed to continue and how the worst of these abuses might be brought under control.

3

The Development of the Exchanges

The discoveries of gold and silver around the turn of the century and the wave of popular interest in mining shares that resulted had a significant impact on Canada's stock exchanges. In the depression of the early 1890s, exchange members in Toronto and Montreal were barely scraping by, surviving only through dealing in real estate, insurance, and other commodities as well as securities. By the time of the First World War the Toronto and Montreal Stock Exchanges had greatly increased trading volumes, which resulted in a sharp rise in seat prices. That very success quickly led to the appearance of competitors. Before long there were stock exchanges in such growing cities as Winnipeg, Vancouver, and Calgary, as well as in many smaller places.

Even in these prosperous times the long-established Montreal and Toronto exchanges faced continuing challenges. If they sought to secure business by emphasizing their concern for the interests of investors through the enforcement of tighter regulations, they risked driving away brokers, promoters, and customers to exchanges with laxer rules. Was it better for the MSE and TSE to come to terms with each other and their upstart rivals, to seek agreements concerning the type of listings that each would accept, and even to explore formal commission-splitting arrangements between their respective members? Or could they freeze their competitors out by ignoring them?

For the newly minted exchanges that sprang up across the country the question was whether to try to attract as much business as possible by the loosest possible rules, or whether they should seek to achieve a position in their own communities similar to that occupied by the MSE and the TSE. Should they go cap in hand to those old-line institutions seeking reciprocal arrangements, knowing that they were likely to be rebuffed?

Hovering over all the exchanges was the continuing public debate about how much protection they themselves ought to afford investors. Were these voluntary, private bodies even equal to the task of imposing such regulation, or might it be necessary for governments to intervene by passing new laws? The first decade of the twentieth century saw little lessening of manipulative trading practices. If putting money into the stock market remained much like betting on a horse race or buying a lottery ticket, was public pressure not bound to force state action? Could a measure of voluntary reform stave off this interference, or was the hour already too late?

I

The Montreal Stock Exchange had the advantage of being located in Canada's major metropolis, home to such great joint-stock enterprises as the Bank of Montreal and the Canadian Pacific Railway. During the boom years before the First World War the MSE was able to establish itself as the country's central marketplace for blue-chip securities. Its members enjoyed increasing prosperity after the turn of the century even though trading volume remained volatile (see appendix, table A.1). Almost 3 million shares were traded in 1902 before a loss of confidence in stocks as a result of the recession the following year knocked volume below 800,000 during 1904. The return of good times brought trading activity back to well above 1 million shares by 1906, but another downturn a year later dropped volume below 700,000. Yet 1909 was a record year for the pre-war era, with almost 3,340,000 shares changing hands, spurred on by heavy dealing in both mines (Crown Reserve alone traded 1,069,829 of 1,161,232 such issues handled) and industrials (Dominion Iron and Steel accounting for 794,886 out of 1,290,340).[1] Thereafter volume settled back to over 2 million shares annually through 1913.

The MSE benefited from the last gasp of the mining boom in western Canada in 1901 and 1902 as over 2 million shares of junior mines (par value under $1) changed hands before the Rossland play finally expired, having accounted for nearly half of all trading in the first year and over one-third in the second. Montreal brokers also enjoyed the fruits of the popular appetite for utility stocks in the middle of the decade; between 1901 and 1911 an average of 355,000 street-railway shares changed hands annually, with volume reaching about half a million in each of the last two years. There was heavy dealing not only in the shares of the Montreal Street Railway and its Toronto counterpart, but in the stocks of the companies that served such U.S. cities as Detroit and Minneapolis–St Paul. Trading in industrials was more volatile, but MSE brokers did capitalize on the optimism of Canadians about the future of the country's iron and steel industry as shares in such companies as Dominion Iron and Steel, Dominion Coal, and Nova Scotia Steel and Coal changed hands rapidly. Mergers and amalgamations in the iron and steel business, culminating in the creation of the Steel Company of Canada, whose shares began trading on the MSE in mid-1911, helped to maintain investor interest.[2]

In the course of time MSE business settled into a fairly stable pattern. The old standbys, bank and railway shares, now accounted for a fairly small proportion of total trading, rarely topping 10 per cent of volume, even though the high values of such stocks meant lucrative commissions for brokers. The new street railways, gas and electric utilities, and telephone and telegraph companies usually made up between a quarter and a third of total trading, while other industrials ranged from about 25 per cent of volume and rose to nearly 40 per cent in 1909 and 1912, when merger rumours flew. Trades in shares of established, dividend-paying mines were never significant and declined to a negligible level after 1910; despite a collapse in mid-decade, junior mines enjoyed a comeback on the strength of the new discoveries in northern Ontario.

As business improved around the turn of the century the price of an MSE seat, which had dropped sharply in the depressed 1890s, rebounded, reaching $12,850 by 1901. In their eagerness to capitalize upon new-found prosperity the members initially refused to add to their numbers, and critics dubbed them the Forty Thieves. Eventually five seats were added in 1901, followed by fifteen more in the banner year of 1902. Two years later the MSE left its rented quarters and moved into a splendid new Classical Revival temple of commerce on rue Saint-François-Xavier (see photos 5 and 6). By that time volume had become sufficient that the antiquated 'call' method of trading was abandoned and replaced by a 'continuous auction' like that used on the New York Stock Exchange. Now traders gathered around 'posts' on the floor where particular stocks were dealt in, calling out offers to one another. Once a deal was struck, a transaction ticket was filled out, initialled, and handed to the exchange staff to record on the chalkboards around the walls. Prices and quantities were speedily transmitted by ticker to other markets. When volume increased sharply in 1909, five more seats were added the following year and another ten in 1912. Seat prices had reached $27,500 by 1908 and they hit $30,000 in 1913, when sixty-six seats were in active use.[3]

The rapid rise in seat prices reflected the MSE's establishment as the main marketplace for Canadian industrial shares. Since Montreal was the country's financial metropolis and the headquarters of many large corporations, it was only natural that trading in the stocks of most major public companies should be centred there. From the point of view of local brokers this was a boon since commission rates were fixed according to share values, so that dealing in relatively high-priced industrials was much more profitable than handling penny mining stocks. In addition, MSE members benefited from trading a sizeable number of industrial bonds; over $7.8 million in par value changed hands in 1902, for example. Despite sharp declines in the recession years of 1903 and 1907, bond trading settled down to an annual volume of about $6 million par value between 1909 and 1912 (see appendix, table A.1).

The MSE does not appear to have suffered any serious competition from rival exchanges in the city. The boom in mining shares did lead to an effort to create a new mining-share market in 1900, but the exchange quickly moved to persuade the Quebec government to limit the charter of the proposed rival so that its members could not deal in other kinds of shares.[4] Because there were few mineral finds in Quebec, mining promoters did not locate in Montreal, and the proposed exchange never seems to have become a serious threat.

When Toronto finally began to challenge Montreal as a national, and not merely a regional, metropolis, securities markets in the nation's second city started to reflect its new status. Nowhere was the impact of the Rossland mining boom more evident. Previously the Toronto Stock Exchange's list had been dominated by local banks, mortage loan companies, railways, and utilities, but in the 1890s more and more of the city's brokers busied themselves in marketing shares of speculative mining companies directly to investors. The trading in such shares was handled outside the formal 'board' meetings of the TSE or over the counter in brokerage offices. Aware that its members were missing out on this business, the TSE's governing committee decided in 1897 to try to encourage trading in unlisted mining shares at the exchange after each of the two daily calls of listed issues. In order to arouse public interest such dealings would be recorded by the exchange secretary and reported in the quotation sheets given to the press under the heading 'Unlisted Mining Securities.'[5]

That concession, however, proved insufficient to satisfy the brokers who specialized in mining shares. Late in 1897 they organized a new Toronto Mining Exchange, which began operation the following January and within a year had forty-four issues listed. To permit its members to compete the TSE soon dropped all restrictions on dealings in unlisted shares with outsiders at any time when it was not in formal session. When the Mining Exchange refused to expand its membership from fifteen to twenty-five, however, a third exchange, the Standard, sprang into existence in the summer of 1899 with over thirty members. The Mining Exchange tried at first to prohibit members of the Standard Stock Exchange from being treated as fellow brokers and insisted that they be charged full commission for any business executed. By early 1900, with the Rossland and Rainy River mining booms past their peak, there was not enough business to justify two separate exchanges; talks aimed at an amalgamation of the Standard and Mining exchanges commenced.[6]

These discussions were 'desultory' at first, but by the summer of 1900 the two upstarts had merged under the name of the Toronto Mining Exchange. Because the volume of trade in mining shares was declining, however, its members decided in the fall of 1901 to seek authority from the provincial government to deal in other types of securities under the name of the Consolidated Toronto Stock Exchange or the Ontario Stock and Mining Exchange. That move aroused the hostility of the TSE, fearful about confusion on the part of the investing public; its lawyers persuaded the provincial authorities that the new body should be called the Standard Stock and Mining Exchange.[7]

The great boom in Cobalt stocks in 1905 and the discoveries that unfolded in northern Ontario thereafter helped to set the Standard exchange firmly on its feet and ensured that the TSE would have a persistent rival (see photo 1). By 1906 business was sufficient to add an afternoon trading session to the Standard's single daily call. Additional stocks, including TSE-listed issues, began to be traded. Volume continued to increase steadily, reaching a pre-war peak of 44 million shares during 1911 and far outpacing the level of trading on the Montreal and Toronto Stock Exchanges combined. Most of the trades were in penny mining stocks, however, as the total value of the shares traded that year was $19,875,000, or an average of 45 cents per share (see appendix, table A.7).[8]

Some efforts were made by the Standard's board to tighten up its listing rules. In 1906 companies were required to demonstrate that they had paid for and actually acquired title to their mining claims. Yet brokers continued to display a casual attitude toward listings. In 1911 the assistant secretary reproved A.E. Osler and Company for issuing instructions directly to the exchange's printer to include a stock on the list without bothering to pay the $25 fee or have the application passed on by the committee.[9] The following year it was decided that only properly listed stocks would be displayed on the boards at the exchange and included in the quotation sheets supplied to the press, though this rule was not strictly adhered to.[10] When applications were submitted by mining companies, not all the information requested was necessarily supplied.[11] Questions arose as to the responsibility that the exchange assumed if it listed issues without requiring applicants to supply all the details required on the form.[12] The assistant secretary admitted in 1913 that the exchange tried to scrutinize its listings,

but, of course, mining stocks being purely speculative we can only do our best to ensure that the investor will have a run for his money; we can never be sure that a mine will ever pay dividends or guard against dishonest management.

We also publish quotations on any stock we can, with the idea that we may thus prevent innocent people being loaded up with stocks of little or no value at fancy prices.[13]

During the decade before the First World War the Standard's members also went through the other debates that the TSE had endured in the late nineteenth century as it had struggled for stability. First of all, there was the question of whether members must trade in person or would be permitted to appoint attorneys to represent them. Some people wanted attorneys banned except when a member was ill or absent from the city, so that those brokers who wished to have a trader on the floor at all times would be compelled to purchase an additional seat to the benefit of the exchange. Eventually it was decided that designated attorneys could be present whenever a member was absent.[14]

Not until 1906 was a bar erected around the Standard's floor on Scott Street to separate the public from the traders, but two years later strangers had to be formally banned from the floor during sessions. Rowdy behaviour remained a problem. In 1908 the presiding secretary was asked to explain the 'want of order' at the sessions which was undermining the 'standing and dignity' of the exchange.[15] Then there was the matter of members violating the rules by quoting prices when advertising stocks; offenders were threatened with expulsion. Other members got into trouble for adding advertising material to the daily sheets that they were permitted to circulate to their clients.[16]

The most delicate matter concerned dealings with members of other exchanges. The Standard's board recognized that it could not successfully enforce a prohibition on doing business with TSE members, but in 1910 a new Dominion Stock Exchange was set up in Toronto. Since it had a federal charter of incorporation, its organizers hoped to establish branches in all the major cities in Canada and in Buffalo, New York. Thirty of the fifty seats were quickly subscribed for. The Standard board considered passing a by-law banning outright any dealings with Dominion members, but there were doubts about its legal powers to regulate its members in this way. When the inevitable happened and a Standard member was detected in such a transaction, the board could only punish him for not charging the full commission rate. Fortunately, the Dominion exchange failed to develop into a serious competitor. *Saturday Night* reported in the spring of 1911 that a man who had had no trouble obtaining a membership had jumped bail on a charge of defrauding his clients. The Dominion exchange lingered on for only a few months longer before it collapsed.[17]

The volume of trading on the Standard exchange declined sharply after 1911, only 20.8 million shares changing hands the following year. The slump caught the exchange at a bad time since it had just moved into specially constructed new premises at 56–8 King Street, which it had leased for five years. Volume remained stable in 1913, but the average price fell from 41 cents the previous year to only 28 cents, which meant lower commission income for members. Those who found themselves in serious difficulties tried to sell their seats at sharply reduced prices without the required permission of the board. When a deceased member's seat was put on the market in the fall of 1913, the assistant secretary admitted that the board was eager to see it in the hands of 'some live member, but the market has been so restricted for some time that seats are not in demand.' Eventually the seat was sold for just $700. Nevertheless, the Standard exchange seemed to be on a fairly firm footing by the eve of the First World War.[18]

Faced with a rival exchange the TSE sought to hold its ground. One means was to try to convince investors that it was a broad, liquid market whose price quotations were reliable. At the 1898 annual meeting President A.E. Ames argued that the exchange should aim to open continuously from 10 a.m. to 3 p.m. and to ban off-floor transactions in listed issues altogether, since the latter were not reported to the secretary until the following day and often created artificial prices that did not reflect current trading. Unfortunately for Ames's plan, volume did not justify continuous trading, and so separate morning and afternoon calls continued to be held.[19]

To avoid losing business to the Toronto Mining Exchange the TSE began accepting mining companies for listing provided that they had a sound reputation. The War Eagle mine in Rossland, control of which had been acquired by Toronto businessmen George Gooderham and George Cox, was listed in 1898, when it traded 620,000 shares out of a total annual volume of 875,000 on the exchange. By 1900 six other mines were listed, but unfortunately, the Rossland boom ended, and a rapid run-up in the price of War Eagle stock on the eve of the mine's closure in February led to allegations of manipulation of share prices. These suspicions were not stilled when the TSE board failed to make any serious investigation into the trading in War Eagle stock, a lack of action that hardly aided the campaign to improve the TSE's reputation for honesty and fair dealing.[20]

By the turn of the century, however, the increasing prosperity of TSE members was underpinned by a growing number of listings from outside the ranks of banks, mortgage loan companies, and railways, which had previously provided the backbone of their activities. Now utilities and industrials began to appear on the list, so that the 'miscellaneous' issues, which had totalled only ten in 1895, reached thirty-six in number by 1901, while overall listings numbered eighty. With much of the trading in new issues such as the common shares of the bicycle producer Canada Cycle and Motor and the 'preferred' stock of other industrials, the issuing of which was legalized by federal legislation in 1899,[21] ownership of a stock exchange seat became an increasingly desirable asset. TSE seats, which had sold for just $1,000 in 1897, were worth $10,000 by 1901. In June 1900 the members celebrated their new-found prosperity with a move into new, specially designed quarters in the National Trust building at 20 King Street West (see photo 7).[22]

Like the Montreal Stock Exchange, the TSE began the new century with a flurry of activity arising out of the last gasp of the mining boom in western Canada. Volume reached about 2 million shares in both 1901 and 1902, the Republic mine alone accounting for 493,300 in 1901 and 175,800 the following year, while War Eagle shares traded 292,567 and 185,700, respectively (see appendix, table A.3). These volumes, however, were never again approached in the pre-war years; trading fell to only 1 million shares in the 1903 recession and dropped to just 575,000 the following year before rebounding. The 1907 recession was another heavy blow, and not until the boom year of 1909 did the TSE's volume recover to 1,440,000, before stablizing around the 1 million share mark in the remaining pre-war years.

A fairly steady pattern of trading developed on the TSE as on the MSE. Banks and financial service companies declined in importance after 1908, representing only 6 per cent of yearly volume, while railways dwindled into comparative insignificance. The new utilities were of great importance to Toronto's brokers, particularly the tramways and power companies that local syndicates had organized in São Paulo and Rio de Janeiro in Brazil, so that street-railway shares accounted for around 40 per cent of total volume between 1910 and 1914. Industrial stocks continued to be fairly heavily traded except in the recession years of 1907–8, but never provided as much of the TSE's volume as they did on the MSE. Junior mining shares (par value under $1 up to 1908 and $5 thereafter), which had dwarfed the rest of the market in volume in 1901, went into steep decline thereafter as the Standard Stock and Mining Exchange grabbed a sizeable share of this business. Eventually, however, the new discoveries at Cobalt and Porcupine did create popular stocks such as Nipissing, North Star, and Trethewey, and by the end of the decade junior mines had regained a sizeable part of trading volume, accounting for almost half the business done in 1909 and an average of 25 per cent of volume in each year thereafter until the war.

Even in the best of times the TSE board kept a wary eye upon the rival exchanges. When applying for membership in 1900, John Croft was required to give assurances that he had severed his relations with the Toronto Mining Exchange.[23] Reported trades in listed junior mines on the TSE had evaporated completely by 1906 in the face of competition from the Standard exchange. The following year the TSE moved to recapture a share of the mining market and respond to the Standard's threat to commence trading in TSE-listed stocks by creating a category called 'unlisted securities,' which would be added to the daily lists supplied to the press (see appendix, table A.4). To secure a place on the formal 'share list' now required payment of a $300 fee plus a 'full statement of the affairs of the company,' and a stock could be delisted at any time by the board. All that was required to join the new class of 'listed unlisteds' was the sponsorship of two TSE members. Once approval was granted, they could be dealt in right after the formal call, with trading being reported to the assistant secretary. Since this type of quotation was so easy to obtain, the TSE board revised its by-laws to ban its members from associating with people who belonged to any other Toronto exchange.[24]

The TSE's 'unlisted section' proved an immediate success: over 7.6 million shares in twenty-eight issues changed hands during its first full year of existence. By 1910 not only were Cobalt mining stocks the backbone of this market (with Cobalt Lake alone trading 1,039,877 shares), but now industrials began to appear, including the first five shares of Max Aitken's newly created iron and steel conglomerate, the Steel Company of Canada. By 1911 there were over one hundred issues being dealt in, including twenty-seven Porcupine mines, of which Dome Extension alone accounted for trading of 1,104,855.[25] That same year a small number of unlisted industrial bonds also began to trade. Although total volume was sharply down in 1912 and 1913, the TSE's unlisteds contributed strongly to the prosperity of the Toronto brokerage fraternity in the decade before the First World War.

The other way in which the TSE tried to ensure that non-members remained at a disadvantage was to deny them up-to-date information to prevent them simply meeting the floor prices. In 1901 outsiders were banned from having telephone connections to the TSE. An experiment with local ticker service was discontinued in 1906 as being of 'no use to the exchange.'[26] It also tried to keep tight control over who received its daily quotation sheets each afternoon before they appeared in the press. Members were permitted to send them only to private clients and not to banks or other financial institutions, but in 1909 printer W.R. Houston complained that members were routinely supplying them to Standard stock exchange members. Despite further reminders, however, it proved very difficult to prevent them from doing so since these outsiders could steer TSE members their business in listed issues if they wished to do so.[27]

By the time of the First World War the TSE had established itself as an institution of more than just local importance, no longer the 'rather exclusive club' that it had been at the turn of the century. By 1913 seat prices had reached $20,000 (two-thirds the level of the MSE) as a growing volume of trading in industrials, utilities, and junior mines helped to make the Toronto exchange a national marketplace for certain issues. In 1914 it had actually outpaced the Montreal Stock Exchange in the number of listed issues by 200 to 182, though Toronto brokers still traded significantly fewer high-priced industrials than their

Montreal counterparts.[28] The TSE board felt sufficiently optimistic that in 1911 it decided to purchase a piece of land on Bay Street from Sir Henry Pellatt and build its own premises. Late the following year the cornerstone for the new building was laid, and the formal opening took place early in 1914 (see photo 8). Because of the increased volume of trading the board decided to abandon the 'call' method. Now, as in New York and Montreal, there would be a continuous auction round the four posts on the floor.[29]

Not only did the exchanges in Toronto and Montreal become firmly established, but local exchanges appeared in other Canadian cities during the first decade of the century. And the trading frenzy even penetrated into many smaller towns. Stephen Leacock recorded that once the news of the Cobalt strike arrived in his mythical Mariposa, 'Within a fortnight they put a partition down Robertson's Coal and Wood office and opened the Mariposa Mining Exchange, and just about every man on Main Street started buying scrip.'[30]

Both Vancouver and Victoria had informal mining exchanges during the Rossland boom, but they soon faded away.[31] In 1907 Donald Von Cramer of the Vancouver Trust Company and real estate broker and mining promoter C.D. Rand secured provincial legislation chartering a Vancouver Stock Exchange. Having sold eighteen of its thirty seats for $125 each and rented a small room in the back of a store on West Pender Street, the exchange commenced business on 1 August (see photos 9 and 10). At the opening ceremonies President Rand declared that the days of the fly-by-night brokers who had loaded up buyers with worthless mining stock would end if the public dealt through the VSE.[32]

The VSE's listing fee was $50, which carried with it the supposed assurance that the application had 'passed the investigating committee whereas an unlisted stock has no such standing.' Yet only fourteen companies were listed by the end of 1908. Even some promoters were unconvinced of the worth of a VSE listing. When invited by the secretary to apply on behalf of the Beaver Valley Oil Company, James Harvey (who styled his business 'Financial Agents, Mines, Real Estate, Insurance and Loans') replied with refreshing frankness that he saw no benefit in doing so: 'This company's stock is a purely speculative one, and the stock is all disposed of ... I beg to differ with you when you state that an unlisted stock has no such standing. The general impression of listed stocks, as I understand the situation, is not in favour of the listed stock.' Beaver Valley was operating in a new oilfield, and its stock was 'a good clear gamble and the shareholders purchased it on that understanding. If oil is struck it will not be necessary to have the stock listed on [a] stock exchange to find purchasers. If oil is not struck the stock will be valueless, and it would be a crime to offer it for sale.'[33]

Fortunately for the VSE, others took a more positive view, particularly after the discovery of gold at Portland Canal in 1909 helped to fuel greater interest in mining stocks. The Pender Street premises were available to the exchange for mornings alone, so it was decided to move into larger quarters that would permit a second 'call' to be held each afternoon. Only after the lease had been signed for rooms in the Exchange Building was it discovered that the upstart Pacific Coast Stock Exchange was planning to operate at the same address. Fortunately this rival venture quickly faded away. During 1910, 1,830,000 listed shares changed hands at an average price of 36 cents apiece, while there was also heavy trading in unlisted issues. All thirty seats had by then been sold, so five new ones were created, the last of which went for $3,250.[34]

Much of the action on the VSE was the work of the flamboyant German remittance man Alvo von Alvensleben, whose brokerage sometimes accounted for half the daily volume of listed trading. Von Alvensleben's tipsheets not only brought in a large flow of funds from his fellow German aristocrats but attracted attention across North America. Fish, timber, mining, oil, and real estate ventures were launched in profusion before the recession of 1913 but the outbreak of war the following year led to von Alvensleben's undoing.[35]

Like all newly established exchanges, the VSE had problems controlling its members' activities. The by-laws prohibited advertisements that quoted prices of shares for sale, but this rule was often flouted. In any event, von Alvensleben's tipsheets were so effective in attracting business that the board had no desire to rein him in. The eventual solution was to make the ban on advertising stock prices apply only to British Columbia publications, leaving the rest of the world open.[36] In an effort to make its published quotations more reliable, the board tried to persuade members to report off-the-floor transactions in listed issues, but it could only rely on their goodwill for compliance.[37]

Some Winnipeg businessmen came to believe that the metropolis of the prairies should also have its own stock exchange. The problem in the Manitoba city, however, was that the brokers in town were already fully occupied in the grain trade. The Winnipeg Grain and Produce Exchange had opened in 1887 and secured a provincial charter in 1891. A decade later futures trading began, a move that aroused much antagonism among farmers, who believed such transactions exploited them.[38] In 1907 a group of brokers came together to establish the Winnipeg Stock Exchange, which began operation some time later. But it always struggled along playing second fiddle to the grain exchange, which provided the main livelihood of most of its members. By 1912 only 7,000 shares valued at $800,000 were traded on the WSE.[39]

The history of the Calgary Stock Exchange demonstrated the importance of a local resource base to the securities business in Canada. Natural gas had been discovered in the Turner valley about twenty-five miles southwest of the city in

1911, and in May 1914 oil was struck, setting off a frenzied rush (see photos 11 and 12). The Dingman well had been drilled by the Calgary Petroleum Company organized by Sir James Lougheed and his law partners, R.B. Bennett and W.H. McLaws.[40] Ten days after the discovery a meeting at the offices of Lougheed, Bennett and McLaws approved the by-laws of the Calgary Stock Exchange, which opened with sixteen members in early June. By that time eighty oil companies capitalized at $70 million had been incorporated despite warnings that the Dingman find was not nearly as large as initially claimed.[41]

Never in Canada would there be such fierce competition amongst exchanges as during the Calgary oil boom. At its organizational meeting the CSE agreed to assume the expenses of the Calgary Petroleum Stock Exchange, but in July the members decided against taking over the Calgary Oil and Stock Exchange or the Standard Oil Stock Exchange. The Vancouver Stock Exchange also tried to capitalize upon the oil boom; within days of the Dingman find it had over twenty-five stocks trading on its unlisted section under the heading 'Calgary Oil Stocks.'[42]

Even the outbreak of the First World War in August 1914 could not rupture this frenzy. The CSE closed for three weeks and suspended construction of its new building, but then work resumed to ready the premises by late October. Another oil discovery near Olds, Alberta, that summer only added to the hysteria; four hundred oil companies capitalized at $400 million were soon offering shares to the public, though a typical oil lease for drilling rights to 160 acres cost no more than $1,000. As a result, no less than thirteen other stock exchanges sprang up, of which five ultimately amalgamated into the Calgary General Stock Exchange.[43]

Many years later old-timer R.A. Carlile recalled that he and his partner Jimmy Robertson had held memberships in both exchanges with an attorney on each floor. 'These two used to do quite a big business buying on one and selling on the other.' And ethical standards were far from high. Tim Buck of Black Diamond Oil, said Carlile, had been so keen to make a discovery that he salted his well. Black Diamond stock took off, with Buck selling shares to CSE members at 50 cents under the market, which the brokers turned around and disposed of on the exchange at a handsome profit.[44]

In addition, Calgary had several 'open call' exchanges on street corners where everyone was welcome to show up and enter a bid; business continued even after dark under the glare of the street lights. So great was the lure that respectable members of the CSE were spotted doing business at the open-call markets. The board discussed fines and suspensions but abandoned the idea since enforcement seemed impossible. When one member of the CSE was hauled onto the carpet for expressing opinions detrimental to the exchange, he defiantly insisted that he was not under its jurisdiction since he had not made the remarks during a session. When evidence was adduced that he had uttered the offensive comments during formal trading, the miscreant was fined $25; but the fine was reduced to $10 on condition that he do all in his power not to harm the CSE, but assist in making it 'above reproach.'[45]

Some oil company promoters took advantage of the sellers' market to bypass the brokers altogether and peddle shares directly to the public. A contemporary photograph shows a shoeshine parlour converted into the head office of the Acme Oil Company, sporting a sign that reads, 'Cap[i]t[al] Stock $300,000. 160 Acres Close To Dingman Well. To Start Drilling After First Issue of Stock, $200,000 Shares. Par Value Of Stock 25 Cents. For A Short Time Only 25 Cents Per Share. Open Saturday at 9 AM. Obsolutely [sic] No Promotion Stock Issued.'[46]

Within a year, however, the boom began to ebb. By July 1915 the trust company that had financed the CSE's new building was threatening to put the exchange into liquidation if it failed to pay its debts. Every effort was made to reduce expenditure as trading volume dropped steadily. In November the public was excluded from the trading sessions and the natural gas heating in the premises cut off. Even the formal prohibition on members trading at open-call exchanges was rescinded. At the end of the year one of the two daily calls was cancelled, and soon after the exchange moved to humbler quarters. Not even the strictest economy could save the day, however, and in February 1917 the CSE closed its doors, not to reopen until another oil boom developed in 1926.[47]

Nowhere was the fragility of stock exchanges more vividly illustrated than in Alberta during the months after the Turner valley oil strike. Attempting to exercise too tight control simply led brokers and investors to set up rival exchanges, to frequent the open-call markets, or to buy shares direct from company promoters and officials. Although such a degree of anarchy never developed in Vancouver, Montreal, or Toronto, it always lurked not far beneath the surface. Any sustained boom in share trading might lead to the defiance of rules and the emergence of competitors for the established exchanges.

II

Despite the fact that stock exchanges remained comparatively weak institutions prior to the First World War, they nevertheless performed increasingly important economic functions. By providing a continuous market for an ever-widening range of securities they ensured the liquidity of these investments. Share buyers could put up their money trusting in the knowledge that they might dispose of their investments at will. That confidence helped to entice savers away from more traditional assets such as real estate and mortgages, which tended to be less liquid. Capital was thus made available for new enterprises, especially industrial ventures, which had previously been shunned as too risky.

A recent history of the New York Stock Exchange notes, 'The existence of this facility made an enormous difference to the willingness of investors to buy and hold not only securities in preference to other investments but also one security rather than another, for it was those with the most active market that were most desirable ... 'The criticism that the New York Stock Exchange absorbed funds that could be more productively employed elsewhere can therefore be seen as an unjust one, since the Stock Exchange's very existence both allowed the mobilization of savings that would have remained unused and allowed other savings to be channelled into activities where finance was in short supply. Obviously the system by which this was achieved was abused, but that did not mean that the Stock Exchange did not perform a necessary and valuable function.'[48] Yet contemporaries remained sharply critical of stock exchanges because too many transactions seemed purely speculative. Rather than 'real' investors buying shares to provide stable financing for productive undertakings, most trading seemed to be aimed solely at taking quick profits from short-term fluctuations. Moreover, these price swings were still believed to be greatly exaggerated by activities such as margin trading, short selling, bear raiding, and plotting corners. Critics questioned whether the exchanges possessed either the desire or the will to clean up the worst abuses.

The extent of speculative trading, for instance, was well known. A study of the stock of the Reading Railroad showed that each share traded an average of twenty-two times annually on the NYSE between 1906 and 1912, and that less than 9 per cent of the stock was ever paid for and delivered to investors, according to the books of the company, more than 90 per cent being handed from one purchaser to another in the form of 'street' certificates. In 1913 the Pujo Committee of the U.S. Congress concluded that of the $15.5 trillion worth of shares traded on the NYSE each year,

but a small part of these transactions is of an investment character; that whilst another part represents wholesome speculation, a far greater part represents speculation indistinguishable in effect from wagering and more hurtful than lotteries or gambling at the race track or the roulette table because practiced on a vastly wider scale and withdrawing from productive industry vastly more capital; that as an adjunct of such speculation quotations of securities are manipulated without regard to real values and false appearances of demand or supply are created, and this not only without hindrance from, but with the approval of the authorities of the exchange, provided only the transactions are not purely fictitious.

The 'facilities of the New York Stock Exchange,' declared the Pujo report, 'are employed largely for transactions producing moral and economic waste and corruption.'[49]

Canadian views of the exchanges were equally jaundiced. In 1902 Edward Trout of the *Monetary Times* complained about a run-up of share prices on the Montreal and Toronto Stock Exchanges, noting that locking up so much money in stocks would only work to the detriment of merchants and manufacturers who needed the scarce capital. 'If they are mere plunging speculators nobody need care very much about what they lose, except for the havoc which the example of their wild ventures plays with otherwise sane people.'[50] Such criticisms stemmed from the persistence of a 'mercantile' point of view common to bankers and businessmen, who valued most highly the exchange of goods – or at least, 'real bills' that represented claims upon such goods – over mere paper title to a portion of the equity in some speculative enterprise.[51]

After 1900, however, a listing on a reputable exchange gradually became a worthwhile asset for a public company. Prospective investors were not prepared to tie up their money indefinitely, and continuous trading permitted them to realize funds in short order. This liquidity made securities less risky and hence more attractive than some other investments. Many listed stocks were purchased with short-term money, borrowed from bankers and brokers in the hope that loans could be rolled over as needed. Aggressive investors used listed securities as collateral for margin accounts, and the greater the volume of trading in a stock, the lower the margin demanded.[52]

Nevertheless, market manipulation remained a problem, though perhaps less common in Canada than in the United States, at least on a large scale. For one thing, 'call' loans[53] to finance stock purchases were more difficult and costly to obtain in Canada, which made mounting bear raids and corners harder. The low volume of trading on Canadian exchanges also made short selling more difficult. Thus one knowledgeable insider explained his preference for dealing on Wall Street: 'The Canadian markets are easy to boom, but hard to take profits in. Our markets are narrow.'[54]

The growing volume of trading in mining shares did make speculation increasingly attractive. In 1911 *Saturday Night* claimed that almost all the dealing on the Standard stock exchange in Toronto was wash trading designed to lure in the unwary and fleece them. W.H.P. Jarvis insisted that the shares of Crown Reserve Mines had long been kept at three times their true value by insiders using matching orders. The *Financial Post* noted that many small-time floor traders operating on their own account on exchanges such as the Standard did little else but sell short. Lacking capital, they borrowed stock to sell from other brokers, putting up little or no money and aiming to take profits at the slightest decline. If share prices went up instead, they might face bankruptcy, leaving their creditors to foot the bill. Brokers could complain that the public was reluctant to buy mining stocks, but the paper thought that they had only themselves to blame when markets seemed so clearly rigged.[55] Stories about insiders manipulating the stock market took firm root in Canadian folklore. Jefferson Thorpe, the barber in Stephen Leacock's Mariposa, complained that short selling by the 'unseen nefarious crowd in the city' had forced down the price of the Northern Star shares he had bought at 32 cents to just 3 cents apiece before a vein of silver 'as thick as a sidewalk' was uncovered and the stock jumped up to $17.[56]

Critics of the stock exchanges could also have pointed out that prior to the First World War very few companies except mining ventures, which were speculative by their very nature, actually raised funds by floating shares directly onto the market. In the nineteenth century no new issues were introduced through the Toronto Stock Exchange.[57] 'Primary' distribution[58] was handled instead by syndicates of insiders who sought to place the shares with investors prepared to allow management time to get a fledgling enterprise off the ground, rather than with speculators who would sell at the first sign of a rising market. Often there were formal 'pooling' agreements that bound shareholders to leave buying and selling decisions to someone with inside knowledge of company affairs.

In 1903, for instance, Max Aitken of Royal Securities organized a pool in the common stock of the Trinidad Electric Company, which he was promoting and underwriting.[59] He sought options to acquire shares from the insiders on a graduated scale from $70 to $100 so that he could place them little by little with 'real' investors. As Aitken put it to one of the other syndicate members, '[I]t is our intention to judiciously handle this security with a view to distributing it as much as possible in the hands of investors. We desire to avoid speculative holdings.' All the directors of Trinidad Electric agreed to join the pool during the first half of 1904.[60] Once a secondary market for such shares had been made, preferably after dividends began to be paid, then a stock-market listing might be obtained.

In the narrow Canadian market, however, caution remained the watchword. Another Aitken promotion, Porto Rico Railways, which controlled the utilities in San Juan, was organized in 1906, but it was not until two years later that broker A.E. Ames proposed to seek listings on the Montreal and Toronto Stock Exchanges. He hoped that doing so would ensure 'transactions in such volumes as would in a short time provide a free market. This would enable those who wish to hold for a period to borrow upon the security of their stock.' He believed that shares were sufficiently widely distributed among investors who would not dump the stock at the first hint of a rising market, but other insiders opposed the idea for fear that the sale of even a small block of shares would cause prices to drop sharply. As late as 1909 Aitken expressed the belief that the market could not absorb even two hundred shares without breaking the current price of $50. Brokers, of course, tended to favour heavy trading, which brought in commissions even if it sometimes made promoters and managers nervous.[61]

During the first decade of the twentieth century, despite the overall growth of the Canadian economy, there were several stern lessons for investors about how rapidly opinion on the 'street' could swing from bullish to bearlike. In the recession summer of 1903 share prices dropped sharply in the United States, trapping A.E. Ames, who had acquired many new issues that he hoped to market to his growing clientele across southern Ontario. The value of his inventory collapsed so rapidly that he was unable to meet his obligations, and his firm was suspended by the TSE. Within six weeks Ames had paid all that he owed to other exchange members and applied to resume his seat. Because he had been able to persuade his creditors not to force him into bankruptcy, he was readmitted, and after considerable travail his firm ultimately recovered.[62]

The gyrations of the market in 1903 sparked renewed criticisms of gambling in stocks. The Baptist Association of Toronto passed a resolution strongly deprecating the speculative tenor of the times, a condemnation echoed by the prominent Methodist cleric S.D. Chown. A Halifax grand jury demanded that the government pass legislation to license stockbrokers.[63] Quebec MP Henri Bourassa urged Parliament to regulate brokers in order to control speculation; he argued that the prevalence of margin trading made stock exchanges little different from bucket shops. Brokers ought to be licensed and minimum margin requirements of at least 25 per cent imposed. These proposals received a lukewarm reception: Opposition leader Robert Borden warned that Canadians would simply shift their business to American brokers. Justice Minister Charles Fitzpatrick pointed out that the federal government lacked jurisdiction over contracts to buy and sell shares. Eventually Bourassa withdrew his motion after a vague promise from Fitzpatrick to consider the problem.[64]

During 1907 shares prices dropped again as another recession developed. A dip in the spring of the year put one Montreal broker out of business. In the summer the upstart Sovereign Bank of Canada found itself in deep trouble. The president had made several ill-advised loans without the knowledge of his board of directors. He was dismissed and a reserve fund of $1,250,000 set aside to meet the losses, while the bank's capital was reduced from $4 million to $3 million. With its shares listed on both the Montreal and Toronto exchanges, the Sovereign's management anticipated a bear raid as soon as the bad news was disclosed at the annual meeting, despite the fact that dividends on the stock were to be maintained at the previous level of 6 per cent. In a highly unusual move the boards of both exchanges agreed to the bank's request that the stock be delisted temporarily on the eve of the annual meeting to help thwart the bears. Attempts were made to trade Sovereign shares on the curb during the brief suspension, but little stock changed hands, and once relisted the stock actually moved upward from $100 to $113. The financial press applauded the exchanges for protecting the interests of real investors against the predations of the speculators, contrary to normal practice.[65]

By the fall of 1907 the economic crisis had worsened, and in October a run developed on several New York trust companies. As share prices slipped, the president of the New York Stock Exchange suggested closing its doors to avoid a wave of selling, as had been done in the panic of 1881. Meanwhile, the Toronto press printed rumours that at least one local brokerage house was in trouble. When the Detroit United Traction Company (in which Canadians were heavily interested) announced that it would skip a dividend payment, share prices in both Montreal and Toronto slumped sharply.[66]

Eventually the blame for triggering the break was laid at the door of an unsuccessful effort to corner the stock of United Copper on the New York Curb. Market insiders, who hated corners (at least when they were not involved), had hoped to punish the raiders by getting their loans called, but had failed to anticipate the runs that resulted on the trust companies which had financed the purchase of United Copper shares. In the end the lordly investment banker J.P. Morgan, who normally steered well clear of seedy stock-market operators, had to be persuaded to step in and avert disaster by helping to restore confidence.[67]

The 1907 slump seemed only to confirm the unsavoury reputation that stock markets already had in many quarters. In a well-publicized decision that year the Supreme Court of Canada had denied the claim of A.E. Ames to recover an unpaid margin call from the prominent Ontario politician James Conmee.[68] In 1902 Conmee had ordered 300 shares of Lake Superior Consolidated on 33 per cent margin, paying $3,000 down. When the stock price dropped, a call for additional funds was made upon Conmee, who had put up an additional $1,800 then declined to pay more. Ames sued for the outstanding $4,200 and was upheld in the Ontario courts. The Supreme Court overturned the decision, noting that upon receiving Conmee's order Ames had purchased 600 shares of Lake Superior from a Philadelphia broker, but instead of holding the stock for delivery to clients, he had himself paid the Americans only half the total cost (i.e., $9,000) and had pledged all 600 shares as collateral for a loan. When share prices declined, the Philadelphia broker demanded repayment of its loan, and Ames refused. The Americans then sold 475 of the shares to recoup the balance owing and sent the remaining 125 shares to Toronto. In his suit Ames admitted that he would have been unable to make delivery to Conmee of all his 300 shares if he had paid the balance owing, but Ames insisted that he could easily have gone into the market and secured the other 175 shares required. Conmee, however, contended that Ames had failed to purchase all the shares he had ordered and hold them for him, as was contractually required, so that he had refused to pay the margin calls.

Since Ames could have recovered his 600 shares from the Philadelphians only upon paying a total of $9,300 while Conmee owed him just $6,000, the Supreme Court held that he should not have been subjected to the contingencies of Ames's solvency (which had, of course, previously evaporated during the slump of 1903). A broker was entitled to pledge shares bought on margin for a loan not exceeding the customer's indebtedness, but could not mingle them with other shares as Ames had done. 'The broker must at all times have on hand stock sufficient in quantity to deliver to his client upon payment by the latter of the amount due by him upon the stock.'[69] The implication seemed to be that even as well-known a broker as A.E. Ames had been guilty of practices that smacked of the bucket shop.

Early in 1907 the newly founded *Financial Post* had proudly announced that the number of shares being carried on margin had probably declined by half in both Montreal and Toronto since 1901. Like the stocks of well-established dividend-paying companies in the United States, shares in enterprises such as the Canadian Pacific Railway and the Hudson's Bay Company were said to be quickly disappearing off the street and into safety deposit boxes, reflecting distrust of the antics of brokers and exchanges. In many of these stocks 'dealings have almost ceased, and it is quite impossible to purchase any considerable amount and the prices have accordingly appreciated.'[70]

At the same time the *Post* reported that many U.S. businessmen were abandoning stock markets in disgust. Why should they put up with call-money rates that oscillated from 50 per cent one day to less than 5 per cent the next without any significant alteration in the economic situation? 'The fact in a nutshell is that Wall Street methods have to a large extent alienated the conservative businessman.' The paper's American correspondent, 'A.J. Canuck,' confirmed that there was widespread disgust about the stock jobbing and market rigging that had been revealed by a New York State investigation into the insurance industry and by the Interstate Commerce Commission's examination of financial practices amongst railroaders.[71]

Could the exchanges themselves be relied upon to clean up such abuses? Efforts to prevent commission splitting with non-members and trading of listed issues off the floor seemed unavailing. The New York Stock Exchange proved unable even to force its members to withdraw from the New York Produce

Exchange when that body changed its charter in 1907 to permit trading in securities. Nor could it deny ticker service to members of the rival Consolidated Stock Exchange.[72] If one exchange tightened its rules too much, dealings in listed issues simply shifted to places with less-restrictive rules or to the totally unregulated 'gutter' markets that existed in all cities.

Following the panic in New York in the autumn of 1907, however, demands for reform of the financial system intensified; the following year state governor Charles Evans Hughes appointed a commission to study speculation in both securities and commodities. The resulting report noted that only a small number of transactions on the NYSE were for investment purposes, the remainder being gambles or speculations, but it admitted that eliminating the latter would seriously interfere with the former by decreasing liquidity. The commission simply recommended more active enforcement of the NYSE rules and the incorporation of the New York Curb so that some internal regulation could be imposed. The *Financial Post* applauded the thrust of the report, since 'Interference by government with the properly conducted operations of a representative stock exchange is apt to be fraught with greater evils than attend upon the waste involved in incidental speculation.' Nonetheless, the paper added that even the mildest of these recommended reforms was unlikely to gain the support of NYSE members.[73]

Another scandal developed early in 1910 when Rock Island Railroad shares rose on the NYSE from $51 to $80 in the space of just fifteen minutes before falling back to the previous level. Investigation revealed that market manipulators had taken advantage of a rule regarding 'all-or-none' bids for 1,000-share lots, which permitted traders to offer to buy such blocks at highly inflated prices while refusing to accept bona fide offers of 100-share blocks at lower prices, no matter how many of the latter were tendered. Insiders had used this rule to mask their operations while rapidly running up prices. Embarrassed, the NYSE board abolished the rule and gave its law committee authority to investigate members suspected of improper dealings.[74]

In the absence of such well-publicized abuses the Canadian exchanges faced less pressure to reform themselves and continued to do business as usual. One Toronto broker tried to argue that there was less need for change because investors had not been taken advantage of to the same extent. 'The way in which Canadian listed stocks hold advances should attract casual traders who do not make a business of watching the ticker, and who have suffered in the past through the sudden and unexpected declines of issues in the New York market, brought about by bear raids and various kinds of rumours with which it is difficult for Canadian houses to keep closely in touch. With the increasing variety of securities on the Toronto and Montreal stock exchanges investors and traders will find the same opportunities of profit in the majority of cases as in the bigger markets without incurring the same risks.'[75]

Such claims were fanciful, particularly in the case of the mining exchanges in Toronto and Vancouver which dealt almost exclusively in speculative issues. A rising tide of criticism in the United States that securities markets favoured speculators over investors had already spilled over into Canada. By 1910 *Saturday Night*, for instance, was leading the campaign for a clean-up of practices that seemed to rig the odds against honest, if naive investors and in favour of speculators and insiders. Many Canadians still hoped to strike it rich by buying mining stocks or other kinds of securities. The stock exchanges themselves seemed unable or unwilling to discipline their members and prevent abuses. As a result, pressure for government regulation of brokers and securities markets was on the increase in the years just prior to the First World War, while the operators on the exchanges continued to do business as usual.

4

Blue Skies

By 1910 the Canadian economy had been booming for more than a decade. Montreal continued to enjoy its place as the country's business and financial metropolis, while Toronto prospered from the rich gold and silver finds in northern Ontario. Hopeful migrants from home and abroad swarmed onto trains bearing them westward to the rich wheat lands of the prairies, where cities and towns, large and small, strained at their seams. Beyond the Rocky Mountains the fisheries, forests, and mines of British Columbia held out equally alluring prospects for development. Boom times, however, played right into the hands of unscrupulous share pedlars. In 1911 Ontario's mines minister grumbled, 'It is very much to be regretted that very objectionable methods continue to be used in floating companies, for the exploitation of the mining districts of Ontario, particularly Porcupine.'[1] Yet shares in mines, oil and gas properties, land companies, and other highly speculative ventures continued to find eager buyers.

I

The unscrupulous company promoter and smooth-talking share pusher became stock figures. J. Rufus Wallingford was the creation of George Randolph Chester, whose stories began to appear in 1908 with *Get-Rich-Quick Wallingford: A Cheerful Account of the Rise and Fall of an American Business Buccaneer*, dedicated to 'The live businessmen of America who have been "stung" and those who have yet to undergo this painful experience.' Chester presents his protagonist as physically large with a confidence-inspiring manner of bluff heartiness that disguised his physical cowardice and sexual predation. From his very first share-selling scam, the Universal Covered Tack Company, supposedly set up to manufacture carpet tacks with little bits of coloured cloth glued to their heads to make them match a rug when driven into it, Wallingford succeeds in arousing the cupidity of investors to lure them into handing over their money.[2]

In *Young Wallingford* his sidekick, Horace G. 'Blackie' Daw, delivers this view of life: 'Why, man, the bulk of this country is composed of suckers that are able to lay hands on from one to ten thousand apiece. They'll spend ten years to get it and can be separated from it in ten minutes. You're one of the born separators. You were cut out for nothing but easy money.'[3] Ritzy hotels, grand houses, cigars, and champagne all float upon schemes like the manufacture of a solar-powered engine developed by one Mr Bang (the Bang Sun Engine Company) or – an even nicer touch – the production of an automobile in which people can both eat and sleep. At times Chester even presents Wallingford fairly sympathetically as one who takes money only from the greedy or from other swindlers or corrupt politicians.[4]

Some of Wallingford's adventures were dramatized by the famous American showman George M. Cohan in 1910, and there were a number of silent movies and even one talkie, which appeared as late as 1931. William Rose Benet observed that Wallingford's name 'has become part of American folklore.'[5] During the twenties and thirties the *Financial Post* continued to warn Canadians against smooth-talking 'Wallingfords' with their fancy offices.[6]

In Canada Stephen Leacock gave these same themes a nice ironic twist in *Arcadian Adventures with the Idle Rich* (1914). 'Tomlinson, the Wizard of Finance,' really hates his vast fortune acquired from the discovery of the Erie Auriferous Consolidated's mine under the family farm. Mrs Tomlinson sets out to lose all their money by buying shares about which she knows nothing, 'like R.O.P. and T.R.R. pfd.; they go down all the time and you know where you are.' But when news spreads that the 'Tomlinson interests' are buying, 'the sluggish R.O.P. and T.R.R. would take as sudden a leap into the air as might a mule with a galvanic shock applied to its tail.' In the end Tomlinson is reduced to giving away all his shares to Plutoria University just before the mine is revealed to have been salted and the company collapses.[7]

Wallingford's real-life counterparts gained great notoriety in the United States. George Graham Rice had once controlled the promotional brokerage house of B.H. Scheftels and Company, which was raided by the authorities for illegal share pushing. In 1911 he published a lengthy confession entitled 'My Adventures with Your Money – Who Got It – and How.' Though the editors of the magazine *Adventure* reported that Rice was now engaged in composing moral tales for boys who might go wrong to appear in the *Youth's Companion*, old habits proved difficult to shake off, and in 1916 Rice was sent to the penitentiary for another stock fraud.[8]

In Canada, too, there were men such as the aptly named A.F.A. Coyne, who sought to make his fortune promoting dubious oil companies. According to a long-standing associate, Coyne was indeed a man of parts.[9] Five years before coming to Canada from Scotland in 1906 at the age of nineteen, he had designed the first modern submarine using diving planes, something he conceived while studying the fish swimming in an Edinburgh museum. His skills did not, however, extend to the ability to swim: that he acquired after he reached Canada when his canoe swamped in fifteen feet of water forty feet from shore on Lake of the Woods. Not only did he learn fast enough to save himself from drowning, but he soon became an expert swimmer, able to remain underwater for three and a half minutes at a time.

Coyne laid claim to equal expertise in the field of geology. During the First World War, when the government was forced to ration imported Pennsylvania anthracite, he took up the hunt and supposedly discovered domestic supplies of this vital fuel. He also declared himself the first man to have discovered radium in Canada and the first to arrive at the conclusion that Devonian limestone was the main oil-bearing stratum in Alberta. Coyne fell afoul of the provincial government in Edmonton in 1917, however, when he claimed to have found over 200 million barrels of oil in the Athabasca River valley. The Alberta authorities were convinced that he had merely acquired title to some of the well-known, but commercially valueless oil sands deposits along the Athabasca, which had been noted by explorers as early as the eighteenth century.[10]

When he was prevented by the provincial Public Utilities Board from selling shares in his oil company, Coyne left Canada in 1919 in a high dudgeon and returned to Britain, but the lure of easy money was so great that he was back before long. This time he unveiled another purported coal discovery near Sudbury, Ontario, and began planting articles in the press, laying the groundwork for a stock-selling scheme. George Bulyea of the Alberta Public Utilities Board noted that his method of operation was to form a company, vote himself a large block of shares for services supposedly rendered, and sell the stock for whatever he could get. Like Wallingford, Coyne understood the value of an impressive suite of offices in wooing prospective investors. One man who visited his Toronto operations reported that he had spotted a door labelled 'Engineering Branch,' but when he opened it he found himself back out in the corridor. Bulyea considered Coyne a man of undoubted ability but 'absolutely lacking in con-science or principle ... He should not be allowed to form any companies as his object in business is purely and simply to fleece the unsuspecting public.'[11]

Later Coyne set himself up in Montreal as a 'consulting petroleum geologist' on the basis of his supposed lectures at Imperial College in London and his appointment as head of the geology branch of the 'Petroleum Extension University' in Fort Wayne, Indiana. By 1927 he was cranking out pamphlets with titles such as *The Oilfields of Eastern Canada* which chronicled the activities of Coyne Geological Surveys, including a photograph of 'Our Own Derrick,' soon to be drilling in Ontario. By then Coyne had convinced himself that that province could produce over 23 million barrels of oil during the next sixty years. In his apt words, 'The time has come when all this effort should be capitalized.'[12]

II

As the pre-war boom reached its height the demand for regulatory action to control company promotion and share pushing became particularly strong in western Canada, where the pages of the newspapers were already crammed with the alluring advertisements of real estate promoters. In 1912 *Saturday Night* reported that the Edmonton Board of Trade had called upon the province to act because land frauds were well on the way to overtaking mining stock scams in separating the unwary from their money.[13] The *Financial Post* singled out Winnipeg as 'unfortunate in coming to be looked upon by American hot air promoters as a good city to locate in and operate from, but it behooves the city fathers of this fast-growing Canadian muncipality to watch the operations of the promoters who are flocking to it, for they can only bring upon it a bad name.'[14]

Identical warnings were being heard in the United States. The problem seemed particularly acute on the western plains, where the Wallingfords were peddling stock in all manner of fly-by-night undertakings. Some credulous farmers, it was said, were even buying shares in the blue sky above. 'Not a tree nor a house broke the broad sweep of flat country that reached the edge of the sky in all directions' on the Kansas prairie whence came the cyclone that took Dorothy and Toto to the land of Oz,[15] and fittingly enough, it was the Kansas legislature, under pressure from farm organizations and local businessmen, that passed the first 'blue-sky' law in 1911. The act aimed at protecting investors by requiring all companies selling shares there to register with the state banking commissioner. This official was given authority to determine whether an offering was fair and to require sellers as well as securities to be registered. The experiment attracted keen interest, and within two years seventeen other American states had passed similar laws. In Canada the *Financial Post* quickly took note of the Kansas law and suggested that it merited careful study.[16]

Within months Manitoba became the first Canadian jurisdiction to act. Why Manitoba? First of all, the 'hot air promoters' were conceived of as outsiders, Americans or easterners who preyed upon the bluff yeomen using a line of smooth talk. The farmers were suspicious of financiers and happy to see their predations reined in. Moreover, with relatively few company promotions, especially in speculative fields such as mining, there was no local community of brokers and dealers to exercise pressure upon government to let them go their own way. The Winnipeg Stock Exchange was small and comparatively feeble, and it was hard to point to the fruits of a resource boom such as the Cobalt rush had brought to northern Ontario. Like their counterparts in Kansas, the Manitobans were ready to experiment with new methods of regulation.

The Manitoba Sale of Shares Act of 1912 reflected these attitudes by requiring all companies incorporated outside the province to obtain a licence to sell shares there. Newspapers were prohibited from accepting advertisements from unlicensed undertakings. Since banking fell exclusively under federal jurisdiction in Canada, the province had no official like a banking commissioner, and responsibility for assessing the required financial information and issuing the licences was given instead to the provincial Public Utilities Commission. The PUC had been set up that same year to control exploitive monopolies in the field of telephones and electricity and was given the added responsibility of administering the blue-sky law.[17]

The new legislation did not escape criticism. The board of the Winnipeg Stock Exchange belatedly mounted a delegation to the PUC to complain of the 'absurdity' of some of the act's provisions and demand its repeal. How, the brokers asked, could they continue to trade in the shares of well-established and highly reputable banks and railways with federal charters if the companies refused to apply for licences in Manitoba? It was pointed out to them, however, that the PUC could grant exemptions for shares listed on recognized stock exchanges.[18]

Other critics raised the argument that registration of a security might actually be used by unscrupulous salesmen to convince prospective buyers of its virtues. Claims might even be made that the province had somehow 'guaranteed' a return on the investment. Nonetheless, the *Financial Post* applauded the action of the Manitoba government, arguing, 'Even with this difficulty, however, there is not the slightest doubt that the Act is a step in the right direction, as although such an Act cannot guarantee the success of the company it goes a long way towards guaranteeing the good faith of the promoters.' Manitobans, the paper concluded, would hold onto their money despite any other problems created.[19]

Judge H.A. Robson, the public utilities commissioner charged with enforcing the new legislation, was somewhat less sanguine (see photo 13). He had not been consulted when the act was being drawn up, and close examination convinced him that it had serious deficiencies. The 1912 legislation actually conferred very narrow regulatory powers, since it was 'only intended to be a revenue act for the Province of Manitoba, and once a company took out a license and was under the provincial law then it got out of the scope of the

Public Utilities Commission. I saw that was simply making a revenue measure of it, of what I thought was a pretty mean type.'[20] Robson therefore approached the government and argued, '"This legislation is deceptive because on the face of being moral legislation it is only revenue legislation," and they immediately changed it by bringing it up to the full status of a law for the prevention of frauds in the sale of shares. I had no great difficulty in getting that change accomplished.' Amendments to the Sale of Shares Act passed in 1914 made its licensing requirements applicable to all companies selling shares in the province. The following year the Public Utilities Commission was granted the power to revoke the registrations of dubious enterprises.[21]

Robson shared the view that the farmers of Manitoba required special protection because they seemed 'particularly susceptible to your glib share-selling artists.' City folk were often 'more sagacious and cunning investors' who knew full well when they were speculating, but in rural areas 'Selling shares seems to be a handy way whereby our smooth ... gentlemen may go through the country and get other people's money for very little ... I think that the investment of money in this country is a serious business, and that we should as far as possible exclude the possibility of money being taken away without value, especially in the farming community.'[22] He therefore insisted that all applicants submit a business plan to meet the test of the act that a company demonstrate that it could offer a fair return on investment. That meant not only that dividends would be paid but that the capital invested would not be frittered away: 'I used to make it my duty to know that that capital was coming back.' Entrepreneurs who promised to invest in Manitoba generally received a warm reception. The size of the commissions to be earned by those distributing the shares was also noted since exorbitant rates were a warning sign of fraud.[23]

Promoters of industrial companies tended to receive a fairly careful hearing, but Robson was always suspicious of speculative resource stocks. He recalled that a mining man once came to see him with a pocketful of nuggets, only to be told, 'Nothing doing; you can put those things back in your pockets, and you won't get a certificate.' Robson drafted a set of rules to apply only to mining companies which required the promoters to show exactly how much money was to be spent on exploration and development and to promise that once the mine was making a profit a fixed percentage would be returned to the shareholders. Issues of additional stock to dilute the claims of the original shareholders were banned. In 1916 the blue-sky act was further tightened to require the money raised by the sale of speculative mining shares to be held in trust in order to ensure that it was used for the purposes specified.[24]

Manitoba's blue-sky law took effect at a critical time, for the spring of 1914 saw the beginnings of the wave of speculation in Alberta oil shares as salesmen fanned out across the country. One of the leading promoters approached Robson and tried to persuade him that investors were going to make millions. The commissioner bluntly replied that he was wasting his time since Robson did not intend to permit the sale of any Alberta oil shares in Manitoba. As a result, Manitobans were largely saved from the losses that many other oil investors suffered, confirming the value of the legislation in the mind of Robson and many others.[25]

The judge clearly relished his task. Reflecting on his experiences a decade later, he told a legislative committee that complaints about administrative heavy-handedness thwarting legitimate enterprise were inevitable: 'There will always be criticism, both of the law and of the administrator of a "blue sky" act, but the good to the country of it is so great that you have got to stand that criticism ... I say that the merits of the legislation are beyond question.' Though disappointed applicants might allege that he had overreached his discretion, 'I believe in the one-man commission ... It was not any bed of roses; you do not have the choice of tyrannical power [in] administering that thing at all.' Still, the PUC did not have to release reasons for refusing a certificate. About that Robson was blunt: 'Quite a complaint was made one time that there was no record of all these things [i.e., applications]. Why should I bother myself with records or keep things like that?'[26]

Strong backing from the cabinet could be critical. One angry promoter threatened to go over Robson's head directly to the premier. 'I said, "Alright. Come back and tell me what he says ..." I got good support from the ... government. We had a couple of fellows in jail, you know, on the thing, and it checked things up in good shape.' One offender was sentenced to six months in prison and another to a shorter term, while a third fled before his premises could be raided by the police. 'There are teeth in that law. I never had any hesitation in getting done what I wanted; it is the best way because it makes your job lighter.' Summing up his experiences Robson was well satisfied with his work: 'I just frankly enjoyed administering that law.'[27]

Next door in Saskatchewan, Canada's second blue-sky law did not work so effectively. Passed in 1914, partly in response to the Alberta oil boom and the wave of share pushers that it spawned, the act required any joint-stock company 'carrying on business' in the province to be licensed by the Local Government Board. Unfortunately, the attorney general soon ruled that corporations chartered outside Saskatchewan which simply sold stock there were not 'carrying on business.' As a result, Alberta oil companies could not be required to register before distributing their stock. Soon there were complaints that the people of Saskatchewan were being flooded with literature about oil promotions as the sharpers thwarted by Robson in Manitoba continued hard at work.[28]

In Atlantic Canada, meanwhile, the stock pushers were trying to capitalize on a fashion for fox furs. Promoters were busy organizing joint-stock companies to purchase pure-bred silver foxes, promising dividends as high as 60 per cent per annum. One Maritime member of Parliament wrote anonymously to the *Financial Times* praising its criticisms of these promotions, which he likened to 'Cobalt Wild-Cats.' A blue-sky bill was introduced in the Nova Scotia legislature which would have required companies selling stock to file prospectuses and financial statements with the provincial secretary, along with certification from two Nova Scotia bankers that the promoters had a good business reputation. In the end, however, the legislation failed to pass.[29]

Saturday Night, meanwhile, supplied heavy coverage of the successes of the blue-sky law in Manitoba, arguing that the province of Ontario ought to bring in similar legislation. Even if such a tribunal cost $50,000 a year, it would be justified by the millions saved by unwary investors.[30] In 1915 the attorney general did commission a study of blue-sky legislation. This report noted that most of the acts in the United States and in Canada had not been in effect long enough to permit a clear assessment of their effectiveness, but that many experts remained sceptical. Such regulation had been considered in Britain during the 1890s and rejected on the grounds of the cost and delay that investigating each applicant entailed. Granting approval to sell securities might create a 'fictitious and unreal sense of security to the investor and might also lead to grave abuses.' The only good results were likely to come from the deterrent effect of an investigation upon shady promoters. In light of this conclusion the Ontario government took no action.[31]

The only other Canadian jurisdiction that actually passed blue-sky legislation during the war was Alberta. Ironically, the provincial government took no action until 1916, by which time the steam had gone out of the oil-share boom.[32] Then the Public Utilities Board was given power to refuse a license to dubious ventures, and in 1917 A.F.A. Coyne's Northern Production Company applied for permission to sell stock on the basis of his supposed oil discovery in the Athabasca valley. When rejected, the pugnacious Coyne immediately charged that he was a victim of prejudice. The PUB, however, pointed out that over 700,000 of the company's 800,000 shares were being given away to insiders in exchange for assets of dubious value, while the public was to be asked to purchase these securities for $1 apiece.[33]

When Coyne persisted in selling shares anyway, he was convicted of violating the Alberta Sale of Shares Act (though the conviction was later overturned on appeal). Nonetheless, he proved a resourceful opponent for the PUB. As the First World War was coming to an end, he announced that he was prepared to give away 100 free shares of Northern Production to any returned soldier, and soon a steady stream of veterans was trooping through his luxurious offices in Edmonton while he reaped a harvest of favourable publicity. Coyne also threatened to descend upon the PUB with 'a committee of returned soldiers.'[34]

In the spring of 1919, however, he left Edmonton for Britain with another warrant for his arrest outstanding. From a Brighton hotel the irascible promoter despatched to the Public Utilities Board a twenty-six-stanza poem of his own composition entitled 'The Knocker,' which included such lines as

Appointed, judges of all things,
You flouting fools, you're flesh.
Like the raven from the tree that sings
'Tis arrogance you caress.

At the bottom of the page he scrawled: 'Read it twice. It will do you good.'[35]

Other promoters echoed Coyne's complaints that the Alberta PUB often turned down applications without giving specific reasons. The secretary of the Skeena Copper Company demanded to know what general principles mining companies should adhere to in allotting stock to insiders who sold them claims. Judge A.A. Carpenter, the head of the PUB, refused to lay down hard-and-fast rules, arguing that each case was considered on its merits and what might be appropriate in one case would not be acceptable in another. In response to a further complaint that Skeena Copper was still 'in the dark' about what was wrong with its application, Carpenter noted that 500,000 shares had been handed over for some oil leases which were admitted to be valueless. He refused to answer hypothetical questions about how much vendor stock might be approved by the board, but did agree to hold informal discussions with the company solicitor.[36]

The experience of the three prairie provinces with blue-sky legislation did not escape attention in British Columbia. In 1914 Attorney General W.J. Bowser received a complaint that one promoter was putting out a tipsheet called the *Daily Oil Gazette* trumpeting the existence of an out-of-control gusher near Calgary in an effort to gull the unwary into buying shares. Before long, reports were circulating that oil had been discovered along the Pitt River in British Columbia, and several real estate offices in Prince Rupert shifted into selling oil stocks. The *Financial Times* contended that a blue-sky law was essential in light of these fake oil promotions and the 'putrid real estate propositions' which were attempting to sell land along the Grand Trunk Pacific Railway that would 'never be anything but very ordinary pasturage for cattle.' Despite urgings from both the *Times* and the *Financial Post*, however, the provincial government did not follow the example of its neighbours on the prairies.[37]

In 1917 a Vancouver trust company executive applauded the Manitoba Sale of Shares Act and urged British Columbia's attorney general to pass a similar law: 'Sooner or later we are almost bound to see a mining boom in this province, with the prospect that many a promoter will be enabled to filch the hard-earned dollars of the working people of this province ... The government certainly owes protection to the innocent investor.' The attorney general who had succeeded Bowser, though admitting that he was unfamiliar with the term 'blue-sky' law, did express interest in the idea of legislation like that in force in Manitoba, but nothing came of the suggestion.[38]

The same year the *Financial Times* reported that Quebec's mines minister had appealed to the Canadian Mining Institute for help in finding the 'correct formula' to end the exploitation of innocent, rural investors by the sale of speculative mining stock. The minister expressed the desire not to hamper legitimate business, but only to clamp down on fraudulent promotions. The *Times* repeated the arguments that Manitoba's blue-sky law had been a decided success and that a similar enactment in Quebec would be highly desirable.[39]

Despite continuing interest in certain quarters, however, no other jurisdiction in Canada moved to enact such a measure during the First World War. The federal government did not amend either the Companies Act or the Criminal Code in order to regulate the financing or promotion of joint-stock corporations to prevent fraud. Under-Secretary of State Thomas Mulvey, the civil servant responsible for administering company law, visited Kansas in 1913 to study the operation of its blue-sky law. He came away unimpressed with the claims that its proponents were making for the legislation in protecting investors against unscrupulous share pushers. Any positive effects, Mulvey concluded, rested solely upon the wide publicity given to the law, which might scare off some of the more disreputable operators: 'If there is any virtue whatever in the statute, it appears to me to be owing to this particular provision.'[40]

Moreover, the impact of war upon the market for Canadian securities lessened the sense of need for action. Outside Alberta, where the oil boom continued into 1915, investors showed little interest in buying new shares of any kind. Brokers moved as quickly as they could to try to protect themselves against dramatic declines in share prices as the fighting in Europe got under way in the summer of 1914. Not until the boom times of the 1920s would the agitation for the passage of blue-sky laws revive in Canada.

5

War Clouds

The First World War had an enormous impact upon securities markets in Canada. First of all, the European crisis in the summer of 1914 led the country's stock exchanges to close completely for several months. When they finally did reopen, they operated under special restrictions for nearly two years. Peacetime rules were reinstated in mid-1916, but a further crisis near the end of 1917 led to the reimposition of controls which were not lifted entirely until after peace had finally returned in 1919. Secondly, the financing of the war effort by the federal government required it to assume a much more interventionist role in securities markets. To sell millions of dollars' worth of war loans in the narrow Canadian capital market caused Ottawa to mobilize the country's bankers, bond dealers, and stockbrokers in unprecedented fashion. Moreover, once these obligations were in the hands of the public, the federal government felt compelled to intervene in the bond market to ensure price stability. The result was that securities markets were to a considerable extent isolated from the play of general market forces between 1914 and 1919.

I

Canadians had little sense of the mounting diplomatic crisis of July 1914; even the prime minister was on holiday beyond the reach of the telephone.[1] When panicky European investors began dumping their stocks and bonds and demanding gold, security prices started to spiral downward. On Tuesday, 28 July, a selling wave caused the closing of the Bourse in Vienna, followed immediately by similar suspensions in Berlin and Paris. The London Stock Exchange remained open but could not absorb the wave of sales, even at sacrifice prices. It closed that afternoon just as the exchanges in eastern North America were starting their morning sessions, and the pressure was telegraphed across the ocean like a tidal wave travelling at the speed of light. Brokers were among the first Canadians to grasp the gravity of the situation as they watched stocks such as Canadian Pacific Railway, widely held in Europe and freely traded in New York, fall 13 points (dollars) while the Montreal Stock Exchange was shut for its lunchtime recess.

Faced with a wave of orders to sell CPR at 15 points below the morning close and with other interlisted stocks showing similar declines, the MSE's members prepared a petition asking the governing committee to close the exchange 'due to the fact that panicky feeling exists.' After a hasty meeting the board decided not to reopen for the afternoon session. Chairman Hartland B. McDougall declared, 'It went very much against the grain to close the Stock Exchange, but we felt, under the circumstances, that it was in the interests of everybody ... To have reopened in the afternoon would have meant a reckless and needless slaughtering of Canadian security holdings.' When traders reconvened at the Toronto Stock Exchange, they found stocks being offered on different parts of the floor at prices varying by as much as 2 points. As sell orders flooded in from Montreal and made Toronto a 'dumping ground,' orderly trading became impossible. Realizing that even the well-margined accounts of people who could not be reached by their brokers to put up additional collateral for their loans were being sold out, the TSE board ordered the closing bell rung just fifteen minutes into the afternoon session, to the profound relief of the members.[2]

The following day, 29 July, the Standard Stock and Mining Exchange in Toronto also decided to close its doors when it became clear that owners of even the soundest Canadian mining issues were being forced to sacrifice their holdings in order to meet margin calls. Two days later the Winnipeg, Calgary, and Vancouver exchanges accepted the inevitable and shut down too, bringing organized securities trading in Canada to a complete halt. On Thursday, 30 July, the board of the New York Stock Exchange conferred with investment banker J.P. Morgan and then announced that it intended to remain open. Morgan departed for a weekend on Long Island to demonstrate his confidence that the situation was under control, but the following day, when it was learned that Germany had formally declared war on Great Britain, the NYSE shut up shop, while the London Stock Exchange held its final session on Saturday, 1 August.[3]

In Canada there was hope that the halt in trading would be brief. Monday, 3 August, was a holiday in most cities. Initially there was talk of reopening the exchanges on Tuesday, but when Britain's ultimatum to the kaiser to withdraw from Belgium was ignored and the British empire found itself at war with Germany and Austro-Hungary, such optimism ebbed away. On 4 August both the MSE and the TSE decided to suspend operations until further notice, and four days later the TSE staff were put on half pay. The *Financial Post* reported brokers gloomily cooling their heels with no commissions coming in, while their private telegraph wires to New York, which cost up to $10,000 a year, carried nothing but a little gossip and some grain prices. The streets of Toronto's financial district were reported to be increasingly quiet as investors dropped their habit of visting brokerage offices; and the traders went off on holiday. Still, everyone believed that before long there would be a climactic naval battle between the British and German North Sea fleets, and that once the British had carried the day, normal life would resume.[4]

The decision to keep the stock exchanges closed rested ultimately with Canada's chartered banks. So many investors dealt on margin, borrowing from their brokers at an interest rate of 7 per cent to fund their purchases, that the loans which the brokers secured from their bankers (at 6 per cent) were absolutely crucial to the functioning of markets. Most banks had favoured stocks upon which they would lend money, though the Bank of Montreal allegedly refused this business altogether. Typically, the banks would advance 80 per cent of the value of stocks trading at over $100 per share. For stocks trading at under $100 some banks would grant the same margin rate (20 per cent), while more cautious lenders demanded a flat $20 margin. Speculative stocks required a higher margin.[5]

Had these loans been called in August 1914, brokers would likely have faced bankruptcy and chaos in the markets as they scrambled to liquidate holdings to cover under-margined accounts. Where the downward spiral of share prices would halt nobody could have predicted. As soon as the decision to suspend trading was taken, exchange officials contacted the Canadian Bankers Association, and an agreement was reached on minimum share prices for all listed issues, based upon trading on 28 July. The bankers agreed to value shares at these prices and not to call their brokers' loans. CBA president D.R. Wilkie of the Imperial Bank immediately declared that there was no cause for alarm since Canadian stocks were sound and markets simply needed time to stabilize.[6] In order to allay any fears about the stability of the banking system itself Finance Minister Thomas White announced that the government stood ready to provide credit to permit the banks to expand their reserves and allowed them to suspend payments in gold to avert a run.[7]

The banks then drew up a list of loan values for all listed stocks, such values being fixed at about 80 per cent of the minimum prices. If brokers would work to bring all accounts into line with these requirements (that is, customers had to put up collateral to the extent of 20 per cent of the loan value of their stocks), no brokers' loans would be called until three months after the stock exchanges had fully reopened for business. Brokers had no choice but to accept these terms, which saved their bacon for the time being.[8]

With this breathing space the brokerage community could set about trying to clean up any dangerously under-margined accounts by securing more collateral from customers. Those who could not put up the required funds might find their stock sold off if the brokers could find any way to dispose of it during the suspension of the exchanges. That, of course, created the temptation to deal privately in listed stocks. The governors of both the Toronto and Montreal exchanges tried to discourage such dealing, apparently with reasonable success. One TSE member was hailed before the committee in mid-September and reprimanded for 'office (private) transactions in the present closed market conditions.'[9] More difficult to control were offers to buy listed stocks at heavy discounts over the prices prevailing when trading ceased. Most of the Toronto press agreed not to carry such advertisements after the TSE closed, but one of the evening papers continued to accept them. Despite protests from the TSE board, in mid-September one non-member broker was advertising for $5,000 worth of CPR at around $100 per share, though the stock was selling in New York for $155. Similar offers of cash or gold were being made for other blue-chip stocks at steeply reduced prices.[10]

The closure of the exchanges demonstrated once again the difficulties of limiting trading to their floors. On 7 August the New York Stock Exchange reopened, though with minimum prices and trading confined to a cash (not margin) basis and limited to the shares of American companies. In Canada the strongest pressure to resume operation came from the members of the Standard exchange. On Monday, 24 August, its board decided to reopen for cash trading only and with minimum prices fixed at 28 July levels to prevent any bear raids. The resumption went off without untoward results, but volume remained insignficant. A month later the *Financial Post* reported scornfully that the Standard's single daily session served for little beyond the exchange of gossip: 'Business is a pure farce, and even the few paltry sales that are effected are merely professional.' The minimum prices held up because there were so few buyers and sellers, but pressure from some brokers to drop the minimums was resisted for fear that doing so would set off an across-the-board slump as investors scrambled to unload.[11]

Action by the Standard tempted the other Canadian exchanges, and at the end of August the MSE announced its reopening then rescinded the decision in hopes that the Allied armies would soon commence a victorious offensive. Members felt it more prudent to lay off personnel and cut expenses to the bone. A month later, however, the pressure to resume operations was becoming more and more intense, a decision 'rendered inevitable by the growth of "outside" transactions in exchange securities.' The board of the MSE was forced to approve its members trading listed stocks with non-members or else see clients turn to an 'independent piratical trader,' who was ready to do business with all comers. The Standard also threatened the stability of the Toronto Stock Exchange by proposing to list some TSE stocks for cash trading, though this plan was finally dropped after discussions between the two boards.[12]

Following consultations between the MSE and the TSE, each exchange drafted special trading rules before reopening on 15 October. Both formalized minimum prices for all stocks. Short selling was banned. Brokers seeking to 'relieve the necessities' of under-margined accounts were permitted to send a list of stocks already held by their customers to the governing committee, which would try to match them with cash buyers. The MSE permitted a one-hour daily session for other trading above the minimums, while the TSE initially restricted dealing to a half-dozen local mining issues and stocks interlisted with the NYSE. Ten days later the Toronto exchange also opened trading in all its listed issues. Naturally, many stocks did not trade at all under such conditions, the unfortunate result being to 'establish very clearly in the public eye the fact that certain stocks are valued below the official minimum.' In an effort to prevent such a loss of confidence the TSE imposed a blackout on quotations; not until December 1914 did it resume publication of prices on selected stocks, and even then it still refused to disclose volume.[13]

The minimum-price system created a great deal of controversy. First of all, the minimums on some stocks differed between the MSE and the TSE, and it took several weeks before most of these differentials were eliminated. There were other complaints that this artifical system distorted share prices: 'Circumstances under which trades are accomplished on the exchanges as at present constituted are such as to preclude the possibility of the transactions interpreting real values.'[14]

The problem facing the boards of the MSE and the TSE was that they could not move to resume free trading more rapidly than their bankers and the actions of the more powerful exchanges in New York and London would permit. Yet at the same time they were being pressured by the steady expansion of off-floor dealing and, particularly in the case of Toronto, the readiness of the bolder spirits on the Standard exchange to relax all the restrictions. In mid-November the Standard resumed its all-day meetings with cash trading on every issue and no minimum prices. Moreover, there were recurrent threats to list all TSE stocks on the Standard.[15]

A month later the New York Stock Exchange reopened its entire list of North American stocks for cash dealing, though minimum prices were maintained. This meant that such important Canadian stocks as CPR began to trade much more freely. The boards of the MSE and the TSE extended their hours as the volume of business picked up and began to discuss with each other the possibility of reopening fully in the new year.[16]

Nothing happened. Early in 1915 the Standard exchange did drop its requirement that trades be for cash, but there was little margin trading since brokers' loans remained scarce. Both the *Financial Post* and the *Financial Times* claimed that the minimum prices on the MSE and TSE were becoming increasingly artificial and simply served to prevent buyers from snapping up shares at bargain prices, but the bankers showed no enthusiasm for ending the restrictions. The TSE continued to trade only a couple of hundred shares daily. By the end of March there were forty-one stocks on the two exchanges that had not been dealt with at all since the crisis the previous July.[17]

The governors finally took their courage in their hands early in April 1915 and announced a relaxation of the trading rules. The MSE permitted free trading in all stocks under $15 and all mining shares. Blue-chip securities trading well above their minimums would be eligible for a 20 per cent margin. The TSE actually dropped minimum prices for half a dozen actively traded issues, but when the exchange board asked the Toronto clearing house of the Canadian Bankers Association for authority to reduce the minimum prices on other shares up to 10 per cent the bankers refused to go along.[18]

To the gratification of members, however, trading volume picked up, and thirty-five of sixty-three stocks listed on the MSE showed gains during April, with fifteen unchanged and only two or three down. Even bad news from the European front and the sinking of the *Lusitania* in May with the loss of hundreds of lives failed to demoralize the Canadian exchanges as much as those elsewhere. Yet confidence remained fragile, and many people in the financial community were convinced that had short selling been permitted, panic might have occurred in both Toronto and Montreal.[19]

By the summer of 1915 the recession in Canada was nearing its end as mobilization intensified. 'War' stocks such as steel, construction, and transportation enjoyed strong demand. In July the TSE tried to persuade the MSE to agree to empower their boards to cut minimum prices on any stocks up to 10 per cent whenever buyers could be found at the new levels and to support a reduction in the minimums for banks and loan and trust company shares equal to the dividends paid by them in the second half of 1914. After consultations with the CBA's Montreal clearing house committee the MSE board rejected the proposal because of hostility on the part of the bankers, and at a general meeting of MSE members only one in ten expressed support for the idea of cutting the minimums. When the TSE's committee approached the Toronto clearing house about cutting the minimums on financial stocks, the bankers insisted that any changes would have to be approved by all their general managers. Some TSE members wanted to move unilaterally, but a general meeting late in the summer simply endorsed further negotiations with the MSE and the CBA in an effort to reach an agreement.[20]

In the fall the TSE made further efforts to persuade the CBA's Toronto clearing house committee to agree to cuts in the minimums for bank stocks equal to the dividends paid over the past two quarters. Once again, however, the Montreal clearing house committee declined to endorse lower minimums, and the TSE board was forced to drop its proposal. Nevertheless, the MSE established a monthly record by trading 335,000 shares in November 1915, reaching a peak of 38,000 in a single day.[21] Trading for the entire year on the MSE totalled 1.5 million shares (versus over 2 million in 1913), while the TSE handled only 600,000 shares (as against 935,000 in 1913). More than 1 million industrials were dealt with in Montreal, demonstrating the demand for war stocks, while Toronto traded another 230,000. The sharpest declines in volume from the pre-war levels on the two exchanges were in bank and railway shares, where only just over 10,000 shares of both types were handled. (See appendix, tables A.1 and A.3.)

Relations between the brokerage community and the bankers remained tense even with the increase in the volume of trading. The Bank of Toronto left no doubt about who had the whip hand when it expressed its unhappiness at the failure of one TSE member to reduce the size of its borrowings as requested, bluntly threatening to sell out the shares that the bank held as collateral. 'When the banks came to the rescue of brokers it was for the purpose of giving them time to turn around and get their accounts put in order, appealing to their clients, if necessary, to put up more margin. It was not the intention then, and not the intention now, that banks shall [sic] allow brokers to lie down upon their loans and not put them in proper shape when called upon.'[22]

By the spring of 1916, wartime prosperity seemed to render the maintenance of minimum prices on the stock exchanges unnecessary. The *Financial Post* argued that the minimums were now simply hurting investors by preventing them from learning the true value of their securities. The rules permitted unscrupulous brokers to buy stock at minimum prices and then make large profits by immediately reselling it as much as 10 points higher. The banks, however, were determined to cling to the minimums on their shares because the rise in interest rates since 1914 had made bonds more attractive as blue-chip investments as their prices fell. The refusal of the banks to raise their dividends had reduced demand for their shares, so that the minimum prices were artificially high.[23]

The TSE continued to take the lead in pressing the banks to agree to a gradual reduction in minimum prices, and in March 1916 negotiations were opened with the general managers of the banks whose head offices were in Toronto (the Commerce, Imperial, Toronto, and Dominion). John Aird of the Commerce, largest of the Toronto banks, raised the matter with the CBA, which now seemed somewhat more sympathetic. After lengthy negotiations between the Toronto and Montreal exchanges and the CBA, it was agreed that the minimum prices on many issues would cease to apply early in May. On the whole the process proceeded smoothly, and a number of stocks that had not traded on the exchanges since July 1914 began to change hands again. Encouraged by this development, the CBA now agreed to drop the remaining minimums on bank shares, and after nearly two years, trading without restrictions on the Canadian exchanges resumed on 23 June 1916. With the Canadian economy operating at full blast a rise in share prices commenced which carried many stocks to new highs in the months that followed. By the fall of 1916 brokers' borrowings from the banks to finance margin accounts had reached record levels.[24] Trading volumes on the MSE reached an all-time high of 3.4 million shares in 1916, while 1.3 million changed hands in Toronto, only narrowly missing the record level of 1909. Montreal brokers also benefited from very heavy trading in bonds. (See appendix, tables A.1 and A.3.)

II

Brokers naturally greeted the resumption of unrestricted share trading in mid-1916 with profound relief. The preceding two years had been pretty bleak. Had it not been for the opportunity offered to sell Canadian government bonds to finance the war effort, the toll of failures in the securities business would have been heavy indeed. Initially expecting only a short conflict ('The war will be over by Christmas'), the Borden government did little to meet costs beyond raising a few luxury taxes in August 1914. At the end of the year Finance Minister Thomas White confidently told the Canadian Club of Montreal that the country's financial future looked rosy. Believing that military expenditures would mainly be incurred abroad, Canada arranged to borrow from the British government to cover most of its needs, and by March 1915 these advances totalled £12 million sterling.[25]

By that time, however, it was clear that the war would be much longer and more costly than anyone had anticipated. Britain could no longer afford to meet the requirements of its former colonies, and London capital markets were closed to outside borrowers in order to supply domestic requirements. Canada therefore shifted its borrowing to New York, and in July 1915 an underwriting syndicate headed by J.P. Morgan and Company took up $45 million worth of one- and two-year notes, bearing interest at 5 per cent. Finance Minister White later noted, 'Prior to the loan the securities market in Canada had been dead.' Canadian dealers, loaded with pre-war municipal bonds paying considerably lower interest, faced losses as these issues fell in price to reflect the higher wartime interest rates, and as a result there was a certain amount of criticism of the government for paying Morgan 5 per cent.[26]

The cost of borrowing in the United States, combined with the inexorable rise of military expenditures, eventually compelled White to consider a war loan in Canada. There were grave doubts that domestic buyers would absorb an issue of any great size, but he took the decision to go to the market in the fall of 1915 without consulting stockbrokers, though he did discuss the matter with the banks. He announced the sale of $50 million worth of ten-year war bonds bearing interest at 5 per cent. Issued in denominations as low as $100, the bonds were priced at 97.5 per cent, payable in monthly instalments until 1 May 1916, which made the effective annual yield almost 5.5 per cent. These interest payments were to be tax-free, which it was hoped would make the bonds particularly attractive to investors.

Nevertheless, doubts persisted. The *Financial Post* reported, 'The officials of the Finance Department would like to know whether there will be a thousand or twenty thousand applications.' For safety's sake White persuaded the chartered banks to agree to underwrite half the issue, but to the government's surprise and gratification Canadians flocked to purchase the bonds and the issue was heavily oversubscribed. The banks themselves applied for $26,350,000 worth of bonds, insurance companies $7,585,000, industrial firms $4,825,000, cities $2,920,000, and trust and loan companies $1,250,000. In addition, 24,862 individuals subscribed for $2,503,000, making a grand total of $45,533,000. One bank manager reported that accounts in his quiet country district were being drawn upon for the first time in twenty years to buy the bonds. Patriotic motives aside, prosperous Canadians obviously saw them as a desirable investment; the press published a list of the twenty largest individual subscribers, who offered to take over $1,750,000 among them. Faced with this unexpected good fortune, White promptly decided to double the size of the issue. All subscriptions under $50,000 were accepted in full, and the banks' allotment was cut slightly to bring in a total of $100 million. (See table 5.1.) In White's words, 'Having received twice the sum asked for, the problem arose [of] what to do with the surplus.' Therefore $50 million was lent to Britain to purchase food and war supplies in Canada, thus further spurring the economic boom.[27]

The unexpected success of the 1915 war loan was as gratifying to financial men as it was to the government. The *Financial Times* expressed some surprise that brokers and bond dealers had thrown themselves so heartily into selling it in light of the low rate of commission, but clearly with the 'street' so quiet, anything was better than nothing. Though individuals had put up only a small proportion of the total raised, the *Financial Post* was now convinced that 'the

TABLE 5.1 Canadian domestic war loans, 1915–19 (monetary figures in $000,000)

	1915 (Nov.)	1916 (Sept.)	1917 (Mar.)	1917 (Nov.)	1918 (Nov.)	1919 (Nov.)
Sum asked	50	100	150	150	300	300
Subscriptions						
Banks	25	50	60			
Public	79	151	201	419	690	678
Total	104	201	261	419	690	678
Allotments						
Banks	21					
Public	79	100	150	398	690	678
No. of subscriptions						
(000s)	25	35	41	820	1,080	830
Rate of interest	5%	5%	5%	5.5%	5.5%	5.5%
Term (years)	10	15	20	5–10	15	5–10
Price	97.5%	97.5%	96%	100%	100%	100%
Status	TE (tax exempt)	TE	TE	TE	TE	taxable

SOURCE: Douglas H. Fullerton, *The Bond Market in Canada* (Toronto, 1960), 40.

small investor will develop in time and be well worth the trouble spent on him.'
Moreover, the brokers were comforted by the thought that a secondary market in
the bonds would develop once investors realized that their money need not be
locked away for the entire ten-year term. By the end of 1915 war bonds were
being traded in both Montreal and Toronto at approximately the issue price.

The only fly in the ointment for the brokers and dealers was the competition
from the banks with their extensive networks of branches. Some subscribers
took application forms issued by bond dealers to their neighbouring banks,
which simply crossed out the dealer's name and secured the commission for
themselves, the first, but by no means the last, time that bankers would interfere
in the retail distribution of securities to the dismay of the Canadian brokerage
community. Ignoring protests from the dealers the Finance Department refused
to interfere or order a split in the commissions.[28]

Despite the success of the first domestic war loan, Finance Minister White
was not convinced that it could be repeated.[29] When the government needed
more money, he decided to return to the U.S. market in the spring of 1916, in
part because the one-year notes from 1915 were falling due, and arranged to
borrow $75 million through another underwriting syndicate headed by J.P.
Morgan and Company. This sum was divided equally between bonds of five,
ten, and fifteen years issued at rates between 5 and 5.5 per cent. The fifteen-year
bonds, in particular, were heavily oversubscribed, leading critics to argue that
the government had overpaid for the funds. Some Canadian brokers and dealers
insisted the money could have been had much more cheaply.[30]

The criticism of the American war loan of 1916 and the inexorable rise of military spending during the battles on the Somme forced the Canadian government to consider new methods of financing. In 1916 White introduced a 'business war profits tax' and in 1917 the first federal income taxation, but neither of these covered more than a fraction of the expenditures. The government was therefore compelled to borrow most of its funds domestically during the final stages of the war. To White's gratification each of the Canadian war loans was heavily oversubscribed, so that altogether he was able to raise $2.116 billion from bond buyers at interest rates ranging between 5 and 5.5 per cent. (See table 5.1.)

White's caution and pessimism about the ability of the market to absorb such comparatively large issues is evident in the fact that he had the banks underwrite a large portion of the first three loans even though this proved unnecessary. Moreover, he accepted only the amount requested for the second and third loans despite heavy oversubscriptions. He later argued that doing so was prudent since Canadians needed to be trained as to the nature of these securities, and that it helped keep the prices and interest rates of later issues firm by not overtaxing the lending capacities of the citizenry. Only the growing prosperity created by the war economy after 1916, he claimed, provided the pools of funds to be tapped.[31]

What is undeniable is that these war loans were a godsend to the investment community in Canada, becalmed by sluggish share markets and minimum prices on the stock exchanges. War financing represented a heaven-sent opportunity to diversify into the marketing and secondary trading of federal government bonds, an area of business that had been non-existent prior to 1914. Spotting this opportunity the bond dealers hastened to organize themselves in order to exert as much influence as possible over the timing, terms of issue, and commission rates of future war loans.

Toronto's bond dealers had actually taken steps to form an organization as early as 1911. Yet some firms were reluctant to join together at that time for fear that the public would regard such activity as a price-fixing combine for marketing municipal issues. Nevertheless, a local Bond Dealers Association was created under the auspices of the Toronto Board of Trade, and when the war broke out the association did take steps to try to ensure that all municipalities (who were the major domestic bond issuers) lived up to their obligations. When Finance Minister White announced his first war loan in the fall of 1915, however, he did not even bother to consult the Toronto group, preferring to deal only with the banks.[32]

The Montreal bond houses had never been formally organized, but in 1916 Quebec municipalities approached the provincial government seeking legislation that would have unilaterally altered the terms of contracts between municipal issuers and bondholders. This spurred the Montrealers to get together and lobby the government, and their success seemed to demonstrate the value of a permanent organization. In June 1916 a group from Montreal travelled to Toronto for discussions with their counterparts and agreed to create the Bond Dealers Association of Canada with William Hanson (of Hanson Brothers, Montreal) as president.[33]

The largest Montreal and Toronto bond dealers were among the thirty-three founding members of the BDAC. These men, who a year earlier had doubted that Canadians would take up an issue worth even $10 million, could now envisage a solid living from marketing and trading government of Canada bonds. Within weeks the government had announced the second Canadian war loan, seeking to raise another $100 million. Finance Minister White, however, resisted pressure from the BDAC to make the issue more saleable to Americans by having it payable in U.S. dollars. The banks again agreed to take up to half the bonds and distribute them amongst themselves in proportion to their capitalization. Thanks to diligent work by the new Bond Dealers Association in appointing local agents and seeking out small subscribers, 34,526 individuals applied for a total of over $150 million. White, however, refused to expand the issue and cancelled the banks' $50 million underwriting. (See table 5.1.) Only individual subscriptions under $25,000 were accepted in full in the hope that those who had not received their full allotments might bid up prices and reduce interest rates.[34]

As Canada's war effort continued to gobble up money, White announced early in 1917 the creation of war savings certificates (modelled on those in Britain), which were designed to tap the savings of people unable to raise the $100 required to purchase a bond. Certificates sold at banks and post offices for $21.50, $45, or $86 would be redeemable in three years for $25, $50, and $100, respectively, or an annual interest rate of just over 5 per cent. This issue attracted little criticism from the brokers and bond dealers, since they believed that it would raise only small sums unless the government were to devote large amounts of money to advertising and promotion, since few people of modest resources were likely to lock up funds for three years without any return in the interim.[35]

By the time that the Bond Dealers Association held its first annual meeting in Montreal in February 1917, it was clear that there would be another flotation before long. A delegation from the BDAC immediately sought a meeting with the finance minister to argue that since American buyers had taken up an estimated 25 per cent of the 1916 bonds, though they were payable only in Canadian funds, White should make the new issue payable in U.S. dollars to render them even more saleable. This time the minister accepted the advice. The loan announced in March 1917 consisted of $150 million worth of twenty-year 5 per cent bonds priced to yield about 5.5 per cent interest; holders of the first Canadian war loan were permitted to convert their bonds (which had eight and one-half years until maturity) into the new series.[36]

Not only did the Finance Department accept the BDAC's advice about making the bonds payable in New York, but its members had grounds for celebration when sellers were formally barred from splitting their commissions with purchasers. Securities salesmen again beat the bushes energetically for small subscribers, and in the end 40,800 applications were received, totalling over $200 million (see table 5.1). Members of the BDAC claimed to have marketed over $100 million of bonds, with a single house, Wood, Gundy, alone recording sales of $34.6 million to 2,500 customers. Again White cancelled the banks' underwriting of $60 million and refused to expand the size of the issue. To encourage small investors, only subscriptions for less than $25,000 worth of bonds were allotted the full amount applied for, larger applications again being scaled back.[37]

After 1917 'Victory' bond issues, which dwarfed anything even imagined in Canada before the war, became annual events, the money raised being used principally to fund British purchases in Canada. More and more Canadians became accustomed to ownership of government bonds. Having imposed conscription in the summer of 1917, the Borden government announced the first Victory loan in November. This issue of $150 million worth of five-, ten-, and twenty-year bonds was to bear interest at 5.5 per cent. After further consultations between the Finance Department and the BDAC there was a bow to small investors as denominations as low as $50 were issued, payable in instalments from December through to May. The government was sufficiently confident of success that for the first time no underwriting was sought from the members of the Canadian Bankers Association, though the banks were permitted to lend money to creditworthy customers to finance the purchase of bonds over a twelve-month period.[38]

A highly elaborate nationwide organization was speedily created to publicize and market Victory bonds, resting primarily upon the brokers, bond dealers, and banks but including insurance companies, schools, church groups, and fraternal societies directed by a central committee. Patriotic fervour was supposed to suppress competition and ensure cooperation amongst salesmen. By early October people on the 'street' were so heavily involved in selling the new issue that there was even discussion of closing down the Toronto and Montreal Stock Exchanges to permit members' employees to devote their full time to the bond campaign, but that idea was eventually dropped.[39]

The first Victory loan campaign coincided with the federal election in which

Sir Robert Borden's coalition Unionist government was returned to office with overwhelming support (at least in English Canada) for its conscriptionist policies. So successful was the bond drive that subscriptions totalling nearly $419 million were secured from 820,000 individuals, or about one in ten of the entire population (see photo 14). The government therefore decided to increase the size of the issue to almost $400 million. (See table 5.1.) All subscriptions up to $1 million were allotted in full.[40]

Nevertheless, the first successful Victory bond campaign was conducted in the shadow of gloomy news. Disastrous defeats in the Italian theatre and the collapse of Russia into revolutionary turmoil jolted stock markets in the autumn of 1917. As share prices declined in New York, the New York Stock Exchange attempted to discourage short selling and prevent bear raids by requiring anyone borrowing shares to report daily to exchange officials. The aim was to stem panic based upon rumours and avoid the reimposition of minimum prices.

Almost at once, downward pressure on the prices of interlisted issues was again felt in Canada. Seeking to stop the fall in CPR, which was widely held locally, the board of the Montreal Stock Exchange delayed its opening on 30 October 1917 and reinstated minimum prices on all stocks, with the aim of preventing losses and marshalling funds to defend the value of CPR. As in 1914 this was done without consultation with the Toronto Stock Exchange. Reluctantly the TSE board felt compelled to follow suit, believing that the bankers had once again endorsed the imposition of minimums. Trading volumes quickly slumped, and most shares dropped back to the minimum prices, thus ending the better times that had prevailed since the exchanges had reopened fully in June 1916.[41]

Volume on the MSE and the TSE fell off sharply to 1,130,000 and 510,000 shares handled respectively during 1917. The drop was particularly pronounced in industrial stocks: Montreal handled just over 700,000 as against 2,350,000 the previous year, while Toronto was off from 700,000 to just over 210,000. Further declines in volume in 1918 saw the MSE trade just over 1 million shares, while Torontonians received orders for only 340,000 shares as the volume of industrials hit just 110,000. Nor did bond trading take up all the slack, for although business on the exchanges remained good in 1917, the volume of bonds handled dropped sharply in 1918. (See appendix, tables A.1 and A.3.)

Toronto brokers were almost universally opposed to the reimposition of minimums, which they believed was simply forcing trading off the floor rather than protecting share values. Not only had the MSE board failed to consult the TSE before acting, but the Torontonians discovered that there had been no prior discussions with the Canadian Bankers Association. Nonetheless, Toronto's bankers advised the TSE in January 1918 that if stocks on which brokers' loans had been advanced were found to be trading off the exchange below their minimums, they might well demand that the brokers put up additional margin. The bankers denied the existence of any arrangement not to call in their loans to brokers of the kind that had been arrived at in 1914, though they declared no present intention to require repayment. The TSE board huffily demanded that Montreal should send a committee to discuss the whole matter and seek an understanding with the bankers. Moreover, the TSE insisted from the outset on deducting any dividends paid out by companies from their minimum share prices, creating differentials between the two exchanges for a small number of interlisted issues when the MSE refused to follow suit. The banks were able to force the TSE to cease this practice in the case of their own shares, demonstrating once again who held the whip hand.[42]

Montreal stuck to its guns on the issue of minimums. At a general meeting on 20 March 1918 the MSE's members decided to retain the minimums, not even deducting dividends as they were declared. Meanwhile, business on the TSE was so slow that the committee had to ban domino playing on the floor. One listed company, Shredded Wheat, took the bull by the horns and demanded that its minimum price be dropped, but for the rest of 1918 the system remained intact as the fighting in Europe dragged to its close.[43]

The armistice on 11 November 1918 redoubled the pressure to drop the minimums on the TSE, but Montreal showed no signs of bending. At last, its patience exhausted, the TSE board decided to repay the other exchange for the unpleasant surprises of 1914 and 1917, and announced unilaterally that free trading would resume on 2 January 1919. Nevertheless, in January the members of the MSE resolved by a vote of 41 to 17 to stick with the minimums until a treaty of peace between the Allies and Germany was actually signed. Not until 2 June did the Montreal exchange finally resume full free trading in all stocks.[44]

The reimposition of minimum prices on the Canadian exchanges in late 1917 had coincided with further intervention in financial markets by the federal government. Finance Minister White had become concerned about the need to reserve the domestic capital market for Victory bonds. In the summer of 1916 rumours had begun to circulate that Ottawa intended to impose special taxes on the purchase of all non-Canadian securities, but nothing happened.[45] One year later White expressed the desire for power 'to conscript or expropriate the right of competition of new securities with Dominion loans.' The Justice Department was therefore asked to draft regulations that would require approval for borrowing by any municipality, province, or company, domestic or foreign.[46] White took no action at that time, but in December 1917, with the Unionist government safely back in office, an order-in-council was passed under the War Measures

Act. When the governments of Ontario, Quebec, Alberta, and Saskatchewan protested at this abrogation of their right to borrow money, White simply replied that the necessities of war finance made federal control of capital markets essential.[47]

Thomas Bradshaw, the city of Toronto's finance commissioner, was appointed by White to pass upon all applications to borrow. Predictions that corporate borrowers might seek to exploit the new regulations by implying that permission was tantamount to government endorsement of the securities being offered proved correct in at least one case. In the summer of 1918 Gold Banner Mines was allowed to offer 2 million of its shares at 40 cents each, and the prospectus noted that the federal regulations were designed 'to prevent any but safe investments getting on the market.' The hint that these shares were as good as gold (or at least Victory bonds) led the Finance Department to revoke Gold Banner's permission to borrow for violating the regulations, which required a statement that sanction did 'not consitute an approval of the issue as regards its merits.' Otherwise the new regulations seem to have operated without serious hitches during the final stages of the war.[48]

By 1918 the government of Canada had issued almost $750 million worth of war bonds. One of Finance Minister White's major concerns became the support of the bond market to keep the various issues trading as near par (100 per cent of face value) as possible in order to keep interest rates low. As more and more people purchased bonds, secondary trading increased as did the temptation to offer heavily discounted prices to those needing to liquidate their holdings in a hurry. Bond prices had slumped with the military reverses in France during 1917, so the third War Loan was selling as low as 91.75 per cent of par, while wartime inflation was nibbling away at the real rate of return. With another $300 million of Victory bonds just coming onto the market, the task of stabilizing secondary trading became more and more important.

Bond dealers in both Toronto and Montreal began discussions on the matter in December 1917, and eventually a meeting of the Bond Dealers Association was held at which it was decided to create a permanent body to deal with the problem. The Victory Loan Special Committee would acquire any 1917 Victory bonds offered for sale at 97.84 per cent using funds from the subscriptions of large institutional buyers who had not received their full allotments and would resell them to permanent investors at a fixed price of 98.84 per cent. Bond dealers numbering 240 in all agreed to work with the committee and abide by these prices for patriotic reasons.[49]

Just as the fighting came to an end in November 1918, the government announced the second Victory loan, which aimed to raise another $300 million at an interest rate of 5.5. per cent. Once again stockbrokers and bond dealers were asked to devote their entire energies to the sales campaign. In Vancouver the campaign organizers agreed to hire salesmen for three weeks at salaries of $400 per week, a most welcome offer for traders caught in the slow markets on the Vancouver Stock Exchange. In the end an astonishing 1,080,000 subscriptions were received for $690 million worth of bonds at 100 per cent of par, and the government decided to accept all the applications. (See table 5.1.)[50]

At the end of November the Finance Department lifted its controls over borrowing by provinces and municipalities but retained control over private borrowers. When the Toronto Stock Exchange resumed trading freely in January 1919, the Victory Loan Special Committee also discontinued its price-support operations after handling about $70 million worth of bonds in over 33,000 transactions during the previous year, leaving the bonds trading above par.[51] With the most urgent tasks of war finance out of the way the seventy-six members of the Bond Dealers Association finally had an opportunity to set their organization on a permanent footing.[52]

The final Victory loan came in November 1919 to pay the costs of demobilization with another $300 million worth of bonds. The Victory Loan Special Committee was revived for a campaign that succeeded in bringing in 830,000 subscriptions totalling $678 million, all of which were accepted. (See table 5.1.) The committee once again intervened to stabilize the prices of all three victory loans, but the market for the bonds was now sufficiently broad and liquid that the committee was able to cease its market-support operations within a month or so.[53]

Early in 1920, however, the government found it necessary to reinstitute controls over financial markets. The British government had 'unpegged' the pound sterling, which rapidly slid to a discount against the dollar and led to a heavy selling of Canadian securities held in Great Britain. On 23 February Finance Minister Sir Henry Drayton, who had succeeded White in the summer of 1919, demanded that banks, stockbrokers, and bond dealers impose an embargo on purchases of Canadian securities from overseas since such purchases were depressing the price of Victory bonds. The brokers complained bitterly that the embargo was both unwise and ineffective, blaming the banks for persuading Drayton to impose it in an effort to protect the value of their large inventories of Victory bonds bought at high prices.[54]

Meanwhile, the Victory Loan Special Committee was again revived to stabilize bond prices. In June 1920 chairman G.H. Wood rejected the Toronto Stock Exchange's request to drop the controls, despite the fact that the Bond Dealers Association of Canada was deeply divided over the issue.[55] But the committee was forced to reduce its support price on five separate occasions during the year. Dealers were further angered by the efforts of the government and the banks to avoid paying Canadians interest on the 1917 war loan in U.S. dollars, which now commanded a healthy premium over Canadian currency. The bonds had been made payable in U.S. funds so that they would be more saleable, but now the government seemed to be trying to evade its contractual obligations.[56]

In October there was an acrimonious meeting between Drayton and Toronto investment dealers about their grievances concerning the embargo on purchasing foreign-held securities and the artificial support prices for Victory bonds. Critics of Drayton's policies dubbed the gathering a 'fiasco' and a 'farce,' but could extract no more from the minister than a promise to try to revoke the embargo early in 1921. Over the next few weeks this discontent led to a heavy sell-off, which brought about a meeting of all Toronto's bankers, brokers, and bond dealers with the finance minister at Sir Thomas White's house late one Saturday afternoon, continued at the National Club the following day. Eventually Drayton was convinced that support for bond prices should be dropped immediately. After a brief decline prices rose above the pegged levels in brisk trading, and the government liquidated the remainder of its inventory.[57]

Thus by the end of 1920 the last of the wartime restrictions on Canadian financial markets, which had been imposed on 28 July 1914 when the stock exchanges closed, had finally come to an end. The war years had seen important and long-lasting changes in the financial system. First of all, there was the remarkable expansion in the ownership of government bonds, in particular by small investors, which had commenced with the surprising success of the first War Loan in 1915 and climaxed with the three Victory loans. More than one out of eight Canadians had submitted applications to purchase the 1918 issue. Not only were there thousands of new bondholders, but bond trading now became big business. The members of the Bond Dealers Association of Canada profited greatly and became key players in the financial community as a result. And the success of the Victory Loan Special Committee in stabilizing the market for the bonds gave these securities an excellent reputation with investors.

The experiments with controlling share prices by imposing minimums on the stock exchanges between 1914 and 1916 and again in 1917 and 1918 were much less successful. As critics noted, a good deal of trading simply shifted off the exchange floors to the offices of brokers. Thus the stock exchanges emerged from the war weaker rather than stronger than they had been prior to 1914. Yet 1920 also saw a hopeful portent as four leading Toronto bond houses decided to purchase seats on the Toronto Stock Exchange.[58] The distinction between those who dealt in more-speculative stocks and those who handled blue-chip bonds seemed to be eroding. With the end of the post-war recession the financial community could look to the future optimistically.

6

Highbinders and Re-Loaders

Joseph Xavier Hearst arrived in Winnipeg from the United States in 1920. He married a local woman, and together they established the Canadian Regalia Company to manufacture ceremonial garb for lodges and fraternal associations. This enterprise did not prove a success and soon went bankrupt, but its failure did not stand in the way of Hearst's other, grander plans. He claimed to be a composer and marketer of popular songs, and in July 1921 he incorporated the Hearst Music Company as the first step towards cornering the market in the publication of sheet music, a rapidly growing business at that time. One year later Hearst increased the authorized capital of his company from $25,000 to $250,000. Then he started selling shares to the public in order to raise the funds required to construct a specialized printing plant to be located in Winnipeg.[1]

Hearst let it be known that he was selling a portion of his stock in the company only in order to escape heavy income taxes by reinvesting his money in tax-free bonds. The share salesmen whom he employed confided to potential buyers that he was related to the great newspaper magnate William Randolph Hearst. The International Music Corporation of New York, which Joseph Hearst also controlled, was said to be working on a similar scheme to dominate the U.S. market. Most important, he promised that the Canadian company would start to pay dividends to share purchasers immediately.

He was as good as his word. Mrs Flora Edie, an elderly Kildonan resident, sold a pair of interest-bearing school-district debentures to buy one share of Hearst Music stock. Over the next couple of years she continued to accumulate Hearst Music shares until she had fourteen in all, bought at prices ranging from $100 to $120. Part of the appeal of this investment was that between January 1923 and July 1924 she received an impressive $739.42 worth of dividends, all of which, plus more of her own money, she promptly ploughed back into Hearst Music.[2]

A.W. Snider of Wawanesa initially put $800 into the company, receiving a 30 per cent dividend along with a 60 per cent bonus in 1922. Eventually he became the largest investor, putting up over $40,000; he joined the board of directors and helped to persuade people in the Wawanesa area to purchase $125,000 worth of stock altogether.[3] The owners of the 5,700 shares of Hearst Music Company stock marketed between 1922 and 1924 received over $65,000 worth of dividends, much of which went to Joseph Hearst himself since he remained a large shareholder. Some investors got dividends as high as 50 per cent while others netted only 15 per cent.[4]

People who approached Hearst in the hope of selling him songs were often persuaded to buy shares instead. Carl Fink tried to market a composition by his wife but ended up purchasing stock, having been guaranteed a 10 per cent return on his investment. Another composer also had his song rejected but bought stock and eventually joined the board of directors of Hearst Music; he was permitted to borrow $2,850 from the company treasury, which was paid off by 'royalties' for subsequent compositions. Altogether the company paid out about $31,000 in royalties to various songwriters.[5]

When the marketing of stock was already well under way, Joseph Hearst realized that he had neglected to register his company under Manitoba's blue-sky law, the Sale of Shares Act. In November 1922 he applied to the Public Utilities Commission for permission to distribute $75,000 worth of stock. The prospectus and financial records indicated that Hearst Music's Chicago printing plant had yielded total receipts of $290,000 during the previous ten months, producing profits of $143,000 and leaving $197,000 in the company's bank account. Yet Commissioner P.A. Macdonald was not impressed. He pointed out that the company's assets were not fixed and were located outside the province, while sufficient funds were already on hand to construct a music printing plant in Winnipeg. Macdonald had interviewed Hearst and found him less than frank and confidence inspiring; he had refused to divulge the name of his banker or to produce any of his music publishing contracts. Registration was refused.[6]

Hearst was outraged and immediately hired lawyer J.W. Wilton to take up his case. Wilton tried to overcome Macdonald's suspicions by producing a glowing endorsement from Hearst's bankers. A letter from the assistant cashier of the Chase National Bank of New York advised that Hearst's accounts totalled $562,340 and, moreover, that he had on deposit 439 shares of the International Music Corporation and 10,000 shares of Studebaker stock. In addition, there existed his 'special' account covering 117 producing oil wells, 143 tank cars, and 12,354,278 barrels of oil. Other oilmen were waiting to join a pool of oil stocks managed by Hearst, 'confident that it will be the biggest thing of its kind in the history of the nation.' As if that were not enough, Chase National offered to lend International Music $150,000, and the letter concluded with a flourish: 'We wish to take this means of congratulating you on the splendid manner in which you have handled this particular proposition ... We certainly regret that [sic] fact that you have again refused to enter our board as one of our directors; perhaps you would prefer such a place on another subsidiary of ours or of our particular correspondent bank in Canada. If so, advise by wire and it will be immediately acted FAVORABLY ON.'[7]

Wilton insisted that if the company did not receive a certificate to sell shares in Manitoba at once, Hearst might well shift his printing operation elsewhere. Why was Commissioner Macdonald being so obdurate? If only the lawyer were given an opportunity to present his case, he could easily demonstrate that Hearst Music would be highly profitable. After all, it was already paying a dividend of 50 per cent to investors who had put up $107,000 during 1922.[8]

When Judge H.A. Robson had begun to administer the Manitoba Sale of Shares Act in 1912, there existed no appeal against a refusal to issue a certificate. Complaints were heard that the legislation gave too much discretionary power to a single individual, and in 1919 the act was amended to permit the commissioner himself to appoint an appeal panel. That too was criticized, and the following year the provincial cabinet was made responsible for appointing a panel which would no longer include the commissioner.[9] Wilton pressured the government to allow an appeal (even threatening to have a private member's bill granting registration to Hearst Music introduced in the legislature), and eventually the cabinet ordered a new hearing in early 1923.[10]

A two-man panel composed of a chartered accountant and a music-store owner heard the appeal. The panelists did not even consult Commissioner Macdonald about his reasons for refusing registration in the first place. After listening to Wilton and examining a certificate from the company's auditor, they granted Hearst Music permission to market $75,000 worth of stock to the public. The share-selling campaign then shifted into even higher gear, with farmers who owned bank stocks being specially targeted by Hearst's salesmen. Before long the company increased its authorized capital further and moved into fancy new offices in Winnipeg. Nevertheless, suspicion lingered. At the end of 1923 Macdonald discovered that Hearst had taken steps to free himself from provincial control by procuring a charter of incorporation from the federal government in Ottawa. Not only that, but he had transferred all the assets of the provincial undertaking to the federal one, something expressly forbidden under the Sale of Shares Act. Macdonald therefore cancelled Hearst Music's registration in Manitoba, but stock selling continued merrily, helped along by the payment of generous dividends.[11]

In August 1924 Joseph Hearst left Winnipeg for points east, supposedly to put the finishing touches on his conglomerate, which would dominate sheet-music publishing throughout North America. Not until November did Toronto's *Saturday Night* raise the alarm about Hearst Music with a long and highly critical story by its Winnipeg correspondent. F.C. Pickwell demanded to know where the money was coming from to pay the huge dividends since the press had been advertising returns between 25 per cent and 100 per cent over the past year and the stock was quoted as high as $260 per share. Hearst Music had tried to place a plug in *Saturday Night* claiming sales of 2 million copies of songs in 1922 and 5 million the following year, but enquiries in the music business had revealed that these figures were highly inflated. If profits were so healthy, why were share salesmen still working so hard to push the stock? 'There is an undoubted atmosphere of mystery about the inner workings of the company which do [*sic*] not impress those accustomed to making sound investments.'

Though Pickwell had not got wind of Hearst's lengthy absence from Winnipeg, he raised tough questions about his business reputation. When Canadian Regalia had gone into bankruptcy in 1920, Joseph Xavier Hearst had been known by another name; perhaps this was just 'a passing musical *nom de plume*,' but a great deal about the man remained mysterious. Almost all the company's funds were supposed to be on deposit in an American bank, yet enquiring shareholders had been refused any details, even the name of the bank. The directors of Hearst Music were not a confidence-inspiring lot, including the likes of a local fireman. The meteoric rise of the company's stock price had been marked by 'a trail of undoubted misrepresentations, if not actual fraud,' and Pickwell believed that prudent investors should make it their business to find out exactly where they stood as soon as possible.[12]

At long last, director A.W. Snider, suspicious about Hearst's lengthy absence, demanded an accounting and almost overnight the whole house of cards collapsed.[13] The account with the Chase National Bank had never existed; Hearst had written a couple of years earlier enquiring about banking by mail and then had had the letterhead on the bank's reply reproduced by a local print shop. Chase National's cashier pointed out the obvious fact that the extravagant testimonial to Joseph Hearst's assets and abilities had been signed with a rubber stamp. A warrant for Hearst's arrest on charges of procuring money by false pretences was issued on 17 December 1924, the Manitoba government offering a reward for $1,000 to anyone supplying information.

Soon it became crystal clear that Joseph Xavier Hearst had been running a classic share-pushing scam. No connection of William Randolph Hearst, he had been born Nathaniel Hirsch in Brooklyn, New York (and sometimes used the aliases Nat Lewis or Nat Osborne). In the words of the police flyer, 'He has a good knowledge of the stock market and will play it wherever he goes. His talk is always in huge figures and practically nothing else, and while talking he always walks about, cannot stand or sit still, gives one the impression that he is a drug addict.'[14] Of the $250,000 realized by share sales up to June 1923, only $99,000 had found its way into the company treasury, while the remaining $151,000 had been paid out as 'royalties' and 'dividends' (mainly to Hearst himself) or been diverted to him personally. Estimates of the total amount of money missing mounted steadily towards $1 million, a good portion of this lost by Hearst selling short in a rising stock market in New York.[15]

How had Hearst gotten away with such huge sums? The company's auditor turned out to be doubling as the corporate secretary and was a member of its board of directors; he believed that there was always at least $450,000 in the bank in New York. Hearst's personal secretary insisted before a legislative committee that he never even had an inkling that anything was wrong. This was too much for one assembly member: 'What I cannot understand is how so many people would sit around an office and simply swallow all this man Hearst happened to tell them, which was absolutely contrary to the first impression which a schoolboy would get about the way of doing business. Hearst is here doing business in Manitoba with a Canadian charter and selling his stock here; he is doing 80% of his business in the United States and he keeps all his money tied up in a bank in New York, and yet nobody ever gets suspicious, nobody ever sees the bank account, nobody ever knows that it is there.'[16]

Displaying that mixture of nerve and self-deception that makes the successful confidence man, Hearst did return to Winnipeg. He surrendered to the police in July 1925, protesting his innocence and claiming to have been in Europe during the past six months soothing his frazzled nerves. The Crown laid eight charges of fraud, false pretences, and theft of $385,000, and Hearst was released on $10,000 bail. His lengthy preliminary hearing commenced in December 1925 but dragged on until the following spring.[17] At his trial in June 1926 Hearst took the stand in his own defence, insisting that he too was an innocent victim. The real villain was another New Yorker, Earl Hampton, who had joined him in a scheme to merge all the sheet-music publishers in North America in December 1921. Hampton had been supposed to handle all the financial arrangements in the United States and deposit the company funds in the Chase National Bank. After they had not seen each other for the next couple of years, Hampton had failed to show up for a meeting in Chicago and had disappeared from his usual haunts in New York, taking the company's assets with him. This attempt to shift the blame onto the imaginary Hampton failed, and Hearst was found guilty on all eight charges. The judge sentenced him to seven years in the penitentiary, noting sternly that he had compounded his offences by perjuring himself.[18] Hearst was revealed as one of the classic 'highbinders' of his era.[19]

He was not alone: the decade of the twenties was something of a heyday for notable con men and swindlers. In 1920 Bostonians lined up to give their money to Charles Ponzi, lured by his promise to pay them 50 per cent interest on forty-five-day loans, or an annual rate of 400 per cent. Ponzi claimed that he was realizing these returns by buying prepaid international postal reply coupons, which could be cashed in Europe at a substantial profit because of exchange-rate fluctuations. Between January and August he took in $15 million before it was revealed that only a few hundred dollars' worth of postal coupons had been sold. When Ponzi brought his pitch to Montreal in August 1920, *Saturday Night* denounced him and compared him to the pre-war crook C.D. Sheldon, from whom Ponzi may have received his inspiration.[20] As public confidence collapsed, Ponzi was found to have liabilities of $7 million but only $4 million in assets and soon was serving a five-year sentence for mail fraud. His most lasting legacy was the term 'Ponzi scheme,' given thereafter to similar financial frauds in which current receipts were used to pay inflated returns to investors.[21]

Hearst Music was among the most widely publicized stock-selling swindles in Canada during the 1920s, but it was by no means the only one. There were plenty of other notorious characters. For instance, on 15 November 1923 Oland J. Brooks told an enthusiastic audience at a venison dinner in the Chamber of Commerce rooms in Stratford, Ontario, about his plans to establish a factory to produce steam-powered cars. Over the next three years he and his salesmen succeeded in persuading 8,000 investors across Canada to put up $4 million to purchase the common and preferred shares of the Brooks Steam Motor Company. At its peak in 1926 the Brooks Securities Company, which handled promotion and sales in return for 25 per cent of the money raised, occupied the entire eighteenth floor of the Metropolitan Building in Toronto. Brooks and his salesmen were 're-loaders' who specialized in persuading current shareholders to take up more and more of the stock, on the promise that the company was poised to soar towards immense profitability if only a few more dollars were raised. By the time that Brooks was forced to resign as company president in October 1927, 95 per cent of the company's assets had been dissipated and fewer than 150 cars had actually been manufactured. Only in the nick of time did the Canadian shareholders prevent him from turning over all the company's remaining assets to its American affiliate and transferring his entire operation to Buffalo, New York. Within months Brooks had reappeared in Montreal, where the People's Holding Company got busy selling stock in a company that would produce hot-water heaters.[22]

Hot air from share pushers seemed to have a natural affinity with heated water. The Instantaneous Electric Heater Company set up a showroom in downtown Toronto with a demonstration tank in the window which produced water warmed as it ran from the tap. Investors flocked to buy shares and profit from this scientific marvel until the arrest and prosecution of the promoters revealed that the flow came from an ordinary boiler in the basement. By that time, however, the funds raised had evaporated like steam.[23]

Revelations about the likes of Hearst and Brooks were more than enough to convince many Canadians that the laws governing company promotion and share selling sorely needed change. But how? Manitoba's blue-sky law had failed to prevent the Hearst Music scam. Should other provinces pass similar (or more drastic) legislation of this sort, or were there better ways to prevent such swindles? What, if anything, should Ottawa do, because it seemed that the provinces had little authority to regulate the activities of federally chartered companies?

I

Even as the final Victory loans were floated at the end of the First World War, new concerns were already being expressed about the need to protect unsophisticated investors. When the federal government's wartime prohibition on issuing unauthorized stocks and bonds was lifted in January 1919, *Saturday Night* immediately began to campaign for a national blue-sky law to protect thousands of Victory bondholders from efforts by shysters to persuade them to exchange these sound investments for shares in all manner of speculative ventures. After Ottawa failed to act, the magazine turned its attention to the provincial government in Ontario, the centre of the country's speculative share markets.[24]

The Conservative cabinet there proved surprisingly receptive. Blue-sky legislation had been investigated in 1915, but following an exhaustive analysis of the recent state and provincial laws, the attorney general's staff had been unenthusiastic. Not only was it too early to tell how effective the legislation would be, but the 1915 report echoed one of the common criticisms of blue-sky laws: that the issuing of licences to sell shares would be misused as a selling tool by salesmen to create 'a fictitious and unreal sense of security to investors and might also lead to grave abuses.'[25] Nevertheless, in early 1919 Ontario attorney general I.B. Lucas submitted draft legislation to the Bond Dealers Association and Toronto's two stock exchanges. The Standard Stock and Mining Exchange declared itself 'opposed to the bill as a whole,' but legal counsel for the Toronto Stock Exchange proposed a number of amendments which were adopted. Introducing the bill, which would require the registration of any company offering shares in Ontario with a securities commissioner, Lucas admitted to the legislature that the government did not intend to force it through over strong resistance. After it received first reading in the house, nothing more was done, since 'owing to the opposition, raised chiefly by mining interests in northern Ontario, it was thought advisable to withdraw it so that further consideration might be given.'[26]

Saturday Night was highly critical of Lucas's timidity, arguing that he might as well try to frame a theft law endorsed by pickpockets as to draw up a blue-sky law approved by mining promoters. When an oil-share boom in the United States led to a growing flood of new company promotions which soon spilled over into Canada, the pressure for action mounted. In the summer of 1919 the Attorney General's Department decided to crack down on those who failed to comply with Ontario's Companies Act by not filing prospectuses before advertising shares for sale. A private law firm was retained to prosecute four promoters of Texas and Oklahoma oil properties, and a press release announced, 'We have no blue sky laws in this province, but the Attorney General says that there is a law on the Statute Books which is there to aid in protecting the public in its investments and prevent wildcatting and the offering to the public of worthless shares, and he is determined that these laws shall be enforced.' Offenders who ceased to advertise would not be pursued, but in future there would be 'wholesale prosecution' of violators, and Lucas promised to pass a blue-sky law at the next session of the legislature.[27]

Convictions were obtained in a number of cases, and the attorney general's stand earned him praise even from a former president of the Standard stock exchange, who argued that most of the money invested in oil shares went straight into promoters' pockets. 'If it were not so serious it would be almost comical to think that they could get sufficient buyers even to keep up their office[s] or pay the agents commission.'[28] But before Lucas could take any further action, the Conservatives were turfed out of office at the provincial election in October 1919 and replaced by a minority government composed of a coalition of the United Farmers of Ontario and Labour representatives.

The new attorney general, W.E. Raney, shared the belief that tighter regulation of securities marketing was needed. He turned for advice to an acknowledged expert on company law, Mr Justice Masten, who went over the Lucas bill and returned a decidedly unenthusiastic report. A blue-sky law might well curtail 'legitimate promotions of speculative enterprises' such as mines, 'where if the company end of the enterprise is absolutely honest, everybody goes into it knowing perfectly well that they are speculating as to whether the mine will turn out [to be] worthwhile or whether they will lose all they put in ... The strong tendency of legislation of the kind suggested is to hamper, and ... sometimes prevent, the securing of the necessary capital for these enterprises.' The attorney general's own staff preferred a different approach, the licensing of all securities salesmen, a provision that had been in the original draft of the earlier legislation but was dropped because the Bond Dealers Association had objected. Opposition to a blue-sky law was reinforced by the senior federal administrator of company law, Under-Secretary of State Thomas Mulvey, who told the Toronto branch of the Canadian Manufacturers Association that he considered such legislation not only ineffective but a blow to freedom of contract and an unwarranted bureaucratic interference in economic life.[29]

As a result, Raney dropped any idea of quick action. To a Liberal back-bencher who raised the issue with him a year later, the attorney general replied that he had been giving the matter thought and discussing regulation with both federal and provincial officials, but the 'difficulties surrounding it are very great, the chief being the risk that any system that might be established would produce more ills that it would cure. However, I have not entirely given up hope of finding some solution.'[30]

The summer of 1921 brought a wave of reports about efforts by unscrupulous salesmen to persuade holders of Victory bonds and other sound securities to trade them in for worthless issues. Many of these share pushers were alleged to be expatriates from the United States who had discovered that they could operate within the law in those Canadian provinces which had no blue-sky legislation. That autumn the Chamber of Commerce in London, Ontario, became the first business group in the province to urge action by the government.[31] At the same time Attorney General Raney retained lawyer A.H. O'Brien to undertake a special investigation of blue-sky laws in other jurisdictions and make recommendations to the government.[32]

After attending a meeting of officials from the prairie provinces charged with administering their blue-sky acts, O'Brien returned from Regina and set to work preparing his report, which was delivered early in 1922. He covered familiar ground in examining the U.S. experience and noted that forty-three of the forty-eight states now had some form of regulation, so that unscrupulous American promoters were beginning to invade Ontario. While mining and oil men generally opposed such interference in their affairs, O'Brien argued that share purchasers were entitled to full disclosure about the uses to which their money would be put, rather than permitting promoters to continue lining their own pockets. He endorsed legislation to appoint an Ontario securities commissioner possessing broad discretion and the right to impose severe penalties for violations.[33]

Raney accepted the recommendations and tabled a bill in the Ontario legislature in the spring of 1922. The Toronto Stock Exchange considered this proposal, but eventually decided to take no action. However, as a result of the strong opposition of mining men centred at the Standard exchange the measure was not proceeded with immediately. Meanwhile, the financial press continued to report a significant number of dubious mining and oil promotions as the Canadian economy revived after the post-war depression.[34]

Part of the reason for the delay probably arose from continued resistance to Raney's proposals within the provincial bureaucracy. The chief inspector of mines argued that his industry should be exempt from such regulation because 'it should be remembered that mining ventures are financed by what might be called "gambling money." A man takes a "flier" in a mining venture with an entirely different mental attitude from that with which he invests in an industrial proposition.' Unorthodox geological theories might attract ridicule, but they sometimes uncovered valuable finds, so that 'the wild cat of today may be the legitimate mining venture of the future.'[35]

In the end, however, Attorney General Raney got his way, and a legislative committee held hearings on the bill in the autumn of 1922. The managing director of the Unlisted Securities Corporation pointed out the increasing prevalence of re-loading; he too suggested that all share salesmen ought to be registered. Claims were heard that bucketing by brokers was still commonplace, particularly among the members of the Standard stock exchange, who accepted orders for mining stocks on one-third margins but never executed the trades, simply making fictitious entries in their accounts. Lawyer Evan Gray, who had done much of the drafting of Raney's bill, suggested that this problem could be eliminated by granting the securities commissioner power to order audits, but E.G. Long, who had been retained by the Toronto Stock Exchange, denounced this proposal as an outrageous interference in private dealings. Eventually, however, the bill was presented to the legislature in a form acceptable to the TSE.[36]

Ontario's blue-sky law was finally passed in the spring of 1923. Company promoters were required to file extensive information with the commissioner of securities. Fraudulent practices were defined to include any promise not made in good faith, any fee or commission so large as to endanger the solvency of the issuing company, any action calculated to deceive as to the nature of a transaction or the value of a security, and any fictitious purchase or sale of a security. Should the commissioner have reasonable grounds to believe that fraud had been or was about to be committed, he could prohibit any sale or offering of shares for sale. Moreover, brokers and salesmen were required to register, including non-residents, who had to post a bond guaranteeing compliance with the act, and registration was subject to cancellation for misconduct. Penalties for second offences were more stringent, the heaviest punishments being reserved for those acting with intent to defraud. The new legislation was to come into effect on 1 September 1923.[37]

By the time the Ontario government acted, a number of other provinces were also considering imposing regulations concerning security sales. At its 1923 session New Brunswick's legislature passed a blue-sky law modelled upon the acts in force in western Canada, which gave the Public Utilities Commission oversight in this field. When the law took effect on 1 June, brokers began lining up to obtain the necessary registration.[38] British Columbia also began considering similar legislation even though the registrar of joint stock companies thought such measures paternalistic and largely ineffective.[39] The Vancouver and Penticton Boards of Trade had endorsed the idea in 1921, but Registrar H.G. Garrett dragged his feet, arguing that tightening up the Companies Act to compel more disclosure and launching prosecutions against the worst offenders was likely to be more salutary. In the end the cabinet accepted his recommendations and simply amended the provincial Companies Act.[40]

A major scandal in the spring of 1923 seemed to demonstrate the need for tighter regulation. Shares in the L.R. Steel chain stores worth $9 million had been sold to some 3,000 people across Canada before the company collapsed into bankruptcy. Steel's network was composed of intertwined Canadian and U.S. companies, and many investors who had bought preferred stock in the Steel Realty Development Company (chartered in Delaware) believed that this firm owned the real estate on which the Steel stores sat, while others thought that they had bought stock in the Canadian company which actually operated the stores. To determine the precise relationship between the companies seemed impossible, and the shareholders were left with nothing. Since L.R. Steel had been forbidden to sell shares in Alberta or Saskatchewan and had had its registration revoked in Manitoba, the value of blue-sky legislation seemed self-evident. Even the president of the Bond Dealers Association of Canada conceded at its annual meeting, 'The heavy losses sustained during the past year by people of modest means, who placed their money in unsound ventures, appear to justify the supporters of "blue sky" legislation. While recognizing the limits of beneficial restrictions by law, I am satisfied that governments should exercise a measure of supervision of the public offering of shares.'[41]

At that very moment, however, a serious challenge to provincial authority over securities marketing developed. Myrylo Lukey of Yorkton, Saskatchewan, agreed to take up shares in the Ruthenian Farmers Elevator Company and then reneged on his payment. The company, which had a federal charter and a head office in Winnipeg, sued Lukey, though admitting that it had failed to register with Saskatchewan's Local Government Board under the Sale of Shares Act before distributing its securities. In the fall of 1922 Judge Ross of the District Court held that this failure to obey valid provincial legislation debarred the elevator company from pursuing its claim against Lukey through the Saskatchewan courts.[42]

The company appealed; rumours circulated that the appeal had been arranged to test the validity of the blue-sky law by promoters who were angry at the enforcement of Saskatchewan's legislation, which they felt was unduly arduous to comply with. The elevator company claimed that it had no need to register with the Local Government Board because it possessed a federal charter of incorporation. Though provincial laws of general application might govern companies doing business in the province, the Judicial Committee of the Privy Council had ruled in *Great West Saddlery v. R.* (1921) that 'provincial legislation cannot, directly or indirectly, expressly or impliedly, destroy or derogate from the status and consequent capacities validly conferred by the authority of Parliament upon a Dominion company either expressly or by necessary implication.' The right to sell shares was an essential component of such status, so that only federal legislation could regulate such activities. In July 1923 all five judges of the Saskatchewan Court of Appeal accepted the company's position, ruling that the Sale of Shares Act was *ultra vires* so far as federally incorporated companies were concerned.[43]

Since any promoter wishing to sell shares in Saskatchewan now seemed able to flout its blue-sky law with impunity simply by procuring incorporation from Ottawa, the provincial government was determined to appeal the decision. In the autumn of 1923 New Brunswick's act was also challenged in the courts. James M. Queen was convicted in magistrate's court of selling shares in the federally chartered J.M. Queen Oil Company without a certificate from the Public Utilities Commission, but this judgment was swiftly overturned by a writ of *certiorari* 'on the ground that it is a right inherent in a company incorporated ... under the Companies Act of the Dominion of Canada to sell its shares ... and that the Sale of Securities Act is *ultra vires* in so far as it proposes to prohibit or restrict the sale of share of companies under such Dominion charters.' Until the Supreme Court of Canada made its ruling upon an appeal in the *Lukey* case, provincial authority to regulate share selling by federal companies remained in limbo.[44]

Meantime, Ontario's newly enacted blue-sky law was supposed to come into effect on 1 September 1923, but the political situation there took a sudden turn. Mining men and members of the provincial legislature from the northern part of the province had been hotly critical of the measure during the assembly debate. Almost as soon as the bill became law, the minority United Farmers of Ontario government dissolved the legislature and called an election. In June 1923 the Conservatives were swept back into power with a large majority. The new premier, Howard Ferguson, and his minister of mines, Charles McCrea from Sudbury, had been among the sternest critics of the blue-sky law; both men had questioned the efficacy of the blue-sky approach, and to these criticisms they could now add serious doubts about the constitutionality of such legislation.

McCrea immediately commissioned a report on the act. Deputy Provincial

Secretary F.V. Johns explained that while he had helped to draft the new Ontario act, he had never been completely persuaded of its constitutionality, and now the *Lukey* decision appeared to render several key sections *ultra vires*. While the legislation was a good specimen of its type, he was far from convinced of the efficacy of blue-sky laws; two of the greatest swindles of recent times had passed muster with state boards in the United States: the Pan Motor Company in Minnesota, which had sold $9.5 million in worthless shares to 70,000 people, and Consumers Packing Company in Illinois, which had been a complete fraud. That was why some states such as Illinois had repealed their blue-sky laws, while an investigation in New York had concluded that legitimate promoters were more likely to suffer harm than crooks.

True, Johns admitted, some dishonest share pushing might be thwarted, but frauds were bound to slip by. All the insistence in the world that a licence to sell shares was not tantamount to approval by the government would not thwart unscrupulous salesmen. The very appointment of a regulatory body to investigate and pass upon security offerings was bound to give a false sense of security to naive investors who were most in need of protection. Yet no commissioner could anticipate all the ups and downs that might bankrupt a company. Most failures were caused by mismanagement, lack of experience, or shortage of capital rather than fraud, but the public were sure to blame the government if any money was lost.

Johns argued that the best way to protect investors was the extension of the disclosure provisions of the Companies Act on the British model. In 1914 Ontario had passed legislation that would have permitted shareholders who were being unfairly dealt with to force an investigation of the internal affairs of a company, but as a result of Ottawa's failure to pass similar regulations for federal companies, these provisions had never been brought into force. If the federal government were persuaded to tighten up the prospectus requirements and amend the Post Office regulations to ban the use of the mails for fraudulent advertising, the province could quickly stiffen its own rules. Once other provinces followed suit, that would prevent shady operators from jumping between jurisdictions in an effort to escape control.[45]

Almost from the moment that the new government took over, talk was heard on the 'street' that the new cabinet would not proclaim the blue-sky act into law as scheduled. J.A. Kingsmill, secretary of the Bond Dealers Association, spoke for the staider and more respectable elements in the investment community when he wrote to the premier to express his hope that action would be taken since BDAC members considered the new regulations 'highly desirable': 'The legislation as passed, it was considered, would operate greatly to the advantage of the people of the province and mean a tremendous saving to them, instead of the losses which have been experienced through unwise speculation and business ventures. Almost every state in the Union and several of the Canadian provinces have found it necessary to pass this type of legislation, and there is no doubt that blue-sky legislation has proved very beneficial to the people in the provinces and states in which it has been in operation.' Mining men, however, had the ear of northerner Charles McCrea. They had always insisted that more stringent controls would make the flotation of any speculative mining company impossible. McCrea and the premier decided to postpone action. After considering F.V. Johns's report, Ferguson told Kingsmill of the BDAC, 'I cannot agree with the view that the blue-sky legislation passed by the House at the last session best meets the situation.' The government had concluded that there were better ways to protect 'the unwary against unscrupulous promoters,' and meanwhile it would encourage local Crown attorneys to prosecute frauds.[46]

The province had little to gain, of course, by proclaiming its legislation before the Supreme Court had pronounced on the *Lukey* case, which was argued in the fall term of 1923. The governments of both Saskatchewan and Ontario intervened in the appeal in support of wide provincial jurisdiction. Saskatchewan attorney general J.A. Cross personally presented the argument that the province could enforce the Sale of Shares Act under its constitutional powers over 'property and civil rights in the province' and the authority to deal with 'matters of a merely local or private nature.' Such regulatory legislation did not interfere unduly with the status or powers of federally chartered companies as defined by the courts. For Ontario, Deputy Attorney General Edward Bayly contended that such a provincial law did not impinge upon any areas of jurisdiction reserved exclusively to the Parliament of Canada under the British North America Act.

Writing for the majority of the court, Chief Justice Sir Louis Davies accepted the argument of counsel for the Ruthenian Farmers Elevator Company that provincial blue-sky regulation of federal companies was *ultra vires*. Citing particularly the decisions of the Judicial Committee of the Privy Council in *John Deere Plow Co. v. Wharton* (1915) and *Great West Saddlery v. R.* (1921) the chief justice contended that the 'power of a Dominion company to sell its own shares throughout the Dominion goes to the root of its essential powers and capacities, and any attempt by a provincial legislature to prohibit altogether the sale by a Dominion company of its own shares ... or to make the legality of such sale depend upon the company's first obtaining a license ... must necessarily be beyond the powers of a provincial legislature.'

The sole dissenter was Judge Idington, who observed, 'I most respectfully submit that a prevalent gross dishonesty such as the Act in question aims at checking, and thereby preventing the ruin of possibly thousands of helpless people, ignorant of financial schemes of our so-called enlightened days is quite as well within the powers of our local legislatures, as the several provincial acts forbidding the sale to anyone of a glass of beer, even by a legal entity clothed, indeed created, by the residuary Dominion powers of incorporation.' Federal companies, noted Idington, were already subject to all manner of provincial regulations covering bills of sale and chattel mortgages with the aim of preventing fraud, none of which had ever been held to be outside the powers of the provinces. But the three other justices who joined the chief were not persuaded, and the claim of the provinces to control federal companies through blue-sky laws such as Saskatchewan's was nullified.[47]

The restrictions on provincial powers to regulate federally chartered companies were quickly seized upon by the courts in New Brunswick, where the refusal to convict James M. Queen for selling shares in his oil company under the Sale of Securities Act was still under appeal. Efforts to argue that the New Brunswick act differed from Saskatchewan's blue-sky law were unavailing. Chief Justice Sir J.D. Hazen's decision held that the distinctions were immaterial and that the *Lukey* decision constituted a 'binding authority' on this issue. Queen's conviction was quashed.[48]

There still remained the possibility, of course, that an appeal of the *Lukey* decision to the Judicial Committee of the Privy Council in London might alter the situation. After all, the highest court within the British empire had often proved more sympathetic to arguments for wider provincial powers than the Supreme Court in Ottawa. When the eminent constitutional lawyer Eugène Lafleur was consulted, however, he recommended against such an appeal because the case raised a number of peripheral issues that the British judges might easily seize upon as grounds for a decision rather than settling the central question. Moreover, an adverse decision could prove almost impossible to overcome, so that governments were always cautious about which cases they brought before the Judicial Committee.[49]

The *Lukey* decision in 1923 took much of the wind out of the sails of those pressing for a blue-sky law in Ontario, since it now seemed that company promoters could escape registration simply by securing charters in Ottawa. The government did intervene in the case before the Supreme Court in the general interest of preserving and expanding provincial jurisdiction over companies, yet Deputy Attorney General Edward Bayly, who handled the argument, had no faith in this kind of regulation: 'Except for the purpose of allowing the public to think a department or government is "doing something," blue sky legislation has been, in jurisdictions which have tried it, pathetically ineffective.'[50]

Still, the amount of publicity being given to swindles such as the L.R. Steel affair made it difficult for the new Ontario government to altogether avoid 'doing something.' The annual meeting of the Western Ontario United Boards of

Trade passed a resolution reminding the premier that he had promised to take some action to stamp out fraudulent stock selling if he was not going to proclaim the blue-sky law. In the spring of 1924 mining broker W.J. Post sent an open letter to all members of the legislature claiming that public confidence in the financial community had been seriously undermined by the collapse of the Home Bank the previous August. Brokers who were heavily engaged in margin trading were widely suspected of bucketing customers' orders, and there were doubts about the solvency of some dealers.[51]

Attorney General W.F. Nickle directed his staff to begin drawing up new legislation to regulate security sales which would take into account the *Lukey* decision. A.H. O'Brien, who had conducted the inquiry for the previous government in 1922, suggested that the bill should be based upon the principle of registration of stockbrokers and share dealers rather than the licensing of securities issuers. At the same time the disclosure requirements under the prospectus sections of the Companies Act could be widened. Not only did such changes avoid the blue-sky approach, about which the government had serious reservations, but they seemed to be better adapted to survive constitutional challenges. Behind the scenes the Bond Dealers Association also lobbied hard, with their counsel, E.G. Long, working hard to persuade Nickle and his officials to adopt these principles.[52]

The Sale of Shares Act that emerged from the Ontario legislature in the spring of 1924 required promoters to file prospectuses with the provincial secretary which accurately described the financial structure of their companies and disclosed any commissions paid to share sellers. They, in turn, had to be registered with the provincial government and to ensure that all buyers received copies of prospectuses. Directors were required to swear to the truth of all statements contained in the prospectus and were liable for any losses suffered by investors which arose from misrepresentations. Violators of the act were liable to fines and jail sentences.

Unlike the blue-sky law passed by the Drury government the previous year, the 1924 act did not create a commissioner of securities but instead left enforcement to the provincial secretary and the attorney general. To avert criticisms that such anti-fraud statutes merely barred the doors after the horses had been stolen, the attorney general and local Crown attorneys were given authority to investigate any security promotion that they considered suspicious and to issue warnings to the public through advertisements if necessary. In order to comply with the *Lukey* decision, federally incorporated companies were not forbidden to sell shares in Ontario without provincial approval. Nonetheless, all companies were required to make full disclosure about their affairs to the provincial secretary, and penalties were created for fraudulent misrepresentations in any prospectus, an approach that it was hoped the courts would accept.[53]

Saturday Night welcomed the passage of the new act with the claim, 'Ontario's doormat no longer carries the words, "Welcome to Crooks" emblazoned in lurid letters for every smooth-tongued salesmen of unsound and fake securities to see.' Attorney General Nickle had withstood a great deal of pressure to water down his legislation, but opposition persisted as officials commenced the task of drafting the regulations before proclaiming the act law.[54] When the news leaked out that mining companies and their securities were to be treated just the same as all other undertakings, the mining fraternity stepped up its complaints. By the late summer of 1924 the government was trying to deflect criticism by claiming that the delay was to permit the drafting of amendments to the act to make it even more stringent. Before long, however, it was clear that the whole process had stalled. When a Cobourg man wrote to complain that dishonest brokers were still getting away with murder, the premier sought to pretend that the problem was opposition from Ottawa to provincial action. 'You are doubtless aware that two years ago we passed some legislation hoping to meet this very situation. The Dominion government, however, questioned the jurisdiction of the province to pass such an act, and we have had to stay our hand until we find some different manner of meeting the situation.' In truth the government simply lacked the stomach to tackle the problem, particularly in light of strong opposition from the mining community in northern Ontario so powerfully represented in the cabinet by Charles McCrea.[55]

Financial interests had similar success in blocking drastic changes to securities legislation in Quebec, where interest in mining stocks was on the upswing because of recent discoveries in the Rouyn district in the northwestern part of the province. Though touted as a blue-sky law, the proposed act did little more than bring Quebec company law into line with Ontario's by requiring the filing of more extensive financial information with the provincial secretary. Even that stipulation provoked outcries in certain quarters, and one leading bond dealer told the *Financial Times* that he saw no reason why the selling of shares should be treated any differently from selling horses or automobiles. In the end Premier A.-L. Taschereau intervened in response to lobbying by the Bond Dealers Association, and the bill was redrafted so that all companies currently in existence were exempted from compliance along with those which obtained listings on Canadian stock exchanges or in Paris, London, or New York. No effort was made to render federally incorporated companies subject to provincial regulation.[56]

The blows to the constitutionality of key sections of the blue-sky laws suffered in the *Lukey* case, combined with doubts about the efficacy of this approach, blocked the implementation of tighter regulation of securities marketing in Ontario, despite the fact that the province passed legislation on this subject in both 1923 and 1924. The stock exchanges themselves took no steps to impose regulations on promotions, while the mining community remained strongly hostile to any interference with their freewheeling methods. As share markets began to heat up in the mid-1920s, the watchword in eastern Canada seemed to be business as usual.

II

The sensational revelations about the Hearst Music swindle that began to unfold at the end of 1924 seemed to make clear the need for tighter regulation. Concern about securities fraud became particularly strong in Alberta, which was on the eve of another oil boom. Exploration companies took advantage of the *Lukey* decision and hastened to secure charters from the federal government so that they might sell shares without registering with the local Public Utilities Board under the province's blue-sky law. In the spring of 1925 the editor of the Calgary *Herald* asked Premier J.E. Brownlee if nothing could be done to protect the public by forcing companies that took out advertisements to disclose whether these concerns were federally or provincially incorporated. Unfortunately, the Alberta Sale of Shares Act expressly forbade companies from referring to their local registration certificates to prevent the unscrupulous from utilizing these as marketing devices.[57]

Judge A.A. Carpenter, head of Alberta's PUB, remained convinced that most criticisms of the blue-sky law were unwarranted. This legislation had been on the books for a decade now, and while it was impossible to calculate the size of the losses prevented, it was clear that such notorious characters as L.R. Steel and Joseph Xavier Hearst had been kept from selling shares in his province. Were there laws of any other sort, he asked, which offered ironclad protection against crime? Wasn't it inevitable that regulators would sometimes make mistakes or be deceived? That was no excuse for abandoning the effort to keep swindlers from peddling their wares to Albertans.[58]

Carpenter and Brownlee were determined to repair the effects of the *Lukey* decision and secure jurisdiction over federal companies. The governments of the three prairie provinces agreed to draft a joint bill to be passed by Parliament in Ottawa delegating federal powers in this area to the provinces. In the autumn of 1925 officials from each of the provinces and from British Columbia met with the federal under-secretary of state, Thomas Mulvey, at the Canadian Bar Association in Winnipeg to try to persuade him to endorse this proposal. Mulvey, of course, was still firmly convinced that blue-sky legislation was ineffective. Moreover, the recent federal election had returned the Liberals to office but only as a shaky minority government, leaving Mulvey, in his own words, 'practically without a minister.' Obviously, in that situation there was little likelihood that Ottawa would respond favourably to the demands of the provinces.[59]

During 1925 a select committee of the Manitoba legislature conducted an extensive inquiry into the collapse of Hearst Music and the Farmers' Packing Company, both of which had initially been refused registration under the Sale of Shares Act but had successfully appealed for certificates.[60] Appearing as a witness, Judge H.A. Robson, the first administrator of the province's blue-sky law, stoutly defended the legislation.[61] He said that he had done his best to convince Mulvey of the virtues of blue-sky legislation for western Canada, arguing: 'It is prairie legislation. It is all right for the prairie people. You could not enforce that law in Wall Street, St. James Street, Montreal or the great broker[age] offices in Toronto; they would have to get back to the law of fraud and prospectuses and that sort of thing there.' Ottawa refused, however, to yield its authority to regulate federal companies, because it 'is jealous of its prestige; all the departments, they like things to be going there to be done, they like things to go down there; they don't mind a bit; they enjoy it.' Robson recommended trying to overturn the *Lukey* decision through a carefully framed reference case in which the Manitoba Court of Appeal was asked to answer a set of questions about provincial powers to regulate companies. The result could then be appealed directly to the Judicial Committee of the Privy Council for a binding decision, thus leapfrogging over the Supreme Court of Canada altogether.[62]

A delegation from the Investment Bankers Association of Canada (the new name of the Bond Dealers Association, which had affiliated with the IBA in the United States in 1925) also appeared before the Manitoba committee but was much more critical of the province's blue-sky law. A.H. Williamson contended that the requirements were too 'burdensome.' If nationwide businesses such as the Canadian Pacific Railway or the Bell Telephone Company had not been exempt from registration under the *Lukey* decision as a result of their federal charters, he said, they would refuse to comply with the act because of the voluminous filings required by the PUC. Moreover, the exemptions from registration that had once been granted to companies whose shares traded on recognized stock exchanges had been cancelled in the aftermath of the Hearst Music affair. Now the minister of municipal affairs would only grant exemptions when all trading was done on the Winnipeg Stock Exchange in order to ensure his jurisdiction over the companies, but this approach was unthinkable for the likes of CPR or Bell. As a result, many first-class securities were not being offered to Manitoba buyers. Nevertheless, the investment dealers did support the idea of provincial regulatory legislation, proposing a uniform act along the lines of Ontario's new law that relied on disclosure and the registration of dealers to avoid constitutional problems.[63]

The Manitoba committee's report endorsed the principles of blue-sky legislation but suggested that a number of amendments were required. First, the appeal procedure needed to be revamped by creating a permanent tribunal. Second, the commissioner should have the power to exempt blue-chip companies from registering with the PUC but should also be able to cancel exemptions if problems arose. Nor should he hesitate to publicize dubious offerings or to require the sellers of such issues to be bonded. The committee adopted Robson's suggestion that the constitutional position should be clarified by a reference case and urged close cooperation with the other western provinces in seeking control over all securities offerings.[64]

With the boom in oil shares heating up following the discovery of the spectacular Royalite well no. 4 in the Turner valley in 1924,[65] Alberta was particularly keen to prevent any repetition of the events of 1914, when many share buyers had lost their shirts. A report to the Public Utilities Board noted that prior to the Sale of Shares Act the minimum sum to be subscribed had normally been fixed as low as possible; at present only $5,000 need be in a company treasury before the shares were allotted to the insiders, even though over $50,000 was then required to drill an exploratory well. Two-thirds of the authorized shares had typically been handed to the vendors of the properties, who immediately set about selling their stock in competition with the company's treasury shares. In one company 333,000 shares had been marketed for a mere 10 cents apiece, leaving only $18,000 in the treasury after commissions at the usual rate of 40 per cent had been paid to the salesmen. Only one company was known to have returned subscriptions to its shareholders when its plans did not pan out, and at least one group of promoters had admitted that their sole objective was to earn commissions from selling stock.[66]

The Public Utilities Board was determined to prevent the recurrence of such abuses. Already new promotions such as Scotia Oils were being floated with a proposed minimum subscription of just $5,000, while the vendors of the drilling leases would receive $7,000 in cash and $97,500 par value worth of $1 shares, of which 27,500 would be available for immediate sale by insiders in competition with the treasury shares. The Scotia prospectus contained glowing predictions, even though Royalite no. 4 was over a mile away and there was no geological report on the area. To the PUB this company had 'so little merit' that it was merely 'a stock-selling concern.'[67]

The board refused to lay down hard-and-fast general rules for applicants but insisted that each one file a 'fair, honest' business plan that included detailed information. The minimum amount subscribed before the stock was allotted to buyers should be about $60,000, sufficient to defray the average cost of drilling a well. Payments of stock and cash to vendors of property or leases were strictly controlled. The objective was to eliminate the 'purely stock-jobbing promoter' and force the insiders to invest some of their own money in their companies as an earnest of good faith. Even when deliberate fraud was not involved, the claims made in prospectuses were often wildly optimistic, and on occasion they were so reckless that they could be explained only by fraudulent intentions. One promoter frankly admitted to the PUB that his company 'could not hope to sell its stock if it adhered to the truth,' while another complained that he could never market his shares if he were compelled to issue accurate financial statements.[68]

In an effort to control such swindles, the PUB required that vendor shares be placed in escrow until the minimum subscription was secured and then released only bit by bit as the company treasury filled up. The maximum commission allowed for selling shares should be limited to 15 per cent. The investor ought to get 'a fair deal and a fair run for his money. The very best prospect is a gamble, and undoubtedly the only one who should invest in such a venture is the person who can afford to lose his money.' If drilling uncovered no oil, at least the money had been properly spent and knowledge of geological formations advanced.[69]

To ensure that it was not being unduly severe and holding back development, the Alberta PUB sought advice from blue-sky regulators in oil states such as Texas, Oklahoma, and California during the summer of 1926. All the replies indicated that similar restrictions were imposed upon American promoters. California reported, for instance, that licences were denied to companies whose promoters had bad records. In addition, promoters must control sufficient acreage that oil could not simply be drained away from neighbouring wells, quickly depleting a field. Maximum commissions to share sellers (including advertizing, travel, and the printing of prospectuses and literature) were limited to 15 per cent or 20 per cent.[70]

Yet there was little that the PUB could do to control the activities of oil companies incorporated elsewhere. During 1926 only sixteen oil companies altogether applied to the province to sell shares there. One oilman, whose proposal was turned down because he planned to pay his share salesmen a 25 per cent commission, bluntly replied, 'We know what it costs to sell this stock, and we will not apply for an Alberta charter unless the Board will reconsider its decision.' Of eleven Alberta companies who applied for registration during 1926 only eight received approval; the lawyer for one of those rejected told the Alberta premier frankly that he intended to do the same thing as the vast majority of oil promoters: take advantage of the *Lukey* decision by seeking incorporation in Ottawa, thus leaving the province with no control over the sale of its shares. The federal Companies Act did not require promoters to deliver a prospectus or to disclose all information of material interest to share buyers, but only to reveal the names of any parties with whom contracts had been entered into, a requirement easy to subvert by using nominees. Soon Fuego Oil of Toronto was selling shares in Ontario, supposedly to finance drilling near Oyen, Alberta, over two hundred miles from the nearest known oilfield.[71]

In March 1926 the Alberta legislature unanimously passed a resolution urging Ottawa to intervene to control share selling by oil companies with federal charters. If there were any more large discoveries, Premier John Brownlee warned Prime Minister Mackenzie King, millions could be lost in a 'riot of speculation' which the provincial government would be powerless to control. Brownlee also urged Progressive members of Parliament from Alberta to put pressure upon the minority Liberal government. That sparked a rumour that the federal authorities were finally preparing to strike a deal with Alberta granting it prior approval of all resource companies intending to operate in the province, but the beleaguered Liberal ministers were far too busy clinging to power to take up a comparatively minor matter in the face of strong opposition to blue-sky laws by a senior civil servant such as Under-Secretary of State Thomas Mulvey.[72]

Early in June that year the premiers gathered in Ottawa for their first formal Interprovincial Conference since 1918. Alberta was unrepresented, but Manitoba and Saskatchewan saw to it that the issue of regulating share selling by federal companies was not ignored. The conference endorsed a draft bill that would delegate federal regulatory authority over the sale of securities by all firms chartered in Ottawa to the provinces. Premier Howard Ferguson of Ontario forwarded the bill to Mackenzie King asking for speedy action, but the prime minister was absorbed with the problems of his faltering minority government and showed little interest.[73]

The pressure from the provinces did produce some results. Acting Secretary of State Charles Murphy announced his intention to hold a conference to discuss a variety of conflicts between Ottawa and the provinces over company law. His under-secretary, Mulvey, remained unwavering in his opposition to blue-sky laws, but told Ferguson that some concessions might be made to placate the western provinces. 'While it is submitted that the investing public cannot be adequately protected by any regulations such as are usually within what is termed "Blue Sky" legislation, yet it may be that in some provinces where financial operations are limited, it is believed by the provincial authorities that some protection might be given. There appears to be no reason why Dominion companies should not be subject, under these circumstances to provincial sale of shares legislation.'[74]

A few days later, however, all hopes of action on this issue were dashed as Ottawa was engulfed by political uproar when King tendered the resignation of his government in order to avoid defeat in the House of Commons. Governor General Lord Byng then refused to grant King a dissolution of Parliament, and

Conservative Arthur Meighen became prime minister only to see his government promptly defeated in turn. The House of Commons was dissolved, and all attention now focused upon the federal election fixed for 14 September 1926.[75]

By the time the election campaign got under way Joseph Xavier Hearst was starting his seven-year term in the pentitentiary for the Hearst Music fraud. Salesmen for Oland J. Brooks's Steam Motor Company were as busy as ever peddling stock. The exposés in *Saturday Night* and the revelations before the select committee of the Manitoba legislature seemed to show that various other 'highbinders' and 're-loaders' were still hard at work pushing worthless shares upon gullible investors in Canada. Why had government regulation failed to address these problems effectively?

Faith in blue-sky laws reached its height in the early 1920s: company promoters should be forced to reveal their business plans to government officials before they could receive permission to market their securities. Just as the Sale of Shares Act had protected the people of Manitoba against crooked oil promoters in 1914, so L.R. Steel would be prevented from marketing worthless shares across the prairies in 1922–3. Yet the revelations about the Hearst Music Company left Manitobans and other Canadians wondering how regulators could have been lulled into accepting such pie in the sky. Even at the height of its popularity the blue-sky approach to securities regulation never lacked critics. In Ottawa Under-Secretary of State Thomas Mulvey remained an ardent opponent of this type of legislation. His study of such acts in the United States before the First World War had convinced him that they did not work, and he stuck to this position unwaveringly during the next fifteen years. Not only that, but he also strongly resisted provincial interference with the activities of federally incorporated companies, and on that score he had the backing of the courts. In the *Lukey* decision in 1923 the Supreme Court of Canada ruled that the provinces could not require federal companies to register under their blue-sky laws in order to sell shares. If promoters could avoid this kind of regulation simply by obtaining a charter in Ottawa, then provincial regulation seemed to offer investors little protection.

Opposition to securities regulation was strong in other quarters too. Oil and mining men insisted that they could never supply the kind of business plans that would satisfy regulators; if blue-sky legislation were strictly enforced, it would simply kill off resource development. These critics were particularly vociferous in Ontario, the centre of mining finance in Canada, where provincial officials also shared Mulvey's reservations about the blue-sky approach. The UFO government toyed with the idea of such regulation in 1919 and passed, but never proclaimed, an act in 1923. A slightly different approach was followed by the new Conservative government a year later, but again the law gathered dust unproclaimed as a result of second thoughts and doubts about its constitutionality. As a later attorney general observed, none of these measures 'seemed to fill the bill so that any Government was prepared to proclaim them.'[76]

By the mid-1920s the regulation of securities markets in Canada was little tighter than it had been prior to the First World War. Yet now the telephone and the automobile were making it increasingly simple for boiler-room operators and their salesmen to penetrate urban areas and to reach out to the small towns and the back concessions. Protests about the activities of con men such as Joseph Xavier Hearst put increasing pressure upon governments to take some action. Otherwise, with the Canadian economy booming throughout the latter part of the decade, it seemed that there would surely be another great 'barbecue' in which investors were stripped of their money.

7

Fighting Fraud

Trading on stock markets in Canada soared to unprecedented levels during the late 1920s. Not only did volume rise sharply on the well-established exchanges in Montreal and Toronto, but there were even more dramatic increases in dealings in speculative mining shares, which were conducted principally on the Standard Stock and Mining Exchange in Toronto and on the Vancouver Stock Exchange. These were palmy days for the brokerage community as people flocked to buy shares on margin in the expectation of continued rises.

As investors poured their money into stocks, pressure increased to make certain that swindles became a thing of the past. In particular, demands mounted that the exchanges themselves ensure that the issues traded on their floors were sound and legitimate, and that their members were not engaged in price manipulation to the disadvantage of customers. As the volume of business – especially margin business – increased, there was also concern to ensure that brokerage houses had sufficient financial resources to meet their obligations, even in hard times. Regulators and brokers agreed that such matters were best left to the exchanges themselves, although there was plenty of room for disagreement about how stringent the rules should be.

This new emphasis upon self-regulation came at a time when widespread doubts had emerged about the validity of the blue-sky approach to controlling securities markets. First of all, the Canadian courts had undermined the ability of the provinces to control the sale of shares in federally chartered companies, and Ottawa had shown little disposition to act itself or to bolster provincial authority. Moreover, in Ontario and British Columbia there were officials who believed that there were other, more effective means of ensuring honesty and fair dealing by registering securities sellers and banning a wider range of fraudulent practices.

Attention therefore shifted during the late 1920s from shady techniques of marketing over-the-counter stocks to the operations of the exchanges themselves. As popular attention centred increasingly upon these markets, even boiler-room operators and tipsheet publishers realized that exchange price quotations were an important selling tool. Regulators therefore focused their concern upon the wash trading and bucketing of orders, which were often used to manipulate prices on the exchanges. Clearer definitions of such improper practices were required, and if the doors were to be barred before rather than after the act, the exchanges themselves had to take on increasing responsibility for enforcement.

Following a serious scandal on the Standard stock exchange in 1927 the government of Ontario began to consider new means of fighting fraud. The challenge was to draft enforceable legislation which would control both primary and secondary trading of securities but be immune to the constitutional challenges that had disabled blue-sky legislation. Day-to-day supervision of trading by the exchanges would be combined with closer enforcement to prevent dishonest activities.

I

Business on the Montreal Stock Exchange picked up sharply once the wartime restrictions on trading were lifted in 1919. From just over 1 million shares in 1918, volume shot up to over 4 million shares in the following two years. Industrials became the bread and butter of Montreal's brokers as the MSE solidified its position as the major marketplace for blue-chip stocks. In addition, the par value of bonds traded rose more than tenfold in 1919 to $71.5 million. (See appendix, table A.1.) As a result, that June an exchange seat was sold for a price equal to the all-time high of $30,000. Membership, which had risen from forty-five to sixty during the decade or so before the war, hit a peak of eighty-five in 1920. The trading floor got so crowded that the posts around which dealers in particular stocks congregated were removed to provide more space, and the floor was divided up into squares above which were blackboards listing the current 'bid' and 'ask' prices of the issues handled there. Traders shouted their needs in 'open cry,' and when identical offers were made simultaneously, stock was allocated by the flip of a coin.[1]

By 1921 the impact of the postwar recession was felt as the MSE's volume was cut in half to 2.1 million shares, though bond trading remained vigorous. Not until 1925 did trading surpass the levels right after the war, but thereafter volume grew by leaps and bounds, doubling between 1927 and 1928 from 10.7 million shares to 20.5 million. At the same time bond trading on the exchange dwindled away to around $20.0 million par value annually. Many bond traders left the floor as the underwriting houses began to employ salesmen to retail large new issues of government and corporate bonds directly. Membership was reduced from eighty-five to eighty in 1927, but the heavy trading of blue-chip issues kept seat prices high; they reached a maximum of $225,000 by 1929. Volume was so heavy that in May 1928 the MSE began to hold a continuous session without breaking for lunch, and in October the hours were extended so that trading ran from 10 a.m. to 3 p.m. on weekdays and from 10 until noon on Saturdays.[2]

Montreal brokers depended heavily upon utility stocks for their commissions since electric railways and light and power companies accounted for more than a quarter and up to two-fifths of total volume in some years in the late 1920s. Brazilian Traction, Light and Power Company, which operated the power, transit, gas, and telephone services in Rio de Janeiro and São Paulo, was a particular favourite. In 1925, when almost 1 million electric railway shares changed hands on the MSE, Brazilian accounted for 745,000 of those, and the following year 1,830,000 out of 2 million; in 1927 Brazilian traded 2,615,000 shares and in 1928, 3,820,000. Senior mining shares became very important for the first time in 1928; trades in International Nickel alone increased from 390,000 shares in 1927 to 4,245,000 the following year.[3]

Dealings on the floor continued to be personal since the MSE rules still required that the member in whose name a seat was held do the actual trading, no attorneys being permitted. Serving those people who were absent or too busy to attend were the so-called $4-brokers, who took no orders from the public. Instead they acted for other members, receiving 10 per cent of the regular commission (which was $4 on a 100-share lot trading between $25 and $125, hence the name). In addition, a few 'professional' traders operated exclusively for their own accounts, while some firms had partners who devoted themselves to arbitrage, seeking to exploit the price differentials between various exchanges.[4]

In 1926 the members of the MSE decided to set up a separate organization to handle less-seasoned issues. The one hundred members of the Montreal Curb Market shared the staff of the MSE but operated in separate premises until 1929, when it moved in next door. The two exchanges had separate boards of directors, but many local firms held seats on both in order to participate in the rapidly growing market for mining shares that developed near the end of the decade. The MCM's trading list originally included thirty-seven utilities and other issues as well as twenty-six mines, providing some serious competition for the Standard exchange in Toronto.[5]

The MSE and the Curb never faced the kind of serious competition from a local exchange that the Standard provided for the TSE. There was a Montreal

Mining Exchange, chartered in 1899, but this organization had led only a shadowy existence before closing its doors during the war. Revived in the spring of 1922, it collapsed again before reopening a year later. Gradually the MME achieved some stability, but most Canadian mining shares continued to trade on the Standard in Toronto despite the opening up of valuable new mineral prospects in the Rouyn district of northwestern Quebec during the early 1920s. The creation of the Montreal Curb Market in 1926 was designed to cut into the business of the Montreal Mining Exchange, which soon found itself mired in scandal because of the scramble to compete.[6]

Brokers in Toronto faced a less rosy situation than those in Montreal during the early 1920s. From a wartime low point of 340,000 shares in 1918, volume rose only to 780,000 in 1919 then dropped back to 670,000 in 1920. Many firms were thankful for the bond business, which increased almost twentyfold in 1919 to more than $60 million par value. (See appendix, table A.3.) Later that year a TSE seat went for $9,500, but the postwar recession put a crimp in trading in 1921 as volume dropped under 550,000.

For the next three years trading on the TSE hovered around the 1-million-share mark before doubling in 1925. Growth was rapid through the later years of the decade and had reached 10 million by 1929, when the MSE's members handled over 25 million shares. A good part of the TSE's growth came from trades in industrial stocks, which rose from 765,000 in 1926 to 3,900,000 the following year. In part this rise reflected heavy trading in International Nickel, which was treated as an industrial on the TSE; its volume rose from 119,000 in 1926 to over 2,260,000 a year later. Yet there were other strong stocks such as the farm-implement maker Massey Harris, which rose from 58,000 to 458,000, and the newly listed shares of the Seagram distillery, which also traded 458,000 in 1927. Mining shares too were important in 1928 and 1929, though the increase for the first year was exaggerated because Inco then seems to have been listed as a mine and over 1.5 million of its shares changed hands.[7]

Since business was fairly slow during the early 1920s, a seat on the TSE, which had sold for as much as $12,500 in late 1920, commanded only $5,300 by the end of 1924; in the spring of 1923 the board rejected a petition to permit domino playing on the trading floor between noon and 2 p.m. Only in 1925 did seat prices again reach $10,000, and they hit $16,000 the following year. As volume increased sharply, so did the cost of a TSE seat, which reached $150,000 in 1928 and $200,000 a year later.[8]

Despite the general prosperity of the brokerage community during the 1920s, problems arose which led to growing demands for tighter self-regulation of members by the stock exchanges. Montreal's Thornton, Davidson and Company failed in 1920, resulting in criticism of the MSE because the firm was reported to have continued to accept margin accounts even after its bankers had learned of financial problems and sent in staff to try to sort them out. *Saturday Night* observed that in the past the exchanges had protected the public from losses when brokers became insolvent, and it suggested that the governing committee needed the authority to step in and investigate the internal affairs of a member at any time to prevent a repetition, but no action was taken by the exchange.[9]

The failure of another Montreal firm, Tousaw, Hart and Anderson, in the spring of 1922 led to discussion about requiring periodic audits of members. Though some brokers insisted that serious financial problems could remain undetected by the auditors, complaints redoubled in the summer when Fairbanks, Gosselin and Company was bankrupted by short selling. Still the MSE declined to take action despite the fact that even the New York Stock Exchange dispatched a team of financial investigators to ascertain the stability of several MSE firms with which its members were dealing. NYSE president Seymour L. Cromwell openly criticized the MSE's rules: 'In Montreal, in an incorporated exchange, working really under the old Napoleonic code, an attempt to discipline members for fraud is a farce. Members are fined and do not pay, members take into partnership with them people with bad reputations, and the Exchange is helpless to prevent it.' Not until the failure of Nash and Company in 1924 was the MSE board finally induced to require all its members to produce an audited statement every six months showing that all securities held for clients were available for delivery if required.[10]

Nor was the TSE's regulation of members' conduct unduly strict. Late in 1920 TSE firms were prohibited from making copies of the shareholders' lists that had to be attached to listing applications to use as marketing tools, but continued abuses eventually led to a ruling that companies need not submit actual names but merely provide the number of stockholders owning up to 100 shares, the number holding between 100 and 200, and so forth up to 500 shares.[11] The prohibition on trading listed shares off the floor had to be reiterated in 1922. Though fines for failing to charge prescribed commissions and interest rates to clients were raised to $1,000, they were almost never imposed.[12] At the end of 1923 the board was given authority to investigate suspicious numbers of 'put throughs' in any stock where the same broker appeared on both sides of a trade, a common indicator of wash trading, but this power was very rarely exercised. In the summer of 1925 there was discussion of requiring members to be regularly audited as was done at the MSE, but the proposal was soon dropped.[13]

Over at the Standard Stock and Mining Exchange business was only slightly livelier than at the TSE during the early 1920s. Seat prices remained stuck at just over $1,000 for the first three years after the return of peace, taking off for unheard-of heights only in 1926. Trading volume remained below pre-war levels in 1920–1 before it too began to climb towards new highs (see appendix, table A.7). The price of an average share rose slowly from 37 cents in 1920 to 49 cents in 1925. About the only effort to tighten up the rules of the exchange seems to have been the creation of a listing committee in 1922 to avoid the overhasty approval of new offerings in an effort to raise the quality of the stocks traded there. Still, the board did not set unduly high standards, directing only that the listing committee should seek to ensure that 'some substantial portion' of the proceeds of the sale of treasury stock should find its way into the company's coffers, leaving room for the customary generous commissions to promoters and brokers.[14]

Ninety per cent of the trading on the SSME was done on margin, with investors putting up about one-third of the purchase price and paying their brokers 6 per cent interest on the borrowed balance. Critics of the exchange pointed out that this practice had a number of harmful consequences. Banks refused to make loans to brokers when low-priced mining stock was offered as collateral, especially non-dividend-paying issues. As a result, brokers were tempted to bucket orders rather than execute them, confident that they could always buy the required shares in the unlikely event that their clients paid the balance and demanded delivery. A tempting practice because few mining brokers possessed the capital resources to finance a large volume of business on their own, this meant, in effect, that brokers were betting against clients who purchased stocks on the recommendation that prices would rise, while the brokers hoped to be able to buy shares at a lower price than their clients if required.

D.E. Cushing, mines editor of the *Financial Post*, was highly critical of promoters and brokers who rushed to secure listings for their companies even before the money had been raised to finance any exploratory work on a prospect. The result was that most issues on the SSME had a very small 'float' of publicly owned shares, which made it easier for insiders to manipulate prices. Once a listing was obtained the price might be pushed upward by wash trading to facilitate sales. When this market support was withdrawn, the usual result was a collapse which would catch margin buyers uncovered, rendering them liable to be sold out and facing large losses.[15]

Complaints about bucketing by SSME brokers became sufficiently serious that the Ontario Attorney General's Department commenced an investigation into several firms in the spring of 1925. By that time a number of exchange members had become concerned about a lack of investor confidence, which had led to a significant drop in trading volume in 1924. Under pressure from the government the exchange board decided to order all members to submit to a twice-yearly audit intended to demonstrate that they were capable of meeting their obligations to clients.[16] The effectiveness of this new test was doubtful, however. Limited companies were not permitted to belong to the exchange, but many had unlimited subsidiaries that were members. Often both companies and their brokerage arms dealt with the public, yet the audits would not cover the corporate books.

The first audit was ordered in May 1925 but did not take place until September, and the general opinion on the 'street' was that this lengthy delay was intended to give the numerous members who had been engaged in bucketing margin orders time to clean up their books. By the time the audit date arrived the *Financial Post* was terming the whole exercise a 'joke'; all members passed without difficulty, but it was pointed out that one auditor's certificate merely stated that 'all stocks are available in the usual course of business,' which might mean that if a client paid the balance owing on a bucketed stock, the dealer could go into the market, buy the required shares, and deliver them in the 'usual' way. Business was expected to continue pretty much as before on the SSME.[17]

Public interest in mining shares mounted during 1926. Not only were there discoveries in the Rouyn district of Quebec, but in the spring a staking rush broke out around Red Lake in northwestern Ontario even though the ground was still blanketed with snow and drilling was impossible.[18] Trading volume on the SSME rose sharply, which quickly translated into higher seat prices; a seat that had brought $4,350 at the beginning of 1926 cost $7,500 in early February and $12,000 by July. At the end of the year the future looked so bright that the members approved leasing new premises at 15 Richmond Street West (see photos 15 and 16).[19]

Elsewhere in Canada during the early 1920s other stock exchanges stumbled along before the boom at the end of the decade brought greater stability. The Calgary Stock Exchange, which had closed during the First World War, remained shut until the spring of 1926, when oil discoveries in the Turner valley offered the hope of renewed prosperity. Unfortunately this prospect proved over-optimistic, and there were suggestions that the exchange might close again towards the end of the year. The manager, Harold W. Riley, blamed oil companies for the lack of investor interest because there had been too many overcapitalized promotions and really attractive propositions were few and far between. In the spring of 1927 it was suggested that the members might hold private trading sessions among themselves, with prices not being reported to the public. Fortunately, cooler heads prevailed, arguing that if own-account trading volume was subtracted from the current 'dribble' of public business, it was sure to sound the exchange's death knell. A year later the president blamed lack of progress upon the slow development of the Alberta oil industry. As always in such difficult circumstances, charges circulated that members were dealing on the other, less-formal exchanges that existed in the city. By the end of the year fifty-two members were in arrears on their dues, and when just ten agreed to pay up, some firms moved to suspend trading, a proposal that was defeated only by a vote of 20 to 8.[20]

In 1928 the situation suddenly began to look up. A couple of Toronto mining houses detected enough investor interest in oils to purchase seats in Calgary, paying up to $1,000 where a few months earlier $50 would have been a good price. Volume shot upward from 40,000 shares monthly in late 1927 to almost 825,000 the following May. Near the end of the year the exchange moved into new, larger premises. When Home Oil's big no. 1 well blew in early in 1929, CSE members felt sufficiently flush to vote $1,000 to help pay for the construction of an all-weather road from Okotoks to the Turner valley so that their cars would no longer get mired en route to showing clients their best prospects. In May 1929 the Calgary Stock Exchange handled over 2 million shares.[21]

The Winnipeg Stock Exchange also had its problems since the major trading action in the city continued to be on the Grain Exchange. Most of the trading on the WSE was in unlisted western Canadian companies and Victory bonds, though under the Manitoba Sale of Shares Act companies listed on the exchange could be exempted from the requirement to be licensed with the Public Utilities Commission in order to sell shares to the public. In 1928 it was rumoured that the two exchanges would amalgamate, but most grain-trading firms did not deal in securities, and in the end the idea was dropped. That same year an effort was made to set up a separate mining exchange in the city, but this move was resisted by the PUC, which preferred to see all share trading done through the WSE. Eventually it was decided that the exchange would set up a mining section to which all members would be admitted, but the Winnipeg exchange continued to find difficulty in establishing itself on a firm foundation.[22]

The Vancouver Stock Exchange had also been more or less moribund during the First World War, though it never officially suspended operations. Not until 1924 was there much effort to reorganize operations, when the listed section was confined to companies that had been traded for some time or had paid a listing fee; all other stocks were to be unlisted. In addition, the public was excluded during the daily auction call to prevent disruptions. Only in 1925 did things begin to improve. In his report to the annual meeting the next year President W.H. Nanson noted the rapid rise in volume and in the average price of shares traded so that fewer issues priced as low as ¼ cent were being dealt in any longer. He boasted about the reputation of the exchange: 'Fair dealing and fair play are more essential in a stock exchange than in any other business because the public is generally nervous and can only be led to deal under the existence of complete confidence. One of the surest methods of keeping the curb broker where he is at the present moment is to make sure that we as members of the only stock exchange – special charter [sic] – west of Toronto are doing our business with scrupulous care and by conforming rigidly to its bylaws. In this regard a noticeable advance has also been made as there have been very few cases before the committee that necessitated censure.' Still, Nanson did admit that members were under increasing pressure to allow the public back in to see what went on on the floor, and a few days later the exclusion was reversed.[23]

A further effort to convince investors that the operations of the Vancouver exchange were above board was the decision late in 1927 to require all members to have their books audited by a chartered accountant who was to report any violation of the by-laws to the board. At the same time President S.W. Miller called upon British Columbia's attorney general to crack down on a number of Vancouver bucket shops as 'a menace to the investing public' and to bring in legislation requiring all non-member brokers and dealers to post bonds with the provincial government. As trading volume shot higher during 1928, passing 1 million shares in a single day, the VSE finally abandoned the antiquated method of calling stocks one by one and set up trading posts like those used on eastern exchanges. (See appendix, table A.8.) A separate committee was created to investigate new listing applications, and a couple of stocks were promptly turned down because they were not widely distributed amongst independent shareholders. Some eastern brokerage houses began to take out memberships, which were selling for $18,000 that spring. A year later, when five additional seats were created, they sold for $35,000 apiece, which seemed to signal that the VSE had finally attained the status of a major exchange by the time it moved into new premises in the summer of 1929 (see photo 17).[24]

II

As share markets boomed in the late 1920s, the impact was felt particularly strongly in Toronto, the centre of mining finance in Canada. Mining stocks were among the hottest, and trading volume on the Standard Stock and Mining Exchange soared from 129 million in 1926 to over 320 million shares a year later. Yet that prosperity brought new problems for the exchange as a public outcry developed in the spring of 1927, and the government of Ontario began to exert strong pressure for a thoroughgoing clean-up. If the exchanges failed to deal with the situation, the government might feel compelled to step in and impose stricter regulations.

In the fall of 1926 the attorney general, W.F. Nickle, claimed that many of the problems of the SSME had been cured by the introduction of the twice-yearly audit of members' books, though he had to admit that it remained difficult to control misrepresentations made to customers by salesmen unless it could be shown that they were acting on instructions from their bosses. At the end of the year the exchange board convened a special meeting of members to approve a letter to broker Morgan U. Kemerer complaining that his employees were making unsolicited telephone calls to non-clients. Kemerer was warned to stop using high-pressure sales tactics, and he promised to comply.[25] He did not do so, however, and it soon became clear that he was by no means the only offender among SSME members. In March 1927 three listed stocks on the exchange suddenly dropped drastically; Bourlamaque Syndicate fell from $1.50 to $1, South Keora from 65 cents to 15, and Vickers Porcupine from $1.47 to 40 cents. Kemerer was known to be the main backer of Bourlamaque, Kiely and Smith of South Keora, and F.G. Oke and Company of Vickers. Charges flew on the 'street' that share prices of the companies had been pushed up artificially and maintained by pooling in order to facilitate high-pressure stock-selling campaigns.[26]

When the news broke, angry protests were heard from buyers all across Ontario who had purchased stock as a result of telephone calls and telegrams from the three firms. One man complained to F.J. Crawford, the president of the exchange, that when he telephoned Kemerer and ordered his Bourlamaque shares sold, his salesman, Woods, had failed to return his calls. Eventually the customer visted the firm's offices. Told that Woods was ill and could not see him, he refused to speak to anyone else, and ultimately the man with whom he had been talking left the room, returned, and admitted that he was Woods. The client was not permitted to see Kemerer himself, but another salesman finally offered to take his Bourlamaque shares off his hands for $1 (instead of the $1.20 prevailing earlier) provided that he would not make any further fuss. Yet no money was forthcoming, and Kemerer had personally telephoned the client to try to persuade him not to complain to the SSME board.[27]

The exchange tried to damp down the outcry by dropping the trio of stocks from its listings; for unlisted issues only daily trading volume was released so that bid and asked prices could not so easily be used as sales tools. The board also summoned the three members to appear and explain the price fluctuations satisfactorily or face suspension. Philip Kiely admitted that he had an option on a large number of South Keora shares at 12 cents apiece, which his salesmen were selling for whatever they could get and keeping half the difference, some stock having gone for 24 cents. F.G. Oke said that he had a block of 350,000 Vickers shares, but he flatly denied that his firm was engaged in high-pressure selling, though he admitted that he knew of a New Jersey firm unconnected to his that was using the long-distance telephone to sell across the province. Morgan Kemerer insisted that he had mended his ways since the rebuke the previous December, but revealed that he did have an option on Bourlamaque shares at $1, that he was selling them on margin, and that on occasion he would even accept other Bourlamaque shares as collateral for loans to buy more. However, each person vigorously denied any wrongdoing.[28]

Damaging allegations continued to leak out. The *Financial Post* claimed that Kiely and Smith had sold 300,000 South Keora shares taken down under option for 5 cents at prices up to 55 cents. Pooling of shares and granting of low-priced options were all too common for SSME issues. The paper argued that brokers should not be permitted to unload penny stocks for ten times the option price since doing so was an open invitation to stock jobbers and raiders to fleece the public. The *Financial Times* complained that brokers were lending on margin purchases of South Keora shares though it was well known that no bank would advance money on the security of such stock. All in all, the market break was the 'most regrettable incident that has occurred in a long time.'[29]

The Ontario Attorney General's Department was determined to prevent a whitewash this time. The new minister, William H. Price, ordered his deputy to keep a close eye on the situation, and Edward Bayly drafted a letter to the SSME demanding a thorough investigation to discover if wash trading or 'put throughs' had been used to artificially inflate the value of shares that never really changed hands.

A careful check of your clearing house records and the accounts of members who appear to be participating in this sort of thing will probably prove that there has been considerable 'bucketing' going on.

There should be no necessity at present for the government to intervene and make a check up of this sort, so long as your exchange continues to exhibit a willingness to clean up the situation, but the steps already taken by you will not constitute a complete cure unless you curb manipulation of this sort.

Eventually Price and Bayly decided to hold their hand for the present, and the letter was not sent, but the exchange board got the message that it would not be allowed to sweep the matter back under the rug and directed its newly appointed solicitor, A.J. Trebilcock, to investigate further. He set about trying to get sworn complaints, something that share buyers who had been swindled were often reluctant to provide.[30]

In view of the uproar in the press the attorney general was also worried about public criticism if the goverment failed to act, so Edward Bayly directed the local Crown attorney to begin his own investigation with a view to laying charges. E.N. Armour bluntly replied that the SSME 'has always been irregular. It has been the means of creating fictitious prices of mining shares by "wash" sales. Some of the firms which are members of the exchange engage in "bucketing" but to prove particular instances is next to impossible.' He pointed out that to prove wash trading under the Criminal Code it would be necessary to seize the books of all the members of the exchange at once, a difficult and expensive operation. A skilful bookkeeper could make bucketing almost impossible to uncover, and complaints were rarely made since brokers used blocks of option stock to meet demands for delivery to customers. Such irregularities were so prevalent that corporate directors made no effort to prevent them. Armour suggested to the attorney general that it would be better to order a public inquiry rather than seek to put the offenders in jail.[31]

Price did not order such an inquiry, but he did meet privately with the exchange president. 'I told him,' he reported to Bayly, 'if they did not clean house we would. The result of this was that Mr. Crawford said that they would at once begin to discipline the brokers who had transgressed the rules of the exchange.' Kiely and Kemerer were called before the board to hear the evidence against them, found guilty of improper conduct, fined $100 each, and suspended from the SSME for thirty and sixty days respectively. Kemerer, however, refused to take his punishment lying down; he sued the exchange, claiming that the board had refused to allow him to cross-examine those who had registered complaints about his firm's high-pressure telephone selling. The exchange decided to leave the case against Oke in limbo until the courts had made a ruling on the validity of its by-laws.[32]

After hearing the case Mr Justice Middleton dismissed the suit on the grounds that Kemerer possessed the right to appeal any penalty to an SSME members' meeting, and because he had failed to do so, the courts ought not to intervene. The judge did note that while the board had acted speedily with the laudable aim of preventing misconduct, it had failed to give Kemerer adequate notice of the precise charges against him, nor had it tried to ascertain if the complaints made against him were true. Middleton added that there was some doubt about whether the by-laws banning improper conduct could be used to penalize high-pressure telephone selling by member firms and suggested that they needed to be rewritten to clarify them. As a result the SSME lifted the penalties levied upon Kemerer and dropped the case against Oke.[33]

Price became determined to force a clean-up at the Standard exchange. President Crawford had promised that the by-laws would be rewritten and that somebody from the attorney general's office would be allowed to sit in on the drafting. 'I am quite certain,' Price told Bayly, 'that we will now make enough progress this way to clean up the whole situation there without interfering with the regular transaction of business ... I think we can now get this exchange on a basis where there will be ample protection for the public ... [I]t is now time for us to start to get everything cleaned up, so that there will be no difficulty when situations of this kind arise in the future.' Bayly immediately wrote to the New York, Montreal, and Toronto Stock Exchanges requesting copies of their rules against bucketing and wash sales to use as models. As soon as Kemerer's lawsuit was dismissed, he stepped up the pressure, writing to the secretary of the SSME to enquire when the process of drawing up the new by-laws would begin.[34]

In late June 1927 A.W. Rogers of the Attorney General's Department attended a meeting of the SSME board to discuss the revised rules. He reported that the proposed by-laws would now specify a number of kinds of improper conduct, such as telephone selling to non-clients, but would also leave the directors considerable discretion. Rogers urged the directors to ban margin trading on stocks below a fixed minimum price, but they persuaded him that doing so would likely drive trading to other, laxer exchanges such as the Montreal Curb Market or to non-member brokers. When the directors maintained that, like everyone else, they normally heard of abuses only after the fact, Rogers was sceptical and delivered a none too veiled warning: 'I told them that I thought perhaps they would be more likely to hear of operators of doubtful repute before we did, and that perhaps a tip in time might save a good deal of trouble.' Having reviewed the draft by-laws Attorney General Price pronounced them a great improvement, though he was still eager to see the SSME be more choosy about those who were admitted as members. Rogers was directed to remind exchange officials that in future they should inform the government immediately about complaints against members which might lead to the laying of charges, so that investigations could commence without delay.[35]

In an effort to deflect some of the embarrassing criticisms directed at the SSME, the board had pointed out to Rogers that, in fact, it was not their members who were causing the worst problems at present, but 'a large number of unscrupulous brokers driven here from the United States [who] are opening offices in hotel rooms, etc. and installing a battery of telephones and serving high-pressure phone salesmanship from various so-called "sucker lists."' Even Standard members became annoyed at the kind of competition they had to deal with: Homer Gibson complained that an over-the-counter firm, Picard and Company, had sent a couple of men with an airplane up to Sturgeon Falls, Ontario, where they were treating the leading citizens to joyrides and liberally dispensing whisky brought in by the caseload in their hotel rooms. Flushed with good cheer the local notables were buying shares, so that Gibson's North Bay branch had lost a number of accounts. He wanted the attorney general to step in and put a stop to this activity.[36]

Canadians seemed to be receiving floods of newsletters and tipsheets from the United States, such as the *Financialistic Debater* and the *Wall Street Icono-*

clast. Each one normally included advice to buy good, solid stocks, so as to inspire confidence, but sooner or later would strongly tip whatever promotion the sponsoring firm was handling at the moment. Those who responded to these publications immediately found themselves deluged with mail, telegrams, and telephone calls pressing them to make a purchase. Before long there appeared a horde of domestic imitators with titles such as the *Financial Advisor*, the *Financial Bulletin*, the *Stock Exchange Mirror*, and the *Dominion Financial News*.[37]

A.H. Munday of Toronto cockily urged people to buy shares in a 'mystery mine.' In that case the Ontario authorities felt compelled to intervene even though they lacked clear legal authority to do so. The Attorney General's Department warned Munday that *Mines and Metals*, 'instead of being as it purports to be, an independent mining paper, is nothing more than a mere tipster sheet.' His ploy, A.W. Rogers told him sternly, 'seems more to indicate an effort on your part to find out who has money than anything else. We have no objection to a mining paper being run as such, but when such activities as these of yours are coupled with it, it is very apt to cause us to find ways and means of putting it out of business.'[38]

'Boiler rooms' utilizing banks of telephones began to appear in Canada, and their salesmen pulled all sorts of stunts. C.J. Conway and Company of Montreal put out the *Stock Exchange Mirror* and used thirty telephone lines to pitch mines. One Montreal businessman was induced to buy shares in highly reputable Chrysler Motors on the prediction of a rise, but a few days later a call advised him to sell and buy 'Pontiac' instead. Imagine his surprise when he discovered that he had bought shares in Pontiac Gold Mines, which Conway and Company was pushing. The police moved in, closed down the operation, and arrested three people on fraud charges.[39]

The SSME board had suggested to Rogers that the best way to uncover these boiler rooms with their banks of telephones was to seek help from the Bell Telephone Company. The Toronto Securities Company and Charles Stewart and Company were identified by the brokers as worthy of investigation. The attorney general directed Rogers to see if he could get the telephone company to assist in identifying 'all these fly-by-night operators who furnish luxurious premises without actually making any effort to comply with our laws.'[40]

In September 1927 the Ontario Provincial Police moved in on Toronto Securities. Though these New Yorkers had fled the day before, officers discovered a bank of fourteen telephones sitting on desks carved with obscene words underneath the motto 'Don't Work.' The principals, Milton and Ira Janis, had been peddling shares in the Dominion Lead Mining Company, which they falsely maintained owned a mining claim near Sault Ste Marie, using fictitious quotations from the Montreal Mining Exchange. When an accounting showed that some $450,000 was missing, Ontario requested the extradition of the Janis brothers from the United States. Eventually Pinkerton men picked up the pair in Atlantic City, New Jersey, in the spring of 1928, and though they managed to fight off extradition for another year, they were finally returned to Toronto and sentenced to three and one-half years in the pentitentiary for fraud.[41]

Tips from the public also helped. In the summer of 1927 a lawyer in Owen Sound complained to the Toronto police about a similar operation. Worthington and Company was bombarding him with publicity using a 'new wrinkle in the fake mining stock game.' Starting with the 'amusingly nervy request' that he send in $100 for a 'mystery' stock that was sure to advance in price, Worthington followed up with daily bulletins in the same vein. A police investigation revealed that seven men were using a dozen telephones to push shares and that business was so good they were planning to expand. Stock in Eastern Metals and Smelting obtained at a cost of $1 was being sold on the basis of a fake quotation of $17 on the Montreal Mining Exchange and had netted the swindlers $75,000. A member of Parliament, Dr Ira D. Cotnam of Pembroke, Ontario, who had bought Eastern Metals stock after reading the *Dominion Financial News*, had been taken for $35,000. He complained indignantly to Ontario attorney general W.H. Price about the lack of protection for investors: 'If any promoter can sell stock on such a basis, not assume any responsibility, then company promotion and stock selling is surely the greatest gamblers' paradise on earth.' In this case, too, charges were laid and the two ringleaders were each sentenced to two years in the pentitentiary, while four other salesmen were ordered deported to the United States.[42]

Despite these successes Attorney General Price was concerned about the lack of deterrence since prosecutions like that of Worthington and Company were usually perceived simply as the work of local Crown attorneys. He advised Rogers, 'If we are going to get action in these cases, then it might be wise to have it appear from a public standpoint that we are actually behind it.' By that time Price was convinced that a new regulatory approach was required to stamp out securities fraud both on and off the exchanges.

This view was reinforced by the serious constitutional flaw in the blue-sky laws. The Supreme Court's 1923 decision in *Ruthenian Farmers Elevator Company v. Lukey* had held that provincial regulations could not require federally chartered companies to register in order to sell shares; in the Alberta oil boom of 1925–6 most promoters took advantage of this ruling by seeking incorporation in Ottawa. Nevertheless, the Manitoba government remained determined to try to exercise power over companies wherever incorporated. The Sale of Shares Act was redrawn in 1924 to require all securities issuers to register, and in 1926 the Public Utility Board Act was also amended. In order to test the constitutionality of these provisions it was decided in the spring of 1927 to mount a reference case in the Manitoba Court of Appeal, which was simply asked whether or not the provisions of the new legislation were *intra vires* so far as federal companies were concerned. Unfortunately, the Manitoba court, adhering to the *Lukey* precedent, returned its answer in a single, discouraging word, 'No.' Though this finding was to be appealed to the Judicial Committee of the Privy Council in London for final decision, the blue-sky approach now seemed fatally flawed.[43]

III

Ontario officials had never had much faith in the efficacy of blue-sky laws anyway. By 1926 Deputy Attorney General Edward Bayly was proposing a different approach to cleaning up share pushing: the licensing of salesmen. Toronto Crown attorney E.N. Armour had also become convinced that 'The only way to stop fly-by-night stock selling is to pass legislation requiring (1) all persons who deal in securities to become licensed; (2) restricting licenses to British subjects resident in Ontario; (3) forbidding the sale of securities by calling at the house (this has been done in England); (4) forbidding the sale of securities by persons not licensed under heavy penalties; and (4) allowing arrest without warrant for infractions of the act.' Price accepted the idea and directed A.W. Rogers to begin drafting a new bill, keeping in mind that 'legislation of this kind should be simple and appeal to the public generally.'[44]

The need for some type of new securities legislation became more and more acute because of the tremendous boom in mining shares in the autumn of 1927. The SSME handled an unprecedented 2,300,000 shares in a single day of trading, and its members sought more business by opening numerous branch offices across the province, a total of thirty altogether by September. Seat prices on the SSME reached a record high of $26,500.[45] In addition, there was heavy action on the Toronto Stock Exchange, which decided to set aside part of its boardroom as a temporary space for dealing in unlisted mining shares; the increase in trading volume helped to push TSE seat prices up to $47,500 by the autumn and led to a demand for quotations to be broadcast over a local radio station in the fall.[46]

The Montreal Stock Exchange, having just created the Curb Market where unlisted mines accounted for a large proportion of trading, also benefited from the boom. The rival Montreal Mining Exchange had maintained an intermittent existence since the turn of the century, but in the fall of 1927 a scandal forced the resignation of its former president, William J. Ball, who was charged with manipulation and conspiracy with various other shady characters, including the Janis brothers of Toronto Securities. Yet the increased interest in mining shares gave the MME a renewed lease on life, and the new executive promised (once again) a clean-up to get rid of undesirable members and listings. The exchanges in Winnipeg, Calgary, and Vancouver and the small Victoria Stock Exchange also did most of their trading in mining shares.[47]

With mining-share markets flourishing the Ontario Attorney General's Department began to keep an even closer eye on the operations of the Standard stock exchange. To increase trading volume the board had allowed non-members to have SSME ticker service, though they had no control over the financial stability of these firms, many of which did a large margin business. Under pressure from the government the SSME decided to require non-members who did not belong to another recognized exchange to demonstrate their soundness by submitting audited financial statements.[48]

Price was annoyed, however, that after a delay of six months the members of the exchange had not yet formally approved the new by-laws, which had been discussed in the summer of 1927. 'With the great number of stocks being sold it is most important that this matter be arranged at an early date. It is just at these times that things occur and need specific handling.' Rogers wrote to the exchange solicitor, A.J. Trebilcock, in October 1927 to urge quick action 'in view of the tremendous public craze for buying mining stocks.' He pressed the lawyer to make sure that the new rules tightened up listing requirements and disclosed commissions and option agreements. Manipulation must be curtailed since it was probably a criminal offence for insiders to maintain share prices artificially by buying up any shares that came on the market without disclosing this fact. The exchange should have the power to delist any stocks about which it had suspicions, and all the audits of members should be held on a single day to prevent them fudging their books by borrowing shares from one another.[49]

Trebilcock replied that the board had already met half a dozen times and had finally agreed upon the by-law changes to be submitted to the members. No new regulations would be added since the exchange already scrutinized all option agreements. Listing requirements had already been tightened to require that at least 10 per cent of the stock was in the hands of public shareholders to ensure an adequate 'float.' The only stocks traded on the unlisted section were those being actively traded on the 'street' or on other exchanges or well-known issues that had never applied for an SSME listing, such as Inco or Noranda. New issues had not been admitted to the unlisted section in recent months because the listing committee believed that all the stocks being dealt in should meet the formal listing requirements.[50]

Rogers kept up the pressure, telling exchange president F.J. Crawford that the new by-laws must be passed as soon as possible. If there was another scandal, the public would be outraged when reminded that half a year had passed without any real action by the SSME. By late November 1927 volume had reached nearly 3 million shares per day; margin trading was believed to account for about half that figure, and it was rumoured that brokers continued to bucket a high proportion of these orders, which created a large short interest. While some traders were trying to push values up further in order to punish the shorts, others were poised for bear raids to take advantage of lower prices to cover themselves. It all added up to a highly unstable situation in which brokers doing a large margin business might find their financial stability imperilled as they scrambled to buy shares to fill orders.[51]

Meanwhile, Rogers tried to keep an eye out for potential problems. Once again the stable of mines being promoted by the Kemerer brokerage firm came under scrutiny. R.E. Kemerer complained that enemies had threatened to have Rogers step in and force him to turn over control of the shares to a holding company, Precious Metals Limited: 'It seems incredible that some of the people quoting you should have the opportunity, to say nothing of the authority, to use your office as a means of legalized blackmail, which is what the efforts of some come close to.' Rogers ignored Kemerer's complaints and tried his best to avert any further scandal.[52]

Early in December 1927 SSME members finally met and approved their new by-laws. At the same time an exchange seat was sold for the unheard-of price of $60,000, just $5,000 less than the price of a newly created seat on the Toronto Stock Exchange, where a section for trading unlisted mines had just been opened on the main trading floor.[53] As often happened when business was particularly good, talk began to circulate about the establishment of a rival exchange; the press reported that lawyer J.R. Roaf was seeking a federal charter for the Canadian Exchange Limited to handle mining shares. Attorney General Price ordered an investigation since the principal promoter was not a stockbroker and was a reputed to have served time in jail in the United States. Investigations by the Ontario Provincial Police revealed that many of the purported backers of the scheme had not given permission for their names to be used. Eventually Ottawa rejected the charter application, and the scheme fizzled out along with a plan to create an independent stock exchange in nearby Hamilton. The proposal to create a National Stock Exchange in Toronto to trade mining shares because of supposed delays and congestion at the SSME likewise came to nothing in the spring of 1928.[54]

Even with the new by-laws in force at the Standard stock exchange the Attorney General's Department continued to watch out for share-price manipulation during the boom in November 1927, which was described by the *Finan-*

cial Post as 'an orgy of speculation.' Early in December W.H. Price ordered the exchange to investigate a sudden rise in the price of Amulet Mines stock, but a check by a chartered accountant could uncover no misconduct.[55] At the same time the price of Bidgood Mines shares also rose meteorically from 5 cents to $1.83 then dropped equally dramatically. Price ordered a full investigation. There were rumours that a pool of 1 million of the 2.3 million issued shares was operating to manipulate prices, and suspicion fell upon a dark, well-dressed man, 'a typical German Jew, not like the average Jew,' who had recently arrived in Toronto and did his trading through the offices of A.E. Pearce and Company. A.W. Rogers despatched the Ontario Provincial Police to investigate, and an inspector moved in next door to the man's room in the King Edward Hotel to shadow him and eavesdrop on his telephone calls. Wash trading designed to alter share prices should show up in the records of the exchange as matching buy and sell orders. There were thirteen large clearing-house sheets for every trading day, and the SSME refused to undertake the analysis, but Rogers thought that it might be worthwhile to put all the members on notice by having government auditors do the job. 'We might say that we are trying to check manipulation by an outsider, not naming him, and if they do not wish to check it we can ask them to deliver the sheets to us and check the activity of all the stocks dealt in [during] November and December, including Bidgood. That would give us a pretty fair picture of the operations of the various brokers.'[56]

Further study revealed, however, that proof would be much more difficult to obtain. The clearing-house records did not reveal which trades involved matching buy and sell orders. Rogers consulted his friends in the New York attorney general's office about how they handled such problems. The response was discouraging: only by checking the books of all the brokers trading a given stock and matching them with the exchange records could wash trading be uncovered.[57]

Attorney General Price concluded that the exchange itself was best equipped to investigate. In January 1928 he persuaded the SSME to appoint a three-member complaints committee and immediately requested that they look into the fluctuations in Bidgood the previous December. An anonymous letter-writer had pointed out that Solloway, Mills and Company had been touting Bidgood in its *News from the Mines*. Yet between 8 and 10 December 1927, as share prices slipped sharply, Solloway, Mills had sold 31,250 Bidgood shares while buying only 10,300. Had the brokerage gone 20,000 shares short on a stock that it was urging its own customers to buy? Were they bucketing buy orders in the knowledge that the market price would fall? After an investigation the SSME complaints committee reported that Solloway, Mills had been able to satisfy them that nothing improper had occurred.[58]

The attorney general was even more concerned by rumours that SSME members had been carrying large amounts of stock for non-member brokers on margins as low as 5 per cent. If these non-members had required their customers to put up between 30 and 50 per cent of the purchase price, they might have the difference to use for their own purposes. But the courts had held that payments from clients were trust funds to be used for the designated purposes, and failure to do so would constitute fraudulent conversion or perhaps even theft.[59] The SSME board promised to look into the matter, though in the absence of specific allegations about members offering margins as low as 5 per cent to non-members nothing much was likely to be discovered.[60]

Even with its newly created complaints committee the SSME failed to come up with definite evidence of wrongdoing by any of its members, which helped to convince Price that the time had finally come to bring in new legislation to control security frauds. Though some of the steam went out of the mining-share boom in the spring of 1928, expectations remained high and a seat sold on the Standard exchange for $65,000 at the beginning of March and for an extraordinary $90,000 only a fortnight later. By the end of the month the price had hit $100,000, and even the creation of five new seats failed to dampen demand. Business continued to be so good that in the summer the members approved the exchange seeking new, larger premises.[61]

Moreover, the federal government had once again demonstrated its lack of interest in granting the provinces regulatory authority over share selling by federally incorporated companies. At the Dominion-Provincial Conference in November 1927 the provinces brought up the idea that Parliament should pass legislation delegating these powers to them as recommended by the premiers at the Interprovincial Conference in 1926. Secretary of State Fernand Rinfret dashed their hopes by declaring that he believed that the problem could best be dealt with by federal regulatory legislation.[62] Unless the Judicial Committee of the Privy Council overturned the decision of the Manitoba Court of Appeal in the reference case concerning the blue-sky law, it looked as though the provinces would not have the power to control share selling by federal companies.[63]

Ontario attorney general Price finally took the decision to bring in a new type of legislation. He told the Canadian Life Insurance Officers Association right after the Dominion-Provincial Conference that the act would be based upon the registration and control of securities sellers, an approach that A.W. Rogers had been developing since the scandal on the Standard stock exchange in mid-1927. After extensive consultations with W.R. Cottingham, Manitoba's public utilities commissioner, Rogers and Bayly produced a bill which they were satisfied would be effective in controlling fraud yet not subject to constitutional challenges. The Investment Bankers Association of Canada was also consulted and signified its approval of the new approach.[64]

The Security Frauds Prevention Act, which Price introduced in the Ontario legislature in March 1928, aimed at controlling the conduct of securities sellers; each broker and salesman would be required to register and to post a bond of at least $500. Applicants could be refused for any 'reasonable' cause, and non-residents or those of dubious reputation could be compelled to obtain bonds from a surety company. Registrations could be cancelled or suspended by a judge of the Ontario Supreme Court. Security fraud was more precisely defined to include any misrepresentation or omission of a material fact and any promise about the future beyond reasonable expectation. Exorbitant commissions were outlawed, and bucketing dealt with by banning any fictitious security transaction. To prevent fly-by-nighters from absconding the attorney general was given power to investigate suspected frauds and freeze any bank account or place any broker in bankruptcy. Price proudly told the legislature that his approach had the support of 'all the better business and financial organizations of the province, who desire to see trading in securities properly safeguarded, so that the small investor will not be fleeced.'[65]

The Toronto Stock Exchange accepted the new approach without complaint. Lawyer E.G. Long, who acted as counsel for the exchange as well as for the Investment Bankers Association, had become a proponent of regulation through the registration of salesmen and had helped to persuade the Ontario government to include some of these provisions in the 1924 Sale of Shares Act, which was never proclaimed into law. Later he had drafted a model statute along these lines, which was submitted to the Manitoba legislative committee that had investigated the Hearst Music Company scam in 1925. The TSE minute books reveal no further debate on the issue in the spring of 1928.[66]

The Standard stock exchange did not oppose the bill either. Indeed, Rogers had reported to the attorney general in the summer of 1927 that 'the directors seem to be rather keen on the idea of licensing brokers of all kinds, and all express the view that legislation along these lines would do more to prevent high-pressure thievery than anything else.' Yet some of the act's provisions did arouse concern, and lawyer A.J. Trebilcock was instructed to prepare amendments to be forwarded to the government. While declaring that the board still 'heartily favours' the principle of the legislation, the secretary of the exchange had several complaints. The power of the attorney general to suspend a broker's registration for up to ten days on suspicion of fraudulent activities would be tantamount to putting a firm out of business because doing so would destroy public confidence. The ban on levying 'unconscionable' fees or commissions was equally sweeping since it left the promoters of speculative stocks uncertain as to how much they might charge to take on risky ventures such as mines.

The government refused to budge. A.W. Rogers replied that the purpose of the legislation was to arm the attorney general with emergency powers if required. Except in the most unusual circumstances no established brokerage need fear a ten-day suspension without having a hearing in court. He defended the prohibition on unconscionable returns as something to be defined by the courts taking account of the facts of a particular situation. Recent investigations had uncovered cases of shares optioned for as little as 10 cents apiece being sold for $1.70. Surely the courts would hold that to be an illegal gain, but the test should be a comparison between the return to the underwriter and the amount received by the company treasury.[67]

When the law came into force in mid-May 1928, Attorney General Price made a point of emphasizing that it was not blue-sky legislation. Rather, it was intended to promote development in sectors such as mining by forcing promoters to file prospectuses that could be checked for false or fraudulent claims. In an article written for *Saturday Night* the attorney general defended the government's record. There would be no draconian enforcement; instead he promised to 'have a talk with brokers and salesmen against whom complaints have been made to see if matters cannot be adjusted before taking extreme action.' That the need to rein in the bolder spirits still existed was emphasized by a report in the *Financial Post* during the summer: an inactive mine in northern Ontario had unexpectedly replaced its lone watchman with a burly 225-pounder twice his predecessor's size. When this news reached a Toronto broker, he immediately sought a listing for the company's shares and pushed prices upward using this news as evidence of a significant discovery on the property.[68]

Still concerned about the problems created by tipsheets, Attorney General Price put pressure on the federal government in the spring of 1928 to deny them the use of the mails. Despite some initial hesitation, the postmaster general eventually agreed to take action against some of the worst offenders, such as the *Financialistic Debater* from Boston; the editor of this paper tried to pretend that he had been falsely accused of wrongdoing for criticizing the operations of several Canadian bucket shops, but the authorities stuck to their guns. Yet postal bans proved a fairly feeble remedy since the shrewder tipsters frequently changed their addresses or enclosed their mailings in plain envelopes.[69]

Although Ontario attempted to clamp down on securities fraud, the province of Quebec did not follow suit. Booming share markets had pushed the price of a seat on the Montreal Stock Exchange from $45,000 to $60,000 by the fall of 1927. The Montreal Mining Exchange was again reorganized in an effort to shake off its sleazy reputation, and by the spring of 1928 seats were selling for $6,500, up from $800 just six months earlier. That summer there was even talk of reopening the long-moribund exchange in Quebec City.[70] Though Montreal remained Canada's financial capital, the regulation of securities markets there still relied mainly upon voluntary action. During the early 1920s the Associated

Advertising Clubs of the World in the United States had created a Better Business Bureau to promote higher standards of conduct. That movement quickly spread, and local BBBs like the one in Boston (home of a notorious Curb Market) did their best to publicize stock-selling scams. In 1928 the Montreal Merchants Association in conjunction with the Investment Bankers Association of Canada, the Montreal Stock Exchange, and the Montreal Curb Market decided to establish a BBB.

Soon the bureau was issuing bulletins warning against purchasing particular stocks and bonds. The Quebec government considered a proposal to require all securities sellers to receive the endorsement of the BBB before securing licences, but the organization baulked at assuming such a heavy responsibility. Nevertheless, within six months the bureau had received nearly four hundred enquiries about over two hundred undertakings and had secured the issuing of nine arrest warrants against securities sellers.[71] In the autumn, for instance, the BBB issued a warning against a well-known Boston boiler-room operator named Todd Larkin, charging that drill cores in a mine which he was promoting had been salted. Larkin attempted to squelch the publicity with a $50,000 libel action, but the courts tossed out the case.[72] The Toronto business community was sufficiently impressed with the work of the BBB that a movement began in 1928 to organize a local branch. The Board of Trade, the two stock exchanges, the Dominion Mortgage and Investment Association, and the Toronto Real Estate Board gave their support, and by the fall of the year the new bureau was starting to issue its own bulletins.[73]

Voluntarism had obvious limitations, however. In western Canada faith in the blue-sky legislation still remained strong. In July 1928 the Judicial Committee of the Privy Council heard the appeal in Manitoba's reference case. Attorney General R.W. Craig reiterated the province's argument that its jurisdiction over property and civil rights, licensing, and local and private matters was sufficient to endow it with the authority to require all companies, whether federally or provincially chartered, to be licensed by the Public Utilities Commission in order to sell shares. Supporting him as intervener was Ontario deputy attorney general Edward Bayly, who insisted that these regulations did not trench upon the exclusive jurisdiction of the federal Parliament under section 91 of the British North America Act. For the respondents Solicitor General Lucien Cannon contended that previous Privy Council decisions had invalidated provincial laws which interfered with the 'status and capacity' conferred by Ottawa's incorporation. In December, 1928 the Judicial Committee rendered its decision, upholding the Manitoba Court of Appeal's finding that the blue-sky law did 'impair the status and powers' of federal companies and was accordingly *ultra vires.*[74]

Ontario officials were convinced that their Security Frauds Prevention Act was proof against this type of constitutional challenge. Federal companies were not required to be licensed in order to sell their shares, but either the person who sold the shares or the company officers did have to be registered under the SFPA. Offences under the act were, therefore, committed by individuals not by the companies themselves. Thus if a company could not get registered because the attorney general objected to its corporate officers, it had the alternative of replacing the officers or of finding a licensed broker to dispose of its shares. Hence the claim that there was no 'interference with the actual getting in of its capital by a Dominion company,' which the courts had objected to.[75]

Following the Privy Council decision, T.C. Davis, the attorney general of Saskatchewan, advised Ontario's Price that he was now thinking of introducing legislation identical to the SFPA. Price's response was highly encouraging. The act had been working well, and so far Ottawa was proving cooperative. 'I think we can get along with this act without getting into any controversy. We have very wide powers. A word from the Attorney General about a company, whether Dominion or Provincial, would pretty nearly stop it selling stock in this province. All of the promoters and exploiters of the public know this fact and are not anxious to get into controversy.'[76] Yet the westerner remained nervous: the Judicial Committee had said that the provinces could not do something indirectly that they lacked the power to do directly. If a federal company wanted to sell stock in Ontario but was required to register beforehand wasn't that an unconstitutional interference with its rights? Price looked at the Judicial Committee's decision and began to have doubts too. 'We do not want,' he wrote to his deputy, 'to get ourselves into a position where we have this new act attacked.'[77]

His officials remained confident. The invalid Manitoba legislation was 'a typical blue-sky law.' If a federal company was refused a certificate by the PUC, it could not sell shares in the province, except perhaps in small transactions spread over a period of years or in one big block.[78] Edward Bayly argued that the SFPA was framed on entirely different principles which did not interfere with essential corporate powers. Moreover, if a federal company did baulk and threaten legal action, he pointed out, it could face adverse publicity, which might prevent it from selling any shares at all. The deputy attorney general contended that if the other provinces followed Ontario's example there could be effective nationwide regulation without any interference by Ottawa or any further court cases.[79]

Davis's fears were assuaged, and Saskatchewan adopted an SFPA in 1929, as did Manitoba, Alberta, and Prince Edward Island soon after.[80] Davis then started a campaign to persuade British Columbia to follow suit. Price chimed in, advising the BC attorney general that the SFPA had proven 'very elastic' and conferred 'great power' when required. He claimed that even Thomas Mulvey reportedly approved of this type of legislation since it was not a blue-sky law. If all the provinces west of Quebec were to present a united front, Price argued, they would be in a much stronger position to demand from Ottawa wider powers to regulate federally chartered companies should these prove to be necessary.[81]

British Columbia officials were not easily convinced. The province's registrar of joint-stock companies, H.G. Garrett, had never been a convert to blue-sky laws, preferring the British approach, which relied upon full disclosure. He remained dubious about the virtues of the SFPA, and in the end the province opted for changes to the Companies Act to require promoters to reveal more of their intentions. Despite pressure from the local branch of the Investment Bankers Association, registration of securities sellers on the Ontario model was not imposed. The act did make door-to-door share selling illegal unless a prospectus had been filed with the authorities.[82]

Thus by 1929 Ontario, Prince Edward Island, and all three prairie provinces had Security Frauds Prevention Acts. New Brunswick still had its constitutionally flawed blue-sky law, and British Columbia's Companies Act had been tightened up to compel broader disclosure. Only Nova Scotia and Quebec had not enacted special legislation; like the federal government, they had so far declined to become involved in closer regulation of securities markets.

In Ontario officials continued to keep a close eye on the operations of the local stock exchanges during 1928. In order to clamp down on market manipulation through wash trading the Attorney General's Department persuaded both the SSME and the TSE to adopt by-laws requiring that brokers' confirmation slips show both the time of the trade and the name of the other party involved. Though it was admitted that heavy trading by house accounts and the use of fronts could still conceal manipulation, these changes made it more difficult.[83]

Meanwhile, stock prices continued to soar. Both the Montreal and Toronto Stock Exchanges had record years in 1928. Seat prices on the TSE reached $125,000 by the end of the year, and with a further rise in trading volume anticipated, members authorized spending $160,000 to purchase the land adjoining their building on Bay Street for future expansion of the trading floor.[84] The Montreal Curb Market moved into new premises next door to its parent in the spring of 1929. At the same time a new Consolidated Mining and Oil Exchange was established in Toronto to trade speculative issues.[85]

In the fall of 1928 the Standard stock exchange laid out $261,000 for a building on Temperance Street and undertook extensive renovations. Seats continued to sell for just under $100,000 in the spring of 1929. At the same time members decided to expand the unlisted section of the exchange for trading issues that were already actively dealt with over the counter in Toronto and the shares of companies that refused to submit listing applications. This move was spurred on by the organization of a rival Unlisted Stock Market in Toronto, which handled over 100,000 shares on its first day of business in April 1929. Eventually the Standard board decided that it would leave the unlisted traders in the old building on Richmond Street when it moved into its new premises.[86]

Not everything was rosy, however. At the beginning of 1929 SSME member H.H. Sutherland was unable to meet his obligations, and the board was forced to suspend him. Just a few weeks later the TSE's Heron and Company went bankrupt, leaving about $2 million in unpaid client balances.[87] As a result Attorney General Price decided that the exchanges should tighten their audit rules. The Standard board expressed concern that it lacked the charter powers to order surprise audits of members' books, and the Security Frauds Prevention Act was therefore amended in 1929 to grant the exchanges the necessary authority to require regular six-monthly audits as well as surprise examinations.[88]

By early May the TSE had passed the necessary by-law giving its board power to appoint an exchange auditor and draw up a list of approved accounting firms to serve its members. Any broker in poor financial condition could be suspended for as long as necessary. Clarkson, Gordon and Company were quickly chosen as exchange auditors for the TSE and by mid-July had rendered the first report. Eleven members were found to have more or less serious problems, mainly a lack of free capital funds in relation to the volume of business transacted. These firms were able to satisfy the auditors of their soundness, either by the injection of additional capital or by the 'subrogation' (or subordination) of claims owed to partners or shareholders to those of other debtors. One brokerage was discovered to have potentially serious difficulties as a result of under-margined accounts and underwriting of speculative shares; a special board committee headed by the TSE president, C.E. Abbs, was created to oversee the drawing up of a plan to liquidate these commitments as quickly as possible.[89]

The Standard stock exchange moved somewhat more slowly, but by the fall of 1929 the board had reached agreement with the Attorney General's Department on the wording of a new audit by-law and the composition of its panel of auditors. Holland Pettit of Oscar Hudson and Company was chosen exchange auditor. Meanwhile, A.W. Rogers remained in charge of monitoring trading on the exchange under the SFPA, and whenever he detected suspicious price movements in a particular stock, he would request details of the trading in order to uncover the cause of these fluctuations. When Rogers and his wife found themselves on a 'sucker' list for a mining promotion, the official threatened to start an immediate publicity campaign against the offender unless he registered his salesman and divulged the source of his list of names.[90]

On 27 June 1929 the Standard Stock and Mining Exchange held a gala opening for its new quarters on Temperance Street in Toronto, attended by Premier Howard Ferguson, Attorney General William H. Price, and Mines Minister Charles McCrea. Addressing a banquet audience of politicians, brokers, and other financial men, Ferguson declared that the exchange had done much to bolster public confidence and to give investors a fair opportunity to put their money in speculative shares, which had greatly helped to develop the province's mining industry. Price thanked the members for cooperating with the government to ensure that all share buyers got a square deal and urged them to ensure that trading was kept on a high plane. McCrea said that the exchange was a credit both to the brokerage fraternity and to the province generally. Flushed with pride the Standard members headed home to await the opening of their brand new trading floor on 2 July.[91]

By 1929 securities markets in Canada seemed to have left the bad old days behind. Having abandoned the blue-sky approach because of constitutional problems, five of the provinces had passed Security Frauds Prevention Acts which gave governments much wider powers to clamp down on dishonest practices. Brokers and salesmen were required to be registered, and suspicious characters could be refused licences altogether or required to post large bonds for good behaviour. Where fraud was suspected, the provincial attorney general had powers to intervene and prevent fly-by-nighters and boiler-room operators from absconding with their ill-gotten gains.

The stock exchanges, basking in the boom of the late 1920s, had also taken some steps towards tighter self-regulation. First, their boards had begun to require periodic audits and in Ontario could now order surprise investigations of members' affairs. New trading rules and tighter scrutiny was supposed to reduce price manipulation by wash trading and bucketing, for which the Standard stock exchange had become particularly notorious. At long last it seemed as though share buyers could expect an even break.

8

Crash

By 1929 I.W.C. Solloway was one of the best-known financial men in Canada. In just three years Solloway, Mills and Company had become the country's largest brokerage, with over 1,000 employees serving up to 70,000 clients through more than thirty offices spread through every province, as well as branches in Newfoundland, Britain, and the United States linked together by more than 13,500 miles of private wire to transmit information and orders. The firm held eighteen seats on various stock exchanges dealing mainly in speculative mining and oil shares. 'Ike' Solloway did more than a quarter of all the trading on Toronto's Standard Stock and Mining exchange and over two-fifths of the business on the Calgary stock exchange. In one six-month period his brokerage handled transactions for 56,248 individuals in shares worth about $170 million.[1]

Solloway's meteoric rise rested upon the stock-market boom that gripped North America during the late 1920s. He had been a prospector in northern Ontario for a dozen years without notable success before joining the army in 1916. When he returned from the war, he found it very difficult to raise money to resume exploration. Then he met Harvey Mills, the owner of a tobacco and newspaper store in Niagara Falls, New York, who occasionally grubstaked men in northern Ontario. Eventually he persuaded Mills to put up a small amount of capital to found a brokerage partnership, and in February 1926 they purchased a seat on the Standard stock exchange for $7,500.[2]

'My main object in going into the brokerage business,' Solloway would later claim, 'was to create some new way of financing mining companies so that a company could obtain sufficient money to accomplish a large program of development work.' Yet he conducted himself like most other Standard members, seeking profits by trading heavily on his own account. Within a month he had lost his entire capital and that of many of his new customers by gambling on

Noranda Mines. Mills had to be persuaded to put up another $7,000 to keep the business afloat.[3]

At that point Solloway decided to change his business strategy. As a prospector making the rounds of mining promoters he had noticed that most brokers did little to try to attract retail customers. Business premises were usually located deep inside downtown office buildings, and when customers did appear to buy over-the-counter stocks, salesmen often spent a great deal of time telephoning around in an effort to get better prices and squeeze out a few more dollars on a deal or simply offered shares in their own current promotion. Solloway decided to inject some theatre into his business to attract a larger clientele. He took space on the ground floor of Toronto's Metropolitan Building behind a large plate-glass window where people heading to the elevators could see the chalkboards which recorded changing prices. He placed his desk out in the open so that customers could hear him telephoning the exchange floor and knew that they were being offered the best current prices. Within six months business had expanded enough to employ a second trader, and the growing crowds in the office required steadily increasing space. By 1929 Solloway, Mills and Company filled almost two floors of the Metropolitan Building with a Toronto staff numbering 225. As the volume of business increased, the firm acquired a second seat on the Standard exchange in mid-1927 and a third (which cost $60,000) in December. Other brokers quickly followed suit, establishing branch offices elsewhere and buying seats on exchanges across the country to capture more local business.[4]

Solloway, Mills rode the wave of growing interest in mining stocks during 1927. The firm established a network of informants in northern Ontario to supply customers with a daily diet of news and rumours. Large profits on Amulet shares attracted many new accounts, but losses on the fluctuation in Bidgood in December 1927 generated sharp complaints. The Ontario authorities demanded that the Standard exchange investigate because the firm appeared to go short on the stock after recommending it to customers, but the company's explanation was eventually accepted.[5] Thereafter customers' men were instructed to be more careful in giving advice and to avoid making any guarantees that stocks would be bought back to erase losses. A visit to western Canada that summer alerted Solloway to the possibilities of Alberta oils and BC mines, which led him to purchase seats on both the Calgary and Vancouver exchanges in 1928 and helped to spring them from the doldrums. In addition, he decided to try to interest Quebeckers in mining shares, from which they had largely held aloof, by running a private wire to his Montreal office carrying the Standard exchange's ticker service. This initiative proved so successful that new staff had to be hastily hired and branch offices were opened across the country.[6]

As an increasingly powerful figure in the brokerage community, Solloway did not hesitate to throw his weight around. In the fall of 1928 he became most unhappy with the board of the Standard stock exchange, particularly for selling its ticker service to the shaky Montreal Mining Exchange, whose members operated in direct competition with his Montreal branch and its expensive private wire link. 'I have to confess I am greatly annoyed at belonging to an exchange to which my firm brings millions of dollars worth of business every year, and to the members of which my firm pays thousands of dollars in commissions each month, but which has never missed an opportunity to check me up on petty technicalities nor to put me to all the trouble possible, but which, on the other hand, allows irresponsible parties to use the privileges of the exchange and so bring discredit upon it.' Eventually the board bowed to this pressure and agreed to sever its relations with the Montreal Mining Exchange.[7]

As the size of his firm grew, Solloway became more and more unhappy with the long-standing practice of the Standard in granting split commissions to members of the Toronto and Montreal stock exchanges. He argued that if these brokers were forced to pay full commissions to purchase mining stocks heavily traded on the Standard exchange, they would soon offer similar splits to Standard members dealing in industrials. Already the other exchanges were trying to capitalize upon the boom in mining shares by opening curb markets to compete directly with the Standard. On this issue, however, he did not get his way since many Standard members depended heavily upon business referred to them by the Toronto and Montreal exchanges and were not prepared to risk open warfare.[8]

In December 1928 Solloway became the sole owner of the firm, acquiring Harvey Mills's interest for $500,000. By that time he was heavily involved in Alberta oil promotions. In the summer of 1929 he persuaded the Standard exchange to add twenty-five Turner valley oil stocks to its unlisted section to broaden the market for them. He joined with Mills to back an airline linking Edmonton to the Mackenzie River valley in the hope of exploiting resources there too. Having hired the mining editor of the *Financial Post* to act as manager of his private wire service, Solloway completed his nationwide network of offices in August of that year by buying Willis Securities of Halifax, which had nine offices across the Maritimes and in Newfoundland, thus giving him an outlet in every province of Canada.[9] In a photograph taken at this time Ike Solloway appears very much the swell, turned out in tailcoat and striped trousers with glossy top hat and white gloves. Leaning on his stick, he stands on the well-manicured gravel in front of a long, low convertible touring car; he looks every inch the captain of high finance (see photo 18).

I

Ike Solloway and other brokers could hardly keep up with business in 1928–9. The weighted monthly index number for a basket of Canadian common stocks compiled by the Dominion Bureau of Statistics (with 1926 levels equalling 100) rose from 150 in August 1928 to 185 at year's end. By February 1929 the index had hit 210; it slipped back a bit then reached 217 in September. People flocked to buy shares as the exchanges traded record volumes. Solloway, Mills benefited particularly because so many of its customers were interested in mines and oils. The DBS index for mining stocks, which began to be compiled in 1927, reached 140 by November of that year. Though it slid back somewhat in 1928, it was over 130 by mid-year and not far below that in early 1929. The sub-index for gold-copper stocks, however, ran up from 110 in April 1928 to 334 in January 1929 and was still at that level in the autumn. (See appendix, figures A.1 and A.2.) Everyone anticipated a rosy future.

On Monday, 21 October 1929, however, American markets suffered a severe downward lurch. Canadian stocks such as International Nickel and Brazilian Traction that were interlisted on the New York Stock Exchange started to drop in heavy trading as the ticker lagged far behind the frantic action on the floor. After a recovery on Tuesday, things went from bad to worse the following day as selling orders poured in and some stocks fell 10 or even 20 points. Then came the 24th, 'Black Thursday.' Despite the efforts of Richard Whitney to turn the tide on the floor of the NYSE by bidding $205 for 10,000 shares of U.S. Steel when it had already fallen under $200, followed by purchases of other blue chips for a consortium headed by J.P. Morgan and Company, the downward momentum proved irreversible.[10]

Friday, 25 October, was a quieter day, and everyone hoped the worst was over. The chair of the Montreal Stock Exchange, Edgar M. Smith, pointed out that all its members were in sound financial shape, while the head of the Toronto Stock Exchange, C.E. Abbs, observed that 'considering everything that happened in New York, I think we can conservatively say that the Toronto market did not give a bad account of itself.' But on Monday, 28 October, a new wave of selling commenced and Tuesday was far worse. What those who worked on the exchanges remembered ever after was the noise; Gordon Bongard, then a young trader, recalled, 'By this time there was a hell of a roar and it was pretty smoky, so it was awfully hard on your voice. What you'd do was go around the floor yelling, for instance, "Nickel going at 50!" And then soon it was "Nickel going at 49 1/2!" and so on. It was hard to find a buyer because everyone wanted to get out fast ... At times there might be two or three different prices being quoted in different corners of the room.' The same thing was true across town at the Standard exchange, where Bill Townsend, a youthful employee, remembered, '[T]hings were really hectic and people were bumping into one another in the thick [cigarette] smoke. It was pretty grim and there were a lot of long faces. Everyone wanted to sell but there were almost no bids. So, to be fair, they put all the brokers' names in a hat and drew one out whenever a bid came in.'[11]

When the exchanges finally closed for the day with the ticker running hours behind, the financial districts in Montreal and Toronto were still thronged with people as the back offices of brokerages struggled to catch up with the flood of paper. The most urgent item of business was putting in margin calls to customers as prices plummeted. Investors watched helplessly as their assets evaporated. When brokers tried to sell out those who could not advance more money, they found few buyers at any price.

Predictions that the downturn was only a market 'correction' and that the upward climb would quickly resume proved false. In such a crisis the instinctive reaction of the brokerage community was to close down the exchanges in the hope that the scare would blow over without too much damage. At noon on 29 October the governors of the New York Stock Exchange met secretly to consider whether or not to close immediately, but following intense debate they decided the show had to go on. Shortly after, however, it was announced that trading hours would be shortened and a number of 'special holidays' would be observed, supposedly to let brokerage staffs catch up with the mountains of back-office paperwork. These limitations continued in place into early November, but they failed to stem the steady decline in share prices.[12]

Once New York had decided to remain open, the Canadian exchanges had little choice in the matter: they had to soldier on or trading would simply shift outside into the 'gutter' market on the 'street.' At first the board of the Toronto Stock Exchange declined even to approve shorter hours, but eventually it decided early in November to open only in the morning (10 a.m. to 1 p.m.) for the next fortnight and to cancel all Saturday sessions. Somewhat reluctantly the Standard exchange followed suit.[13]

Nothing could stop the disastrous slump, however. From its September high of 217 the DBS index of common stocks fell to 155 by year's end where it stayed into the spring of 1930, while the mining-stock index dropped from over 100 to around 75 (see appendix, figures A.1 and A.2). Soon scapegoats were being sought, and public attention quickly focused upon the brokers and the stock exchanges themselves. Evidence of misconduct was all too ready to hand. Even the lordly members of the New York Stock Exchange found themselves the focus of unwanted attention, for they too had been guilty of a number of dubious actions during the preceding decade. In 1920, for instance, when the governing committee was criticized because it had intervened to break a corner that had trapped a number of prominent NYSE members who were shorting the stock of the Stutz Motor Car Company, a spokesman had grandly declared, 'The stock exchange can do anything.' John Brooks notes, 'Unshackled by any sort of public regulation, and governed by rules of its own devising, [the NYSE] was fully capable of summarily changing those rules to its own advantage, carrying on vindictive vendettas, and explaining itself to the public in terms so patently preposterous as to seem to express contempt.'[14]

Wall Street insiders thought nothing of taking well-known stocks with small floats and through a pool, often managed by the exchange's 'specialist' member responsible for ensuring orderly trading, pushing up prices artificially by wash sales which were prohibited but seemed impossible of detection by the exchange. Then as the rubes and suckers began to take up shares, the 'plug was pulled' and the pool dumped its shares at a handsome profit. In March 1929 the *Wall Street Journal* reported a 1-million-share pool in Radio Corporation of America involving a Rockefeller, a Chrysler, a Schwab, and Mrs Sarnoff (wife of RCA's president) managed by the NYSE specialist in RCA, Michael J. Meehan, which pushed up prices from $90 to $109 in a single week before a sell-off, earning Meehan $500,000 and the others $5 million. Over at the New York Curb Market (which had finally moved indoors in 1921) such operations were even more common, the specialists being a particular source of problems. Faced with such behaviour the investing public could do no more than seek to find out about such ramps and try to profit by joining in at the right moment.[15]

Lower trading volumes made such operations more difficult on the Montreal and Toronto stock exchanges during the 1920s (which was why some aggressive Canadian investors sent their money to New York). Nevertheless, in August 1929 the *Financial Post* reported that pool operators had pushed the stock of Famous Players Theatres of Canada from $50 to $75, and some people believed that it might double again. Doubts about the trustworthiness of markets were only reinforced by the operations on the Standard stock exchange, which had attracted the attention of the provincial authorities in Ontario during the late 1920s.[16] After the crash many Canadian investors wondered if they had not been victimized by manipulation on the part of insiders. At the end of October the *Financial Post* noted that Canada was fundamentally sound economically; Canadian stocks had not been trading at the unrealistic levels that had been reached in the United States. Some of the rush to liquidate had obviously been sparked by the break in New York, but surely there was more to it than that: brokers and insiders such as Ike Solloway must be to blame for the extent of the catastrophe.[17]

II

As the mining-share market picked up steam the Standard stock exchange remained notorious for price manipulation through wash trading and pooling. Every time there was an unusual fluctuation in the shares of a mining company during 1929 A.W. Rogers of the Ontario Attorney General's Department would despatch a letter to the exchange seeking information. The results were scant. When members of the public complained directly to the exchange, they were usually fobbed off with a request for more details so that the matter could be referred to the complaints committee, which had been set up under pressure from the government at the beginning of 1928.[18]

The problems on the Standard exchange stemmed mainly from the laxity of its rules. To obtain a listing a company was required only to have 10 per cent of its shares in the hands of the public and $25,000 in its treasury, and few applicants were ever rejected. There was also an 'unlisted' section where established companies that refused to apply for listings could be traded, some of them being quite well known, such as International Nickel and Home Oil. Yet in the spring of 1929 the Standard opened its doors even wider by creating a 'curb' section, where any security could be posted for trading provided that the board felt there was sufficient public interest. Even if the exchange was unable to secure information from the company itself, unofficial news about its internal affairs (which usually came from interested brokers or promoters) was considered sufficient. The argument in favour of the curb was that over-the-counter stocks typically had wide spreads between 'bid' and 'ask' prices which might be narrowed by a more active and liquid market. When listed stocks became inactive, they could simply be dropped to the curb and then reinstated if interest revived. The result was that of over one hundred stocks on the listed and unlisted sections only about twenty-odd were actively producing either ore or oil, while most of the seventy stocks traded on the curb were completely inactive.[19]

The internal administrative structure of the Standard exchange was equally shaky. On 3 July 1929, the day after it moved into its new premises on Temperance Street, auditors for the federal government reported serious underpayments of the stock-transfer taxes that were supposed to be remitted for each trade. The senior employee was J.J. Kingsmill, the assistant secretary, who quickly admitted that for several years past he had failed to forward any taxes on behalf of several brokerage firms and had spent the money on himself. Kingsmill was hastily fired, but the Department of National Revenue demanded $51,800 in arrears dating as far back as 1922, while the provincial government wanted another $18,400. The federal government also sought recover $28,700 paid to the exchange as a commission for collecting the taxes, since it had promised in 1920 to indemnify Ottawa against any losses. In the end National Revenue settled for $61,816.31 (of which $32,975.00 was written off the exchange books as a loss with the faint hope that the rest might be recouped from the hapless Kingsmill), but this payment plus those to Ontario and a cost overrun on the new building absorbed the entire surplus of $106,000 in hand at the beginning of 1929. The only bright side to this incident was that the embarrassing news did not leak out to the public just at the time the crash occurred.[20]

Meanwhile, Rogers was becoming increasingly testy because the exchange had failed to put in place the new audit system designed to guarantee the solvency of its members. Ontario had amended the Security Frauds Prevention Act in 1929 in order to empower the Toronto and Standard exchanges to compel their members submit to both regular and surprise audits. While the TSE had moved fairly quickly and completed its audit in July the other exchange dragged its feet. Early in October President Norman C. Urquhart tried to persuade Rogers that in view of 'depressed market conditions plans for the audit be proceeded with, but that the first audit be held up for the time being.' When the crash came a fortnight later, suspicion about the stability of some brokerages flourished, and eventually the government insisted that an audit be held on 30 November. Oscar Hudson and Company, the new exchange auditors, reported that they could not make a full examination, but each member was required to submit a recent balance sheet and to answer a questionnaire concerning securities on hand. At long last a formal audit system was set up with a panel of auditors responsible for every member.[21]

By that time, however, share prices had collapsed disastrously, and many investors were convinced that the brokers and the exchanges were to blame. On 7 November 1929 Floyd Chalmers, the youthful editor of the *Financial Post*, began a ten-week series in which he dilated upon the evils of the Standard exchange and its members (though prudently naming no names on account of the stringent libel laws). Like many before him, Chalmers quickly concluded that the intertwined practices of margin buying and short selling lay at the root of the problem. In 1926 the *Post* had recorded that three women had been overheard in a Toronto theatre discussing a shopping spree financed by the quick profits from a margin purchase of stock in a mining company about which they knew nothing. Over a year before the crash the attorney general's staff was trying to persuade Standard members that they ought to demand a minimum margin of 40 per cent; this would prevent shares selling under 40 cents from being margined and eliminate the 'young girls' who were gambling on penny shares. Some of the big brokers seemed disposed to agree, but Solloway, Mills, which was aggressively building up its business, refused to go along. When the break came, margin accounts were sold out wholsesale and investors often found themselves deep in debt.[22]

Equally serious, in Chalmers's view, were the concerns about the way in which brokerage houses handled their margin accounts. Charges had frequently been levelled that orders for penny stocks were not being executed but simply bucketed. Customers might receive fictitious confirmation slips recording a purchase, and in the few cases where companies were earning dividends they might even get payments. All accounts were charged 7.5 per cent interest on the balance of the loan (which was usually about two-thirds of the purchase price of mining shares in the 1920s but might range as high as four-fifths for prized customers). In reality, many orders were never executed. Since no bank would lend money to brokers on the security of such speculative stocks, the brokers simply bucketed most of these orders, confident that they could go into the market and buy the shares required in the unlikely event that the customer paid off the balance owing and demanded delivery. This method had two advantages for the brokers: their scarce capital was not tied up in share purchases and they were earning interest on loan balances which they had not had to borrow and thus paid no interest on. Even if they had to hand over small sums in dividends to deceive the customers, this business was highly profitable.

Though every brokerage's total position in a given stock fluctuated cease-lessly, Floyd Chalmers alleged that some firms normally had on hand as few as one-third of the shares carried on their books. When a stock was rising and clients were buying, this position might decline to as little as one-tenth of the required, leaving a huge short position, and when the price of a stock slipped, firms would build up their long positions. These brokers were encouraging purchases of certain shares on which they were simultaneously going short, thus profiting from their customers' losses. When these clients themselves tried to sell short, Standard exchange members often refused to accept such business, reserving it for themselves.[23] Since bucketing and wash trading were apparently so difficult to detect, Chalmers believed that only a royal commission with broad investigatory powers could ensure a real clean-up at the Standard, particularly in light of the fact that many smaller firms were said to be controlled by larger ones, so that only about twenty-five of the fifty members were truly independent. Asked about the possibility of such a wide-ranging inquiry one broker told the *Post* that he would rather quit the business than face such a probe.[24]

Ike Solloway was an obvious target. Publicly he insisted that the criticisms in the press were the work of rival firms at the Montreal and Toronto stock exchanges, jealous of his success in the mining business and eager to deflect attention from themselves in the aftermath of the crash. Yet the outcry showed no signs of abating. On 19 November A.W. Rogers of the attorney general's staff attended a meeting of the Standard board and reminded it that while the courts had never defined exactly how far a broker might go short, to fail to buy any of the stock ordered by a customer might be deemed to be evidence of an intention not to make delivery of the shares if required, a practice banned by the anti-bucketing section of the Criminal Code.[25]

While Chalmers kept up his campaign, Premier John Brownlee of Alberta wrote to his Ontario counterpart, Howard Ferguson, to enquire whether he intended to commence an investigation into the operations of the large Toronto-based brokerage. Solloway, Mills did a very large proportion of the oil-share trading on the Calgary Stock Exchange, and Brownlee's officials were convinced that there had been serious violations of the Security Frauds Prevention Act. The problem was that they had no way of verifying evidence about transactions occurring outside Alberta at other offices of the brokerage firm.[26]

This suggestion was by no means welcome to Attorney General William Price. On 29 October the Ferguson government had successfully secured re-election. Afterwards Price's officials reported just how serious was the situation at the Standard. He later tried to excuse his failure to intervene sooner: 'At this time the market had reached its highest, and it was impossible to try and curb a thing which no one in the province under any government or any Attorney General had tried to curb in fifty years. If we had started a year earlier, or two years earlier, we could have met with greater success.'[27]

Thirty years after the event Price was somewhat franker: 'What I figured was if I yelled a lot and told everybody about it, it would only do the situation more harm and what I should do is find out about it and keep it confidential.' Once it was clear that many of the leading firms on the exchange had indeed gone heavily short on stocks owned by their customers, Price 'called a representative of each of them up in my office at the Parliament Buildings. I told them ... that I knew without mentioning anything [in detail]. I said, "It is quite evident what I could do right now if I wanted to, [but] I don't think that's in the public interest. You've been slipping along because the world is slipping along at the present time. Now I'll tell you what I'll do with you. I'll give you 6 months to clean up, and then if you can clean up so that I get a good report on you I'll be governed by what I find out."'[28]

Price therefore tried to put Brownlee off by explaining in confidence that if there was any formal inquiry, not only would both stock exchanges in Toronto have to be examined, but that such an investigation was certain to alarm already skittish investors further. The result might be further steep falls in share prices, for there was no guarantee that the low point had been reached. Price's real fear, of course, was that if he moved against such big operators as Solloway, Mills he could trigger the virtual collapse of the Standard exchange in the face of a flood of unfillable selling orders. He therefore offered only to cooperate with Alberta in a private investigation of wrongdoing which might require evidence to be taken in Toronto following the seizure of the records of the Calgary branch of Solloway, Mills at the beginning of December.[29]

By Christmas time, however, the *Financial Post* was reporting rumours that backbench Conservative members in the Ontario legislature were pressing Price for more action, one of them having suffered considerable losses on his mining investments. The government was also embarrassed by the fact that a leading mining promoter, John E. Hammell, had launched a private campaign against the bucketing and short selling of shares in his Howey Gold Mines. He was convinced that there was a plot to drive down the value of the stock and demanded that the 'delousing machinery' be brought in. Early in January 1930 the provincial Opposition leader, Liberal W.E.N. Sinclair, added his voice to demands for an inquiry in order to calm the fears of the public.[30]

The attorney general could point to the fact that the Standard exchange had already begun to take some of the steps which he had demanded. In early December eight mining issues were dropped from the listings to the curb section because they no longer met requirements. At the same time a rule was passed banning margin trading by customers on shares valued under 60 cents. Yet the rule was not made retroactive, and customers were to be carried unless the price of their shares slipped below 25 cents, when they would either have to pay up or be sold out.[31]

Meanwhile, the Toronto Stock Exchange tried to keep its own skirts clean by reiterating its general prohibition on commission splitting with Standard members; the TSE board also cancelled a special agreement that did permit splits on trades in four interlisted issues which were dealt with on both exchanges.[32] This move angered some SSME members, particularly since the TSE was also witholding its ticker service from them as a sign of disapproval. Solloway, Mills even argued that the time had come for the Standard to compete directly by listing a number of high-grade stocks normally traded only on the Montreal and Toronto Stock Exchanges. The firm's large clientele guaranteed it frequent orders for industrials, which it was forced to pass on to members of the other exchanges to have executed but for which it received no income since the MSE and TSE had refused to endorse any general commission-splitting arrangements. Many of the smaller Standard houses, however, opposed any change because they relied heavily upon orders for mining stocks sent to them for execution by MSE and TSE members, on which they took one-half the regular commission and rebated the rest. In the end their wishes carried the day.[33]

Matters came to a head early in January 1930. Following the seizure of the records of the Calgary branch of his firm, Solloway held several meetings with Alberta officials. He claimed that he had been trying for several years to reform the brokerage business and that he welcomed the investigation. After a visit to Edmonton at the beginning of the year he believed that he had an understanding that he would be consulted once a report on the situation had been prepared. However, having uncovered abundant evidence that Solloway, Mills had persistently bucketed orders during 1929 and gone short against its clients, the Brownlee government screwed up its courage and issued warrants for the arrest of both Ike Solloway and Harvey Mills.

Solloway was shocked when the police came to arrest him in Vancouver for conspiracy to defraud while Mills was brought from Ontario to face similar charges. He told the press that the Alberta government was simply picking on the largest brokerage firm in Canada as a public-relations exercise and in doing so risking serious damage to the interests of thousands of investors. Privately, Price basically agreed with Solloway, grumbling that Brownlee was trying to grab all the credit for cleaning up the securities business: 'I had cooperated with them ... and given them a chance at the things I had [evidence of]. Do you know they arrested him before I had done anything on it? They arrested him as if they had done everything.' Solloway and Mills were swiftly released on bail pending a preliminary hearing in March. Despite fears that prices for oil stocks on the Calgary exchange would plunge, the market soon steadied and the firm was permitted to continue trading there.[34]

Price refused to take action despite mounting criticism from the press because he still feared a disastrous slump in prices on the Standard stock exchange. Its new president, F.J. Crawford, was believed to favour wide-ranging reforms but was rumoured to have been elected by only a 26-to-25 vote of the members, so that he lacked a strong mandate. In any event, Crawford was absent on holiday in Florida and refused to return to Toronto until the end of January, pleading illness in his family, despite a personal request from the attorney general that he make himself available at once.[35]

Matters came to a head, however, when the federal government revealed that it had discovered widespread bucketing and wash trading while auditing Toronto brokers for stock-transfer taxes. The brokers claimed that they had simply fallen behind in their remittances as a result of the volume of recent business, but Revenue Minister W.D. Euler demanded $300,000 in unpaid taxes on customer orders that had been confirmed but not actually executed, up to 70 per cent of total business in the case of one firm. He told the *Financial Post* that he was relying upon the province to take action to end such fraudulent practices.[36]

Finally, charges of conspiracy to defraud were laid in Ontario against William

J. Smart, who did business as Homer L. Gibson and Company. He was alleged to have collected $181,000 in interest on loans to margin customers when he had actually paid out only $8,500 for his borrowings. His clients had received $86,500 in dividends on shares for which the firm had received only $25,600, so that $60,900 of its own funds had been used to maintain the deception. Homer L. Gibson and Company had thereby secured access to about $4 million from margin clients to trade with for its own account.

Despite these revelations, Price still tried privately to convince his Alberta counterpart that the situation in Toronto was nothing like as bad as that in Calgary since short selling had been discovered but no bucketing of orders. He did admit that his main worry remained that a thorough clean-up might put a number of Standard members out of business. Since he believed that they had as many as 500,000 clients on their books (a wildly inflated estimate), he wondered how many prosecutions were advisable if these investors were to avoid huge losses.[37]

Meanwhile, an eerie calm settled over the Standard and share prices even rose a bit. Some brokers made efforts to cover their short positions; the rumour on the 'street,' however, was that they were only asking their weaker customers to pay up knowing that the forced selling following failure to meet margin calls would push prices down further. This would make it easier for the shorts to secure cheaper stock and fill orders from their stronger clients who were paying off their loans and demanding delivery. Confident that no further action by the government was imminent, most of the brokerage community continued with business as usual despite calls from the *Financial Post* for the creation of a royal commission or the laying of further charges. The only response by the exchange itself was to agree to the request of the attorney general that two highly respected accountants, Geoffrey Clarkson and George Edwards of Clarkson, Gordon, should undertake a comparison of its trading rules with those of the New York stock exchange with a view to making recommendations about amendments. At the same time the accountants were granted access to the recent member audits and clearing sheets. The Toronto Stock Exchange hastened to disassociate itself from the whole mess by issuing a statement declaring itself in 'entire sympathy' with the actions of the government; TSE rules, it was claimed, already forbade the practices complained of and a recent surprise audit of members had found everything in good order.[38]

Ever optimistic, the Standard brokers still hoped to avoid any radical reform. An internal committee was established to review recent clearing sheets and reported that it had found a number of suspicious trades which either had the same broker or the same price on both sides or used a third party, which might conceal a wash trade. Called before the board to explain these transactions, the members involved supplied a variety of unconvincing explanations. A.E. Butler and F.V. Collins both declared that they never instructed their floor traders to deal with anyone in particular, while W.L. Christie said his 'boy' didn't even know who was placing the orders he handled. L.J. Moore, J.C. Colling, and exchange directors Austin Campbell and Malcolm Stobie all insisted that orders that had crossed between the same buyer and seller were mere coincidences. The board accepted these feeble excuses but did immediately revise the by-laws to require that when a trade was 'put through' at an identical bid-and-ask price, the bell must be rung on the exchange floor and an announcement made so that if there were other higher or lower offers, other traders could intervene. The minimum price of a marginable share was also increased from 60 cents to $1 as of 1 February 1930.[39]

By then, however, the situation was spinning out of the exchange's control. The auditors had uncovered indications of widespread bucketing and short selling, which the authorities could no longer afford to ignore. At long last Price called in the head of the Ontario Provincial Police and told him to be ready to act on 30 January: '"Get in three or four of your men from other parts of the province. Don't tell them anything [about] what you're to do. Ask them to go to your house at 5 o'clock in the morning and you'll have warrants for a certain number of people." I told him the whole truth. That was done and representatives of ... five firms were arrested.' A dozen principals from the largest mining brokerages on the Standard were charged with conspiracy to defraud: altogether Solloway, Mills, Homer L. Gibson and Company, D.S. Paterson and Company, A.E. Moysey and Company, and Stobie, Forlong and Company held fourteen seats and accounted for three-quarters of trading on behalf of almost 40,000 customers. What was more, they were rumoured to control at least eleven other seat holders, giving them power over almost half of the fifty-one members.[40]

Ike Solloway was particularly outraged when he was charged a second time for the same kind of offences complained of in Calgary. He preferred to think of himself as a force for the reform of abuses in the brokerage business and concluded (rightly) that Attorney General Price had acted only because his hand had been forced. When he was returned to Toronto from Alberta for arraignment, Solloway recorded that he demanded a meeting with Price, who confessed, 'Yes, Solloway, I've got to. If I could have kept the brokerage situation out of politics I would have faced public opinion and eventually carried out my own policy, but now that these fellows in Alberta have made political capital out of the brokerage business I intend to prosecute.' The broker even insisted that the attorney general had expressed doubt about the likelihood of his conviction by the Ontario courts.[41]

The arrests of its leading members tipped the Standard exchange into a deep crisis from which it appeared impossible that it would ever emerge without severe damage. Stobie, Forlong and Company promptly declared bankruptcy and was suspended. Even more alarming, the attorney general's officials informed the exchange board on 30 January that the other four firms must also be suspended, cease trading, and withdraw from the floor, while all their securities, cash, and cheques were to be frozen indefinitely under the Security Frauds Prevention Act. Price took this step because he was convinced that the accused might simply dump all the shares they controlled on the market and start an irreversible downward price spiral or else abscond to the United States with whatever assets they could lay their hands on.

A.J. Trebilcock, the exchange's assistant secretary (who had replaced the disgraced J.J. Kingsmill the previous July), pleaded with A.W. Rogers that suspending these firms would make them unable to complete the day's clearings with other members, which would certainly have catapulted most of the rest into bankruptcy too. An approach to the attorney general himself was unavailing; he suggested that the exchange simply close for the next five days, but doing so would certainly have wrecked it. Eventually, exchange lawyer I.F. Hellmuth persuaded him to relent, and enough funds were released to auditor Geoffrey Clarkson to permit him to make the daily settlement, but Strachan Johnston, the lawyer acting for the government, insisted that not another dollar or another share would be forthcoming.[42]

Still facing disaster on the morning of Friday, 31 January, the Standard board fought back panic and decided to open for business as usual. Past president Norman Urquhart was chosen to plead with the government and succeeded in convincing Price and Rogers to meet that afternoon with the managers of the four offending houses still in operation, to see if they could arrive at an understanding that would permit them to resume trading. The government insisted that each firm sign an agreement providing that any securities and cash would be handed back to the firms only on condition that all spending be approved by the government's auditors, Clarkson and Edwards, with the aim of conserving assets for the benefit of customers and other creditors. Short interests were to be liquidated as rapidly as possible without disrupting the market unduly, and all future trading by these firms was placed on a cash basis. Partners and shareholders were to return all recent dividends or withdrawals except salaries. Once agreements had been signed, the four firms would be permitted to resume trading on the exchange.[43]

When the Standard board reconvened at eight o'clock in the evening of 31 January (with the president, F.J. Crawford, finally back from his holiday in Florida), there was a faint hope that the situation might be saved. The directors now recognized that they had no choice but to cooperate with the government if they were going to save their skins. It was admitted that the present situation had arisen because 'the way things had been run in the past had not been in the interests of the exchange.' The resignation of director Austin Campbell, one of those facing charges, was accepted to show good faith.

Representatives of the four suspended firms were then summoned to appear before a special confidential session of the board. D.S. Paterson complained, 'They had not camouflaged short trading as it had been done on other exchanges ... The government now insisted on their doing what they could have done themselves.' But he and the others agreed to cooperate and try to liquidate their short positions with as little disruption as possible, provided that other Standard members did not attempt to take advantage of them, since, in Paterson's words, 'If other members got the idea they must cover up their short position they might rush up the prices.' All four formally applied for reinstatement. President Crawford replied that the board was sympathetic, but felt that it must protect the other members against any future loss by securing a $25,000 bond from each of the houses. This was agreed to and auditor Clarkson was telephoned to approve the release of the necessary funds. With that done each exchange member was assessed $500 to raise a war chest, and the directors approved a press release before dragging themselves home to bed in the small hours.[44]

As soon as Geoffrey Clarkson signified his agreement, the four suspended firms provided their $25,000 deposits and resumed trading when the exchange opened for its regular Saturday morning session on 1 February.[45] There were fears that the news from Toronto might create dangerous instability on other Canadian stock exchanges. When it was learned in Calgary on 31 January that Solloway, Mills had been suspended by the Standard exchange, the firm agreed to cease operations there voluntarily, but after it was reinstated the following day, business resumed as usual. The Vancouver Stock Exchange had considered suspending Solloway, Mills in mid-January when the charges were first laid in Alberta, but had not acted on the urging of the Calgary Stock Exchange, whose president reported that the attorney general was eager to prevent any general liquidation with large losses for investors. Like the CSE, the VSE did suspend the firm on 30 January and considered closing the following Friday and Saturday until the situation stablized. In the end the Vancouver board decided to stay open and quickly reinstated Solloway, Mills when the firm was readmitted to the Standard.[46]

The situation in Winnipeg appeared even more dangerous because the bankrupt Stobie, Forlong and Company had an associated firm in the city (Stobie, Forlong, Mathews), which did a sizeable business there and was providing the financing for one local mining company as well as a number of BC properties. Winnipeg brokers were afraid that when the Stobie, Forlong office was closed a panic might ensue. The Standard exchange agreed to provide its ticker service to another Winnnipeg house so that investors could follow prices in the hope that doing so would dampen fears. Work at the mining properties was quickly closed down, but a run did not develop on the Winnipeg Stock Exchange as had been feared.[47]

When the Standard stock exchange reopened on Monday, 3 February, the situation seemed stable. Under the supervision of the auditors, brokers began the process of covering short positions, calling upon margin clients to put up more money or pay for shares and take delivery, but giving them a reasonable amount of time before selling them out if they failed to do so. Behind the scenes, however, the exchange had been shaken to its foundations. Its auditor, Holland Pettit of Oscar Hudson and Company, had been ordered to examine thirty-nine of the members and began to file reports which indicated that a number of them were teetering on the edge of bankruptcy. On the Monday six of the nineteen completed audits revealed serious deficiencies, and several members were told to secure additional capital, reduce their short positions, and refuse to take on any new accounts. By Wednesday, 5 February, twenty-eight audits were complete and a dozen firms were revealed to be on the brink of default, including the four against whom charges had been laid.[48]

The attorney general decided that new regulations were required to ensure stability, and the government auditors, Geoffrey Clarkson and George Edwards, were despatched to New York to examine the trading rules of the NYSE and the Curb, accompanied by past president Norman Urquhart of the SSME. Meanwhile, the exchange continued to function while all the members held their breath and hoped that a run would not develop among customers of any one firm which might topple the whole house of cards. In hopes of maintaining calm, Attorney General Price publicly declared that the worst was over. Meanwhile, he accepted a suggestion from Alberta premier Brownlee and set about organizing a conference of provincial representatives to discuss the regulation of exchanges and brokers, which was scheduled to meet in Toronto on 10 February.[49]

Gradually the situation seemed to improve. One Ottawa broker who had been in financial trouble reported to the Standard board, 'The run on his office had quieted down'; he had raised additional capital to bolster his position. At long last, considering the broader issues at stake, the chastened directors formally resolved that although short selling was not unethical in itself and could cushion market swings, brokers should not go short against their own customers. On the instructions of A.W. Rogers the exchange prepared a list of 'constructive suggestions' that could be laid before the provincial officials at their meeting, which was also to be attended by Crawford, Urquhart, and Vice-president G.W.

Nicholson, along with representatives of the Montreal, Toronto, and Vancouver exchanges and the official auditors of the two Ontario exchanges.[50]

All the provinces from Quebec westward were represented at the Toronto conference, which met at the provincial Parliament Buildings from 10 through 14 February. Reports were delivered by each provincial official, as well as by the auditors and exchange leaders. A number of recommendations were adopted unanimously. First of all, it was agreed that the Security Frauds Prevention Acts in force in Prince Edward Island, Ontario, and the three prairie provinces ought to be amended to ban the practice of brokers going short against customer orders. To do so would entitle clients to recover their funds or securities with interest. The provinces which to date had not enacted an SFPA were urged to pass a uniform statute (though Quebec's law would have to be framed somewhat differently because of the existence of the Civil Code).[51]

Officials complained that to date they had experienced 'great difficulty' in successfully prosecuting bucketing under the federal Criminal Code. In order to improve enforcement they drafted an amendment to section 231 identical in terms to the proposed amendment of the SFPAs. The hope was that by giving local Crown attorneys 'an opportunity to investigate complaints when made, there would be a greater opportunity of getting evidence for the laying of charges and their proof in the courts.' Such criminal prosecutions would then supersede offences under the provincial laws, though the right of customers to recover money or securities under the SFPAs would remain intact.[52]

The conference also returned to the long-standing problem of the division of jurisdiction over the incorporation of companies between Ottawa and the provinces. It was argued that blue-sky laws in western Canada had 'worked out very well so far as provincial companies were concerned but when the Dominion companies attacked the various acts in Manitoba and Saskatchewan the courts decided that these provincial acts were, in respect of Dominion companies, *ultra vires*. The result was that Dominion companies, without any provincial supervision, often sold spurious securities through [*sic*] the province.' After reviewing the intergovernmental discussions on this issue the official conference *Report* noted that while the SFPAs had worked 'reasonably well' since 1928, it was still desirable that Ottawa should make most federally chartered companies subject to provincial regulations concerning securities sales.[53]

Finally, the conference recommended that in provinces where stock exchanges existed there should be immediate discussions 'with the idea of having them put into force rules for improved trading methods.' Tightening of listing requirements (including disclosure about the number of vendor shares granted for properties and the existence of pooling agreements), banning of short selling against clients, firmer control of 'put through' trades, the keeping of better brokerage records, and the issuing of prompt confirmations showing the names of buyers and sellers and the time of the trade would cure many of the worst abuses that had been revealed by recent investigations. 'In addition, the board of each exchange was to be given full power to control the trading practices and business methods of its members and possess the power to suspend or expel any member who is unwilling or unable to comply with any financial or other requirement of the exchange.' To prevent the evasion of obligations to customers and exchanges, limited companies should no longer be permitted to hold memberships (as they were still allowed to do on most Canadian exchanges).[54] These rules 'should be placed before the stock exchanges with the suggestion that they are expected to adopt them where not already force.' To cope with any problems that might arise in future, each province should include in its SFPA 'ample power to make any regulations that may be necessary to deal with certain matters of trading on the various exchanges. Experience only will show the method of curbing certain abuses, and it is desirable that sufficient powers be given so that these things may be dealt with without the delays occasioned by further amendments to the act.'[55]

After five days of meetings the provincial delegates felt well satisfied with their achievements in devising new rules that would 'protect the investor and at the same time not interfere with practical methods of trading.' Their report concluded with the ritual reminder 'The development of mining and other natural resources of the country must always be kept in mind, and care must be taken in the remedying of abuses not to create others which would only stifle business and not advance the general interests of the public.' Attorney General Price expressed confidence that his own actions since late January had been salutary. However reluctant he had been to intervene, he now confided to his Alberta counterpart that taking control of both the Standard exchange and the offending brokers had prevented them from 'running riot.' He suggested that Alberta might demand similar powers over the Calgary exchange so as to stabilize oil-share markets if necessary. As for the conference, it had gone 'exceptionally well' and its recommendations were certain to be 'beneficial,' particularly if Ottawa could be persuaded to act on the requests made to it.[56]

The brokerage community, of course, was less thrilled with the new regime. Homer L. Gibson and Company complained to the SSME that some 'smart alecs' were trying to organize a shareholders' protective association and collect $20 from every customer of the firms accused of wrongdoing, the money to be used to finance an investigation. Over at the TSE some brokers wanted to profit from the travails of the Standard exchange by expanding the mining section to take over its business. The board decided unanimously that this was not an opportune time to put the matter before a general meeting of members. To deal with customer complaints that confirmations often carried unrealistic prices, at the end of February the SSME installed time clocks on its floor to stamp orders and permit the exact moment of a trade to be fixed, and the TSE followed suit a few days later.[57]

Worries about the financial condition of some Standard members persisted, and the twelve most troubled firms were required to file monthly statements with the exchange auditor. Investigators from the Ontario Provincial Police continued to poke through trading records. By the end of February, however, with the amendments to the Security Frauds Prevention Act being debated in the Ontario legislature, the attorney general discontinued supervision of the day-to-day operations of the four houses whose principals had been charged, and by early March the SSME board agreed to return their $25,000 bonds to them. The situation was stable enough that the bankruptcy of the member firm of Mowat and MacGillivray of Ottawa created little uproar.[58]

With their preliminary hearing in Calgary due to start in mid-March, Ike Solloway and Harvey Mills decided to sell two of their three seats on Standard stock exchange for $20,000 each.[59] There had been criticism in the eastern press about Alberta's decision to go ahead and lay charges against Solloway, Mills rather than leaving prosecution to the Ontario authorities, but Attorney General J.F. Lymburn insisted that in light of the evidence of misconduct discovered on the Calgary Stock Exchange, he had had no alternative but to act. When the preliminary hearing got under way, evidence was presented that between May and December 1929 the firm had frequently gone short. On 26 July 1929, for instance, clients were advised that 4,440 shares of Dallas stock had been bought and were charged commissions when no purchases had actually been made. Solloway, Mills employees defended their actions, arguing that it was common practice for oil and mining brokerages to go short and fill orders from house accounts when required, but Solloway and Mills were bound over for trial in June.[60]

By the end of March 1930 the board of the Standard stock exchange had approved sweeping amendments to its by-laws covering the matters discussed at the Inter-Provincial Conference, and a special general meeting was scheduled for early June to formally approve the changes.[61] Late in April both D.S. Paterson and Company and A.E. Moysey and Company created a small furor by advertising that they would once more accept margin business. Government auditor Geoffrey Clarkson demanded that all new margin accounts be segregated from other business, but the board decided simply to give its president discretion to permit members to take on new margin accounts provided that they had eliminated their short positions. This decision provoked an angry protest from Ike Solloway, who insisted that there were members of both the SSME and the TSE taking on speculative mining stocks on margin without possessing the required financial capacity to ride out a downturn. He claimed that the government had turned the problem over to the exchanges, which opened the way to favouritism. Nevertheless, the lifting of the ban on margin trading by Paterson and Moysey did not have the desired effect of increasing volume, which remained stuck at about 260,000 shares daily.[62]

A number of Standard members continued in serious financial difficulty in the spring of 1930. On 30 April H.S. Shannon and Company declared bankruptcy and was suspended, and three weeks later Fairlie and Company reported serious problems. The Fairlie firm was kept alive throughout the rest of the year at the request of the Attorney General's Department by a direct loan of $6,500 from the exchange itself (secured by a lien on Fairlie's seat) in the hope that a merger with some other member might permit a workout of its debts. In the end the effort was unsuccessful and the firm went into bankruptcy in November. H.P. Bellingham and Company, for which a similar rescue was attempted, finally folded in the late summer. Nevertheless, it appeared that the Standard had survived the worst of its travails. The point of maximum danger had come not at the time of the crash of 1929 but three months later. William Price could congratulate himself that his instinct to hush up the scandal at first had eventually allowed the exchange to survive while some of its worst abuses were finally being remedied.[63]

III

The Canadian financial community's attention was riveted on Calgary when the trial of Ike Solloway and Harvey Mills started on 2 June 1930. The prosecution put forward evidence showing that their firm had frequently carried a large short interest in various mining and oil shares and argued that there was fraudulent intent to make profits by speculating with customers' funds which were supposed to be used for purchases for their margin accounts. Witnesses for the defence responded that the firm had simply followed accepted practice since there were no rules against brokers going short or using the stock in margin accounts. In fact, it was claimed that this was the only prudent way to manage trading in speculative shares on which the banks refused to lend money. Attempts to liquidate large shareholdings in falling markets if margin customers failed to pay up might bankrupt a brokerage. There was no attempt to deceive and everybody knew what was going on. By maintaining short positions, Solloway, Mills had guaranteed that it would be a buyer if there were no others, taking up customers' stock and thus ensuring liquidity. One accountant argued, 'That is why I think there is some justification for this new method ... of financing which has sprung up among the Standard brokers. I do not believe it has been from any spirit of dishonesty on their part. It has been from a spirit of honesty and a desire to keep themselves financially sound.'[64] Mr Justice Ives (who admitted little prior knowledge of the stock-market) refused, however, to admit evidence that the defence had collected regarding exchange practices in other countries.

The two accused were found guilty of conspiracy to defraud and of bucketing. Solloway was fined $225,000 and sentenced to four months in jail, while Mills (who had largely retired from the brokerage business by the start of 1929) had to pay $25,000 and received a one-month term. Solloway, Mills and Company clearly had little future. As soon as the news of the convictions was received, the board of the Standard stock exchange voted its 'disapproval' of Solloway and Mills as directors or shareholders of the firm. Unless they were removed within a fortnight, the firm's membership in the exchange would be suspended. A few days later a new by-law was passed which gave the directors power to suspend or expel any member or partner convicted of crimes involving securities trading. Both the Calgary and Vancouver stock exchanges moved even more swiftly to suspend Solloway, Mills.[65]

Both men appealed their convictions, but Ike Solloway immediately announced his retirement from stockbroking: 'Speaking for myself I am through with business. I feel that our contribution to the development of Alberta's oil resources has been received somewhat ungratefully, and that a great many people in the West have not appreciated the assistance we have given in this regard.' The entire assets of Solloway, Mills were put up for sale. Though the number of branches and employees had been scaled back in the aftermath of the October 1929 crash, there were still 250 people working at head office and the twenty nationwide branches. Now just 50 key personnel were retained.[66]

The conviction of the two men strongly reinforced the belief of many investors that they had lost money in the stock-market crash because of misconduct and dishonesty by brokers. So many aggrieved people wrote to the attorney general of Ontario to complain that A.W. Rogers had to devise a form letter explaining that his staff had analysed all transactions on the Standard exchange for the week of 17 September 1929, but had found it very difficult to tell if particular orders had been bucketed without access to the books of the broker concerned. If the transaction complained of did show up in the exchange records, it was almost impossible to ascertain if there had been any improper dealing. Public opinion remained strongly hostile towards brokers.[67]

Solloway and Mills still had to face charges in Ontario. When the two men came to trial in Toronto in October 1930, their lawyer contended that the conspiracy to defraud charges should be nullified on the grounds of *autrefois convict* on the same evidence. Mr Justice Jeffrey studied the evidence in the Alberta trials and discovered that some of it had been supplied by the Ontario attorney general. He therefore suggested to the prosecution that the conspiracy charges be dropped and this was done, so that the men faced only charges of bucketing. Solloway and Mills agreed to plead guilty to those charges, expecting a small fine, and were shocked when the former was fined $200,000 and the latter $50,000.[68]

Solloway later claimed that the decision to plead guilty was taken because the appeal of their Alberta convictions was about to come on, and they wished to avoid the cost and effort of another full-scale trial in Toronto. The Ontario authorities were very concerned about this appeal since Attorney General Price considered Solloway's four-month sentence in Alberta extremely lenient, especially as the Ontario courts were about to hear the cases against the other mining brokers. In the end, however, Solloway and Mills withdrew their appeals and began serving their sentences at the pentitentiary in Lethbridge in mid-November.[69]

The trials of the other Toronto brokers led to convictions for two principals from each of the four firms. W.T.H. Shutt and James Hepplestone of A.E. Moysey and Company entered guilty pleas, so no trial was required. Malcolm Stobie and Charles Forlong of the bankrupt firm bearing their name, D.S. Paterson and Austin Campbell of D.S. Paterson and Company, and William Smart and Maurice Young of Homer L. Gibson and Company were all tried and found guilty of conspiracy to defraud and received jail sentences ranging between two and three years. These six appealed their convictions, but in the spring of 1931 the Ontario Court of Appeal unanimously confirmed both the admissibility of the evidence and the jury charges by Judge Jeffrey in each of the cases, and the men went off to begin serving their time.[70]

Clearly, none of these brokerages could operate successfully under their old names. Stobie, Forlong, which had ceased business as soon as the charges were laid, underwent a lengthy process of trying to realizing assets to pay off its creditors, its stock exchange seats being acquired by Doherty, Roadhouse and Company.[71] Paterson transferred all his accounts to others, closed his firm, and surrendered his exchange seat. A.E. Moysey and Company gave up its Standard seat soon after Solloway and Mills were first convicted, and its assets were eventually taken over by R.E. Jackson and Company, which traded through other brokers. Homer Gibson became Elwin and Company with an entirely new management, though by the end of the year it too had sold its exchange seats and gone out of business.[72]

Ontario attorney general Price remained sufficiently dismayed at the short sentences handed down to Solloway and Mills in comparison to the other brokers that he laid fifteen additional charges of unlawful conversion against the two men for having used client assets as their own. They were tried once more in Toronto in June 1931 and found not guilty. The British Columbia government also laid conspiracy charges against Solloway, which were eventually withdrawn on grounds of *autrefois convict*, but Solloway, Mills and Company was found guilty of fraudulent conversion and fined another $100,000.[73]

Ike Solloway remained unrepentant. When released from the pentitentiary in Lethbridge in the spring of 1931, he issued a 2,000-word statement contending that he had been 'persecuted' rather than 'prosecuted.' In the book that he published the following year to set forth his side of the story, Solloway insisted that Mr Justice Ives had not found him and Mills guilty of any criminal offence: 'He convicted us of employing the customs and usages that had been established in this country since Confederation ... I might have taken the same view myself had I been in his position. In those days public opinion was prejudiced against the brokers, and behind public opinion was all the power and prestige of the Alberta government and the press.'[74]

This air of injured innocence was hardly born out, however, by a series of revelations stemming from lawsuits concerning the collapse of Solloway, Mills and Company which dragged on over the next five or six years. In 1932 and 1933 two aggrieved former customers, D.B. Rochester and J.P. McLaughlin, obtained judgments of $162,000 and $65,000 respectively against the company for trading losses and damages. These cases revealed that there had actually been two separate Solloway, Mills companies, one incorporated in Ottawa and the other in Ontario, the federal company having taken over the assets of the brokerage partnership at the end of 1928. Solloway's defence against the suits was that the provincial company had been the firm with which clients dealt, the federal company being another customer of the brokerage, so that it could not be accused of trading against the clients' interests by going short on share purchases. This defence was flatly rejected since nobody, with the exception of a few employees, had even known of the existence of the Ontario company; it kept no separate books or bank accounts and was merely a phantom operation that was not even registered under Ontario's Security Frauds Prevention Act.[75]

These suits also revealed some distinctly shady aspects of Ike Solloway's management of the firm. He had acquired Mills's interest in their brokerage partnership at the end of 1928 for $500,000, money that he had obtained from Solloway, Mills and Company in exchange for 500,000 shares of McDermott Gold Mines. These McDermott shares (which ultimately proved worthless) had originally been acquired in 1927 at five cents apiece, and the courts held that Solloway's self-dealing was indefensible, improvident, and fraught with conflict of interest. The valuation placed upon the brokerage was also generous since the company's free capital on 31 January 1928 was a mere $6,000; shares on hand were worth only $2.3 million, whereas if all customer orders at that date had actually been executed, they would have totalled $13 million, a measure of the extent to which Solloway, Mills had gone short against its clients. By the end of 1929 there had been a deficit of working capital totalling nearly $350,000. Solloway still refused to concede any wrongdoing; at one point in the McLaughlin trial he became so annoyed by aggressive questioning that he threatened to punch the plaintiff's lawyer in the nose.[76]

The evidence also revealed that Ike Solloway had treated himself extremely generously. Just after the Alberta authorities began their investigations into the affairs of Solloway, Mills in December 1929, as the sole shareholder (except for a few qualifying shares held by other directors) Solloway declared a dividend of $30 per share, or $750,000, at a time when the company had only $6 million on hand, though $9.9 million was owed to customers. Another dividend of $35 per share, totalling $875,000, was paid out at the end of August 1930, which was even more controversial since it not only followed Solloway's conviction in Calgary but also seemed to contravene the agreement that he had signed with the Ontario government the previous January to preserve all the firm's assets for the benefit of customers and other creditors. Altogether he had drawn out some $2.5 million from the company in this period, $900,000 being advances taken from accumulated profits in house trading accounts at various branches, to which he had contributed no capital, along with huge sums for personal and travelling expenses. This despite the fact that up to the end of 1931 the firm showed an accumulated loss of $6 million on the brokerage business, though this figure was more than offset by an $8 million profit on the company's stock-trading account, earned by short selling.[77]

When the suits by Rochester and McLaughlin uncovered this information, it set the company's creditors abuzz. First in line was the government, which demanded $700,000 in unpaid personal income taxes. Solloway resisted in court but eventually settled for a one-time payment of only $100,000, which provoked angry comment in the press.[78] The federally incorporated Solloway, Mills and Company entered bankruptcy in March 1932, leaving accountant Geoffrey Clarkson to preside over its liquidation with assets of only $20,000. Rumours circulated among the creditors, unable to recover anything from the bankrupt firm, that large sums had been spirited out to Nassau in the Bahamas or were being held by nominees. Eventually a writ was issued in June 1934 for Solloway's arrest on further charges of misfeasance and fraudulent breach of trust, but the hearing was not held until a year later.

The court ordered O.E. Lennox, an assistant master of the Supreme Court of

Ontario, to undertaken a thorough analysis of Solloway's affairs. In February 1936 he confirmed that Solloway, Mills had financed itself by improperly using the money in margin accounts. In one four-day period the firm had gone short on at least four different companies to the tune of at least $1 million each rather than executing customers' orders. Lennox concluded, 'A very substantial part of the operations under consideration were nothing more than pretence.'[79]

On the basis of Lennox's findings, Ike Solloway was again arrested in June 1936 and charged with theft of $2.1 million from Solloway, Mills and Company. He was eventually found not guilty of the theft of the dividends and payments for McDermott Gold Mines shares in January 1938 after the jury had deliberated all night long. He was less successful in the civil actions, and in the spring of 1937 was ordered to pay over $3.3 million by Mr Justice Makins, who rejected the defence that all payments had been duly authorized by the company's board of directors. The judge noted that Solloway, Mills executed only 15 to 20 per cent of the orders received from customers, treating the remainder of the funds received as its own. Since the money belonged to the clients, not the company, there existed no right to pay it out to Solloway or anyone else. His appeal to the Ontario Supreme Court was unsuccessful, though it is unclear how much money the creditors received at the end of this long drawn-out process. Ike Solloway's claim that 'Solloway, Mills had no dummy or fictitious companies, no dummy or fictitious book-keeping' had certainly been exploded and his business reputation severely tarnished.[80]

Solloway became the focus of much of the criticism for the misconduct by the Canadian brokerage community, which many people blamed for the severity of the crash of 1929. What he had done, however, was no different from many others. When he decided to re-enter the brokerage business twenty years later, his lawyer, by now the chief justice of British Columbia, argued that brokers going short on speculative mining and oil stocks ordered by margin customers had then been 'a recognized general practice.' The Alberta government must have known that he was operating in this way, yet the attorney general had attended a testimonial dinner for Solloway only a few days before charges were laid. It was aroused public opinion, which blamed the crash, however mistakenly, upon the brokers, that forced the hand of the politicians and led to the arrests. At that time 'no suggestion of wrongdoing was made against Solloway other than of following the practice of the other brokers.' His misfortune (along with that of his fellow brokers, who, after all, served much longer jail sentences) was to pay the price of a sudden alteration in what was considered acceptable. The result was a speedy change in regulations which banned these long-standing customs.[81]

IV

The publicity surrounding the trials and convictions of the brokers who had once so thoroughly dominated Toronto's Standard stock exchange left it severely battered in reputation as well as wounded from the low volume of trading as a result of the economic downturn. In the fall of 1930 a general meeting of members was convened to discuss ways of improving the situation. The board did not escape criticism; D.J. Lorsch complained that the very act of convening such a meeting showed that the directors had 'acknowledged they were not capable of running the exchange.' Past president Norman Urquhart defended the board's performance in these awful times: 'Artificial measures to increase public interest would not help. Nature must be allowed to take its course and the renewal of public interest would come of its own accord. One reason for the lack of activity was the lack of new mines.'[82]

In the end the only concrete step taken was the hiring of a publicity manager in an effort to get more attention, as well as the decision to send round a list of the current members to other exchanges and financial institutions, making clear that the seats once held by the disgraced, such as Solloway, Mills and Stobie, Forlong, had been 'removed out of the names of the existing holders.' Meanwhile, trading remained so slow that the exchange tried to rent out three vacant rooms in its building to a golf school until the prospective tenant had second thoughts and backed out. It seemed impolitic to advertise heavily in the press at a time when the local papers were already full of stories about the trials of former members, though $2,000 was put up for an advertisement in a special issue of *Saturday Night.*[83]

A change in the by-laws that occurred as a result of the Inter-Provincial Conference in February 1930 provided that after year's end memberships in the SSME could be held only by individuals or partnerships and not by limited companies. The aim was to prevent brokers from sheltering their assets from claims by customers in the event of financial difficulties. As a result, six limited companies ceased to be members of the exchange; the Toronto Stock Exchange followed suit and changed its rules at the same time.[84]

Other Canadian stock exchanges did not face a much rosier outlook than the Standard in the fall of 1930, though the TSE could at least report that all its members had passed their annual audits successfully. In Montreal J. Pitblado and Company became the second MSE member to go into bankruptcy in less than a year with the expectation that creditors would get only 50 cents on the dollar. Quebec finally passed a Security Frauds Prevention Act, which required the exchanges to set up an system of twice-yearly audits for members, one at a fixed date, the other a surprise.[85]

Meanwhile, the exchanges in western Canada struggled along with sharply lower trading volumes. The president of the Winnipeg Stock Exchange bemoaned the loss of business at the 1931 annual meeting; about the only comfort he could draw was that Manitoba's new SFPA had given the exchange broad powers to grant registration to all brokers, members and non-members alike, and those who were refused would be required to post substantial bonds with the provincial Public Utilities Commission. This display of confidence by the government, he claimed, was a 'matter of pride' which would make the exchange stronger once good times finally returned.[86]

On the Calgary Stock Exchange, hard hit by the Solloway, Mills affair, trading fell from over 3 million shares in January 1930 to about 1 million by May, even though oil exploration in the province was continuing. By the time of the 1931 annual meeting only 86 of the 160 members were in good standing, and it was decided to confiscate the seats of all those in arrears on their dues by more than three months. At the same time the afternoon sessions of the exchange were cancelled because of lack of business.[87]

The Vancouver Stock Exchange closed its public gallery again for the summer of 1930 and established an indigent members fund. Several staff members were let go to save money since only about thirty-five of the fifty seat holders were actively trading. Seats, which had cost over $30,000 before the crash, were selling for under $6,000 less than a year later. In the fall of 1930 two members, R.P. Clark and Company and Branson, Brown and Company, defaulted on their obligations and were suspended. An investigation by the registrar of companies, H.G. Garrett, revealed that both firms had been using client funds for underwritings and share speculation. He argued, however, that since deceit or the intent to deceive was absent, these actions did not constitute fraud: 'Looked at from the criminal [law] standpoint I do not think there would be the slightest chance of convicting any of these brokers of criminal fraud.' Still, these failures hardly burnished the image of the exchange.[88]

After the ordeals of 1929–30 every segment of the brokerage community in Canada seemed to be in disarray. Even the relatively staid bond business was shaken by the collapse of G.A. Stimson and Company and the arrest of its three leading principals on charges of conspiracy to defraud. Founded in 1883 by the bursar of the University of Toronto (who handled that institution's investments), Stimson advertised as 'The Oldest Bond House in Canada,' claiming never to have marketed an issue that had failed to repay its interest and principal. But after Stimson died in 1919, the firm had been carried on by others and specialized in lower-grade issues than previously. In the late 1920s its president, F. Graham Johnston, became interested in real estate and undertook the construction of the Commerce and Transportation Building in Toronto and the Marine

Building, one of Vancouver's first skyscrapers. A flock of interrelated companies was established and stock sold supposedly to finance construction, but in reality each building was also mortgaged, though this fact was not disclosed to investors. After the stock-market crash, real estate values nosedived, and before long additional stock was sold in order to pay sales commissions and dividends. Eventually the Ontario authorities stepped in and laid charges.[89] Accountant Geoffrey Clarkson was called in as receiver and discovered that almost no assets remained to creditors and shareholders, who had put up several million dollars, since all the buildings were fully mortgaged. After a trial in June 1931 Johnston was sent to the pentitentiary for three years and his two principal associates for two and a half years each. At the annual meeting of the Investment Bankers Association of Canada that summer there was much hand wringing that 'legitimate and bona fide investment houses' might be 'made to suffer' as a result of Stimson's widely publicized claim to be the oldest bond firm in the country.[90]

Looking back over the year that had followed the stock-market crash of 1929, H.G. Garrett, who was now responsible for enforcing British Columbia's new Security Frauds Prevention Act, reflected that the blame for the disastrous events could not be confined just to a few sinners such as Ike Solloway: 'The severity of the crash was due not only to the unscrupulous methods of people like Solloway, Mills and Co., but also to the unprecedented desire of the public to gamble and to the inexperience of most firms engaged in the stock-broking business.' The machinery of the stock exchanges had not been adequate to control the problems which had mushroomed in a period when unheard-of profits had led to rapid expansion of the brokerage business. Investors had been none too particular when faced with the lure of easy money. 'The lesson,' thought Garrett, 'perhaps is that we must recognize that a desire to speculate is a human instinct which cannot be suppressed, and that a regulated stock exchange is better than a gaming house.'[91]

That lesson was a hard one to learn and even harder to keep in mind in the heat of a boom as everybody rushed to leap aboard the bandwagon. Investors had to swallow a bitter pill as share prices collapsed and margin accounts were sold out. The ten principals of Canada's largest mining brokerages were given plenty of time to reflect upon what they had learned in their cells at the penitentiary. By the beginning of 1931 the question was what the future held for Canada: was economic recovery finally just around the corner?

9

Into the Depths

The stock-market crash of 1929 and the arrest and conviction of many of Canada's leading mining brokers in 1930 seemed the sternest possible test that the financial community could be asked to face, but the next couple of years proved an even stiffer trial. The reputation of the brokerage fraternity had already sunk pretty low, since it was blamed for bringing about the crash by pooling, bear raiding, short selling, and bucketing. Yet with the economic depression worsening, share prices continued to slide, and in the autumn of 1931 an international economic crisis threatened to overturn the entire capitalist system when Britain left the gold standard and many currencies, including the Canadian dollar, were devalued. Terrified about what the future might hold, stock exchanges around the world considered closing up altogether, as they had done in 1914. In the end, however, they decided to soldier on rather than lose all their remaining credibility. Yet in Canada severe trading restrictions were imposed, including the reintroduction of minimum prices along the lines tried during the First World War.

Destroying the liquidity of the stock exchanges quickly undermined the financial stability of a number of brokerages and forced them into bankruptcy. Trading volume declined sharply, which cut into the commission income of the surviving firms. Not only that, but it also left them at the beck and call of their bankers, upon whom they depended for their brokers' loans and quickly exacerbated long-standing tensions between the banks and the brokers. Moreover, in late 1931 the federal government attempted to defend the value of the Canadian dollar by banning the purchase of foreign securities, a restriction that only hurt the brokers further.

Unfortunately for the securities business, times which had appeared so bad in 1930 and 1931 got no better during the next couple of years. What had seemed no more than a temporary market correction on the eve of a recession in 1930 had turned into a full-fledged disaster a couple of years later. While trading volume on the exchanges picked up sharply in 1933, it slumped equally quickly the following year and did not recover to previous levels until 1936. Mining stocks enjoyed a brief recovery in 1933 and 1934, but there, too, declines occurred in the following couple of years, and by late 1937 the index of mining-share prices was no higher than three years earlier. Brokers could do little but struggle to survive and wonder when their sufferings would finally end.

I

Salesmen are incurable optimists. Eighteen months after the crash of 1929 brokers and customers' men had convinced themselves that recovery was just around the corner. On Toronto's Standard Stock and Mining Exchange, for example, trading volume had fallen from 300 million shares valued at $710 million in 1929 to just over 90 million with a value of only $140 million in 1930 (see appendix, table A.7). Surely, felt the men on the 'street,' good news was overdue. Even Floyd Chalmers of the *Financial Post*, who had done so much to expose the abuses on the Standard in late 1929, underwent a change of heart. In February 1931 he and two members of his staff attended a meeting of the Standard board to discuss a series of articles about the exchange. Within a week the paper had switched from condemning the bad old days to cheerleading for this key mart now under responsible management. New rules, new fairness, meant new money could be raised to get on with the essential business of mining. And so forth.[1]

Unfortunately the market took no notice of this flackery as share prices continued to slide during the spring and summer of 1931. Then came news that shook the financial community to its very foundation: on Sunday, 20 September, Britain decided to leave the gold standard, and the value of the pound sterling against the dollar quickly declined by 25 per cent.[2] The news reached North America before the eastern exchanges opened on Monday, 21 September. With the London Stock Exchange closed for the next two days, the New York Stock Exchange discussed shutting up shop too, but rejected the idea, although short selling was banned to thwart any bear raids. Feverish board meetings in Toronto and Montreal led the exchanges to open for business, though with the closing prices from Saturday, 19 September, as minimums and a similar ban on short sales.[3] On Tuesday the minimum prices on interlisted issues that traded in New York were lifted, but dealing remained listless. The only spur to business was that many brokers began to make calls upon their margin customers anticipating further declines when the minimums were dropped. When these calls could not be answered, the clients were sold out.[4]

In the meantime everybody remained on tenterhooks, wondering if there was even worse to come. In this situation Canada's chartered banks assumed a role of central importance, since they were the major source of brokers' loans, which firms relied upon to carry their margin clients. At the end of September W.E.J. Luther, chairman of the Montreal Stock Exchange, was called in by Beaudry Leman, president of the Canadian Bankers Association, and told in no uncertain terms that the exchanges should maintain the system of minimum prices. If they did so, the banks would continue to value securities pledged as collateral for brokers' loans at the pegs and not demand repayment. The Montreal and Toronto exchanges quickly accepted this ultimatum.[5]

On the Standard exchange, however, many members wished to end the minimums and return to business as usual in the hopes of reviving trading and raising commission income. These dissidents were quickly brought to heel when the Bank of Commerce called a Standard member's loan, valuing the shares pledged as collateral at less than the minimums. The CBA's Toronto vice-president blandly declared that while his members would continue to grant loans equal to half the minimum values on most stocks, they retained the right to exercise discretion in dealing with individual borrowers. The Standard's short-lived rebellion quickly fizzled out.[6]

The CBA's high-handed action revived the simmering resentment that brokers already felt towards bankers. This had surfaced earlier in the summer of 1931 when the federal government launched a refunding campaign to replace its wartime Victory bonds with a new conversion loan. The bond houses in the Investment Bankers Association of Canada grumbled that the banks were relying upon their nationwide network of 4,000 branches to compete unfairly in selling to the public, a complaint that had been heard intermittently throughout the 1920s. Stories of bank managers using their knowledge of customers to secure sales or refusing to approve bond purchases through brokers flooded in to the *Financial Post*. With the depressed state of the securities business the sight of $3 million in commissions being snapped up largely by others was too much for IBAC members to bear, though few dared criticize openly since they too depended upon their lines of credit with the banks. At the same time there were criticisms of the increasing involvement of the banks in securities underwriting, which created so many problems in the United States that a complete divorce of commercial and investment banking would be imposed by the 1933 Glass-Steagall Act.[7]

The vulnerability of the Canadian financial system became all too painfully evident as the aftershocks of Britain's departure from the gold standard reverberated around the globe. On 5 October McDougall and Cowans, believed to be the largest brokerage house in the country, announced its suspension. Another long-established member of the Montreal Stock Exchange, Greenshields and Company, immediately followed it into receivership. Both firms, it turned out, had been borrowing from New England financial institutions because American interest rates were only 4.5 per cent as against 6 per cent charged by Canadian banks. But the British move sparked a 10 per cent decline in the value of the Canadian dollar, and panicky American lenders demanded additional collateral. With the Canadian exchanges virtually paralysed by the imposition of minimum prices, the brokers could not secure the required funds and turned to their Canadian bankers for help.

When the CBA first learned of these problems, a meeting was hastily arranged with Prime Minister R.B. Bennett on 4 October at which the government was urged to intervene but declined to act. The following day the CBA met again and concluded that the only way to save the two firms would be to shut down the stock exchanges altogether. In the end the bankers concluded this would be 'too great a blow to Canadian credit.' Both McDougall and Greenshields were forced to suspend, which immediately brought down a smaller Montreal house, Watson and Chambers. With the Royal Bank (which was closely linked to McDougall and Cowans) suffering withdrawals of $10 million and facing a potential run, Bennett called in newsmen on 6 October to try to bolster confidence by telling them that the banks 'had protected themselves as far as brokerage houses were concerned and had ruthlessly kept a margin on all broker loans. At the present time Canadian banks, therefore, were not to be considered shaky but under some circumstances the situation might become very menacing.'[8]

As the receivers picked through the wreckage, they discovered that together the three brokerage firms owed their secured creditors $19,425,000 and their 4,366 clients $5,700,000 in unpaid balances. McDougall and Cowans, which had had a net worth of $50 million at the top of the bull market in 1928–9, had been bleeding steadily as share prices declined through 1930 and 1931. Customers were heavily invested in such Canadian blue chips as International Nickel, Brazilian Traction, Montreal Light, Heat and Power, and Dominion Bridge. In an effort to stem share-price declines the firm had bought back stock from disillusioned customers. At the same time holders of margin accounts who could not put up more funds received more credit rather than being sold out for fear that prices would only slide further. Customers, whose credit balances averaged $1,850 each, discovered that a single person owed as much as $600,000 to the firm, while partners and employees were reputed to be heavily indebted as well.[9]

These failures in Montreal set off a ripple of brokerage collapses across the country. On the Montreal Curb Market W.H. Magill and Beaulieu and Duncan went bankrupt, while on the Standard exchange Millyard and Company failed.

The long-established firm of J.M. Robinson and Sons in Saint John, New Brunswick, closed its doors to reorganize, and Royal Financial Corporation, a municipal bond house with headquarters in Vancouver, also disappeared. E.J. Bawlf and Company, the old-time grain and stock brokers in Winnipeg that had acted as correspondent for one of the Montreal casualties, had to be liquidated. The Calgary Stock Exchange came near to complete collapse after Bawlf's local branch closed; during the next month three other Calgary firms went bankrupt, and by the end of 1931 forty-three exchange memberships had had to be cancelled.[10]

Members of the Toronto Stock Exchange appeared to have escaped unscathed. Publicly, their survival was attributed to the rigorous system of periodic audits instituted in 1929, though (as chapter 10 shows) it really owed more to the willingness of auditors and bankers to turn a blind eye to problems. In an effort to revive trading the TSE board decided on 13 October to lift the price pegs on all issues trading under $3, a move that was promptly copied in Montreal. The Standard stock exchange also lifted its minimums on a couple of gold-producing mines and within a week or so had added about twenty of its sounder issues to the list. The president was given discretion to unpeg any stock, and on 17 October he freed all those trading under 25 cents. At the same time he announced that short selling would resume on all unpegged issues on 26 October. The Canadian Bankers Association ignored these minor acts of defiance, perhaps because its members realized that they too might have a good deal to lose from another round of brokerage failures.[11]

Gradually the brokerage business recovered some semblance of stability. By early November the receivers for both the McDougall and Greenshields firms had announced reorganization plans. The former was restructured, with secured creditors receiving one share for every $100 of debts and 60 per cent of future profits going to pay them off. This arrangement was approved by over three-quarters of the creditors, representing 99 per cent of total debt. Once it was approved by the courts, the receivership ended, and on 21 March 1932 McDougall reopened and was readmitted to the Montreal Stock Exchange.[12]

After some wrangling a similar plan was approved for Greenshields and Company by which secured creditors would receive debentures entitling them to 60 per cent of the profits of the revived brokerage with the aim of repayment by 1939. This plan was also approved by the courts. The smaller firm of Watson and Chambers was wound up because the trustees believed that about 70 per cent of its debts could be paid by liquidating its securities. Unfortunately, further falls in share prices reduced the sums realized, but by the summer of 1932 two instalments had returned 25 cents on the dollar to the secured creditors.[13]

Meanwhile, the brokerage community struggled to restore its business. The

Montreal Curb Market dropped a number of minimum prices on 26 October, and the Standard abolished all pegging on 4 November. The members of the Toronto Stock Exchange were also keen on ending the restrictions as they watched what business there was slipping off the floor and into the 'street.' Late in October, for instance, President G.C. Mitchell suggested to his Montreal counterpart that the peg on Goodyear Tire preferred be dropped, since 'failure to do so is likely to give street brokers an opportunity of dealing in the stock below the pegged price.' Only strenuous efforts by bankers and brokers prevented over-the-counter trading in unlisted stocks from expanding further.[14]

The Torontonians were convinced that keeping the minimums simply undermined the confidence of investors and made them think that pegged shares had hidden weaknesses. As a result the TSE board moved steadily to drop as many pegs as possible, and by the third week of November minimum prices remained in force on only seventy-eight issues. Of these, twenty-two had their primary markets elsewhere (mainly in Montreal, so that action must come from the MSE), while nine were interlisted with other exchanges that still had pegs. Banks and other financial institutions accounted for another seventeen because the Canadian Bankers Association, spooked by the run on the Royal when McDougall and Cowans had failed, was strongly in favour of keeping these minimums to prevent price declines from undermining confidence in the banking system. Because of the banks' hold over the brokerage community the exchanges did not dare to defy the CBA's wishes. That left only thirty issues traded mainly in Toronto for the TSE to act on, and by the end of the month another twenty-one pegs had been lifted.[15]

While the Torontonians hoped to see all the minimums ended by the New Year, the Montreal Stock Exchange, where most blue-chip industrials and banks had their main markets in Canada, remained much more skittish in the aftermath of the brokerage failures there. In mid-December MSE members held a general meeting and voted to maintain the pegs for the time being. All that they would agree to was the formation of a committee to consider each security and see whether prices might be unpegged at some future date. Late in December the minimums were lifted on a number of inactive issues and the pegs on some other stocks revised downward. The MSE refused to go further, however, despite warnings from the *Financial Post* that price-fixing only served as a warning to sophisticated investors that shares were due for a further sharp decline, while the unsophisticated were being lured into margin purchases of pegged stocks on the assumption that there were no downside risks. The paper claimed that by timidly clinging to the pegs while New York had refused to abandon unrestricted trading and even allowed short selling to resume before long, the Canadian exchanges had pushed good stocks to pegged levels or else driven dealers out onto the 'street.' Exchange members were running up heavy losses as commission income had evaporated, with 1931 volume on the MSE running at one-third of the previous year's level.[16]

In addition, the brokerage community found itself engulfed by other waves from the international financial crisis. Since September the Canadian dollar had traded at a sharp discount to the U.S. dollar. With Canada facing interest and principal payments of $260 million in New York during 1932, the federal government became extremely concerned about the additional burden imposed by the adverse exchange rate. Prime Minister Bennett was convinced that downward pressure on the Canadian dollar was being exerted by purchases of foreign securities. On 16 December 1931 he summoned the executive of the Canadian Bankers Association to a meeting in Ottawa and ordered them to do everything in their power, directly or indirectly, to prevent Canadians from buying U.S. dollars for such purposes. The prime minister bluntly added that he expected full cooperation from the financial community without the necessity of the government taking formal steps to enforce such an embargo.[17]

This message was promptly passed on to the stock exchanges by the CBA, and the beleaguered brokers were faced with the need to tell clients that they could not purchase American securities even if they wished to do so. The TSE board tried to shift the onus for enforcement onto the CBA by asking that the banks require all purchasers of foreign exchange to fill out declarations stating their reasons. The CBA, however, preferred others to do its dirty work; the president insisted that he would rather see verbal commitments than signed declarations.[18]

The embargo on foreign securities purchases sparked a lively debate. Those with long memories harked back to a similar effort by Ottawa in 1920, which had engendered much ill feeling (see chapter 5 above). Others argued that the flight of capital from Canada was myth and that there was a good deal of evidence that U.S. buyers had been purchasing more Canadian securities in recent months than vice versa. Without this flow of funds the Canadian dollar might have fallen even lower. There were plenty of ways to get around a voluntary ban, and stories were soon circulating that while large brokerages might be playing by the government's rules, there were cash-starved smaller firms and individuals who had no scruples about turning a profit by bootlegging American securities into Canada.[19]

By mid-January the CBA tacitly admitted that both the rationale for and the implementation of the embargo were decidedly shaky; President J.A. McLeod approached Prime Minister Bennett and persuaded him to relax the outright ban on purchases of foreign securities. In return the bankers promised to discourage the use of foreign exchange for these purposes and to ask the brokerage community to do likewise until the exchange rate on the Canadian dollar improved. The federal government retreated to simply monitoring the situation by requiring the stock exchanges to submit fortnightly statements concerning purchases of American and other foreign securities.[20]

While this skirmish was playing itself out, brokers continued to struggle with the problem of how and when to lift the remaining pegs on share prices. Dissident members of the Montreal Stock Exchange sought advice from their lawyers as to whether the board even had the power to fix minimum prices. While the pegs were perhaps a defensible response to an emergency such as that in September 1931, it was argued that any by-law had to be reasonable in the light of the purposes for which the exchange was established. The prohibition on trading below the minimums had now extended for over three months and was preventing members from operating as intended. Volume was down sharply, listed stocks were being widely traded off the floor, and brokers were unable to protect themselves by selling out margin clients who failed to meet calls. The legal opinion declared that there was a good chance that the continuation of the minimum prices could be successfully challenged in court.[21]

Even more important was the changing attitude of the Canadian Bankers Association, whose members had finally been compelled to accept that the current minimum prices, even on bank stocks, were becoming increasingly artificial. On 30 December CBA president J.A. McLeod had agreed that the pegs on all bank shares could be cut by $10 provided that the MSE and the TSE gave no publicity to the cuts. Anyone expressing interested in buying bank shares could quietly be accommodated at any price above the new minimum, though this effort to conceal the dismantling of the pegs on bank stocks predictably proved futile.[22]

The move seemed to break the logjam, and the Montreal Stock Exchange soon announced the unpegging of all shares trading between $3 and $5 and in mid-January dropped the minimums for 24 additional issues. After two further lots were unpegged, 131 of the 212 stocks traded on the MSE had been freed, including 14 interlisted stocks that had never been pegged. Of the remaining 81 issues, 19 had had their minimums revised downward; but critics complained that the 62 stocks whose pegs were unchanged included such local standbys as Montreal Light, Heat and Power, Shawinigan Power, Quebec Power, Bell Telephone, Power Corporation, Price Brothers, National Breweries, Dominion Bridge, and Steel Company of Canada.[23]

By mid-February the Montreal Curb Market had moved to end almost all its pegs and even permitted short selling on some stocks. The minimums were increasingly being ignored; company managers were becoming convinced that they were fruitless. Opponents of pegging forced a vote of confidence on the

MSE's president and board of directors; their policies were sustained on a secret ballot but the process of ending the minimums continued.[24]

A month later the eastern district of the Investment Bankers Association warned that it would advise the MSE that its members no longer felt obliged to adhere to the minimum prices. The problem was that the Canadian Bankers Association remained adamant that bank shares should not be unpegged even though street brokers were quoting prices of between $8 and $15 below the pegs. The MSE remained unwilling to take the plunge and free the prices of the six major banks and a dozen popular blue-chip industrials without the CBA's consent.[25]

The board of the Montreal Curb Market forced the issue in early April by announcing plans to thwart the 'very active' street market that had developed in all the pegged stocks by amending its rules to lift the ban on MSE-listed issues trading on the Curb; the other exchange raised no objection. Faced with competition not only from the street traders but also from the Montreal Curb, the TSE decided to drop all remaining pegs to protect its share of the market. Still the CBA resisted, agreeing to cuts in the minimum prices on bank shares but refusing to drop them altogether.[26]

By the beginning on May the writing was on the wall: nobody, whether exchange members or not, was paying the slightest attention to the minimums any longer. The MSE announced its intention to drop most of the remaining pegs on industrials. After further cuts in their minimums, the CBA finally agreed to allow bank stocks to trade freely beginning on 18 May. The TSE lifted its few remaining minimums at the end of the month, with Canadian Canners and George Weston Bakeries sharing the dubious honour of being unpegged last. By that time only a handful of stocks such as Ottawa Power, Ogilvie Milling, and Price Brothers remained pegged on the MSE. The exchange board argued that these were 'inactive' stocks, a claim which the *Financial Post* scornfully dismissed on the grounds that trading in these issues was dormant only because they were still pegged. Before long the last pegs were finally dropped.[27]

Looking back on the experiment with minimum prices which had begun when Britain left the gold standard in September 1931, the *Post* concluded that the whole effort to recreate the kind of controls imposed during the First World War had been a disastrous error. Why did sound stocks need protection from market forces? The sole result had been to create uncertainty and apprehension in the minds of investors, which helped to depress prices further. If the stock exchanges in Toronto and Montreal wished to bolster their positions as the country's primary share markets, they should never contemplate such a move again. As though it were an omen, the paper reported the following week that W.E.J. Luther, who had just retired after leading the MSE through these grave difficulties, had died suddenly. His brokerage firm, Craig, Luther and Company, immediately collapsed into bankruptcy.[28]

II

The impact of the depression upon the brokerage community can be measured in a variety of ways. By the 1930s the government of Canada was producing a range of statistics that served as guides to the extent of the decline in the price of an average share of stock during the early 1930s and the excruciating slowness of the recovery that followed. In addition, the stock exchanges in both Montreal and Toronto compiled their own statistics on the volume and types of trading that occurred. These figures show the fall in the level of business to which brokers had to adapt as they watched their commission income ebb away in the early 1930s and only very gradually creep upward again later in the decade.

Not only was the economic crisis severe and long-lasting, but brokers still had to contend with a widespread lack of confidence among customers. Investors were so thoroughly alarmed by the crash and its painful aftermath that some of them came to believe that securities markets would never again attain the prices and trading volume reached in the late 1920s. Thus even when there were stock-market rallies, these were quickly snuffed out by bad news or a lack of momentum to make gains permanent. As a result, recovery from the declines suffered between 1929 and 1932 proved painfully slow.

Since 1913 the Dominion Bureau of Statistics had been compiling monthly index numbers based upon the selling price of a small basket of common stocks. In 1926 the size of the sample had been expanded to over one hundred Canadian industrials, utilities, banks, and companies operating abroad, and the historical data recalculated on a base of 1926 equalling 100 (see appendix, chart A.1). At the height of the boom in September 1929 the index had reached 217, so that the price of an average share had more than doubled in just over three years. No wonder investors were flocking to put their money into the stock-market and stretching their margin borrowing to the limit in many cases.

Thereafter, however, share prices began a long, melancholy slide. Within a few weeks the crash had reduced this index by one-quarter of its value, and it hovered around 155 from November 1929 through the following spring. When markets rebounded slightly in April 1930 optimists predicted that the painful correction was over and a recovery was due. Instead values started to slip rapidly once more, and by the end of the year the index registered just over 100, wiping out almost the entire rise registered during the boom years. Yet even that figure turned out to be just the first dose of bad news. After stabilizing in the early months of 1931, prices again started downward. Britain's departure from the gold standard in September sparked a sharp new decline. Though the imposition of minimum share prices by the stock exchanges eventually helped to steady the index at around 64 until the spring of 1932, the removal of these controls quickly led to the erosion of these artificial values. By June 1932 the index had hit its all-time low of 43.

A slight improvement near the end of that year carried the figure up around 50, where it hovered into the spring of 1933 before a steady advance began which took it to over 80 by September. After a slight fall back near the end of the year, the index rose to near 90 in the spring of 1934 as markets rallied with the inauguration of President Franklin Roosevelt in the United States. But those gains did not continue, and the figure lingered in the mid-80s into the spring of 1935. Only then did some improvement in the economic situation bring about another boost, which pushed the number up over 120 in February 1936. Still the bears outnumbered the bulls in the spring of that year, so the index slid backward again before resuming its slow climb in the fall, which carried it over 140 by February 1937; it finally reached the level of the spring of 1930 after seven lean years.

Traders and dealers in mining stocks, who, of course, played such an important role in Canadian securities markets, experienced an equally bumpy ride through the early 1930s. For those who chose to buy and sell unlisted mining shares, there are no measures of the general trend of prices. Typically a mining issue would appear, be nursed along by propaganda from its promoter, and seek to attract buyers on the basis of well-crafted rumours about discoveries, and if successful, it would rise from pennies a share to more substantial value. If there was a sizeable discovery, the company might be transformed into a dividend-paying worthy; more often the value of such securities dwindled away as their backers lost interest and moved on to another range of hills where metals glimmered. The more responsible promoter might consolidate an old share issue with a newer one and carry his shareholders along, while the fly-by-nighters simply decamped with the money. This process had gone on in good times and in bad, but with many share buyers lacking confidence or money (or both) during the early 1930s business languished. Not until 1933 and again in 1934, when the United States raised the price of gold from $20 to $35 per ounce, did mining stocks recover some of their pre-crash lustre.

Since 1927 the Dominion Bureau of Statistics had calculated an index number (1926=100) based upon the price of seventeen stocks of producing or about-to-produce mines (see appendix, figure A.2). By the time of the crash of 1929 the index had already dropped back into the 90s, and it touched 60 by the end of 1930 despite a brief upward flurry in the spring. There was some up-and-down movement the following year, but by the end of 1931 the index was again lodged at 60 before begining a downward path that carried it below 50 in mid-1932. A year later mining-share prices finally began to improve enough to carry the index up over 100 again and keep it there. The rise in gold prices helped to push it up to 140 in the summer of 1934 before it slipped off again. In 1935 it lingered between 115 and 135, but the following year it moved up steadily before sliding down to 130 again in the 1937 recession.

A similar kind of up-and-down fluctuation was evident on Toronto's Standard Stock and Mining Exchange, which remained the country's leading mining-share market. In 1929 trading volume passed 300 million shares before a precipitous decline to just 90 million the following year. After a modest recovery in 1931 came another crunch the next year, when fewer than 80 million shares were handled. Volume revived to over 250 million shares in 1933. Early in 1934 the Standard merged to become the mining section of the TSE with another healthy increase in volume, largely as a result of a boom in gold stocks, but the following year fewer than half as many shares were handled. During the remainder of the 1930s the prices of mining shares drifted sideways, leaving mining brokers scrambling for business. (See appendix, tables A.6 and A.7.)

The index numbers for share prices show why investors remained discouraged during the 1930s. At the time of the crash the Montreal Stock Exchange was the country's major market for blue-chip shares, with about 7 million industrials changing hands in both 1928 and 1929. Total volume in those years was 20.5 million and 25.7 million respectively, and large amounts of utility and mining stock also traded. In 1930 volume dropped to 15.6 million (about one-fifth being industrials), but in the following two years there was another plunge to just 5.3 million shares and then to a mere 2.9 million in 1932, about the same level as in 1924. Only utility stocks continued to trade in anything like their pre-crash volume. Once the low point of the Depression was passed, there was a healthy rebound in total volume to almost 7.7 million shares in 1933, but this level was not sustained as just over 4.5 million shares changed hands in both 1934 and 1935. At the same time bond sales, which had once accounted for a sizeable volume of business, dwindled into insignificance as a source of commissions. By 1936 total volume had reached only about 9 million shares, less than in 1927. (See appendix, table A.1.)

The Montreal Curb Market, created in 1926 by MSE members to handle less-seasoned and unlisted issues, continued to trade over 5 million shares annually after the crash, a large proportion being mining shares. When the market for mining shares revived in 1933, the Curb's volume shot up rapidly, but it fell back again in 1935 before another big increase the following year. Most of the issues traded there, however, were penny stocks that earned only meagre commissions for brokers. (See appendix, table A.2.)

The Toronto Stock Exchange did not handle anything like the trading in industrials done on the Montreal Stock Exchange, never surpassing a volume of 4 million such shares annually during the 1920s and falling to a low of just 1,250,000 in 1932. After an upsurge to over 6 million industrials in 1933 the TSE dropped back again. Only electrical utility stocks showed themselves fairly steady traders, except in 1932 and 1934. Throughout the 1920s mining shares had become increasingly important in Toronto, and after the crash junior mines continued to account for a sizeable proportion of business despite the competition from the Standard stock exchange, though volume dropped to just 640,000 mining shares in 1932. Oil stocks also became significant in the mid-1930s. Bond trading, which had begun to shrink in the late 1920s, dwindled away and disappeared altogether by 1933. Business on the TSE's unlisted section (sometimes called the Toronto Curb) was always much smaller than on the Montreal Curb Market, especially after an agreement between the TSE and the Standard stock exchange ended all trading in mining shares on the Toronto Curb early in 1932. (See appendix, tables A.3, A.5.)

Thus the brokerage business was in dire straits during the Depression, particularly after Britain left the gold standard in September 1931. The low point came in mid-1932, when the indices of share prices even fell below levels reached in the post-war recession of 1921. Trading volume on the stock exchanges also plummeted to pitiful lows compared to the pre-crash period. Though a boom in mining stocks helped to bring slightly better times in 1933 and 1934, recovery proved painfully slow. No wonder many brokers were forced to give up the game, squeezed inexorably by their creditors' demands and the stubborn slowness of the economy to emerge from the depths of depression.

10

The Ordeal of F.H. Deacon

Why was the brokerage community in Canda so severely wounded by the depression of the early 1930s? Theoretically, brokers simply executed orders to buy and sell securities. True, the serious decline in the volume of trading cut deeply into commission income and necessitated the letting go of many of the customers' men and clerks hired to handle the volume of business before the crash. Beyond this, however, could most firms not have weathered the storm without undue hardship? In practice, of course, the situation was much more complex and difficult. First of all, there was the matter of margin business: as share prices collapsed many account holders saw their equity vanishing and were unable to put up the additional cash required. Brokers faced the dilemma of whether to sell off these shares while they could (though at the risk of driving prices still lower) or of living with the situation in hopes that the dip was only temporary and that good times would soon come back. But prosperity fled in 1929 and showed no signs of returning after several years; yet the banks, which had supplied the brokers with the funds lent to their customers, still had to be paid off. The bankers might be prepared to wait for a while, but could not be put off indefinitely, so brokers found themselves ground between the inability (or unwillingness) of their customers to make things right and the banks' implacable determination to collect what was owed them.

Ironically, the gleams of renewed fortune that flashed when share prices did turn upward briefly in 1933 and 1937 actually made the plight of many brokers worse. If customers did re-enter the market, many of them still wanted to buy on margin to leverage their gains. Suddenly the brokers were faced with the need to approach their bankers and ask them to open the vaults once more. When requested to extend larger loans to struggling brokers to permit them to expand their margin business, however, most bankers were unenthusiastic if not downright hostile.

Equally serious was the fact that many brokers did much more than an agency business, buying and selling securities for others. They traded on their own account; they had inventories of stocks and bonds which also had to be financed by loans; they underwrote and promoted share issues for which they had made commitments. All of these activities required capital, most of which had also been borrowed from the banks, but debts were very hard to meet when share prices became so depressed and buyers so demoralized. In order to keep a flood of red ink off their own books, the banks did not call most of their brokers' loans and precipitate carnage in the securities industry. Many brokers survived to fight another day, but only because of the forbearance of their bankers, who calculated that there was less to lose from nursing the invalids along than from summarily putting them out of their misery and into bankruptcy. Moreover, it was far from clear where any funds recovered could be more profitably reinvested in the desperate times of the early 1930s; better to treat all but the worst basket cases leniently in the hope of eventual recovery.

Thus as a result of shared self-interest the brokerage business survived the 1930s as a kind of tottering lean-to propped against the wall of the bankers' own none too stable mansion. In theory, this should not have occurred. Beginning in 1929 Ontario had required all stock exchange members to undergo periodic audits to determine their solvency and to ensure that brokerage clients would not suffer losses in the event of a firm getting into difficulties; Quebec had imposed similar regulations in 1931. The problem was by that time most brokers would have been insolvent if their securities had been valued at current market prices and their customers sold out for whatever their holdings would bring. Thus bankers and brokers conspired to pretend that many of these securities were worth much more than their current market values. Presiding over this uneasy union were the accountants, a profession that perhaps enjoyed its greatest influence during this unhappy decade. These auditors gave their imprimatur to fictions except in the most serious cases.

Chartered accountants were, of course, bound by the rules of their self-governing profession, but they were able to take part in this charade for several reasons. First of all, the banks clearly did not want to call their brokers' loans in most cases, and if the lenders were prepared to attribute fictitious values to securities, it surely was not the role of the auditors to protest too much. (The same thing occurred in the life insurance industry, where Sun Life of Montreal, which had invested heavily in shares during the1920s, became clearly insolvent after the crash, but the federal superintendent of insurance permitted the company to attribute mythical 'authorized values' to its stocks and so avert a day of reckoning.)[1] Secondly, neither provincial regulators nor stock exchanges had made hard-and-fast rules concerning the ratio of brokers' working capital to customers' debit balances or other forms of indebtedness. Each firm was thus allowed to continue to set its own margin requirements for every customer and for every class of securities.

Of course, the brokers had never really had the whip hand, for it was the banks that decided whom to lend to and on what security. In the 1920s the Bank of Nova Scotia, for instance, discouraged its managers from accepting stocks and bonds as collateral from individuals because in the event of a demand for repayment a person might be 'actively unfriendly to the Bank. Such is not the case with loans to ... stock brokers who well understand that they may be called upon for payment at any time.' But the bank's *Manual of Rules and Procedure* specifically noted, 'Banking credit may be said to rest on character, capacity and capital and it would appear precisely in that order.' Thus the banks retained great discretion in granting and extending loans.[2]

Typically, the banks had accepted as collateral (in addition to bonds) only widely traded securities of companies with a well-established record of dividend payments. During the bull market of the late 1920s good clients could purchase such stocks on margin by supplying about 30 per cent of their current prices, though it is clear that highly valued customers (possessing greater 'character' or 'capacity' if not always 'capital') might be permitted to put up as little as 10 per cent. Brokerage firms, which were usually very lightly capitalized, borrowed the remainder of the funds from the banks on the collateral of an ever-shifting portfolio of firm- and client-owned securities. Although the banks generally discouraged lending on more-speculative issues like non-dividend paying mines, it is clear that even bankers were not immune to surges of optimism, and branch managers could be hard to control. Defenders of I.W.C. Solloway argued that he and his fellow mining brokers had been forced to go short against their own customers in the late 1920s in order to procure the funds to deal in mining shares, on which the banks would lend only 50 per cent of the price, while customers were being granted 70 per cent margins, so that brokerages could remain competitive.

Even after the crash of 1929 the securities business continued much as usual except for those enmeshed in the scandals that sent Solloway and others to jail. Britain's departure from the gold standard in the autumn of 1931, however, dealt a stunning blow to the brokerage industry. As we have seen, McDougall and Cowans of Montreal, reputedly the largest firm in the country, was forced into receivership, followed by Greenshields and Company and Watson and Chambers. Though Beaudry Leman, president of the Canadian Bankers Association, tried to calm fears about further collapses by claiming 'certain knowledge' that the majority of Montreal houses were in excellent shape, such was clearly not the case. For public consumption the Toronto Stock Exchange boasted that the audit system which it had established in 1929 had prevented the failure of any of its members. A more accurate and nuanced statement about the travails faced by TSE members during the early 1930s appears in the official history of the exchange published over a half century later: 'To a surprising degree the Toronto Stock Exchange and its members were able to shield themselves from the slipstream of the depression. No Member Firm defaulted on its obligations to clients (although it might be inaccurate to state that every firm remained solvent through the early 1930s; accommodations with banks and other institutions were not uncommon).'[3]

A list compiled by one TSE insider near the end of 1932 told a depressing story:

Changes in TSE Membership, August 1929–November 1932

Out of business:

Brown, Fleming and Co. (Fleming still owns seat.)
Caldow Easson and Co.
Campbell Stratton and Lindsay
Cochran Hay and Co. (Hay still owns seat.)
Cronyn and Co.
DaCosta Phippen and Co. (Phippen still owns seat.)
Daly and Co.
L.M. Green and Co.
Harley Milner and Co. (Milner still owns seat.)
Aemilius Jarvis Jr.
Padmore Lockhart and Co.
Pellatt and Pellatt Ltd.
W.G. Shedden and Co.
G.A. Somerville and Co. (Somerville still owns seat.)
Stanton and Co. (Stanton still owns seat.)
Stark and Co.
Tovell and Co.
J.F.H. Ussher and Co.
Wood, Gundy and Co.

New firms since 1929:

J.R. Barber (not operating)
Cameron Pointon and Merritt
Dickson Jolliffe and Co.

R.L. Merry (not operating)
G.S. Osler (not operating)
Plummer and Co.
Wills Bickle and Robertson[4]

Nineteen brokers had retired from business in the previous three years, some on instructions from the exchange, while only four new firms had become active, so that the trading membership had shrunk by fully one-quarter from fifty-eight to forty-three.

Those caught up in this maelstrom were not just the weaklings either. Wood, Gundy and Company had been founded a decade before the First World War and had quickly become one of the leading bond dealers in Canada. During the boom of the 1920s it became 'the dominant underwriter of securities issues,' being active in promoting corporate mergers. Though the firm did not go 'out of business' as the above list records, it was forced to give up its TSE membership (acquired in 1920) during the early 1930s, when it found itself in 'a serious financial crisis ... (one apparently overcome only through the patience of its banker).'[5]

Historical records concerning the internal operations of brokerages in Canada are scarce, however, and the period of the 1930s is no exception. So long as that remains true, and so long as the chartered banks and the Canadian Bankers Association continue to keep a firm lock on what their records might reveal, the travails of the brokers are hard to document in detail. Indeed, there seems to be only one major exception: the records of F.H. Deacon and Company, a member of the Toronto Stock Exchange. Deacon appears to have suffered through the problems like most of his contemporaries in the business, so his story must stand for the experience of the rest of the brokerage community during the Depression.[6]

I

Frederick Deacon had built his firm into a mid-sized investment dealer with a well-to-do clientele and a fairly conservative outlook. Like many brokerages, however, it was hardly a model of efficient, centralized management. In 1909 Deacon took in John Campbell Fraser as a partner, and Jack Fraser held the firm's TSE seat in his name, oversaw the trading, and managed the office diligently. Deacon spent his time dealing with his own select clientele and handling his affairs as an underwriter, investor, and corporate director. As he later put it, 'I had never kept a set of books in my life.' When Fraser and another Deacon partner, R.G. Dingman, left to start their own firm in 1925, Deacon simply accepted Fraser's accounting. Elwell C. Reade became his new partner, but never assumed the kind of controlling position that Fraser had occupied.

At the same time Thomas G. Drew-Brook was appointed manager of the bond department and gradually came to play a leading role in the firm.[7] Fred Deacon recognized himself as a salesman rather than a manager and continued to rely upon his staff for routine matters. Drew-Brook was made a partner in 1927 and formally assumed control of the office in 1930, despite the fact that Fraser had often been heard to complain that he was carefree, inefficient, and erratic.[8] But during the late 1920s a loose managerial rein hardly seemed to matter at a brokerage as business increased handsomely.

Deacon had a fairly elevated conception of his own role in the financial world. He wanted 'the conduct of the office to be on an investment banking plan rather than on [the plan of] a gambling den,' he told Tommy Drew-Brook. He saw himself more in the mould of a J.P. Morgan than a hard-driving broker like Ike Solloway, who believed in luring in people who might become small-time margin customers by locating his office behind a plate-glass window at street level. Drew-Brook shared more of Solloway's attitudes. When the Deacons went off on an extended Mediterranean cruise early in 1929, Tommy Drew-Brook set up a board showing the the rise and fall of share prices in the firm's offices for the first time. The business was now located on the ground floor of a building on Bay Street right across from the Toronto Stock Exchange, and the aim was to draw in clients and other passers-by. The rules against the thirty staff members smoking in the office were ignored then dropped altogether. Margin accounts were handled in a relaxed fashion too; naturally, Deacon's well-heeled friends could buy and sell on margin, but Drew-Brook allowed the firm's employees to do so too.

And, finally, there was the matter of drinking. While Fred Deacon was a staunch, teetotal member of the Sherbourne Street Methodist Church, Tommy Drew-Brook had joined the Royal Flying Corps as a teenager, been shot down, wounded, and spent months as a prisoner of war; he returned to Canada with a steel plate in his back to a job at Deacon and Company. Not only was he well known on the 'street' for his wit and charm,[9] but through his father-in-law, the editor of the Toronto *Daily Star*, he was acquainted with many journalists who were not above spending time in the speakeasies that flourished on Queen Street after the Ontario Temperance Act of 1916 closed the bars. Drew-Brook's relaxed attitude towards drinking and smoking extended to the conduct of business, and the atmosphere in the office was easygoing. The chief floor trader was kept on for a considerable time even though he was known to be too fond of the bottle. The firm's books were often months behind as the volume of trading mounted in the late 1920s, and salesmen were pretty much allowed to go their

TABLE 10.1   Commissions earned by
Deacon and Company, 1925–31

Year	Commissions
1925	$ 71,638.30
1926	50,933.80
1927	103,488.83
1928	119,839.10
1929	186,989.63
1930	105,095.39
1931	62,871.36

SOURCE: PAO, F.H. Deacon, box 3, Bank of
Montreal, 1932–3, Memorandum for E.A.W.,
25 November 1932.

own way, but nobody cared very much with business increasing so hand-somely.[10]

Not surprisingly, therefore, the audit required by Ontario's Security Frauds Prevention Act in September 1929 revealed that some potentially serious problems existed at the firm even before the crash. Though Deacon had recently borrowed $290,000 from his bankers to beef up the capital account to $400,000 in light of the increase of business, the firm's auditors, Clarkson, Gordon, still expressed some concerns. The debit balances of clients had been reduced from about $8 million a few months earlier to $5.5 million, but less than half the accounts were fully margined and even at pre-crash values the remainder owed $600,000 which ought to be collected. Some 100 of the 678 clients had large 'overboard' or 'under-margined' accounts, the worst offenders being friends or associates of Drew-Brook and other members of the staff. Outstanding debts included $2.35 million borrowed from Canadian banks and $3 million from American lenders, loans whose collateral, of course, dropped sharply in value by the end of October 1929. Deacon later discovered that the situation would have appeared even worse had it not been for the fact that between 1927 and 1929 thousands of dollars of losses caused by failed trades and bookkeeping errors had been charged to him personally rather than to the firm's suspense account.[11]

Nevertheless, in 1929 Clarkson, Gordon merely noted that Deacon and Company's situation was 'Fair but capable of considerable improvement – now being effected.' The head of the accounting firm, H.D.L. Gordon, in his role as the TSE's exchange auditor, did not feel it necessary to recommend drastic action against his client Deacon. For his part, Deacon took no steps to tighten up the firm's management or to replace Drew-Brook. After 'Black Thursday' most clients who were asked proved able to put up a bit more margin, and others who were working to cut their liabilities were left alone for the time being. After all, everybody assumed that the dip was only temporary and that better times would soon return. And by the end of the year, share prices had steadied. In March 1930 Deacon and Company issued an optimistic brochure, which argued that markets 'have been advancing slowly but steadily for several months and yet bank loans to brokers are practically at bottom levels. Is this not a pretty clear indication that buying is coming from "big interests" such as banks, investment trusts, wealthy private investors who are able to pay cash for their purchases? Are these people not better informed and more experienced than the general public?' Since the answers were clearly affirmative, purchases of blue chips such as Imperial Oil, General Motors, and International Nickel were recommended on a cash or conservative margin basis.[12]

Unfortunately, share prices did not begin to rise again in the spring of 1930 but instead commenced a relentless downward slide that was to last for the next two years. As trading volumes declined, so did Deacon's revenues, and a small loss in 1930 had become a sizeable deficit the following year, though the firm continued to do a substantial business. Meanwhile, Deacon's personal debts, against which he had pledged various securities, increased steadily, and in April and October 1930 he borrowed another $290,000 from the Royal Bank to balance the books. After consolidating other small debts he personally owed the bank $300,000, yet a year or more after the crash the situation seemed manageable.[13]

Sound investments could still be sold even in 1931. Fred Deacon had been a director of the Morrow Screw and Nut Company since 1898 and its president since 1921 while it earned steady profits. On 1 June 1931, $1 million worth of bonds secured by a first mortgage on Morrow's property matured, and Deacon decided to raise new capital by issuing $600,000 worth of preferred shares paying a 7 per cent dividend. His firm underwrote this issue by borrowing from the banks, pledging the unsold Morrow preferred as collateral and retiring the debt as it was sold. During the summer of 1931 Deacon succeeded in disposing of about half the preferred shares to his clients for around $90 each.

On 20 September Britain went off the gold standard, and Fred Deacon found himself trapped in a financial nightmare. After twenty-five years as a member of the Toronto Stock Exchange he had to face the bitter truth that he could not repay his brokers' loans from the banks on Monday, the 21st. When he bemoaned his fate to S.H. Logan of the Bank of Commerce, he recalled that the banker responded as though shell-shocked, 'People are doing a lot of things today they never did before.'[14] Most other brokers in Canada were clearly in the same dire straits at that point.

For Deacon, as for other firms that were also involved in underwriting, the difficulty was that overnight the rest of the Morrow preferred shares became unsaleable, and the bankers who had supplied him with the funds began to press him to repay. The only way Deacon could think of raising a sizeable amount of cash quickly was by mortgaging Glenhurst, the vast house that he had acquired in 1918, which stood on eight and one-half acres of land in Toronto's fashionable Rosedale district. On 22 September he turned for help to his fellow Methodist Sir Joseph Flavelle, who had made his fortune in meat packing and still held large interests in both the Bank of Commerce and Simpson's department store. The canny Flavelle agreed to lend him $125,000, secured by a mortgage on Glenhurst, but only if somebody else would take over one-half of the loan. The semi-retired stockbroker E.R. Wood (founder of Wood, Gundy) agreed to participate, but only if additional collateral was provided. Deacon agreed to include his 600–acre country estate, Glenburn, near Unionville, Ontario, where he raised prize shorthorn cattle (see photo 19). The deal was signed on 3 October 1931, and Wood and Flavelle each tendered a preliminary amount of $25,000.

Two days later McDougall and Cowans and Greenshields and Company shut their doors in Montreal. Well-founded rumours circulated that many other brokerage houses were in serious trouble. Quick as a flash Eddie Wood and Joe Flavelle, who had not gotten rich by being soft-hearted, refused to hand over the other $75,000 owing on the mortgage. With bankruptcy staring him in the face, Fred Deacon was infuriated to discover that the two old men had reneged because his own auditor, Harry Gordon, had told them that he 'could not get through anyway.'[15]

Deacon was finally able to borrow more from the banks by pledging part of his $1 million in life insurance. His friend E.J. Davis agreed to accept only quarterly payments on an $80,000 loan due in mid-October. Associates lent him what money they could, and more was dredged up by putting up his wife's inheritance. Other brokers were hurting too; in November the TSE suspended one of its members and bought back four seats that were 'over-hanging' the market.[16]

Times did not improve, and on 5 January 1932 Gordon met with Deacon to express his growing concern about the further erosion of the firm's financial position. Fred Deacon insisted that things were much better than they appeared. The market for Morrow shares was bound to pick up again before long. Because of its confidence in him the Royal Bank was prepared to wait a year or eighteen months for repayment of his $300,000 personal loan. In addition, with a group of clients and friends he controlled a holding company called Northern Canada Mining. Its major asset, in turn, was 1.7 million shares of the successful Kirkland

Lake Gold Mine, in addition to smaller holdings of other northern Ontario gold producers such as Lake Shore and Hollinger and some promising properties. Though the stock had declined from a high of $2.25 to about 25 cents the company had a bright future. Deacon personally owned 175,000 of the 2.5 million Northern Canada shares, which had cost him $1.75 each on average, and he desperately wanted to avoid selling out at the bottom of the market.

As for Deacon and Company its under-margined clients were paying off what they could, and being investors rather than speculators, he told Gordon, most of them would eventually make good. Even the ones who had had to be told to pay off their loans or be sold out had been friendly and understanding. Many securities had lost between 65 and 95 per cent of their pre-crash values, so that there was nowhere for prices to go but up. Releasing any news about the firm's difficulties would only make matters worse: 'If we are publicly discredited financially, it would seriously decrease our ability to place unlisted securities and to produce earnings in the conduct of our general brokerage business.'

Gordon was insistent: Deacon and Company needed more capital. Once again the only source of funds seemed a mortgage on Deacon's real estate, which he claimed was still worth at least $400,000. He was already severing some lots from his city property in hopes of raising $50,000 to pay off the mortgage taken out the previous September. Under pressure from the accountant, he once again approached Eddie Wood to see if he could get the other $75,000 that he had been promised. Wood said he would speak to Gordon, and the following day Deacon was told that he was not going to get any more money, nor would either the farm or the town house be released so that it could be mortgaged separately. Once again the reason given was that the auditor himself was convinced that Deacon could not escape from his current financial difficulties.[17]

About the only comfort that he could draw from his situation was that Gordon did not compel him either to liquidate his shareholdings or to give up his TSE membership. But stock prices continued to slide in the spring of 1932. In April calls for additional margin had to go out to clients, and not even the willingness of Deacon's staff to forgo a month's salary could staunch the firm's heavy losses. On 21 April 1932 he was summoned to a meeting of representatives of the five chartered banks, chaired by Gordon as the TSE's auditor. Once more Deacon rehearsed the misfortunes, such as the unfortunate timing of the Morrow preferred underwriting, but insisted that he would get through if given leeway. Then he left the room; the bankers deliberated and called him in to hear Geoffrey Clarkson tell him that he must retire from the exchange and call a meeting of his creditors to settle with them. Deacon defiantly refused to do so, reminding them that it had taken A.E. Ames ten years to repay his debts in full after he had suspended his business in 1903.

The bankers apparently believed that a night of reflection would lead Deacon to see the error of his ways. On 22 April he was called to the auditors' offices to meet with Clarkson, Gordon and the latter's youthful son, Walter, in order to formalize his resignation from the stock exchange. The accountants were flabbergasted when Deacon refused point-blank, announcing that he would find a way to pay off the mortgage on his real estate and use it as collateral to borrow enough to get him off the hook with his most insistent creditors. He then stormed off back to Deacon and Company.[18]

Fred Deacon's efforts to borrow from two different life insurance companies failed. Well disposed as they were to him, neither one was prepared to take the risk. Eventually, C.A. Birge of Hamilton, the son of a long-time client, agreed to give him $55,000 worth of bonds on the security of the Glenburn farm. Almost immediately, $20,000 of this money had to be used to pay off some importunate creditors in New York. Worse still, share prices continued to slide.[19]

A month later, on 20 May, Deacon was again called before a meeting of bankers, trust company executives, and TSE officials in the boardroom of the Bank of Nova Scotia. Geoffrey Clarkson laid out the increasingly gloomy situation. Deacon and Company had nearly $500,000 in loans outstanding and was 'going behind' to the tune of $5,000–6,000 per month, a large part of this being interest on borrowed funds. Debts to customers totalled nearly $175,000, and there was $435,000 owing on 'overboard' accounts. Merely cutting salaries and rents could never rectify the problem. Deacon again insisted that he could climb out of this hole by year's end; after all, he had succeeded in reducing his total indebtedness by $2 million over the last seven months. The bankers sent him out of the room and deliberated for an hour before deciding to chance it and allow Deacon to continue in business, provided that he could scrounge up enough money from other sources to meet his operating deficit, the interest on his personal loans, and the premiums on his $1 million life insurance policy. He was required to pledge $300,000 worth of that insurance to the Royal Bank to cover his personal loan, while the Toronto Stock Exchange received a claim on an additional $260,000 to cover potential losses to Deacon's clients in the event of his death.[20]

Fred Deacon was fortunate that he enjoyed considerable personal sympathy among the bankers who controlled his fate so completely. J.A. McLeod of the Bank of Nova Scotia, who was also president of the Canadian Bankers Association and thus an influential figure, was prepared not to press Deacon too hard, calculating that it was better to allow him to continue in business than to force him to close up shop, especially as his loan was not very large. The Bank of Commerce was also resigned to waiting for $65,000 that it had been owed since September 1931. The Royal Bank was equally patient; privately its assistant general manager had already tried to buck Deacon up by saying, 'Considering what you have come through in the past two years, you are a damned good sport.'[21]

Deacon's biggest headaches came from Bank of Montreal, his second largest creditor. His debt of over $200,000 was almost entirely secured by just two types of shares: Northern Canada Mining and Morrow Screw and Nut preferred. Since the Morrow stock was completely unsaleable, the bank's local manager, F.W.C.C. Clark, started pressing Deacon in the spring of 1932 to sell off Northern Canada for as little as 15 cents per share. Deacon resisted strenuously. Not only had the shares cost him more than ten times that much, but Northern Canada's president, J.B. Tyrrell, insisted that the company had a break-up value of at least 31 cents per share. Letting the stock go at fire-sale prices would only destroy its value for the other investors while netting little for Deacon or his bankers.[22]

Though Deacon might insist that his loan was well secured, that was true only if the Morrow preferred continued to be valued at the $90 per share at which it had traded prior to September 1931. The only way he could persuade the bank not to start selling the Northern Canada stock was to agree to begin paying off his loan at the rate of $10,000 per month in the fall of 1932. He regarded this as a breach of the standstill arrangement that he had obtained with such difficulty from his major creditors the previous spring, but all he could do was to threaten to tell the friendlier folk at the Royal that the Bank of Montreal was trying to get a leg up on its competitor by demanding immediate repayment. Yet the bankers knew that they had to live and let live with each other; the Royal's assistant general manager declined to interfere, simply observing sourly, 'There's that damned Bank of Montreal; [they] wouldn't live up to their agreement.'[23]

By 1 November 1932 Deacon had paid off the Bank of Montreal to the tune of $34,000, but the pressure was unyielding. He heard from his old friend S.C. Mewburn, who was a member of the bank's board, that its president, Sir Charles Gordon, had convened a meeting of his fellow bankers to warn that if they didn't cease to call brokers' loans as many as eight firms would fail. If these Montreal brokers were being carried, why was he being pressed so hard? On Mewburn's advice he went to see the bank's Ontario supervisor, W.T.A. MacFadyen, and complained about the daily badgering to pay up or else to agree to sell the Northern Canada shares. MacFadyen blandly told him that he had his orders from head office and badgering people was what he got paid for.[24]

Deacon's protests did eventually gain him some breathing room. The bank cut its monthly demands in half to $5,000, though he insisted to Assistant General Manager S.C. Norsworthy, a boyhood friend, that he would have paid up just as rapidly even if he had not been harassed so much. But when Deacon fell behind on his repayments in the summer of 1933, the pressure was quickly renewed. He complained that he had 'played the game' with the bank by doing his utmost, but if forced to the wall he would call a meeting of all his creditors and explain how the Bank of Montreal was trying to take advantage of the rest of them. Out of either prudence or mercy the bank dropped its demands to $3,000 per month, having by that time recovered slightly more than one-quarter of the $200,000 owing.[25] The Bank of Montreal's conduct remained a sore point with Fred Deacon. He always insisted that it had reneged on a commitment in May 1932 not to press for repayment; one year later he was still demanding (without success) that its exact demands be put in writing. His bitterness about his treatment by the bank festered for years afterwards.[26]

The other person who emerged as Fred Deacon's principal demon and tormentor as he struggled for survival was Harry Duncan Lockhart Gordon.[27] With his partner, Geoffrey T. Clarkson, Gordon was among the most prominent and influential chartered accountants in Canada during the first half of the twentieth century.[28] That was precisely why they had been chosen as official auditors of the Toronto Stock Exchange in 1929 to cast their aura of respectability over that institution by enforcing the provisions of the Security Frauds Prevention Act. Deacon's resentment against Gordon had been born when he learned that Eddie Wood and Joe Flavelle had reneged on their agreement to pay the final $75,000 instalment on the mortgage on his home and farm in the fall of 1931, because the auditor had told them that Deacon 'could not get through' the crisis. In January 1932, as auditor of Deacon and Company, Gordon had suggested privately that the firm ought to be wound up, but Deacon had refused. In April the TSE auditors had summoned him to a meeting of bankers, after which Clarkson had told him that he must give up his exchange seat.[29] A month later Deacon again found himself on the carpet at another meeting chaired by Clarkson. After the meeting one of his friends remarked to him that the only people who would benefit from the bankruptcy of Deacon and Company were Clarkson, Gordon as the likely receivers.[30] Thereafter Fred Deacon brooded about what he came to feel was a determination on the part of the auditors, and Gordon in particular, to put him out of business despite his frantic efforts to engineer a recovery.

II

There was finally some good news around the offices of Deacon and Company in the summer of 1932. When the market began to inch upward, some cautious circulars were issued advising clients to buy, and commission income rose rapidly, even exceeding expenses in September. Clarkson, Gordon reported that the half-yearly audit showed a small profit in the past month and a marked improvement in the capital account as the 'leaning position' on under-margined accounts had been substantially reduced. Even during dismal 1932, two hundred new clients had been signed up, and most of the old ones remained faithful to the firm.[31]

Yet this good news contained the seeds of a problem that was to plague the firm during the next two years and must have bedevilled all brokers who were being propped up by their creditors. Whenever times looked better and new accounts were opened, customers bought more stock on margin so the need for brokers' loans increased. By the end of September 1932 clients owed an additional $90,000, and the firm's borrowings from the banks and in New York had therefore risen by $75,000. That set the alarm bells ringing at the Toronto Stock Exchange. Deacon and Drew-Brook were haled before Gordon and a small subcommittee of the board, composed of the president, G.C. 'Mike' Mitchell, and Harold Franks of Osler and Hammond, to account for this rise. Drew-Brook claimed that except for three cases where 'mistakes' had been made, no new accounts had been opened. All that had happened was that old clients who had closed up their margin accounts had re-entered the market. Mitchell and Franks were equally insistent that this was indeed 'new' business which accounted for the $50,000 worth of additional margin loans. Rather than Deacon's borrowings from the banks being steadily cut, as had been agreed at the May meeting, they were once more expanding rapidly.

More threatening still to the survival of the firm, the TSE officials argued that Deacon had already agreed in May 1932 to accept no more margin business and to put the company's affairs on a strict cash basis. The exchange ignored the fact that total debt had been cut from $4 million to $1 million over the past fifteen months, and that to refuse to do margin business would only drive away those asked to repay their debts. Drew-Brook, whose friends and clients accounted for a good proportion of the under-margined accounts, responded that at present they couldn't even do enough business on a cash basis to cover operating expenses. Not our problem, said the committee; the bankers and brokers had realized in May that expenses were not being covered and that was why Deacon had been made personally responsible for meeting them.

Now the exchange issued an ultimatum: cease all margin business because the firm lacked sufficient capital to finance it and supply an undertaking to get all 'new' clients who had opened accounts since the beginning of September to pay off their loans as soon as possible and put their affairs on a cash basis. Only about a dozen or so customers would be permitted to continue to trade on margin once the situation had been fully explained to them. Whatever else happened, Deacon and Company was not to take on any additional debt, or the TSE would suspend it and put it out of business. Deacon was ordered to initial the minutes of the meeting as a sign that he accepted these conditions.[32]

In the circumstances what could Drew-Brook and Deacon do? Stalling seemed the only answer, in the hope that business might continue to improve or the TSE would relax its demands. But Harry Gordon was insistent: a few days later he called Tommy Drew-Brook in to ask why the initialled minutes had not been returned. Drew-Brook tried to put him off by saying that Deacon was consulting his lawyers about legal action against the TSE, since 'membership on the Stock Exchange was not like membership in a club or society. It was [Deacon's] ... livelihood.' The exchange auditor would have none of that; he briskly replied that 'it wasn't a matter of legal opinion but the opinion of the Stock Exchange Committee.' Deacon and Company had better get on with the business of reducing its loans if it wanted to retain its membership. Drew-Brook could only reply huffily that he and Deacon were doing their best to restore the firm to a sound basis, but 'that it was evident to him from Colonel Gordon's remarks that they were working at cross purposes.'[33]

Fred Deacon did indeed consult his lawyer and fellow Methodist, Newton Wesley Rowell. Gordon's audit had shown that on 30 September 1932 Deacon and Company owed its creditors $362,643 more than it possessed in readily saleable shares, but the firm also had assets with a face value of $523,039, some of which could not be disposed of at present. Yet if they could be realized at full value over time, there existed a potential surplus of $160,395. 'We are solvent but not liquid,' he told Rowell, 'and are therefore said not to measure up to the Toronto Stock Exchange requirements as to cash capital.' Deacon wanted to keep debts at the present level and was prepared to refuse all new margin business, but if he followed the exchange's instructions to put all his accounts on a cash basis as quickly as possible he would drive away all his margin customers, perhaps forever. This ultimatum had come at the very time when Deacon and Company had succeeded in taking in enough commissions to break even on operating expenses over the past five months. Left alone, the firm would have no trouble showing a profit during the rest of the year if times continued to improve. The chief source of his difficulties, he claimed, was his own accounting firm, Clarkson, Gordon ('Our Auditors'), to whom he had paid $4,000 during the past year while they had also compelled him to bear the cost of employing several staff memebers for long periods of time preparing figures for them.[34]

He got little comfort from the lawyer. Rowell replied that he could see nothing which would make trading by Deacon and Company illegal, but he added cannily, 'I am not passing upon the question of whether these transactions are in accordance with the bylaws of the Toronto Stock Exchange or not. I assume you have subscribed to the bylaws of the exchange.' Though Rowell claimed he did not have a copy of those by-laws, he reminded Deacon that actions which were legal might still contravene the exchange's rules. About that Deacon should not be under any 'misunderstanding or misapprehension.' With this unpromising response Deacon had to be content, though he would later claim that another lawyer had advised him that if the TSE did take any action against him, he had grounds to file a suit claiming at least $100,000 in damages.[35]

Fred Deacon also sought to get Gordon and the exchange off his back by appealing to his most sympathetic creditor, J.A. McLeod of the Bank of Nova Scotia. He laid out all the progress that he had made since the previous May; considering the state of the stock market the situation was better than he had ever expected. 'If we did all the business on the Toronto Exchange in recent days,' he told McLeod, 'our commissions would amount to less than we earned formerly for [single] months in 1928 and 1929.' He threatened that he would appeal to Ontario attorney general William Price if his competitors at the TSE persisted in trying to wreck his business.[36]

Fortunately, McLeod, who was after all the president of the Canadian Bankers Association, agreed with Deacon that his creditors had not flatly told him to stop doing margin business back in May. Nothing about this had been formally recorded in the minutes of the fateful meeting in the boardroom of the Bank of Nova Scotia. Faced with Deacon's stubborn refusal to put his firm on a straight cash basis, Gordon and the stock exchange committee apparently decided to back off for the time being and see what would happen. Fred Deacon continued to do business in accordance with what he deemed to be the spirit of his agreement with his creditors; he remained cautious about opening new margin accounts, and he aimed to keep his total indebtedness under $1 million and not permit it to balloon as had happened in September 1932.[37]

The future continued to look brighter in the spring of 1933 as the price of mining shares improved, including Northern Canada Mining, which hit 50 cents or better. Franklin D. Roosevelt's inauguration as president of the United States in March took place amidst a growing financial panic, but his stirring rhetoric ('nothing to fear but fear itself'), followed by the week-long 'bank holiday' which also closed the New York Stock Exchange, steadied the markets. By late April the TSE was reporting the heaviest trading in several years; Deacon and Company succeeded in snaring 150 new clients in 1933 to go with the 200 added the previous year.[38] Commission income leapt upward from a dismal $29,000 in 1932 to almost $96,000 in 1933, while expenses rose from just $52,000 to $65,000 (see table 10.2).

TABLE 10.2 F.H. Deacon and Company's commissions and expenses, 1929–37

Year	Commissions	Expenses
1929	$225,032.57*	$140,564.82
1930	108,239.57*	115,888.03
1931	66,196.46	99,168.37
1932	29,035.43	51,840.97
1933	95,976.44	64,722.92
1934	63,316.70	95,597.26
1935	85,765.23	104,647.97
1936	121,177.21	100,994.58
1937	94,702.42	101,623.20

SOURCE: PAO, F.H. Deacon, box 2, Company History, 1938, Memorandum re Commissions and Operating Expenses of F.H.D. and Co., 1929–37, n.d.
*These figures do not square with the amounts cited in table 10.1, which is drawn from another source, though the discrepancy might have arisen from the inclusion of commissions on bond sales here.

When business improved in April, however, the firm's borrowings began to inch upward as margin business increased, just as had happened in the fall of 1932. From $837,000 at the start of that month they rose to $1,037,000 by the end of May. As a result, Fred Deacon quickly found himself in front of the 'small committee' at the Toronto Stock Exchange, once more trying to justify this development to Mike Mitchell and Harold Franks. Gordon, as exchange auditor, began their meeting by complimenting him on the way things seemed to be improving, but he quickly demanded an explanation for the opening of five new margin accounts which had debit balances totalling $33,000. Deacon explained that these clients were all well-to-do people (including a Samuel and a Gairdner). In a dig at Gordon, he added that they could hardly fail to know about the problems that his firm was having since the auditor had frequently said that everyone was well aware of the situation.[39]

Gordon was nettled. Deacon later reported, 'He said he did not think that possibly I appreciated the action of the Committee and himself in having permitted me to continue, and he said that they had given more time to my account than all the rest of the members of the Exchange put together.' The angry Deacon snapped back that he had been so tried by the interference of the exchange the previous November that he had nearly gone to the attorney general. Gordon's only response was that since Mitchell would be stepping down as president at the TSE's annual meeting within a few weeks, he wanted a written record of the understanding between Deacon and the 'small committee.' 'Colonel Gordon emphasized that the Committee and he had gone beyond what they should have done in failing to report to the General Committee concerning our affairs.' Deacon replied that he had no objection to writing a letter, but that Gordon seemed to want praise for helping Deacon and Company to solve its problems. Mitchell and Franks might be owed his gratitude, but he certainly 'wasn't going to give any credit to Colonel Gordon.' If Deacon had not followed his own instincts and ignored the accountant's wishes, he would have been out of business long ago rather than recovering rapidly. On that unedifying note the meeting ended.[40]

Deacon lived up to his commitment to put his side of the case on paper. In a personal letter addressed to TSE president Mitchell that same day, he refused flat out to commit himself to putting Deacon and Company on a cash basis as the exchange wished. He promised only to be 'most careful in taking on new margin accounts ... We have steadily eliminated undesirable margin accounts, and I can assure you that I shall be most careful not to have any more of them.' As a backhanded slap at his nemesis, Gordon, Deacon went out of his way to heap praise upon Mitchell and Franks for the 'splendid treatment' that they had accorded him over the past two years.[41]

With business improving, Deacon and Company's clients were allowed to run up their total debit balances to $1,114,000 by the end of August 1933. Indeed, Deacon even tried to persuade the Royal Bank to grant the firm a $300,000 line of credit so that he could take on more margin business. Despite the argument that a large loan would permit him to raise earnings significantly and thus pay the bank off sooner, his friends at the Royal declined to go along.[42]

By the end of 1933 the odds that Fred Deacon's firm would survive seemed better than at any time since Britain had left the gold standard. Perhaps his mixture of courage and bravado and the patience of his bankers really would see him through despite all the obstacles placed in his path by the likes of Harry Gordon. It soon turned out that Deacon's troubles were far from over, but the source of his immediate problems lay within the firm itself. Under the stresses and strains imposed by the Depression, Deacon and Company seemed about to fly apart.

The trouble was rooted, like so many of Deacon's difficulties during the early 1930s, in the preferred shares in Morrow Screw and Nut, which had been underwritten in the summer of 1931. About half the 6,000 shares remained unsold, but Deacon was convinced that once the economy recovered the remaining stock could easily be disposed of. Yet it was essential, he believed, that the 7 per cent dividend on the preferred shares should continue to be paid even though Morrow was no longer earning a profit, or else those who had bought the stock for $90 in 1931 would dump it for whatever they could get and he would never be able to sell the other 3,000 shares.

From the beginning his bankers were dubious about the idea of his borrowing funds to pay dividends for a money-losing company. When Deacon faced the crunch in the spring of 1932, he pleaded with his friends at the Royal Bank to lend him the necessary funds, contending that this was a 'life and death matter.' They refused. At the climactic meeting at the Bank of Nova Scotia three days later his creditors insisted that he must raise this money personally from friends or relatives rather than drawing upon them.[43]

Somehow Deacon scraped together the $10,500 required to pay the dividend every quarter. In February 1933 the long-suffering local manager of the Royal Bank again complained about Deacon borrowing to pay the dividend. D.C. Rea pointed out that nobody in his right mind would buy these shares at present, to which Deacon replied in lordly fashion that 'the type of person who bought that stock would buy whatever I told him.' By that summer he had to abandon the fiction that the Morrow preferred should continue to be valued as collateral by the Bank of Montreal at $90 per share, but he still insisted that as soon as good times returned, he would have no difficulty placing it with 'real investors' for that amount.[44]

Yet the most serious trouble over the Morrow preferred eventually came from his own partners in Deacon and Company. Not a peep had previously been heard from them about continuing the dividend, but on 30 November 1933 Tommy Drew-Brook burst into Deacon's office to protest that the firm's money was being used to pay the December dividend. Deacon replied that he had requested the money from the banks, but if they refused to go along, he had made alternative arrangements. Meanwhile, the cheques had to go out the following day. On 2 December Drew-Brook resigned his partnership and joined Wills, Bickle and Robertson, where another former Deacon partner had recently established himself. Ten days later George Jennison followed Drew-Brook out the door, complaining that the firm's funds had not been repaid as agreed.[45]

Whether Drew-Brook really jumped ship of his own accord or was pushed overboard by Deacon remains unclear. Not surprisingly, the two men had had their disagreements over the years. Deacon frequently grumbled that it was Drew-Brook's customers and friends who had the largest under-margined accounts when the crisis occurred in 1931–2, whereas his own clients were 'investors' not 'speculators.' With the banks and the stock exchange pressing the firm to reduce its borrowings, Deacon suggested that all 'overboard' clients with inactive accounts should be interviewed with a view to getting them to pay up their debts. Drew-Brook refused to spend time on this task, arguing that the only way to make money was to trade speculative stocks for margin customers. Since the TSE was constantly pressing the firm not to open any new margin accounts, Deacon huffed that Drew-Brook spent a lot of time sitting around the office without much to do.[46] Nonetheless, it is easy to exaggerate the differences between the two men. When the exchange auditor, Gordon, tried to get them to agree to put Deacon and Company on a strict cash basis in the fall of 1932, both of them had insisted that they could not make any money that way and carried on as before. Drew-Brook even stood up to Gordon's pressure to the point of telling the auditor that he was 'working at cross purposes' with their efforts to restore Deacon and Company's soundness.[47]

Fred Deacon, of course, had always had some reservations about Drew-Brook's casual managerial style. And then there was the question of drinking. When Drew-Brook left, Deacon wrote himself a long self-justificatory memorandum in which he explained that he had become increasingly concerned about this problem. A magistrate of his acquaintance had hinted to him that several of the staff had been caught in a raid on a speakeasy on Queen Street. Investigating, Deacon discovered to his dismay this to be true and fired the chief culprit. Moreover, he learned it was common knowledge that there were after-hours drinking parties in the office. Plenty of liquor was kept in a handy storeroom. Confronted with this state of affairs, Drew-Brook admitted that he had sent a nineteen-year-old minor out to buy supplies, and one young staff member's liquor permit recorded the purchase of no less than seven bottles during the first week of November 1933 alone.[48]

More than likely, however, Drew-Brook left because he saw that the worm had turned: Fred Deacon had decided that he was dispensable, and the row over the Morrow preferred dividend was only the final straw. Drew-Brook and Jennison were shortly followed by another partner, Elwell Reade, who had been with Deacon and Company since 1909. Over the next three months, nine senior and three junior staff, many of them long-time employees, left. Deacon, who had few personal clients and knew little of the day-to-day business of dealing in securities, was left with a small group from the firm's accounting department to try and pick up the pieces. Could these people become effective customers' men?[49]

As was common practice in the investment business, the departed sought to take their account holders with them. A copy of Deacon and Company's mailing list went missing, and 'intense efforts' were made to poach customers. Friends of Fred Deacon reported to him that Elwell Reade was even trying to snare the business of people with whom he had never previously dealt. Doing so proved all the easier in this case, because hints could be dropped about the financial problems at Deacon and Company which lay behind the 'mass exodus,' while other, stronger firms could offer to take on new margin business without risking the ire of their bankers or the stock exchange. Deacon was particularly annoyed because he claimed that the three partners had been responsible for many clients who had suffered losses from unsuccessful speculations and owed him over $200,000 for under-margined accounts. As if that were not bad enough, his former partners and their families remained personally indebted to the firm, two of them having 'overboard' accounts totalling $8,300.[50]

III

Deacon's sense of grievance was intensified because by 1934 there were signs that share prices were picking up and recovery might have arrived at long last. As always, however, better times brought their own problems. By the begining of February 1934 customers past and present still owed Deacon and Company a great deal of money: of 242 margin accounts 42 were overboard to the tune of $240,000. Only 53 customers had settled their outstanding debts or enjoyed a cash surplus, despite the fact that at long last 18 accounts had been completely written off during January. The only good sign was that total debit balances for clients had declined from over $1 million at the end of November 1933 to about $760,000 at the beginning of February.

Once more Deacon was called in by the 'small committee' of the TSE board of directors, now chaired by President Harold Franks backed up by the exchange auditors, Harry Gordon for the TSE and Holland Pettit for the Standard stock exchange (the two exchanges being on the eve of amalgamating). Fearing that Deacon and Company might be unable to meet its obligations, the exchange proposed to place the firm in virtual trusteeship. As in the spring and fall of 1932, Deacon was asked to agree not to open any new margin accounts or do any new business that would increase the debit balance in an existing account. Closed margin accounts were not to be reopened and additional margin might be called for on any account; all future business was to be on a strict cash basis. Bad debts would be written off as soon as they proved uncollectable. Meanwhile, under the supervision of the exchange auditors all securities owned by the firm or by Deacon or his partners personally were to be sold as rapidly as possible; no new securities were to be purchased (except federal and provincial bonds and industrial and municipal bonds valued at less than $5,000 for immediate resale). Deacon was not to do any underwriting and to draw no more than $1,000 in salary per month, monitored by a new bookkeeper approved by the exchange auditors.[51]

Fred Deacon made one final effort to preserve his independence. He appealed for assistance to George Drew, who had been appointed commissioner to oversee the industry under Ontario's Security Frauds Prevention Act in 1931. Deacon claimed that under the guise of ensuring his solvency through self-regulation his rivals were trying to put him out of business: 'Suggest the wisdom of the Attorney General considering the supervision of the Stock Exchange through his Department instead of by the Stock Exchange Committee and present Auditors. The Stock Exchange Committee is composed of competitors, and one of the Committee remarked when all the others were present, that my clients' accounts should not be "mulled over," as one member of the Committee was doing at the time. He said, "It isn't fair, [because] some of our clients might be among those names." '

Laboriously Deacon laid out for Drew the background of his troubles since September 1931. He insisted that his firm's difficulties had arisen not from reckless speculation but from 'our undertaking to take care of over one hundred clients accounts that were insufficiently margined.' In 1932 the auditors had agreed that Deacon and Company could continue to do margin business provided that customers' debit balances were held below $1 million, down from ten times that level prior to 1929. Deacon had kept his side of the bargain and at the same time had been able to eliminate the firm's capital deficit (or 'leaning position'), which had reached $99,000 in 1932, but was reduced to $29,000 in 1933 and transformed into a modest surplus of $8,400 by the beginning of 1934.

The banks were giving him no trouble at present, not even the Bank of Montreal, as interest payments had been made on time, sometimes even early. Clients had received all securities delivered or funds owed on schedule. The exchange had his life insurance pledged to it to cover any losses that might be incurred if Deacon and Company had to be wound up. Why then was he continually being harassed, subjected to ever-changing demands? The answer could only be the animosity of his competitors on the TSE committee and in particular of Harry Gordon: 'The Exchange is my livelihood, not a club, and therefore should not be subject to the whims of competitors or auditors, who at times have shown themselves unfriendly and prevented loans being made.'[52]

Having gone to so much trouble during the late 1920s to establish the principle that the stock exchanges must regulate the conduct of their own members, the Ontario authorities were unwilling to intervene in this squabble. All the more so as George Drew might have to shoulder the blame if Deacon and Company was ultimately forced to suspend and liquidate. Indeed, on the eve of his meeting with Deacon, he had sat down with the board of the Toronto Stock Exchange for a wide-ranging discussion of possible revisions to the by-laws, the exchange practices, and the auditing of brokers which would make clear where the ultimate responsibility lay. Rebuffed by government, Fred Deacon had no choice but to accept the 'small committee's' ultimatum and place the fate of his firm in the hands of the exchange.[53]

Over the next few months Deacon and Company underwent a roller-coaster ride. Business increased handsomely even while a new sales staff was trained to replace those who had left. Harold Edmonds, an accountant and bank manager who had served with Deacon during the war, was made a partner; he had no experience with the securities business, but he set about to alter Tommy Drew-Brook's relaxed style and get a firm grip on the office. Certainly, customers' debit balances continued to be steadily reduced, hitting $630,000 by the end of May and down over $130,000 from the time when the TSE had imposed the new controls. Bad debts totalling $55,000 were written off, while money owed on accounts by under-margined clients, delinquent partners, and the firm itself was cut by $10,000 to $188,000. Call loans in Canada were down from $990,000 to $695,000. Commissions were almost sufficient to cover expenses.[54]

In January 1934 the United States raised the price of gold from $20 to $35 an ounce, which set off a boom in mining stocks that spring reminiscent of 1927–8. The value of Deacon's shares in Northern Canada Mining rose to 54 cents. The TSE's 'small committee' immediately pressed for the sale of this stock while the chance offered, but Deacon refused. The committee considered this a 'grave mistake,' and their annoyance redoubled when the exchange auditors discovered that his customers' debit balances had shot up by $22,000 during May even after share prices had begun to slump again. They therefore demanded an analysis of every account where debts had increased, a process that proved costly and time-consuming. Harold Edmonds complained that if this were to happen every time there was the slightest rise in debits, it would be 'intolerable and the Committee's action would be tantamount to hounding us out of business.' But accountant Holland Pettit was firm, telling Edmonds that 'their responsibility was to see that no client's position became more hazardous through allowing him to increase his dealings on a marginal basis. That was in effect what was being done when we bought for a client and did not at the same time sell sufficient securities to offset the purchases.'[55]

Near the end of June 1934 Fred Deacon was called before the 'small committee' once again. He repeated his now-familiar arguments that the position of Deacon and Company was steadily improving since debit balances had been cut 40 per cent from the previous August and the Morrow preferred was selling again, while the accountants had radically undervalued his real estate and his exchange seat. The committee was not impressed: Deacon was given a month to clean up his balance sheet by reducing certain customers' debit balances from $423,000 to $360,000. Deacon and Company was also to file a partnership agreement with the exchange, making clear which assets and liabilities belonged to the firm and which to individuals. Failure to comply with this demand before the meeting of the TSE managing committee scheduled for 24 July would lead to a report being filed by the 'small committee' advising on the gravity of the situation at Deacon and Company, the implication being that the firm might be suspended from the exchange.[56]

Deacon did his best to persuade the 'small committee' to relent. He asked his long-time associate, the Montreal financier J.W. McConnell, and Morris Wilson, the president of the Royal Bank, to intercede and try to persuade the members of the committee that if he was able to refinance his loan from the banks secured by the remaining Morrow preferred shares, he should be allowed to carry debit balances higher than $360,000. He got the venerable A.E. Ames, who certainly knew the implications of suspension from the exchange, to put in a good word for him. Harry Gordon listened to Ames, McConnell, and Wilson but could not be convinced that Deacon's solution was acceptable.[57]

The ultimatum issued by 'small committee' expired on 24 July 1934. At the managing committee's meeting that day, President Harold Franks reported in detail on the affairs of Deacon and Company to the full board for the first time. He told the directors that the firm had been under scrutiny by the exchange auditor for several years past, but the situation had now reached a point where he felt that they ought to be fully briefed. While the auditors had no hesitation in declaring Deacon and Company solvent, some of its assets were of a character which might cause problems if they had to be liquidated quickly, though efforts were being made to improve matters. In light of this fairly positive account, the exchange directors agreed to postpone any immediate action but to monitor the situation carefully.[58]

A meeting between Deacon and Franks at Gordon's office the following day was stormy. Deacon claimed that A.E. Ames had told him that nothing further would be done until he had been notified; the exchange officials brushed that assertion aside: he had been given a deadline of 24 July and had failed to meet it. Franks told him sternly 'that now the General Committee were in the picture they had to be kept advised periodically, and that, "They won't be as patient with you as we have been."' After listening to so many complaints, Gordon angrily told Deacon that 'I [Deacon] appeared to think that he had not done what he could to help me. He said he had done all he could do for three years, and I appeared to think he opposed me.'

Turning to the business at hand, Gordon told Deacon he had made a great error in not selling his Northern Canada shares when the 'small committee' had told him to do so. Now there were to be no more evasions and delays. Within a week he must file a partnership agreement detailing precisely how the shares in Deacon and Company were allocated. Customers' debit balances were to be cut from $423,000 to $360,000: 'This does not mean immediately but there will not be any latitude shown.' The exchange would keep a close eye on the situation, and if more operating losses occurred, debit balances would have to be reduced further.[59]

The TSE still had no formal regulations concerning the capitalization of brokerage firms vis-à-vis their customers debts or the amount of margin that could be granted. In the fall of 1934 the *Financial Post* reported that for the past year most Canadian brokers had been demanding 50 per cent margin on higher-priced stocks, while shares under $3 were mainly on a cash basis and few would lend at all on those under $1. But these were not mandatory requirements. In order to strengthen its hand the TSE board passed its first by-law specifying the value at which various classes of margined securities could be valued; a special committee would fix the audit value of unlisted shares or bonds held by TSE members as security. This regulation gave the exchange wider powers to deal with the kind of situation that had arisen at Deacon and Company (and at many other brokerages too).[60]

For Fred Deacon 1934 marked a new low: he had effectively lost control of his business. His bitterness at this turn of events was reflected in his careful preservation of a clipping from the scurrilous tabloid *Hush*, dated 1 September 1934, which recorded that 'Handsome Harry' Franks had been arrested for reckless driving and held in a suburban jail after his car bounced down a 125–foot embankment. According to *Hush*, Franks had also been charged with drunk driving, but this charge had been dropped and the name of his lady companion withheld. Bailed out, he paid a fine of just $10 for his offence, which had occurred, as the paper gleefully noted, while he was speeding north from Toronto, having just fined a member of the TSE $1,000 for a breach of its rules in his capacity as exchange president. Around the same time Fred Deacon drew whatever bitter satisfaction he could from firing Clarkson, Gordon as his firm's auditors and replacing them with Campbell, Lawless, Parker and Black.[61]

IV

The outlook for Deacon and Company looked particularly bleak when the upturn in 1934 proved short-lived. Annual commission income plunged to $63,000, while expenses soared to over $95,000, almost exactly reversing the figures for 1933 and turning a $31,000 surplus into a $32,000 operating loss (see table 10.2 above). The firm's capital surplus of about $20,000 in the spring had again turned into a $23,000 'leaning position' by the end of October because the shares of Northern Canada Mining in the firm account had declined in value and 'overboard' customers had failed to pay their debts. Since the start of the year the auditors had insisted that the premiums on Deacon's life insurance, which was pledged to his creditors, and the mortgage payments on his real estate had to be charged to the firm so long as these assets were being used for business purposes. This accounting change increased the flow of red ink onto the books.[62]

Paradoxically, the brightest spot was the Morrow Screw and Nut preferred. At long last Fred Deacon's dogged determination to borrow money in order to keep paying the dividends on this stock began to pay off. During February 1934 he had managed to dispose of the first 300 of the 3,000 unsold shares at $90. By the autumn Morrow was showing improved earnings, and in December the last stock pledged to the banks was sold. By that time Northern Canada Mining had declared a dividend of 2 cents per share and its future was also looking bright.[63]

Not that things weren't still tight. When his friends at the Royal Bank asked him for some more collateral for his personal loan of $300,000 in the spring of 1935, he had to tell them that every penny of his assets was still pledged to the credit of Deacon and Company. On the Toronto Stock Exchange trading continued sluggish that year as industrials maintained their 1934 levels while the volume of mining stocks fell by half. The firm earned over $85,000 in commissions, the best level since 1930, but expenses of just under $105,000 meant another sizeable operating loss (see table 10.2 above).[64]

Little by little, however, the Canadian economy was recovering, though shares prices were slow to follow more buoyant American markets. The overwhelming victory of Mackenzie King's Liberals in the federal election in October 1935 had a stabilizing effect. Commission income picked up, and from then until May 1936 Deacon and Company showed a healthy monthly surplus. That year the firm turned its first operating profit since 1929 as expenses hovered around $100,000 while commissions passed $121,000. As in past spurts, however, more business meant higher debit balances in customer accounts when margin trading expanded, though the TSE seemed content to turn a blind eye for the time being. Deacon and Company was by no means the only exchange member on whom the auditors were keeping close tabs. In December 1935 Harry Gordon reported to the board that Jenkin Evans was unable to meet the financial requirements, and the firm was forced to resign its membership, though all its creditors were paid off.[65]

After a slump in the summer of 1936 share trading picked up strongly towards the end of the year, and by early 1937 there was a full-fledged bull market again. The TSE's board became concerned that members might lack sufficient capital for the growing volume of business that they were doing, so the directors finally decided to fix formal requirements in time for the 31 March audit. Firms were required to have free capital available equal to 5 per cent of customer debit balances up to a total of $250,000 (i.e., $12,500) plus 7.5 per cent above that amount.[66] Deacon and Company remained a particular worry, and the exchange auditors insisted that Deacon put up $54,000 in additional capital. He did so by borrowing further on the security of his Northern Canada Mining shares, complaining that the TSE had forced him to sell almost all the firm's shareholdings while writing off its bad debts.[67]

Within weeks the stock market had slumped sharply as the 'Roosevelt recession' took hold in the United States and trading volume declined, followed by a wave of selling in the fall. Commission income at Deacon and Company for the latter half of 1937 was as bad as in the dark days of 1931, though the firm did finish the year with earnings of almost $95,000 as against expenses of $100,000. More seriously, however, the years of stress and strain caught up with Fred Deacon, causing a heart attack that summer. His young sons, Coulter and John, who had recently become partners, struggled to hold the business together while he recuperated. Then came another roundhouse blow. In September TSE members were subjected to their first genuine surprise audit (ten days prior to the regular six-month check-up), and on the eve of Thanksgiving in early October Harry Gordon announced that the total debit balance must be reduced by one-fifth to $400,000 or the firm would have to suspend operators.[68]

Over the holiday weekend the Deacon boys scoured the countryside by car asking customers and friends to pay up their loans or shift their borrowings to the banks themselves. Finally, one long-standing client, whose dealings with Fred Deacon dated back to the turn of the century, agreed to help out. Even though the Deacons had not been able to raise the entire $100,000, Gordon softened his demands and gave them another week to bring the firm into compliance with the TSE's new capital requirements. Once again Deacon and Company had survived by the skin of its teeth.[69]

Fred Deacon never fully recovered from his heart attack, though he returned to his tasks as fully as he could. Then a series of strokes so undermined his energy that he often had to work in bed at home. Stock markets stagnated again after the recession of 1937, and in the spring of 1938 A.D. Watts and Company was forced to discontinue business on the TSE.[70] Fear of a European war following the Munich crisis in the autumn dampened any recovery. The next spring Deacon's old nemesis, Harry Gordon, was heard from once more; he insisted that the firm needed at least $37,500 to raise its free capital to the required 7.5 per cent of client debit balances over $500,000.[71] On the instructions of the TSE board its auditors moved into Deacon and Company's offices, working twenty-four hours a day in preparation for its liquidation.[72]

Deacon and his partner, Harold Edmonds, hastened to Montreal to see Sydney Dobson, general manager of the Royal Bank. Morrow Screw and Nut still owed Deacon the $56,000 that he had personally advanced to pay the dividends on the company's preferred shares, but in 1933 he had promised that he would not seek repayment without the approval of the bank. Gordon therefore had refused to consider this loan as one of Deacon and Company's assets. Would Dobson now permit the repayment of the money so that it could be used to satisfy the exchange's demands? The banker agreed, remarking, 'Colonel Gordon has been giving you one hell of a ride for nearly ten years.'

Still there was a hitch. Both the Royal Bank's local manager and E.A. Wilson, who had taken over Deacon's interest in Morrow Screw and Nut in 1937, were on holiday in Florida. But Gordon would not wait, and Wilson had to be pursued to instruct the bank to advance the money to Deacon. When he returned, he quickly forwarded a cheque for $50,000. Fred Deacon had fended off business failure one more time as the dismal decade of the 1930s dragged to a close.[73]

Deacon and Company survived; though Fred Deacon may have felt ill-used, he was actually treated quite leniently. TSE auditor Harry Gordon once complained to him that exchange officials had 'given more time to [Deacon's] account than all the rest of the members of the Exchange put together.'[74] Even so, his problems were no different in kind from those under which the entire brokerage community laboured during the early 1930s. In truth, virtually every firm seems to have been insolvent and dependent upon the forbearance of the banks and the Canadian Bankers Association for their continued operation. A good number of brokers were less fortunate than Deacon and were compelled to suspend business or to declare bankruptcy. About them we have little detailed information, and that is why Fred Deacon's story must stand for the experience of many brokers during the terrible times of the 1930s.

It was not so much the crash of 1929 that sandbagged most brokers but Britain's departure from the gold standard in September 1931. That move bankrupted a number of securities dealers immediately, and it left those who survived the first blows scrambling hard to avoid a similar fate over the next two or three years. The principles of self-regulation of members by the stock exchanges also underwent a stern test. After the crash the boards of the two exchanges in Toronto and the two in Montreal found themselves devoting more and more attention to the solvency of their members. As a result, the role of the auditors assumed ever-increasing importance.[75]

That, of course, was why Fred Deacon came to focus so much antagonism upon Harry Gordon. Because precise regulations concerning the financial capacities of brokers were lacking, the TSE's exchange auditor possessed unparalleled discretion during the early 1930s. On several occasions it fell to Gordon to give Deacon the bad news that he must reduce his customers' debts and curtail margin accounts or face suspension from membership. Deacon therefore convinced himself that these threats arose as a result of pressure from competitors upon the accountant or from personal animosity towards him on Gordon's part, but there is little evidence to support this notion. Gordon was constrained by his professional standards as a chartered accountant and by his duty as TSE exchange auditor to ensure that a member's suspension did not leave clients out of pocket. Deacon might claim, 'We are solvent but not liquid,'[76] but this was not true. If nobody would buy a security such as Morrow preferred, then (at least for the time being) it was worth nothing and Deacon and Company *was* insolvent.

All-powerful over the fate of the Canadian securities business in the 1930s were the large chartered banks. Their brokers' loans were the lifeblood of the industry without which the collapse would have been even more disastrous than it was. Fortunately for most brokers, the banks (and the Canadian Bankers Association) decided not to call their notes. For months after Britain left the gold standard, bankers and brokers collaborated in the fiction that minimum share prices on listed stocks reflected real market values. Even after minimums were dropped, the bankers refused to press these borrowers too hard (except in a few cases) and allowed them to survive in the hope that recovery would occur. Fred Deacon was fortunate that his bankers (and on occasion the auditor, Gordon) chose to turn a blind eye to the fact of insolvency. That was what enabled him to survive the ordeal of the 1930s with his firm (if not his health) intact.

11

Reform

Although the volume and the value of share trading declined sharply during the early 1930s, the impetus for the reform of securities markets remained strong. Investors who blamed the brokers and the exchanges for the crash of 1929 and its aftermath sought to punish the culprits and ensure that there could be no repetition. Though the Depression almost ended the flotation of new issues, the determination to impose regulation in order to prevent the reappearance of abuses did not evaporate. Doubts persisted, however, about the constitutionality of key sections of the provincial Security Frauds Prevention Acts. Because Ottawa refused to delegate the responsibility for regulating federally incorporated companies to the provinces, it was eventually decided to test the issue in the courts to see if the SFPAs were valid, and an Alberta case became the chosen vehicle. Meanwhile, the federal government had decided that better investor protection required a uniform Companies Act which could be passed in all ten Canadian jurisdictions to ensure fuller disclosure.

The Ontario government continued to play a leading regulatory role. In 1931 George Drew was appointed to head a new board specifically created to enforce the SFPA. He persisted in emphasizing self-regulation and trying to make sure that the stock exchanges controlled their own members rather than relying upon direct government intervention. Drew soon concluded, however, that this oversight would be more effective if the Toronto Stock Exchange and the Standard Stock and Mining Exchange merged with one another, and he pressed the exchanges to come to some agreement. A short-lived boom in mining shares in 1933 and 1934 saw the revival of some of the shady practices that had been common before the crash. Drew therefore moved to tighten regulation of the over-the-counter markets as well, but before long he became embroiled in a serious conflict with the new Liberal provincial government over his activities. This wrangle, in turn, raised the question of whether the province intended to adopt an American model in which the executive held a tighter rein over regulators and supplied clearer direction as to the problems that were to be urgently addressed.

I

As soon as the delegates to the Inter-Provincial conference on securities regulation had dispersed in February 1930, A.W. Rogers of the Ontario attorney general's staff forwarded the report of the proceedings to the federal justice minister, Ernest Lapointe. The provincial representatives had agreed upon the passage of a uniform Security Frauds Prevention Act, and Rogers also noted the renewal of the recommendation that Ottawa hand jurisdiction over virtually all securities marketing to the provinces.[1] He also tried to persuade Under-Secretary of State Thomas Mulvey that Ontario had no intention of using these powers to harass federally chartered companies. An investigation under the SFPA would be ordered only if the promoters were suspected of 'seeking to line their own pockets.' Ottawa would immediately be informed about any suspicious activities. Rogers urged Mulvey to support the revamping of regulatory legislation, because 'some wealthy promoters would like nothing better than to attempt to test the validity of existing provincial legislation for the mere purpose of restricting our efforts and leaving themselves free to do as they like regardless of the interests of the public, of the shareholders and of the company.' The response was not encouraging. Attorney General William Price recorded that Mulvey 'seemed not to understand the manner in which the Fraud Acts were being administered in the different provinces or the necessity of enacting the suggested legislation.' Evidently, the federal bureaucrats would only act upon the request of the provinces if compelled to do so by their political masters.[2]

Doubts about the constitutionality of provincial regulatory legislation persisted. In its 1928 decision the Judicial Committee of the Privy Council had nullified Manitoba's blue-sky law because it interfered with the charter powers of federal companies. To counter this obstacle the Security Frauds Prevention Acts rested upon the principle of registering individual brokers who offered securities for sale. In Rogers's words, 'The provinces take the view that even Dominion companies must get their capital through men who are trustworthy, and not through persons who from their past records are prone to use fraudulent methods, which may even by criminal.' He was convinced that the SFPA would be upheld by the courts if an appropriate test case could be found: 'With this elastic and flexible statute the provinces can long evade an attack on constitutional grounds and can wait until they find a battleground to their liking.'[3]

Eventually the right opportunity offered itself in Alberta. Near the end of

1930 oilman A.H. Mayland attempted to turn over the assets of Mill City Petroleum to another federal company, called Mercury Oils, which he controlled, thus freeing the underwriters, Solloway, Mills and Company (also federally incorporated), from certain obligations. The minority shareholders of Mill City protested. Though at first somewhat reluctant to take up the complaint on the grounds that he might be portrayed as harassing a legitimate undertaking in a time of economic depression, Attorney General J.F. Lymburn concluded that he ought to act and ordered his departmental solicitor, J.J. Frawley, to investigate both the underwriting and the proposed transaction even though no public trading in securities was involved. Mayland promptly challenged the validity of the province's SFPA in a suit naming Lymburn and Frawley as defendants.[4]

In April 1931 Alberta chief justice Harvey delivered the unanimous decision of the Court of Appeal. The judge began by noting that the SFPA granted very broad investigatory powers: the home or office of any person could be searched and witnesses compelled to come from anywhere in the province at their own expense to give evidence under oath, even when there were no grounds to suspect their misconduct. Failure to appear or making any revelations concerning the proceedings could result in a fine of up to $1,000. Not that investigators should be presumed to be going to act unfairly, said Harvey, adding with some asperity, 'though such things have happened in history.' Still, he held that the provincial legislature possessed the authority to make such a law. Judicial notice was taken of the fact 'that in recent years there has been much speculation in stocks and shares, and that in this and other provinces there have been prosecutions of brokers for frauds in connection with the sales of securities and that convictions and imprisonments have resulted.' These convictions, however, had been secured under the federal Criminal Code, not the SFPA, so that the court must still consider whether such legislation lay within provincial jurisdiction.

Mercury Oils was a federally chartered company. While the province could compel such corporations 'to submit to competent general provincial legislation,' Harvey argued that it could not demand unlimited information as to their internal affairs, which the SFPA purported to authorize, 'apart altogether from its inquisitorial and oppressive features.' The Privy Council had held that provincial laws could not interfere in this way with the activities of federal companies, and the court therefore found that the attorney general lacked the power to order such an investigation into the affairs of Mercury Oils, so that the SFPA was *ultra vires* of the provincial legislature.[5]

This decision was a serious setback for the provinces, since it came at a time when they were becoming increasingly frustrated by the federal government's refusal to assist them in regulating the securities business. In January 1931 British Columbia's attorney general, R.H. Pooley, had complained to Price of

Ontario that Ottawa was doing nothing, even though lawyers for I.W.C. Solloway and Harvey Mills were challenging his authority to investigate the affairs of their federally incorporated brokerage firm under the SFPA. Price therefore decided to organize a lobbying effort by the provinces to persuade the federal government to sort out the situation once and for all.[6] He pointed out to Justice Minister Hugh Guthrie that Ottawa had acknowledged the need for reforms in 1930 by responding promptly to the request of the Inter-Provincial conference for an amendment to the Criminal Code to make it an offence for a broker to go short against his own clients. Yet nothing had been done about the other proposals of the conference to strengthen provincial powers over federal companies. The Solloway, Mills case showed how important it was to deal with this problem, since the brokers had been hiding behind federal charters and submitting false information to the provinces to avoid regulatory control.

Secretary of State C.H. Cahan's response was not encouraging. First of all, he raised doubts about the authority of Parliament to delegate to the provinces powers that lay outside their constitutional authority. Even if this could be done, it might mean that federal companies would be subject to nine different sets of requirements among the provinces. Cahan therefore insisted that if regulatory legislation covering federal companies was required, it should be passed and administered directly by Ottawa, but he showed no inclination to take immediate action. When Alberta also raised the issue, he argued that an amendment to the British North America Act would be required to grant the provinces authority to regulate federal companies.[7]

Faced with another rebuff, Alberta and Ontario decided upon an immediate appeal of the *Mayland* decision to the Privy Council, bypassing the Supreme Court of Canada. Price and Ontario premier George Henry advised Guthrie and Prime Minister R.B. Bennett of their intentions at a meeting in the spring of 1931, and Bennett endorsed the idea of a speedy settlement of the constitutional issue before any further legislation was passed. The provinces hastened to retain the eminent Toronto lawyer W.N. Tilley to put their case in London.[8]

The hearing before the Judicial Committee took place in December 1931, with counsel for the government of Canada intervening on Mayland's side to defend broad federal jurisdiction. Ottawa's lawyers argued, as in the 1928 Manitoba reference case, that provincial regulation interfered with the 'status and capacities' of federal companies. In addition, it was claimed that the creation of new securities trading 'offences' by the SFPA was an interference with exclusive federal power over criminal law.[9]

With some difficulty, provincial officials succeeded in persuading Tilley that the SFPA rested upon entirely different principles from earlier Sale of Shares Acts, since no attempt was made to prevent federal companies from selling securities provided that they operated through a registered broker. Thus there was no interference with the charter powers of a company to raise capital. Before the Judicial Committtee Tilley contended that the SFPA was simply general regulatory legislation passed by the province of Alberta under its constitutional jurisdiction over property and civil rights.[10]

Lord Atkin's decision vindicated this claim. The Privy Council held that the SFPA did not 'destroy' or 'sterilize' charter powers like earlier blue-sky legislation. 'A Dominion company constituted with powers to carry on a particular business is subject to the competent legislation of the Province as to that business and may find its special activities completely paralyzed, as by legislation against drink traffic or by the laws as to holding land. If it is formed to trade in securities there appears no reason why it should not be subject to the competent laws of the Province as to the business of all persons who trade in securities.' Moreover, there was 'no reason to suppose that any honest company would have any difficulty in finding registered persons in the Province through whom it could lawfully issue its capital.'

As for the sweeping definition of 'fraudulent acts' which might be investigated under the SFPA, Atkin accepted claims that such wide authority might be necessary. Since the law fell 'within the scope of legislation dealing with property and civil rights, the legislature of the Province, sovereign in this respect, has the sole power and responsibility of determining what degree of protection it will afford the public.' Perhaps reflecting the staider nature of securities markets in Britain, Atkin added a significant *obiter dictum*: 'There is no reason to doubt that the main object sought to be secured ... is ... that persons who carry on the business of dealing in securities shall be honest and of good repute, and in this way to protect the public from being defrauded.'[11]

The provincial victory in *Lymburn v. Mayland* went far beyond even the most optimistic expectations of provincial officials. British Columbia's registrar of companies, H.G. Garrett, who had been concerned that the Privy Council's earlier decisions might lead it to hold the SFPA *ultra vires*, called the decision 'astounding,' 'a sweeping victory' that ought to leave Ottawa 'shivering in its shoes.' J.J. Frawley of Alberta confided that he would have been quite satisfied merely to have the key provisions of the province's SFPA validated. W.N. Tilley, who had always disliked the broad scope of the legislation, even believed that the Judicial Committee was quite mistaken and that part of the act was indeed unconstitutional; he therefore advised Frawley to be cautious in handling future investigations to avoid violating the principles of natural justice. He went so far as to suggest that the provinces ought to repeal the legislation and revise it drastically, though that did not prevent him from accepting a $10,000 fee for his successful advocacy.[12]

In the circumstances, there was little likelihood of provincial officials adopting Tilley's advice. *Lymburn v. Mayland* brought to an end more than a decade of efforts by the provinces to gain regulatory control over the sale of shares by federally chartered companies. Lord Atkin's *obiter dictum* that the 'main object' of the SFPA was 'to secure that persons who carry on the business of dealing in securities shall be honest and of good repute' was a positive invitation to provincial officials to expand their regulatory sphere. All such legislation could in future be justified on the same grounds, safe from constitutional challenge. As Ontario's deputy attorney general put it, no longer was there any doubt that the provinces had 'all the power to legislate for the protection of investors.'[13]

Despite this decision the two levels of government continued to wrangle over company law during the next couple of years. Many lawyers, bankers, and businessmen believed that all Canadian jurisdictions required a new, uniform Companies Act modelled upon the British legislation of 1929. At a Dominion-Provincial Conference held in January 1933 the federal government proposed this as a means of protecting the rights of investors. After the first ministers had discussed the matter briefly, it was agreed that Ottawa should convene another conference to draft such a bill.[14]

Eventually Secretary of State C.H. Cahan did submit a draft bill to a Dominion-Provincial Conference in January 1934, but the provincial representatives unanimously requested more time to study the matter. Several of the provinces were not enthusiastic about the federal proposals, preferring to retain their existing regulations. In fact, none even bothered to make representations to Cahan. As a result, Ottawa finally decided to go it alone, and a new Companies Act following the British model was passed during the 1934 session of Parliament. Promoters of federal companies were now required to file more detailed prospectuses and copies of sales literature before offering securities to the public. In addition, all considerations paid to vendors of property conveyed to companies and the existence of all options for the sale of shares from the treasury had to be disclosed.[15]

The federal government thus followed a regulatory approach which bore some similarity to that recently adopted in the United States. Since 1929 pressure had been growing upon Washington to end the same sort of abuses in securities markets complained of in Canada. In the spring of 1933 the new Roosevelt administration passed the first federal Securities Act (sometimes called the 'Truth in Lending' law), which required borrowers to disclose all material facts to investors through filings with the Federal Trade Commission. The Canadian Companies Act of 1934 did not establish a separate regulatory agency, but it did rely upon the principle of full disclosure which also underlay American regulation.

Up to that point stock exchanges and brokers in the United States had successfully fended off federal regulation, but then came damaging revelations about stock pools and price manipulation in testimony before a Senate committee, largely as a result of aggressive questioning by its chief counsel, Ferdinand Pecora. Early in February 1934 President Roosevelt suddenly sent a message to Congress demanding action, and soon afterwards a bill was introduced to extend regulatory authority. The 1934 Securities Exchange Act, drafted by some of Roosevelt's young 'brains trusters,' including Thomas Corcoran and James M. Landis, handed the task of regulating brokers, exchanges, and securities issuers alike to a new, five-member Securities and Exchange Commission (SEC) appointed by the president. Disclosure remained the fundamental regulatory principle, but rather than fixing detailed rules the 1934 act left much discretion to this new commission, a fact that made the choice of a person to head it all the more critical. Roosevelt surprised everyone by turning to Joseph P. Kennedy, himself a millionaire Wall Street speculator and a notorious manipulator during the 1920s. The SEC then set about the massive task of registering the hundreds of brokers and securities on the nation's twenty-four stock exchanges, though at first interfering hardly at all in their internal affairs and simply approving existing by-laws. Despite Kennedy's generally conciliatory approach, however, investment bankers staged a 'capital strike' and refused to undertake any new share flotations until the spring of 1935 in protest against the federal government's interference with their business.[16]

In Canada the federal government played a much more limited role. The Privy Council's 1932 decision in *Lymburn v. Mayland* awarded jurisdiction for the regulation of securities markets to the provinces. Lord Atkin's *dictum* that the 'main object' of the Security Frauds Prevention Acts was to protect the public by ensuring that 'persons who carry on business shall be honest and of good repute' seemed to sanction broad administrative discretion. Ottawa's resistance to the provinces intervening in this aspect of the affairs of federally incorporated companies could no longer be sustained. The new federal Companies Act of 1934 did impose somewhat tighter controls over the organization and financing of such undertakings, but regulation of the marketing of securities clearly became primarily a provincial responsibility thereafter.

II

Even before the Privy Council had rendered its decision in *Lymburn v. Mayland*, the province of Ontario had moved to beef up its regulatory capabilities. Oversight had previously been exercised by the staff of the Attorney General's Department in addition to their many other responsibilities for administering and enforcing both civil and criminal law. In 1931 the government of George Henry (who had succeeded Howard Ferguson) concluded that securities regulation was sufficiently complex and time-consuming that it required a full-time overseer. As a result, the Security Frauds Prevention Act was amended to provide for the appointment of a Security Frauds Prevention Board to deal with such matters. Attorney General William Price chose George Drew, a well-known Conservative who currently occupied the quasi-judicial post of master of the Supreme Court of Ontario, as a one-man regulator. Rather than simply pursuing fraudulent operators, Drew was expected to scrutinize new promotions from the outset and step in to prevent abuses in advance wherever possible.[17] The following year the provincial government passed an amendment that re-named its legislation the Securities Act to indicate that fraud prevention was no longer the sole aim, and the year after that another change altered the name of Drew's agency to the Ontario Securities Commission (OSC).[18]

Although Ontario appointed a full-time regulator and created a securities commission even before the American SEC came into existence, George Drew and Attorney General Price always favoured self-regulation by the stock exchanges as the first line of defence against misconduct. In addition, a merger between the Standard Stock and Mining Exchange and its less-tarnished rival, the Toronto Stock Exchange, seemed one simple but effective means of raising the standards of business conduct and restoring the reputation of securities markets. This idea, much favoured by Price, was first floated in the spring of 1931.

F.J. Crawford, who had been re-elected president of the Standard after leading it through the terrible crisis of 1930, managed to persuade his board to consider closer cooperation between the exchanges. He approached the TSE and offered to drop several integrated oil companies from the SSME listings and to stop trading industrials on its unlisted section. In return, it was hoped that TSE members would agree not to tread on Standard turf by dropping all mining companies from its listings and ceasing to trade them on its unlisted section.[19] Then the exchanges would open their doors to each other's members, creating one large organization with two different sections for mines and for industrials. Unfortunately, this plan foundered because some Standard members tried to pretend that their seats were now worth more than those on the TSE, even though the price of Standard memberships had fallen as low as $12,000 by 1930 from a high of nearly $100,000 in 1929 (see appendix, table A.7). When the Standard offered simply to amalgamate with the other exchange, it was rebuffed by the TSE's annual meeting. Though unofficial discussions between the two exchanges continued during the summer of 1931, the SSME board eventually decided that any further amalgamation proposals would have to come from the TSE.[20]

In truth, the SSME was not really in a very strong bargaining position since a number of its members were in extremely rough shape. The year-end audit for 1930 revealed that F.G. Oke and Company was in a serious difficulties and a desperate search for new capital was under way during the spring of 1931. The May audit showed that six firms were having problems, and in June the banks refused to honour cheques drawn by Fleming and Marvin, forcing the firm to surrender its membership. A month later Colonel G.F. Morrison committed suicide, his brokerage firm insolvent, and near the end of the summer Carroll and Wright went into receivership. By that time the exchange's deficit had risen to $14,000, and Canada Life had to be asked to waive the half-yearly payment on the principal of the mortgage on the Temperance Street premises, opened with such fanfare in the summer of 1929.[21]

Moreover, signs that the wicked doings on the Standard exchange's floor were not entirely a thing of the past surfaced at the same time. The Chemical Research Corporation controlled the Gyro process for producing gasoline, but as no refiners were using it, the predicted royalty payments had not materialized. Though this company was traded on the unlisted section of the Standard, management refused to release any financial information. When complaints led the head of the new Ontario Security Frauds Prevention Board, George Drew, to enquire of the Standard's board what it knew about the affairs of Chemical Research, he had to be told that since it was unlisted the exchange had no information whatever about its operations.[22]

Britain's departure from the gold standard in September 1931 was a body blow to both exchanges, extinguishing all talk of amalgamation for several months while brokers struggled to survive under the minimum-price rules. Yet with trading volume and commission income in steep decline the idea was revived by the Standard at the end of the year. TSE members, however, believed that they now held the upper hand since their exchange was more prestigious and had a better building and $135,000 in its treasury. The Standard people countered that mining brokers were bigger commission generators and that they had the largest trading floor in Canada, which could easily accommodate double the current number of members. A general meeting of TSE members was unable to reach a decision on a union in December 1931, though negotiations between representatives of the two boards continued in a desultory way in the new year.[23]

When it became clear that a merger was 'definitely off,' the new Standard president, G.W. Nicholson, called his members together early in 1932 and warned that the TSE might end commission splitting altogether. This would severely hurt Standard members, who received a 50–50 commission split on trades in mining shares executed for TSE members, an important source of business. Such a 'war' could bankrupt some members of both exchanges in the present depressed times. Faced with this threat the Standard members voted to resume discussions with the TSE, though only by a margin of 13 to 9.[24]

Before long an agreement that fell short of a merger was hammered out. The Standard consented to delist four oil producers (British American, Imperial Oil, International Petroleum and Crown Dominion), while the TSE would cease to list or to permit unlisted trading in any mining shares. Only the mineral producers International Nickel and Consolidated Mining and Smelting would be listed on both exchanges, members being free to charge full commissions on trades in them. As in the past, TSE members who bought other stocks through SSME firms would split commissions 50–50. This 'delisting agreement' came into force on 30 April 1932. Members of the two exchanges were hopeful that it would raise both the value and volume of their business.[25]

Meanwhile, George Drew worked to persuade the exchanges to regulate their own members more closely. Audits to ensure solvency were the first line of defence, and the 1931 amendments to the SFPA which created the regulatory board also empowered the exchanges to require their members to adopt any system of book- or record-keeping specified by the executive.[26] Drew was also determined to force the exchanges to deal vigorously with any suspected misconduct. This applied particularly to the Standard exchange. In January 1932 he wrote to G.W. Nicholson, the new president, to complain that the directors had approved a loan to the now-defunct Fairlie and Company on the basis of a balance sheet that showed the firm's seat valued at $100,000, at a time when it was common knowledge that it was not worth even one-third that amount. He reminded Nicholson that under the SFPA the auditors reported not to Drew but to the exchange board: 'It was intended ... that there should be no direct interference with members of the exchange by the Security Frauds Prevention Board, and that the discipline over its members should be carried on by the exchange itself.' If the SSME board had merely accepted figures as submitted by Fairlie, then the public was not receiving the protection to which it was entitled under the SFPA.[27]

To make certain that the Standard clearly understood his position, Drew met privately with the board in February 1932. To president Nicholson, who had missed the meeting, he reported that he believed this discussion had 'ironed out some of the difficulties in relation to the Act, which I hope were mostly a matter of misunderstanding.' Drew also kept up the pressure upon the exchange to investigate any suspicious fluctuations in share prices. Masterson and Company of Montreal was aggressively marketing Buffalo Canadian Gold Mines, which traded on the SSME. As the stock moved up from 20 to 35 cents, Drew complained that Masterson's firm was 'carrying on a high pressure selling system, creating a fictitious value on the market for the securities they are handling, and on the basis of this unloading to the public.' Telephone salesmen were promising that the shares would soon go as high as 75 cents. Drew referred the matter to the Standard confidentially on the basis of his undertanding with the board to 'leave the discipline of brokers and securities with the Exchange in the hands of the Exchange itself.'[28]

He also compelled the Standard to require listed companies to file all underwriting and option agreements with the exchange and to notify his agency whenever there was any significant change in capital structure or internal organization. At the same time he tried to persuade the board to pass general regulations regarding advertisements run by members, ruling out any claims that a rise in the price of a stock was imminent. The governors, however, refused to adopt such rules and merely considered each case on its merits whenever there were complaints. Drew was particularly annoyed when one SSME member issued a circular in April 1932 alleging that there had been a bear raid on Teck Hughes which had driven the stock down from $5 to $3, yet the board had refused to punish the offender even though he admitted that he had acted ill-advisedly. In the end, however, Drew allowed the matter to drop.[29]

Relations with the exchange had, after all, to be conducted fairly diplomatically in order to secure cooperation. When Hughson Brothers gave up its seat on the SSME in June 1932, Drew's deputy, Miss H.B. Palen, tried to discover privately whether or not the firm was in serious financial trouble. She reminded the Standard's assistant secretary, A.J. Trebilock, that exchange members were not required to submit their auditor's report to the government in order to renew their registration as brokers, since the exchanges were responsible for overseeing their solvency. Should Drew use his general powers under the SFPA to order an audit, she asked? Trebilcock, however, was giving nothing away and blandly replied that he did not even know whether Hughson Brothers intended to continue in business as a non-member broker. All he could suggest was to consult the people who were taking over the seat on the exchange.[30]

Though Drew spent much of his time and energy trying to get the exchanges to cooperate, he could not ignore the over-the-counter markets. The problem for a regulator in the early 1930s was to prevent dishonest dealing without cracking down so hard as to provoke charges that over zealousness was blocking economic recovery. Drew's counterpart in British Columbia observed that he had to use his wide powers with a very light hand. The public liked to cry fraud and demand punishment whenever shareholders lost money. 'Here the task is to satisfy the public that the act is effective and being enforced and yet to refuse to deal with more or less groundless complaints.' Still, regulators must not shrink from ordering investigations where necessary. 'The province ... has now taken the dragon by the tail and cannot well let it go.'[31]

The mining fraternity was particularly prone to complaints about over-regulation. In the spring of 1932 a meeting of lawyers, businessmen, and prospectors in Haileybury, Ontario, passed a whole series of resolutions alleging that the rules were impeding mineral exploration by discouraging grubstaking. Calling upon local Conservative organizations to pressure the provincial government, the gathering demanded that the law 'be administered in future according to its literal meaning and not on the interpretation of an individual.' Soon afterwards Drew promised a joint meeting of the Canadian Institute of Mining and Metallurgy and the Ontario Prospectors Association in Toronto that he would form an advisory committee to consider changes in the legislation. The local branch of the CIMM, the OPA, and the Standard stock exchange were all invited to nominate members to this body. The committee recommended that prospectors be permitted to form exploration syndicates with capital up to $35,000 without going through the formal registration process. Drew agreed to allow them to do so and had the regulations altered by order-in-council. Only if shares were to be sold to the public was a prospectus required to be filed, along with detailed information about company organization.[32]

By mid-1932 the Canadian stock exchanges were finally abandoning the last of the minimum prices imposed when Britain left the gold standard. Unfortunately, freeing prices did little to revive securities markets, and both share values and volume remained low. For example, the TSE's exchange auditor in the spring of 1932 twice recommended that Fred Deacon suspend his business because of his scant commission income and his staggering burden of debt (see chapter 10). Times were so bad that by September 1932 the idea of merging the TSE and the Standard exchange was revived in the hope that a union might improve the brokerage business.

This time the Toronto Stock Exchange took the initiative. On 20 September a special meeting of TSE members voted to amend its by-laws to permit them to purchase seats on the SSME, provided that the Standard reciprocated and the 'delisting agreement' dividing mines and industrials between the two remained in force. The Standard board therefore convened a meeting of members to consider the proposal. Although amicable feelings were expressed, a majority still preferred amalgamation rather than dual membership, which they believed would only stand in the way of an ultimate merger. Even if no immediate union was likely, they preferred the status quo to a permanent division; so the TSE proposal was voted down by a 20-to-7 margin, as a result of which it lapsed.[33]

This lack of enthusiasm among Standard members for a merger on the TSE's terms was reinforced by a short-lived boom in gold stocks early in 1933. With 1.5 million shares changing hands on some days, there was new life at the building on Temperance Street, where 150 people thronged the floor. Traders were reported to be carrying bottles of 'cough medicine' to soothe throats hoarsened by shouting. Business was so good that two members of the New York Stock Exchange, Jenks Gwynne and Company and J.R. Timmins and Company, purchased seats on the SSME for about $16,000 each in order to cash in on the bull market.[34]

This upturn caused some grumbling at the Toronto Stock Exchange since the 'delisting agreement' of April 1932 had ended trading in mining shares on Bay Street. At a general meeting of members in January 1933 a motion was made to terminate the arrangement immediately. TSE president 'Mike' Mitchell argued against the idea, contending that it was more desirable to continue to cooperate, and the motion eventually failed for lack of a seconder. Negotiations concerning a merger were revived in April, and the members of both exchanges formally authorized their representatives to continue the discussions.[35]

By this time George Drew had become convinced that he would have to involve himself directly in the negotiations between the two stock exchanges if any progress was to be made. For him the advantages of a single self-regulating exchange were obvious: he hoped that a new board's policies would reflect the slightly more conservative views of TSE members rather than the buccaneering attitudes still common at the SSME. Drew therefore began attending all the meetings between the executive committees of the exchanges. Though little detailed information on these negotiations is available, the issues were fairly clear: SSME members might be doing a larger volume of business (though mainly in penny stocks) but stood to gain prestige from a union that would blur the memories of the scandalous events of 1930. The TSE's members might like a cut of the Standard's business in mining shares during such dismal times but clearly were not going to be granted this without agreeing to a complete amalgamation.

By the end of November 1933 an agreement had been hammered out. The SSME's fifty-odd members would be permitted to join the Toronto Stock Exchange's sixty-two seat holders in a single organization governed by a merged executive committee. The Standard agreed to contribute $51,000 to add to the $62,000 in the treasury of the new TSE. Harold Franks of the TSE would remain president, while the SSME's G.W. Nicholson took over as vice-president, and the offices of secretary and treasurer would be divided between the exchanges until the 1934 annual meeting in June. A.J. Trebilcock of the Standard became the senior paid official (first assistant secretary with a salary of $5,000 per annum), while his TSE counterpart, A.E. Marks, became second assistant secretary. Simultaneous members' meetings approved these arrangements on 5 December 1933.[36]

Since neither of the existing trading floors could accommodate all of the hundred-odd members and their floor traders, the initial plan was that a two-floor exchange should start operation on 2 January 1934. For the time being mines would continue to be handled in the old Standard building on Temperance Street, while industrials alone traded on Bay Street until the TSE could expand its premises onto an adjoining property (see photo 20). It soon became clear, however, that the formal merger would have to be delayed for a month since a number of members were determined to operate on both floors simultaneously. With minor renovations completed the first meetings of the two sections of the expanded TSE occurred on 5 February as forty-six SSME members took on their new roles amidst great self-congratulation.[37]

The amalgamation of the Standard stock exchange into the Toronto Stock Exchange came about just as a boom developed in Canadian mining shares, helped along by the rise in the price of gold in the United States from $20 to $35 per ounce at the beginning of 1934. Volume picked up and gold stocks advanced sharply. A couple of months after the merger, President Harold Franks declared that the marriage had gone 'surprisingly smoothly' and the prestige of the TSE had increased by 'leaps and bounds.' In truth, however, the exchange would suffer some serious growing pains.[38]

Ontario securities commissioner George Drew had worked so hard to bring about the merger because he believed that it would tighten self-regulation of members. Soon afterwards he met with the new TSE executive to remind them of their obligations. As the market for mining shares picked up, he pressured the exchange to ride herd on companies by insisting upon the filing of up-to-date information regarding options and underwriting agreements. At the end of February Algonquin Mines was delisted for failing to supply this information. When the price of Arno Mines shares suddenly shot up from 8 cents to 20 then quickly collapsed back to 4 cents, the stock was removed from the TSE's unlisted section (though it quickly found a new home on the Montreal Curb Market). At the same time, members were reminded to submit all advertising material to the exchange for approval in advance to ensure that exaggerated claims were not being made.[39]

Early in April the TSE board decided to launch an investigation whenever there were sharp price fluctuations and immediately authorized an examination of trading records for Bagamac Rouyn, Columario Consolidated, and Maple Leaf Mines. In an effort to end some of the freewheeling practices that had been carried over from the Standard exchange, the floor committee also threatened to discipline two experienced mining traders who were using their know-how to break in on orders being filled by less-seasoned operators. At the same time the listings underwent a 'spring cleaning' in which a dozen or so stocks were suspended or delisted for failure to comply with various exchange rules.[40]

Drew was still not satisfied. He requested another meeting with the board to express his unhappiness at the way in which promoters and brokers were using the exchange to assist in the primary distribution of stock controlled by them through the manipulation of share prices. A stock-exchange listing was now regarded by the public as evidence of soundness and a guarantee that the prices quoted represented real values, but mining companies, in particular, were employing their listings as selling tools in tipsheets and high-pressure telephone campaigns. Members who held low-priced options on treasury shares were urging clients to buy the stock without disclosing their interest, which constituted misrepresentation. Drew told the board, 'He considered that the financing of a company by the sale of treasury stock based on exchange quotations is absolutely divergent from the ordinary functions of a stock exchange, which is to provide a readily available market for securities ... in the hands of the public.' He warned the directors that if public criticism of these practices developed, the government would be under strong pressure to end self-regulation and introduce tight control over the exchange.[41]

At Drew's suggestion a committee of the board was struck to consider what might be done to alter long-accepted practices, but it failed to reach agreement. Directors from the old TSE who specialized in industrial stocks shared his antagonism towards brokers' options on treasury stock because of abuses. The president of one TSE-listed mining company was known to control a securities firm that held a large number of low-priced options on treasury shares in the mine. Over a period of a few months the stock was run up from just pennies to over 50 cents, but the mine held onto its listing because it was impossible to secure conclusive proof of the insider trading. The mining men from the Standard exchange insisted that there was nothing wrong with taking out options and feeding low-priced shares onto the market as the stock price rose. A.J. Trebilcock pointed out that the SSME had considered requiring the disclosure of every option agreement but had decided against it, though the TSE did require all listed companies to file this information and permitted members to reveal it to clients. He contended that the firms which specialized in industrials simply didn't grasp the way in which mine financing worked, while the critics were convinced that they understood all too well. Since the brokerage community was unable to agree upon new rules, Drew apparently decided to let matters stand for the time being. Self-regulation had its limits.[42]

With the market for mining shares booming, George Drew also took steps to clean up over-the-counter markets. Calling at private residences to sell securities was banned in 1933. Salesmen were required to deliver written confirmations of all orders within twenty-four hours (which helped to stamp out false verbal representations). Distributors operating on commission had to disclose this fact, and the OSC was given authority to fix 'reasonable' commissions. Vendor shares of mining companies given in exchange for properties could not be sold by insiders or promoters unless this fact was disclosed to purchasers, since they netted company treasuries nothing.[43]

As a result of the ban on door-to-door selling, however, by 1934 investors were being bombarded with mailings, tipsheets, telegrams, and telephone calls urging them to buy shares, mainly in mines. The *Financial Post* received an impressive registered letter bearing 13 cents' worth of stamps and several 'Rush' marks which advised buying gold stocks for wondrous profits; the paper recommended that Drew do some 'furious thinking' about how to cope with such problems. Editor Floyd Chalmers later expressed the view that the commissioner himself was partly to blame: 'George Drew always seemed to me a person who would get very inflamed and angry about some situation and he'd enter upon a new job, particularly a job of cleaning up a situation with a tremendous enthusiasm and then the enthusiasm would gradually diminish. I think this was true of his regime as Chairman of the Ontario Securities Commision. He did accomplish something of very considerable importance in the merger of the exchanges, but I never felt he was pursuing it, following up all the little crooked brokers that were around at that time.'[44]

Certainly, there were plenty of brand new problems, such as radio broadcasts, to cope with. John H. Roberts, publisher of a tipsheet called the *Canadian Mining Recorder*, started up a program; on his 6 April 1934 show he displayed the evangelical fervour that had once carried him to a leading position in the Dominion Alliance for the Total Suppression of the Liquor Traffic. He blasted people who discouraged investment in mining shares as 'grossly ignorant' and condemned those who said that share prices were inflated as 'public enemies.' Though he denied being an expert, Roberts made positive recommendations on no less than nineteen different issues. Listeners following his advice helped to push these stocks significantly higher since he suggested that some of them might triple in value.[45]

The falling costs of telephone service also permitted share pushing on a new scale. After the Ontario Securities Commission announced that it had closed three Toronto boiler rooms in the summer of 1934 (sparking an exodus of salesmen to Montreal), a *Financial Post* reporter visited one of the remaining operations. A dozen men were working the phones calling 'suckers,' names from purchased shareholders' lists being the most productive of orders. After Roosevelt's regulatory legislation in 1933 and 1934 there emerged a long-running theme in such Canadian exposes as the *Post*'s: the claim was always made that most of the salesmen were Americans who had fled to less harsh Canadian climes.[46]

By no means everybody agreed that a crackdown was required. In the spring of 1934 the Canadian Institute of Mining and Metallurgy heard an engineer make the familiar charge that the Securities Act was blocking mine development. He said that the Security Frauds Prevention Acts had been drawn up to cater to public agitation by those who knew nothing of the mining business. Even the changes in 1932 to permit small exploration syndicates to operate free of registration had left legitimate prospectors tied up in red tape and fearful of malicious prosecution without seriously hampering the crooks. In July the Toronto *Telegram* took up this cry, calling for the abolition of the OSC and arguing that the Criminal Code could deal better with fraudulent operators than a regulatory tribunal.[47]

George Drew continued to make efforts to police the trading of mining shares. In August 1934 he pressured the TSE into taking a closer look at its unlisted section (which shaded imperceptibly into the over-the-counter market). The board agreed to undertake to discover which companies met the listing requirements with a view to pressing them to apply for listing, which would thus make them more closely controlled. After a meeting between Drew and the directors the following month, each one was asked to prepare written proposals for tighter regulation over unlisted trading. Eventually the TSE did agree that details of all options and underwriting agreements for listed companies would have to be disclosed and published in the TSE *Bulletin* and could be released to the press. The board could refuse to approve such agreements and suspend trading if companies were unwilling to modify them. Of course, that still left unlisted and over-the-counter stocks free of such restrictions.[48] Despite Drew's efforts, however, there continued to be criticisms about the regulation of securities markets by the Ontario Securities Commission, as papers such as the *Financial Post* complained that he was doing too little to stamp out misconduct and demanded more drastic action.

III

The complaints about George Drew found a receptive audience after the election of a new Liberal government in Ontario in June 1934. Taking its cue from Premier Mitchell Hepburn, the cabinet adopted a highly partisan stance towards the provincial civil service. This 'spoils' approach to office holding owed more to American than to Canadian models, but the Liberals were keen to impress the Depression-weary voters with their frugality and determination to prune out

Tory dead wood accumulated over the past decade.[49] Almost inevitably, George Drew, a high-profile official with well-known Conservative connections and a big salary, became involved in a nasty wrangle with his political superior, Attorney General Arthur Roebuck.

In many ways the two men were mirror images of one another, differing in little except their political affiliations. Both were partisan thoroughbreds. Drew had been born in Guelph, Ontario, in 1894, the grandson of a member of Canada's first parliament following Confederation; he joined the militia at sixteen, enlisted in the Canadian Expeditionary Force when war broke out in 1914, was wounded fighting as an artilleryman, and was ultimately promoted to the rank of colonel as commander of a training battery. After attending Osgoode Hall Law School, he was called to the bar in 1920, and while practising law in his home town, he entered municipal politics as alderman and later mayor. A committed Conservative, Drew was appointed to the patronage post of assistant master of the Supreme Court of Ontario in 1926 and promoted to master three years later, before William Price tapped him to head the new Security Frauds Prevention Board in 1931.[50]

Roebuck was older, having been born in 1878, and was proud to call himself the great-nephew of the outstanding radical British parliamentarian J.A. Roebuck. He worked for many years as a journalist, first on the editorial staff of the Toronto *Daily Star* and then as owner and editor of the Temiskaming *Herald* and Cobalt *Citizen* in the northern mining country. Twice he stood unsuccessfully for the Liberals as a candidate for the provincial legislature and was defeated in the federal election of 1917. Also a graduate of Osgoode Hall, he entered legal practice in Toronto, and during the early 1920s he acted as adviser to the Lands and Forests Department following an investigation that had been highly critical of Conservative Howard Ferguson's conduct in granting timber licences. Roebuck was elected for a Toronto riding in 1934 and was chosen by Hepburn to be his attorney general. Slimmer and slighter than Drew, he could nonetheless wield a mean partisan knife which was every bit the equal of the artilleryman's heavy guns at close quarters.[51]

Thus it was hardly a surprise when Roebuck dispatched a brief, abrupt letter to Drew on 15 September 1934 demanding his immediate resignation as Ontario securities commissioner in light of the amount of money being spent and the comparative lack of regulatory success achieved. Drew's reply bristled with resentment at what he considered these false accusations. On the matter of costs he pointed out that most of the OSC's budget came from registration fees. No law could protect the public against every kind of ingenious swindler, but he was convinced of his effectiveness as a regulator and suggested a number of legislative changes that would improve matters even further. To Premier Hepburn,

Drew affected pained surprise: of course he would not stay on if unwanted, but why was his conduct now deemed unsatisfactory when he had always sought to serve the province with scrupulous care?[52]

There was no immediate reply. Over the next ten days the premier was ill and Roebuck absent on a trip. As soon as he got back to town, the attorney general turned up the heat; he sent for certain OSC files and allegedly removed a memorandum from Drew explaining why it would be an 'outrage' to give a licence to a certain person to sell securities, purportedly to shield a Liberal crony. Drew instantly conveyed his 'utter astonishment and indignation' to the premier. How could he be expected to administer the act properly in light of Roebuck's interference, made worse by his refusal to accept recommendations about new regulations that urgently needed cabinet approval? In fact, Drew complained, Roebuck had treated him with 'calculated discourtesy' from the outset. The attorney general had refused even to see the commissioner, keeping him hanging around for hours in an outer office on a couple of occasions; their only consultation had been a brief conversation while Roebuck hurried from his office to the cabinet room.

Drew sought to turn the conflict into one of high principle. The OSC might receive its funding through the attorney general, but that did not make it a branch of his department or give him the right to interfere in administration: 'Careful analysis of the Securities Act indicates that it contemplates an independent commission, over which the commissioner has complete supervision, subject only to the control of the courts in the event of excess of authority. Unless such completely independent control of the act is granted, I am satisfied from three and a half years' rather extensive experience that it would be infinitely better to do away with the act entirely.' Though he must have known that he was sealing his fate as Ontario's securities commissioner, Drew ended his salvo with a spectacular burst of high explosives: so that he wouldn't be blamed for any regulatory failures from now on, he told the premier, he was sending copies of his letter directly to all the Toronto newspapers for publication on the following day, Saturday, 29 September 1934.[53]

That turned the fight into *une guerre à l'outrance*. The violently partisan *Daily Star* had already floated the rumour that Drew was considering the Conservative nomination in the federal riding of Wellington North (which he had equally promptly denied). From his sickbed Hepburn told the paper that Drew was in no position to complain of discourtesy in light of his 'publicity stunt' in releasing his letter. Denying that this was a personal vendetta, the premier said that the provincial government would 'get along' fine without the commissioner, whose responsibilities would be handled by Roebuck for the time being.[54]

The attorney general immediately briefed the premier on the background to Drew's 'newspaper torpedo,' seizing the opportunity to try out some choice insults in private before unleashing them upon the public. By making the 'scandalous imputation' that Roebuck had pilfered letters from the OSC's file, Drew had shown 'the manners of a boor or the venom of a traducer.' 'His slur is as ungentlemanly as it is unjust ... One who would stoop to such tactics is quite unfit to sit in judgement on the business community.' As for the claims made for the independence of the OSC, 'Mr. Drew has been undisputed cock of the securities loft for three and one-half years,' having drawn up the regulatory legislation and regulations and administered them like an absolute monarch. Playing the tribune of the people, the attorney general rejected Drew's conception of his 'absolutism and freedom from responsibility' to the government and legislature. The old Tory government might have used him to deflect criticism of the securities business, but Roebuck would never allow Drew to waste money or 'sacrifice the public interests at his own sweet will. He has a queer conception of the status of a public service.'

Drew could not have it both ways, said the attorney general. If Roebuck was not allowed to interfere in the OSC's affairs, then he was merely an onlooker while the commissioner 'pursued his literary and speaking career, and the selling of securities showed signs of developing into a public disaster.' Dubious stocks and dishonest salesmen were threatening to overwhelm markets, creating 'genuine alarm for the public safety.' Drew was concealing the fact that he had been asked to resign for failing to do his job properly and now he must go.[55]

The premier gave his approval, and at a hastily convened cabinet meeting on the morning of Monday, 1 October, acting premier Harry Nixon and five other ministers signed the order-in-council relieving Drew of his position. After the meeting Roebuck had a chance to toss off some of his carefully rehearsed insults for reporters ('manners of a boor ... venom of a traducer'). Drew got a chance to air his side of the story again in the Tory Toronto *Telegram*: Roebuck was casting 'cowardly' slurs on his competence, using this 'contemptible insult' to conceal the lack of cause for the dismissal.[56]

In a letter to the premier, Drew again took a high-and-mighty line: he had no desire to see his firing reversed and, indeed, would never serve while the present ministers held office. All that he asked for was the British justice which 60,000 Canadians had died fighting for in the First World War: the right to know the charges against him and the opportunity to answer them. Trying to shift the issue to his competence was 'both malicious and dishonest'; the suggestion that he had been motivated by partisanship 'as contemptible as it is false.' Roebuck should not be permitted to get away with this un-British conduct: 'Above all, the Attorney General should no longer be permitted to suppress justice at its very source.' He now claimed that Roebuck was trying to get rid of him because he had refused to be coerced into improperly granting registration to a man with twelve criminal convictions.[57]

That claim led to a whole new round of charges and countercharges. Roebuck had sent a letter to Drew about registering one F.B. Carey, a client of the attorney general's former law partner, E.A. Newsom. The minister insisted that he had only asked Drew to give a man denied that the opportunity to pursue his livelihood a 'sympathetic rehearing.' Where was British justice when a person could be dealt with summarily without any right of appeal against the commissioner's decision? If OSC staff now denied that Roebuck had sent for and tampered with confidential files, replied Drew, the attorney general must have started a 'reign of terror among the civil service.'[58]

Roebuck finally recaptured the spotlight by announcing on 3 October that the new Ontario securities commissioner would be John M. Godfrey, described by *Saturday Night* as 'one of the most prominent Liberal lawyers in Toronto without a seat in the legislature.' Godfrey agreed to accept a salary of only $7,500 as compared with Drew's $8,000.[59] A week later Hepburn, now recovered from his illness, told reporters after cabinet, 'This government is determined to do what its predecessor has never done, namely wage war without quarter through its Securities Commission on financial racketeers and all persons engaging in improper financial practices.' Godfrey announced new regulations under the Securities Act which prohibited telephoning private residences to sell securities. The government claimed that Drew ought to have realized the need for such a ban over a year earlier when boiler rooms had once more become a serious problem: 'Even if Colonal Drew had not willfully put an end to his career as Commissioner, his ... lack of efficiency in not taking the only possible means to eradicate boiler-rooms would have left the Attorney General with no alternative but to ask for his resignation, and the government with no alternative but to dismiss him in the absence of his resignation. Not to have foreseen the inevitable consequences of prohibiting canvassing from door to door, namely that telephones would be employed to sell spurious securities is in the case of a highly paid public official an act of omission that can only be classified as gross negligence.'[60]

George Drew now tried to regain the initiative by alleging that Arthur Roebuck himself was guilty of shady business conduct. He had acted as president of the Diversified Investment Trust Limited, into which investors had paid $186,000. Before the crash of 1929 the trust had assets worth $220,000, all of which had evaporated. Interviewed, Roebuck admitted that the Diversified Trust had suffered after the crash, but he would only give Drew 'credit for his nerve.' He pointed out that the OSC's failure to investigate this case sooner only showed how 'woefully lax' was its management. He added that Drew, 'With his utter lack of any sense of the fitness of things ought to make an excellent leader for the Conservative party.'[61]

The attacks on Drew brought other critics of him out of the woodwork; W.J. Beckett and Company charged that the OSC's 'sleuths' had persecuted the brokerage even though all that Beckett had done was to sign a petition calling for the establishment of a new stock exchange. Drew responded in a speech to the Electric Club of Toronto in which he charged that tipsheets issued by the likes of John H. Roberts (*Canadian Mining Recorder*), Denby Lloyd (*Mining World*), and Strathearn Boyd Thompson (*Hush*) and radio broadcasts by Beckett and Leigh Brooks (the 'Old Counsellor') were swindling investors out of thousands. These men had dubious reputations at best and criminal records at worst. At least he had kept Brooks from doing business in Ontario by denying him registration, but now the 'Old Counsellor' was 'hanging around Queen's Park and not just admiring the architecture.'[62]

By the middle of October 1934 this unseemly wrangle was beginning to run out of steam, though Drew again tried to give it new life by claiming that Roebuck's brother-in-law and secretary, Donald D. Walkinshaw, had been deprived of his insurance licence back in 1930; Walkinshaw responded with a libel suit.[63] Meanwhile, John Godfrey was settling in at the Ontario Securities Commission. He soon fired Norman Harris, who had acted as Drew's 'financial assistant' at the commission. Harris, the former financial editor of *Saturday Night*, responded with a lengthy (if none too coherent) series of articles in the *Financial Post* claiming that the lawyers at the OSC (like Drew and Godfrey) would never be able to clean up the securities business as he could have done. But by that time the whole tempest in a teapot stirred up by Arthur Roebuck and George Drew was finally subsiding.[64]

Before long Premier Hepburn's drinking buddy George McCullagh, who ran the brokerage house of R.P. Barrett and Company, was writing to tell his friend how well Godfrey was working out at the OSC. By his steady effort he was weeding out the wildcat promoters who had supposedly flourished under Drew's lax regime, while his humane treatment of offenders was making many friends for the Liberal government in the financial community. (McCullagh was certainly in a position to speak for those who had fallen afoul of the regulations: in October 1934 the TSE board fined him $500 for conduct detrimental to the exchange over trading in Sakoose Gold Mines; in April 1935 Barrett was one of the firms found to have an unauthorized telephone line linking it to the promoters at the Natural Resources Company, but he was let off without punishment after promising to disconnect the link; in July McCullagh was fined $100 for disturbing the market at the TSE and creating unrealistic expectations by bidding 65 cents a share for Bear Exploration and Radium when it was trading at only 60 cents. When the latter event occurred, McCullagh telephoned a member of the mining floor committee and used 'unbecoming and threatening language'; he was let off that charge with a warning that any repetition would lead to severe disciplinary action.) McCullagh therefore knew what he was talking about when he told the premier that the new man, Godfrey, was doing a good job and winning the government many friends within the financial community, though McCullagh's opinion that George Drew's inefficiency had encouraged many wildcat promoters to misbehave may be taken with a grain of salt.[65]

The question was whether or not Drew's departure would bring about a significant change in the relationship between the OSC and the provincial government. In the United States the five-member Securities and Exchange Commission created in 1934 was mandated by law to have no more that three appointees from one political party, giving the president the opportunity to shape the membership and thus determine the high-priority issues. Politicizing securities regulation might open the way for administrative abuses, yet at the same time it provided an avenue for the expression of popular concerns. Would Ontario follow this model?

The answer turned out to be negative. Once rid of Drew, his partisan foe, Attorney General Arthur Roebuck turned his attention elsewhere; he began the preparation of legislation which would permit the Hydro-Electric Power Commission to repudiate unilaterally the power-supply contracts that had been signed with private Quebec companies by the previous Conservative government during the 1920s because they refused to lower prices and reduce quantities to a level that he deemed affordable in these depressed times. This threat of repudiation, of course, caused outrage in the financial community because it might undermine confidence in every Canadian security, but Roebuck refused to be dissuaded and pressed ahead with the legislation during 1935.[66]

Meanwhile, John Godfrey was allowed to go his own way in regulatory matters at the OSC. When rumours started to circulate in 1936 that cabinet ministers were exercising influence over administrative decisions regarding the licensing of brokers and salesmen, he hotly denied that this was so. Godfrey admitted that there were some people licensed who had previously been found guilty of offences under the Securities Act, but he insisted that he had taken the decision to give them a second chance after a careful review. Applicants who approached the attorney general or other cabinet members were turned aside, and the OSC accepted full responsibility for its own decisions.[67]

Neverthless, John Godfrey did not forget that he owed his appointment to his solid Liberal credentials or that he needed to keep on good terms with the government. When Mitchell Hepburn brought down his budget in 1937 (he was also provincial treasurer), the Ontario securities commissioner wrote him a letter of praise so fulsome as to be positively embarrassing:

I think I have told you several times that what first made me think of you as leader of the provincial [Liberal] party was your sound knowledge of fundamental economic principles. I must now add something to this, namely, that in the budget you carried out those principles impressed upon Liberalism by the grand old man of Liberalism, William Ewart Gladstone. Gladstone's budgets as Chancellor the Exchequer were the most famous in English history. He strove for three things, strict economy, a balanced budget which always means a surplus and the distribution of the surplus by reduction of taxes. The greatest compliment I can pay you is to say that you are the Gladstone of Ontario.[68]

It never hurt to have the premier on one's side, especially one as mercurial as Mitch Hepburn. Yet little evidence exists of continuing ministerial interference in the day-to-day administration at the OSC. Once the furor over George Drew's dismissal in 1934 died away, lost in the flow of events, Godfrey was able to turn his attention to regulating securities markets without significant political interference.

12

Challenges

Securities markets in Canada enjoyed a brief revival in 1933 and 1934 as a result of a boom in mining shares. Almost at once securities regulators found themselves facing renewed challenges to their authority as fly-by-night promoters materialized just as bold and brassy as before the crash. In British Columbia, for instance, two complaints about mining promotions led to the launching of formal investigations under the provincial Security Frauds Prevention Act. The response of the promoters, however, was to go to court and try to block the release of the results of the investigations, claiming that their legal rights had been violated because they had not been permitted to cross-examine witnesses at closed-door hearings. The provincial government felt compelled to fight this battle strenuously in order to validate the method of conducting inquiries into suspected wrongdoing.

When John Godfrey took over as Ontario securities commissioner in 1934, he quickly moved to tighten controls because high-pressure share-selling methods had reappeared. There, too, aggressive promoters proved ready to challenge his authority. Godfrey decided that the most effective way to control boiler rooms, share-price manipulation, and insider trading was to launch a series of well-publicized investigations that would give the public as much information as possible about these operations. Even when no charges could be laid against miscreants, he hoped that the public airing of such activities would help to prevent any repetition. Godfrey also continued the effort to compel the Toronto Stock Exchange to control the activities of its members more closely, but here he achieved little more success than his predecessor, George Drew. All in all, the brief flurry of revived prosperity during the mid-1930s seemed to demonstrate that the shady operators were only awaiting the revival of investor confidence to resume their activities, which posed new challenges to regulators.

I

British Columbia's superintendent of brokers, H.G. Garrett, began to be concerned about a revival of sharp practices following gold discoveries in the Bridge River district near Lillooet. The Vancouver Stock Exchange suddenly leapt back to life in 1933 as trading volume soared to pre-Depression levels once again, with over 88,250,000 shares worth nearly $29 million changing hands as against just 16,640,000, valued at a mere $2.5 million the previous year (see appendix, table A.8). On some days in May 1933 more than 2 million shares were traded. VSE members, half of whom had been technically insolvent, began taking on new staff. Some of the large firms were soon employing sixty or seventy people in place of fifteen or twenty just a few months earlier, while brokers suddenly found themselves working sixteen-hour days and eating meals at their desks.[1]

Almost immediately rumours began to reach Garrett that some VSE members were up to their old tricks of wash selling and price manipulation; some popular stocks had too small a 'float' of available shares for a truly free market to exist. Privately, he warned the exchange board to enforce its by-laws about the lending and delivery of shares and to discipline any violators: 'If it should transpire that prices have been boosted or manipulated and that the process has been facilitated by your exchange not enforcing its own rules, there is likely to be a bad reaction.' The VSE did make a gesture at reform by suspending a couple of stocks, but one of these was reinstated before long.[2]

Garrett still felt he had to move cautiously, however, because the mining and brokerage community was certain to raise a fierce outcry if he intervened too much in an industry that looked as though it might actually create some new prosperity in the midst of a savage depression. Attempting to clamp down would only create demands for the repeal of the SFPA and a return to the good old days before the crash. He reminded Attorney General R.H. Pooley that for this very reason he had largely confined himself during the past couple of years to trying to drive out the dishonest brokers selling worthless shares simply by denying them registration. The superintendent was convinced that the 'large gambling element of the public' would never support too rigorous a crackdown; already there were murmurings in the legislature. The government therefore contented itself with issuing a mild warning against fraudulent mining promotions and advising investors to exercise discretion.[3]

The VSE did its best to fend off any further interference. President A.E. Jukes wrote Pooley to complain about rumours that a formal investigation of misconduct was planned. The exchange auditor was busy performing the surprise audits of members required by the by-laws, and if there were charges against any members, he wanted the VSE to look into them rather than letting the public know what was going on.[4] Pooley had to admit that no direct complaints had been received about VSE members and agreed that investigations should be private; rather than leaving this job to the exchange's own auditors, he appointed accountant Mark Cosgrove to examine the operations of a representative sample of Vancouver's brokers. Garrett and his staff suggested that four leading VSE members and four non-member brokers be studied, and the attorney general added the name of Jukes's own firm for good measure. Cosgrove was directed to look at their books to see if share certificates corresponding to account records were actually on hand and to make sure that there was none of the bucketing and short selling against clients of the kind that had landed Solloway, Mills and Company and the other mining brokers in trouble in 1930. Cosgrove was also to try to find out if 'sales in a ring' or wash selling were being used to manipulate share prices.[5]

As it turned out, Cosgrove's inquiry proved no serious threat to expose any misconduct. His work lasted less than two weeks before he delivered a short report to the attorney general in August 1933. A cursory look at the books had shown that there was little margin trading going on (which was hardly suprising since the banks would not lend funds on the security of most speculative mining stocks). The only real problem uncovered was that one leading firm, Miller, Court and Company, had pledged some client securities as collateral at the bank even though the customers themselves had no outstanding loans from the broker. Miller, Court, however, claimed that this situation had arisen simply because clients' liabilities fluctuated continuously, and it was not always possible to readjust their borrowings from the banks to reflect the precise debit balance of each individual at any given moment.

Not surprisingly, Cosgrove did discover that certain brokers were hand in glove with (or even identical to) particular mining promoters. When insiders controlled virtually all the shares in a new mining venture, they could option a block of low-priced stock and then leak the news that the issue was oversubscribed. Using wash sales and other techniques to raise prices, the brokers could peddle the rest of the issue to a gullible public. In this way the brokers and promoters might earn four or five times the profits permitted by the superintendent of brokers, who usually aimed to restrict commissions on sales to 20 or 25 per cent of share prices. Cosgrove advised, however, that he would have to examine the books of the brokers in much more detail to detect such operations; but he had not done so since he understood his task as merely to send a wake-up call to brokers and remind them they were under scrutiny in case the expected boom in mining shares continued during the fall of 1933.[6]

This rather half-hearted effort not only did little to check misconduct but succeeded in infuriating the superintendent of brokers. Cosgrove's report was delivered just as the Conservative government was forced to dissolve the legislature after five years in office and embark upon the hopeless task of trying to convince the people to re-elect it in the midst of an awful depression. The outgoing attorney general, Pooley, did not even bother to pass the report along to Garrett, and Cosgrove himself waited until after the election on 2 November had swept the Liberals into power before submitting his bill for $232 to the new attorney general, Gordon Sloan. The superintendent was enraged when he finally saw the document; it contained little information that he could not have provided himself and supplied no useful advice. Angrily he scribbled, 'I cannot understand this business of not letting your right hand know what the left is doing. I sh[oul]d certainly appreciate the ... money that Cosgrove will get for finding out nothing. It makes me feel sore.'[7]

Garrett therefore set about to educate his new political master concerning the operation of the SFPA. His first objective, he told Sloan, had been to use his broad discretion to keep out bad eggs by granting first-time applicants only temporary registration and requiring that all new brokers show that they possessed at least $1,000 in liquid assets. 'While the amount of the capital is of no real value,' he admitted, 'it has the effect of keeping out people who might commence business on a shoestring and through lack of any capital might soon become insolvent.' Companies wishing to issue securities had to obtain approval for their capitalization, the number of vendor shares granted, and commissions to be paid for raising funds. These commissions were limited to between 20 and 25 per cent of the sums raised, though Garrett admitted that brokers were evading this cap by demanding low-priced options which could be taken up if share prices rose.

A particular problem was that many large issues were mainly marketed outside British Columbia, where the final price paid by buyers was not subject to his control. Even over the Vancouver Stock Exchange he had no direct authority, though its members were constrained to some degree by the threat of suspension or cancellation of registration. Garrett believed that while outright fraud was less common than previously, the exchange was still 'more or less a betting house' where brokers continued to engage in short selling and wash trading. The legislation passed in 1930 had had some positive benefits, and without its protection investors would have been much more reluctant to put their capital into the province, but there was still room for much improvement.[8]

Early in 1934 George Drew of the Ontario Securities Commission proposed a conference of provincial officials to discuss securities regulation on the grounds that amendments had destroyed the legislative uniformity which had once existed. Superintendent Garrett might have been expected to be sympathetic, since he had just told Attorney General Sloan, 'Personally, I would like to tear up the whole Act and reconstruct it as it is one of the worst-drawn statutes that I know of. Owing to the crash of 1930 it was more or less forced on us as a uniform piece of legislation.' But now he complained that it was Ontario which was at fault for changing both the act itself and its regulations on several occasions without consulting the other provinces. Moreover, Drew wanted to focus upon issues about which there was little concern in western Canada, such as the contents of prospectuses and the increase in telephone selling. Without knowing what changes Drew had in mind, Garrett had little enthusiasm for discussions. Sloan accepted this advice and replied to Ontario that more information was needed on what was being proposed before any meeting was held. Drew did not pursue the matter.[9]

Any notion that tighter regulation in British Columbia since 1930 had put an end to abuses was abruptly refuted in mid-1934. The syndicate of Ben Smith, Victor Spencer, and David Sloan (the so-called Triple-S crowd) had acquired some 450,000 shares of Wayside Consolidated Gold Mines in the Bridge River district at 30 cents apiece and set about marketing them through the Vancouver Stock and Bond Company, a member of the VSE. At first the promotion went splendidly as the stock rose as high as 75 cents on the basis of glowing reports from the site, and more shares were pumped onto the market, trading on both the Vancouver and Toronto Stock Exchanges. Then unfavourable news from a mining engineer brought about a sickening slide and between 5 and 15 June prices fell as low as 7 cents. Smelling a rat, a group of Toronto investors holding almost 300,000 shares got together and demanded that the new Liberal premier, T.D. Pattullo, order an immediate investigation to discover if they had been defrauded. Initially the BC government resisted this pressure, despite the fact that news soon leaked out that a report had already found the company to be a purely speculative prospect with no commercial ore body in the area explored to date. The company tried to damp down the protest by commissioning another engineering study, but the outcry from investors proved sufficient that in August lawyer G.L. Fraser was appointed to conduct an investigation under the provincial Security Frauds Prevention Act.[10]

A few weeks later similar complaints arose about Nicola Mines and Metals. M.E. Erdofy of Seattle and Bartley and Company of New York (represented in Vancouver by Henry Benson) had acquired options on a large number of shares and begun to market them aggressively. Before long some shareholders began to get suspicious about the value of the property. Even Peter Bancroft, who had once been president of Nicola and in charge of its operations near Merritt, complained that he had been denied access to the books and kept away from the mine site. Bancroft underwrote a private investigation into the company's affairs, but the other insiders obtained an injunction preventing its release. When Bancroft complained to the provincial government, J.A. Russell was ordered to conduct an investigation under the SFPA.

The authority of Fraser and Russell to investigate the affairs of Wayside and Nicola rested upon section 10 of the 1930 Security Frauds Prevention Act, under which the attorney general or his delegated representative could 'examine any person, company, property or thing whatsoever at any time in order to ascertain whether any fraudulent act, or any offence against this Act or its regulations, has been, is being or is about to be committed, and for such purposes shall have the ... power to summon and enforce the attendance of witnesses.' The two investigators called various insiders to appear before them during the fall of 1934 and compelled them to testify; but when it appeared that adverse reports were about to be rendered, both George St. John of the Vancouver Stock and Bond Company and M.E. Erdofy and Henry Benson of Bartley and Company sought injunctions to stall any further proceedings. The lawyers for the plaintiffs argued that Fraser and Russell were operating in a judicial capacity but had failed to grant them the right to cross-examine witnesses who might give evidence against their clients, thus denying them natural justice. If investigations under the SFPA must henceforth be conducted with all the trappings of a trial, the process would obviously be slowed down and it might become far more difficult to uncover fraud.

The two applications for injunctions were rejected by different judges of the BC Supreme Court sitting alone. Chief Justice Morrison held in the Wayside case that the investigator was acting as 'bureaucratic offspring of the Legislature' and that there were no grounds to suspect Fraser of bias or prejudice in carrying out his task. In the Nicola case, heard a few days later, it was pointed out that the plaintiffs were not even directors or officers of the company, but had acquired its shares outright and were dealing in them as they saw fit. That argument failed to convince Mr Justice Lucas since the attorney general had very broad powers under section 10 to order the examination of 'any person ... whatsover at any time.' Moreover, the judge pointed out that section 29 of the SFPA specifically forbade anyone from trying to block such an investigation by seeking an injunction or other type of writ. Both Fraser and Russell were freed to pursue their inquiries.[11]

Appeals were immediately launched in both cases, however, so that the release of the reports was again stalled. Attorney General Sloan became so unhappy with this obstruction and the unfavourable publicity being generated that he threatened the VSE with drastic legislation to control its operations (even though the exchange's lawyer tried to argue that the existing rules were adequate to cope with any problems). Superintendent Garrett drafted a series of amendments to the SFPA to be tabled in the legislature in the spring of 1935, but Sloan ultimately decided to take no action pending the decision of the courts in the Wayside and Nicola cases.[12]

The two actions were heard together by the provincial Court of Appeal in March 1935. In the Nicola case the appellants again contended that their actions could not be investigated since they owned the stock outright, and 'What the brokers do with their own shares has nothing to do with the company.' The main thrust of the argument was that an investigation under the SFPA was 'quasi-judicial' and so must be conducted 'in accordance with the principles of natural justice.' Not to permit cross-examination was contrary to 'British fair play.' Acting for George St. John in the Wayside case, former BC attorney general J.W. Farris insisted that he was not seeking to overturn the Privy Council decision in the case of *Lymburn v. Mayland*, which had legitimized provincial claims to extensive regulatory authority over the securities business. What St. John was complaining of was that 'In his absence and without his knowledge there is an enquiry and a conclusion arrived at. It means destroying his reputation and business interests. He is in a position as if he had asked for cross-examination and was refused.' As a result the investigator 'is going to find that St. John and another conspired to give false value of shares. We are about to be convicted of a violation of the Criminal Code without a chance to cross-examine.'[13]

Counsel for the investigators, Fraser and Russell, responded that they were not judges conducting a trial; rather, 'This is a departmental investigation of inquisitorial character.' 'The investigator has discretion as to how to conduct the enquiry,' and both had chosen to hold in camera hearings. 'We are not dealing with the criminal law or purporting to make criminal findings.' The purpose of the process was to provide 'a measure of protection to the public in matters leading to crime.' Under the SFPA only the attorney general had the discretion to lay charges or impose punishment.[14]

Justices Martin and Macdonald proved sympathetic to the challenge to the attorney general's sweeping powers under the SFPA. In his decision Martin argued that 'the fundamentals of justice have not been observed. Matters were allowed to drag in both cases to the stage where these brokers concerned did not know, even at the time of the injunction[s] which restrained further proceedings ..., what definite charges were brought or to be brought against them, and they were not given proper particulars or the opportunity to meet any charges.' This situation arose because the investigators 'treated the plaintiffs throughout as being persons to whom favours might arbitrarily be "allowed," instead of their being entitled to fundamental rights when certain stages were reached.' Judge Macdonald added that both investigators had promised that before they reported, each plaintiff would have the right to appear and make any representations they desired: 'This, of course, was wholly unsatisfactory. It was equivalent to hearing charges *in camera* against someone and allowing him to appear only after all the evidence was given to make his answer and do so without knowing the nature of the evidence against him ... [I]t was incumbent upon the investigator to give the plaintiffs adversely affected by evidence notice of the alleged fraudulent act or acts and reasonable opportunity to be heard and to defend.' It was essential, in Martin's view, 'that safeguards ought to thrown about these loose and ill-defined proceedings, so that the accused person shall have that fair hearing which he is entitled to.'[15]

Mr Justice Macdonald elaborated this point, particularly concerning G.L. Fraser's conduct of the Wayside inquiry. The judge observed that from an early date the investigator seemed to have formed the conviction that criminal offences had been committed by the promoters, remarking to one witness, 'I have no objection to telling you ... there has been a campaign carried on of misrepresentation by the underwriters and by the company, talking about mills and the construction of mills, when the mine is not in [such] a position.' The judge considered that Fraser 'was not willing to give, and in fact did not give, to plaintiffs a fair opportunity to reply to evidence of so serious a nature that it might be the basis of a criminal charge or to permit its [i.e., their] counsel to cross-examine witnesses giving evidence of that character.' Macdonald contended, 'I would not for a moment put difficulties in the way of the working of a useful Act. The Act should be valuable as an aid in suppressing fraudulent practices, but dishonest traders engaged in rigging the market and in mining a credulous public may be exposed – as I hope they will – with greater certainty after obtaining a fair hearing and a reasonable opportunity to explain and to defend, while at the same time the legitimate trader will be more surely protected.' His forceful dissent ended with the observation that 'a proposition of law long established and embedded in the common law is that a man (or company) cannot suffer loss of liberty or have his reputation sullied until he or it have a fair opportunity of answering the charge, unless the Legislature has expressly or impliedly taken away that salutary right.' Since nothing in the SFPA indicated such an intention, Martin joined Macdonald in endorsing the continuation of both injunctions blocking the release of the reports.[16]

British Columbia's chief justice Macdonald, however, accepted the government's argument that an SFPA investigation was not a judicial proceeding; it could be held in secret, was not a court, and did not require that the right to cross-examine witnesses be granted. The attorney general could accept or reject the recommendations of the investigator. During the trial Mr Justice McPhillips had been heard to complain that the Wayside promoters seemed intent upon 'rooking the public' by unloading shares at artificially high prices. Supporting the chief justice, he noted in a concurring opinion that the object of the legislation was to discover if fraud was imminent or had already occurred and to prevent that. After a secret investigation the attorney general could suspend any registered broker or company for up to ten days and publicize the fraud that had been uncovered to warn off other investors. 'No doubt the circumstances of the times warrant legislation in this direction,' wrote McPhillips, 'and in any case the Court cannot in any way question the wisdom of the Legislature – it is supreme in the matter.' He and Justice McQuarrie joined with the chief justice in a majority finding that the injunctions should be dissolved and the investigators' reports released so that proceedings under the SFPA might proceed.[17]

George St. John was sufficiently encouraged by the arguments of the minority on the Court of Appeal that he decided to take his case to the Supreme Court of Canada. The hearing was held in May 1935, but the judges in Ottawa proved unsympathetic. Mr Justice Davis smartly slapped down the notion that the failure to allow cross-examination of the witnesses called by investigator Fraser represented a denial of 'natural justice.' First of all, said Davis, the phrase was 'rather loose and vague,' and he approvingly quoted Lord Dunfermline's words in a Privy Council decision: 'In so far as the term "natural justice" means that a result or process should be just, it is a harmless though it may be a high-sounding expression; in so far as it attempts to reflect the old *jus naturale* it is a confused and unwarranted transer into the ethical sphere of a term employed for other distinctions.'[18] Davis observed that J.W. Farris had contended 'that it was against natural justice that the plaintiffs should have been denied the right they claim of cross-examining every witness who was heard by the investigator. The right was asserted as a right to which every witness against whom a finding might possibly be made was entitled. I do not think that any such right exists at common law. The investigation was primarily an administrative function under the statute, and while the investigator was bound to act judicially in the sense of being fair and impartial, that, it seems to me, is something quite different from the right asserted by the appellants of freedom of cross-examination of all the witnesses.' To the claim that such an inquiry was 'a quasi-judicial tribunal' and so bound to follow the rules of a court, Davis countered, 'Fundamentally, the investigator in this case was an administrative officer ... not a court of law nor was he a court in law ... An administrative tribunal must act to a certain extent in a judicial manner, but that does not mean that it must act in every detail in its procedure the same as a court of law.'[19]

Mr Justice Crocket turned his attention to whether the right to cross-examine witnesses was granted by the BC legislation and concluded 'that the only reasonable inference ... is that the Legislature never intended that notice should be given to any and every person, whose status and reputation might be affected thereby, of the examination of any other witness or witnesses, and that any and all such persons should be afforded the privilege of cross-examining any such witness or witnesses. The whole tenor of the statute in my judgment points quite the other way.' Crocket (like Davis) made much of the fact that investigations were intended to be conducted in private and that the Security Frauds Prevention Act made it an offence for anyone other than the attorney general (or his delegate) to disclose 'any information or evidence' obtained from a witness: 'I find it quite impossible to avoid the conclusion, not only that the investigation provided for was not a judicial proceeding in any sense of the term, but that it was intended to be conducted by the investigator in private and that no person or company should have the right of cross-examining any witness or witnesses brought before the investigator, whether the evidence should affect the status or reputation of such person or company or not.' The investigator was 'given no power to make any adjudication which is ... in any sense binding upon the Attorney General or upon anyone else,' but merely to communicate 'the opinion he has formed as the result of the examination he has made.' Thus it was left to the attorney general to decide whether to suspend a broker's registration, apply to a judge for an order restraining fraudulent conduct, or lay charges; therefore the 'investigation is in no sense a judicial proceeding for the trial of any offence, but merely an enquiry conducted for the information of the Attorney General.'[20]

The other three judges of the Supreme Court hearing the case concurred with Crocket and Davis. Once the constitutionality of the BC Security Frauds Prevention Act was clearly affirmed, charges were quickly laid against the insiders at Wayside Consolidated. Within days the Vancouver Stock and Bond Company, its manager, St. John, and mine manager Purves E. Ritchie were found guilty in police court of manipulating the price of the shares through wash trading, the brokerage being fined $17,000 and the two men $1,000 each. St. John was forced to resign from the VSE, and his seat was bought back from him for $6,000.[21]

The province's victory in the courts also permitted the release of the report on Nicola Mines and Metals, which minced no words in its condemnation of this share-pushing operation. Russell's investigation had revealed that the insiders, Erdofy and Bartley and Company (through Benson) had acquired options on 1 million shares at 10 cents, along with two further 500,000 share options at 16 and 24 cents respectively. An elaborate selling organization had been set up in Toronto, Montreal, and Halifax, salemen being guaranteed commissions of at least 25 per cent plus any expenses incurred for advertising and publicity. Before long, orders had begun to roll in for Nicola stock at prices ranging from 60 cents to $1.34, which were relayed to D.A. Hamilton and Company, a VSE member, and to G.R. Davidson and Company, a non-member broker. They were supplied by the insiders with enough stock to sell on the VSE floor to meet demand. The role played by Hamilton and Davidson was concealed by distributing the buy orders among a number of local brokers. To fill orders in Vancouver drummed up by sales circulars written 'in the usual tipster vein style,' the promoters actually set up a new firm, R.A. Wylie and Company, which employed as many as a dozen salesmen; these people were allowed to retain 10 per cent of the sale price (out of Wylie's 25 per cent commission) provided that buyers held onto their shares for at least three months. Investors in Nicola Mines, of course, believed that the prices they were paying were fixed by the trading on the VSE, when in fact the insiders were distributing the stock for whatever they could get.[22]

The activities of the two Vancouver brokerages, G.R. Davidson and Company and D.A. Hamilton and Company, in feeding out the optioned stock onto the VSE through a web of brokers so as to conceal its source were denounced as a 'brazen fraud.' Over all, wrote G.L. Fraser, who should have known since he had also conducted the investigation into Wayside Consolidated, the Nicola promotion established 'a new high-water mark in dishonesty and ... unless a speedy end is put to the tactics employed, British Columbia will be the last place in the world [in] which an investor will seek to place his capital.' Unfortunately, however, since the insiders had owned the shares that they sold outright, they did not appear to have committed any offence under the SFPA. In a debate among members of the Law Society of British Columbia J.W. Farris, who had carried St. John's appeal to the Supreme Court, continued to argue that the SFPA was unjust, but Fraser contended that the province's reputation had been placed under a cloud and quick action was required if the confidence of investors was to be re-established.[23]

Despite all this bad publicity the members of the Vancouver Stock Exchange continued their antics, even though trading volume fell off from over 92 million shares in 1934 to about 47 million shares in 1935 (see appendix, table A.8). When the price of Reno Gold Mines fluctuated sharply that summer, the superintendent of brokers wondered if the VSE should be required to file a complete list of all transactions daily so that he and his officials could have 'our finger on the pulse of any particular stock' and be ready to commence an investigation whenever it was felt to be necessary. The problem was, Garrett pointed out, that such supervision would not only present a major administrative burden for his staff, but if the government took this drastic step 'there would be a direct responsibility to take some action.' Though Attorney General Sloan expressed approval in principle of the idea of daily reporting, no steps seem to have been taken to compel it, probably for the reason identified by Garrett.[24]

Some members of the Vancouver financial community remained determined to portray themselves as the victims of bureaucratic harassment which was blocking legitimate mining development. When Garrett addressed the state of Washington's Mining Institute on the subject of 'British Columbia's Blue Sky Law' early in 1936, he argued that securities regulation had become imperative in the early 1930s because mining promoters had been bilking the public during an 'orgy of speculation.' Since then efforts had been made to curtail the 'vicious' practice of short selling. The power to order the investigation of suspicious activities sometimes permitted the government to bar the door before any horses were stolen, but Garrett insisted that he never presumed to pronounce directly on the merits of a given mining prospect. Yet Sidney Norman, the mining editor of the Vancouver *Sun*, took him to task in a strongly worded rebuttal, trotting out all the old claims that the Security Frauds Prevention Act was the major obstacle to the discovery of new mines.[25]

Despite the scandals over Wayside and Nicola, which had blackened the reputation of mining promoters in British Columbia, this kind of propaganda kept the regulators on the defensive. In the spring of 1936 the Ontario Securities Commission issued new regulations to control mining promoters by restricting the type of information that could be included in advertising. The OSC insisted that maps must be accurate and should not attempt to mislead by showing adjacent mines even when ore bodies dipped or stopped; all references to assays must specify whether they were obtained from large 'bulk' or isolated 'grab' samples, since rich results from the latter had been used to convey false implications about the value of ore bodies. Superintendent Garrett observed that the new Ontario rules were 'far more stringent than anything attempted in this province. If this office had laid down any such restrictions there would most certainly have been a storm of opposition. On the other hand, the provisions are in most respects needed for the protection of the public and indicate the tendency of development in this type of legislation.'[26]

Old habits died hard. When one promoter tried to incorporate a 3-million share company and hand over 1.35 million shares to the vendors of the property, Garrett intervened to limit the capitalization to 2 million shares, of which just 750,000 could go to the vendors. The Farris law firm wrote to the attorney general to complain that the superintendent had no authority to do so, since granting compensation in the form of shares did not constitute 'trading in securities' because this was an isolated transaction. The superintendent pointed out that such an interpretation would nullify the key provisions of the SFPA, which made no distinction between shares handed over in exchange for properties and those sold to the public for cash. The lawyers then retreated to the claim that restricting the number of vendor shares was equivalent to valuing the property involved and that it was 'pure impudence' on Garrett's part to try to limit this compensation. For the government to intervene in such dealings between private parties was 'utter idiocy' which could only hamper mine development and bring the administration of the SFPA into disrepute. Having observed the operations of the legislation since 1930, the Farris firm argued that it had done 'interminable' harm to the provincial economy.[27]

In the autumn of 1936 the local branch of the Canadian Institute of Mining and Metallurgy took up the cudgels, claiming that the superintendent of brokers had too much discretionary power and too little expertise. As a result, the Security Frauds Prevention Act was being administered in a fashion that was 'dangerously bureaucratic' and decidedly 'un-British.' For instance, Garrett was condemned for requiring that promoters should actually own and control the properties involved when they sought to register new mining companies; this stipulation forced them to spend too much money on the premature acquisition of claims, funds that would otherwise go to exploration and development.[28] In such a hostile climate British Columbia's securities regulators had to move with a good deal of circumspection.

II

John Godfrey started his term at the Ontario Securities Commission in October 1934. His predecessor, George Drew, having been dismissed amidst allegations of laxity, Godfrey was determined to show his zeal and energy; so he immediately ordered a series of inquiries and made certain that his findings received maximum publicity. In Ontario, unlike British Columbia, nobody publicly voiced strong objections to the refusal to grant those accused the right to cross-examine witnesses at hearings under the SFPA, even though that issue was still before the courts on the west coast. Nevertheless, Godfrey soon encountered other challenges.

He was keen to demonstrate that the SFPA already provided ample authority to deal with current problems. In a speech to the Canadian Club during the spring of 1935 he argued that the legislation was 'flexible, and constitutional difficulties so far as Dominion companies were concerned were gone around by putting in the Commissioner's hands the power of licensing salesmen, security issuers and brokers. By that power you can practically control the situation. You can administer the act either as a Fraud Act or as a Blue Sky Act. I have chosen to administer it as a Blue Sky Act. The powers which it confers on the Commissioner are these: he can say who shall or shall not sell securities.'[29]

Within a fortnight of taking over, Godfrey had beefed up the earlier prohibition on door-to-door sales, banning the selling of securities by telephoning a private residence. George Drew grumbled that *he* had really drafted this regulation, but that his political master, Attorney General Arthur Roebuck, had refused even to discuss the matter with him. Godfrey, however, claimed full credit, telling the press that within just a couple of days no fewer than twenty boiler rooms in Toronto had closed up shop. He advised the general counsel of the newly created United States Securities and Exchange Commission that these bans had 'put out of business a large number of undesirable securities sellers, many of whom I regret to say, were importations from your country,' though he had to admit that some of these people had promptly turned their talents to peddling Canadian shares in the United States, activity that he had no means to control.[30]

At the same time the OSC commenced an inquiry into the operations of one of the few remaining local boiler rooms, John White and Company, which was pushing shares in Macfarlane Long Lac Gold Mines. Godfrey soon reported that Macfarlane's promoter had paid a prospector just $400 for a dozen undeveloped mining claims, incorporated a 3-million-share company, and taken half the stock as vendor of the property, while White and Company was set to work marketing the shares. During August and September 1934 (right at the end of Drew's term) the brokerage has spent $16,000 on long-distance charges for its twenty-three telephones to peddle stock as far afield as New Brunswick, Saskatchewan, and even California. One of White's more enterprising salesmen had called a farm outside Winnipeg and demanded to speak to the hired hand, keeping the line open for forty minutes while the man was fetched from the fields. The farm owner was so impressed that he sent White some valuable securities to be exchanged for these worthless shares. By the time the OSC stepped in about 600,000 shares had been sold, netting $192,000, of which only about $50,000 was ultimately recovered. The new Ontario mines minister, Paul Leduc, endorsed Godfrey's crackdown and warned the Toronto branch of the Canadian Institute of Mining and Metallurgy that high-pressure selling of worthless shares was the bane of the industry: 'We don't object to an honest gamble, but the public must have a run for its money.'[31]

In this flurry of activity Godfrey also announced an inquiry into the sharp drop in the stock of the well-established Teck Hughes Mine, whose price on the Toronto Stock Exchange had fallen precipitously in mid-September. In this case investigation quickly revealed that the general manager had discovered a fall in the quality of the ore and decided to cut back production. Fearing a decline in the shares, a couple of the directors dumped thousands of them before the news was made public, which had helped bring about the slide. The need for disclosure and control over the use of insider information seemed to be reinforced by reports about other companies in the financial press, which turned a small spring in a mine shaft into a major flood, while the president of a large gold mining company was falsely reported to be in a straitjacket attended by nurses round the clock in another. In the Teck Hughes case, however, there was nothing illegal about the actions of the company's directors, so the commissioner could do no more than suggest that the offenders ought to be dropped from the board at the next annual meeting.[32]

Even this mild slap, however, caused enough alarm that one prominent Liberal lawyer in Toronto did write to Premier Mitchell Hepburn to complain, 'The situation is serious, full of dynamite.' James Day echoed the criticisms raised in British Columbia, complaining that public hearings at which the OSC could compel witnesses to appear and answer questions and even to incriminate themselves were a grave violation of British justice and private rights. But Day, a leading mining lawyer, was really most concerned that such interference with the free play of markets might make mine financing impossible. Hepburn agreed to see the agitated Grit, yet did nothing to rein in Godfrey, whose actions were earning his government a good deal of favourable publicity.[33]

Godfrey ordered an investigation into Gunnar Gold Mines after its price dropped from $1.43 to 94 cents in just two hours of heavy trading on the TSE on 31 October 1934, knocking over $1,125,000 off share values. Immediately the usual rumours of bear raiders and short sellers began to circulate, along with claims that insiders had dumped a load of vendor shares. One newspaper even alleged that Gunnar's president, Gilbert LaBine, the respected mining man who had discovered the rich Eldorado uranium lode on Great Bear Lake in 1929, was himself responsible. When LaBine requested an OSC investigation to clear his name, Godfrey seized the chance to undertake a full-scale inquiry.

The commissioner used this opportunity to send a message to the financial community by having his report on Gunnar published for the widest possible distribution in February 1935 (apparently the first time that this had been done).[34] What Godfrey uncovered suggested that operations were still occurring on the Toronto Stock Exchange which bore an unhealthy resemblance to the manipulation on the old Standard exchange in pre-Depression days. Gilbert and Charles LaBine and Joseph Hirshhorn, a promoter in New York and Toronto, had taken an option on some promising gold claims in 1933. Gunnar Gold Mines issued 3 million shares, half of them being paid to the insiders for the properties, with 10 per cent going to the prospectors and the rest split between the LaBines and Hirshhorn. These vendor shares were to be pooled until $400,000 was raised for development, and by January 1934, 800,000 of the treasury shares had been disposed of to the public at 55 cents, netting the company 50 cents, and the vendor pool was dissolved. To that point the promotion had been, in Godfrey's words, 'clean-cut and legitimate,' raising a sizeable sum for the exploration of a promising find for a modest commission of 10 per cent.

Thereafter, however, the depredations began. Hirshhorn still controlled 598,000 vendor shares (which had cost him just 8 cents apiece), and he immediately set about to inflate the stock artificially by wash trading. With great skill he pushed the price as high as $2.50 by June 1934 before starting gradually to withdraw his support. During September and October he sold 105,000 shares and bought back only 22,600. The brokerage community at the TSE was well aware that Gunnar was being supported, and the professional floor traders, who made their living by moving in and out of issues aiming to leave themselves without a position (or 'flat') at the close of each trading day, were keeping a sharp eye on it. On 30 October Gunnar fell by 7 cents, and the floor operators expected the market would move up again the following day. 'For this reason many of them began to buy shares at the opening. They soon discovered, however, that while shares were being offered for sale no one was bidding for the stock. They immediately began to feel the market out and found that there were practically no bids. To save themselves from loss they began to sell and they also notified their offices that Gunnar was not being supported. The offices in turn called their clients, and the clients who had to protect their margins began to sell. By noon and before the panic was over the stock had reached a low of ninety-four cents.' At that point Gilbert LaBine, to his credit, had entered the market with a buy order for 15,000 shares, which steadied the situation and started Gunnar share prices moving back upward again.

Had Hirshhorn violated section 444 of the Criminal Code, which made it an offence to conspire 'with any other person by deceit or falsehood or other fraudulent means ... to affect the public market price of stocks'? Certainly he had manipulated the price to his advantage, but that in itself was not a crime since supporting the market for a stock was not illegal. The law envisaged at least two people arranging to carry out wash sales, but 'with the complicated mechanism of the modern stock exchange' it was now possible for somebody using the telephone to carry out 'a three or four way jitney' so that the buying and selling brokers need not even realize what was going on. 'A skillful manipulator can cover his tracks so that the brokers he uses in the transaction may never have a guilty knowledge of his operations and without that guilty knowledge there can be no unlawful conspiracy.'

Godfrey waxed indignant that there was nothing he could do: 'Under the present law the lone wolf may commit any depredation. It is only when he hunts with the pack that he becomes a criminal.' In view of the prevalence of share-price manipulation in Canada, he found it 'inconceivable' that the Criminal Code had not been amended previously and expressed the hope that in 'its present reforming mood' the federal Parliament would take speedy action. Meanwhile, at least nine hundred Canadians who had bought Gunnar shares at

$1.50 or more were out over $500,000. The formal publication of the OSC report in February 1935 was intended to send a message to the members of the mining fraternity to clean up their conduct.

In December 1934 Godfrey investigated another share-selling scam. Thompson-Cadillac Gold Mines had collapsed into bankruptcy right after announcing plans to build an expensive mill to process its ore despite the existence of an unfavourable report on its reserves from a mining engineer. Godfrey quickly discovered that this was part of a plan by the company's president to market his own shares. The commissioner told a meeting of the Advertising Club of Toronto that he thought he was now well on the way to eliminating the crooks and racketeers from the mining business; he was confident that he had the powers required to exercise 'birth control' over new companies and new securities in future. Godfrey observed that the laws had 'plenty of sharp teeth in them' to protect investors and drive out dishonest promoters, insuring the average investor 'a run for his money.'[35]

One way to protect investors, of course, was to make sure that the stock exchanges did not permit shares of dubious quality to be dealt in, a particular temptation in times of depressed volume. The Montreal Curb Market, for instance, still allowed traders to handle any stock in which there was the slightest interest. Soon after the crash in 1930 the Curb had decided to permit trading in any oil or mining stock upon the application of any two members without charging a fee and even without the consent of the issuer. In the spring of 1931 efforts were made to encourage dealing in inactive unlisted securities to 'replace the present unsatisfactory street market.' By the fall of 1932 members had approved efforts to expand the unlisted section in order to increase the volume of trading, which had fallen so low that the percentage of commissions on unlisteds paid to the exchange by all the members totalled only $10.23 during the week ended 22 October. A few weeks later, when Sun Life protested against its shares being traded on the unlisted section of the Curb, the board replied that the stock was dealt with both on the New York Curb and over the counter in Montreal and that it seemed in the interests of Canadian shareholders that it be handled in a public market to enhance liquidity and make pricing fairer. In the summer of 1933 the Montreal Curb board decided to permit its unlisted section to trade in any high-grade stocks listed on other exchanges without any prior approval, noting that 'no publicity whatsoever' should be given to such transactions to avoid retaliation from rival exchanges.[36]

Only in 1933 did the Curb create a listing committee to vet applicants. The board argued that the exchange had no obligation to ensure the soundness of a stock traded on its unlisted section, but conceded that there existed a 'moral responsibility' to do so in order to avoid losing credibility. Otherwise the danger remained that the Curb might be used to 'foist worthless stocks on the public through manipulation of prices and to dump out treasury stocks without the public being aware that they are buying such.' In future the committee would examine all such applications to commence trading, and companies must disclose whether or not there were pooling agreements that covered their shares. A year later, when a proposal was made to list the shares of Canadian Marconi, the company objected on the grounds that this might 'encourage speculation in the shares on the part of the public.' As a result the exchange finally required that issuers should confirm in writing that they had no objection to their shares being dealt in.[37]

The problem with relying on the exchanges to regulate the quality of issues was that once a stock began trading the exchange had relatively limited powers to investigate suspected improprieties. For instance, after complaints about price fluctuations in Normont Gold Mines in November 1933, the stock was suspended by the Montreal Curb and all members were required to provide details of their trades to see if there had been violations of the rules. When no such infractions were uncovered, pressure was applied to have trading in Normont resume even though the provincial regulator was still looking into the situation. The exchange's lawyer argued against resumption on the grounds that there was sure to be criticism if any wrongdoing should be uncovered, observing, 'The public do not appreciate that the principals in these transactions could not be examined by the exchange. We do not want to get ourselves into a position where we have to define our restricted jurisdiction in a matter of this kind, particularly thru [sic] the newspapers ... On the whole, therefore, my suggestion would be that we had better take the criticism resulting from inaction instead of any action which may prove to be a *faux pas*.'[38]

The merger between the Standard and Toronto stock exchanges in February 1934 created concern that a more intense rivalry might develop between the Montreal and Toronto exchanges to win business away from one another. The Montreal Curb attempted to enhance its prestige by changing its listing application form to require companies to disclose more financial information. Some unlisted companies were asked to seek formal listings, with a warning that otherwise the unlisted section might have to be closed under pressure from the Quebec authorities. Eventually, discussions between the MSE, the Curb, and the TSE in May 1934 led to an agreement between them to charge uniform listing fees to reduce the temptation to compete by lowering their requirements. Nevertheless, in the fall of 1934 there continued to be complaints that the MSE was canvassing companies listed on the Curb in an effort to persuade them to shift to the other exchange. At the same time the Curb dispatched a committee to Toronto to try to persuade various mining companies to have their shares listed in Montreal.[39]

John Godfrey did his best to prevent the TSE from allowing trading in the shares of dubious undertakings. Early in 1935 he met with William Amyot, the registrar under Quebec's Security Frauds Prevention Act. Amyot was convinced that tighter controls over which stocks were granted listings on the exchanges would eliminate many problems. He had therefore persuaded both the Curb and the Montreal Stock Exchange to allow him to vet all listing applications, on the understanding that none would be accepted from companies that were not registered in at least one jurisdiction in Canada or the United States. Though these recommendations were not binding on the exchanges, it was assumed that fly-by-nighters would be deterred from applying. After meeting with Amyot, Godfrey persuaded the TSE to adopt the same system.[40]

In the spring of 1935, however, a dispute broke out when the Montreal Curb began to permit unlisted trading in eighteen new stocks. The Torontonians complained that this was a violation of the non-competition agreement, while the Curb board contended that almost all these issues had a purely local market in Monteal and had been admitted to trading only at the behest of the Quebec authorities in order to 'counteract a street market.' Moreover, the Curb insisted that it had no record of any non-competition agreement, but the MSE deflated that claim by pointing out that the chair of the Curb's board had been party to the agreement of May 1934. After a certain amount of backing and filling a further meeting was arranged between representatives of the three exchanges, and a new uniform listing policy was hammered out in July 1935. Henceforth no listings were to be granted without an application from the company itself and the payment of a fee. In recognition of this arrangement each of the exchanges agreed to permit its members to split commissions on a 50–50 basis on any orders forwarded to them from members of the other exchanges, a privilege refused to the Vancouver and Winnipeg exchanges despite their requests.[41]

Godfrey also pressured the Toronto Stock Exchange to impose closer supervision on companies whose shares were already listed. Early in 1935 the board delisted nine oils and mines and placed forty-three other mining companies on notice that if they did not hold the required annual meetings and issue proper financial statements, they would be dropped. Eventually all but three of the companies complied.[42]

During the summer of 1935 Godfrey turned his attention to stocks traded on the unlisted section of the TSE. An OSC investigation had disclosed that price quotations were frequently falsified, even by some well-known TSE member houses, whose unlisted departments were headed by aggressive, young traders operating with little supervision. Quoting prices that were a few points below the market for sales and above for purchases allowed the difference to be channelled directly into the pockets of the traders. As a result, criminal charges were laid and several brokers had their registration suspended.

In addition, Godfrey became concerned about non-member brokers. While exchange members had to put up capital to purchase their seats, as well as submitting to semi-annual audits to ensure that they had at least $25,000 in liquid assets plus 5 per cent of the total value of securities held by their clients on margin, approximately one thousand non-member brokers had not been required to demonstrate their soundness. The OSC therefore decided to institute a system of twice-yearly surprise audits to ensure that they were properly financed, segregated trust funds and clients' securities from their own funds, and possessed extra capital if they did margin business. By the end of 1935 the first round of surprise audits had been completed, and Godfrey was pleasantly surprised at the results. A few problems had been uncovered which were being rectified, but the threat of the audits had eliminated most of the undesirable elements from the business. After just over a year at the head of the OSC, Godfrey believed that his new broom had swept pretty clean and most of the problems were a thing of the past.[43]

The upsurge in securities markets which began in 1933 demonstrated that Canada's securities regulators still had their work cut out for them. The powers they possessed under the Security Frauds Prevention Acts passed in 1930 proved insufficient to stamp out renewed abuses once the prices of mining shares began to move strongly upward. When John Godfrey was appointed to head the OSC in 1934 he was determined to take an active role. Boiler rooms were closed down and telephone selling to private residences was banned; he investigated a number of dubious promotions and worked to publicize his findings. At the same time he sought closer collaboration with his counterpart in Quebec in order to control shady operators. Pressure was applied to the Toronto Stock Exchange to crack down on price manipulation and other improper practices and to carefully vet applications for listings. Finally, Godfrey turned his attention to non-member brokers and dealers in unlisted shares to try to prevent them from swindling the public. Canadian securities regulators never seemed to lack for challenges to their authority.

In British Columbia the government proved cautious at first about cracking down on mining promoters in the midst of a depression, but eventually decided to order formal investigations into both Wayside Consolidated and Nicola Mines and Metals. That provoked a challenge to the authority of the attorney general to order investigations under the Security Frauds Prevention Act without granting those summoned the right to cross-examine witnesses. Eventually, however, the legislation was sustained by the courts. While civil libertarians might find little to celebrate in the upholding of a process that allowed the examination of witnesses in private without the right to cross-examine, the

Supreme Court decision in the case of *St. John v. Fraser* legitimized a type of inquiry that became standard under securities legislation across Canada for more than a generation. Investigators were empowered to seize and examine records, compel witnesses to testify, and report findings which might lead to the laying of charges either under provincial legislation or the federal Criminal Code. The courts proved prepared to grant these investigations a wide degree of latitude in the interests of investor protection because of the abuses that had developed in the late 1920s and reappeared in the mid-1930s.

13

Revival Stalled

March 20, 1937, gave the members of the Toronto Stock Exchange more to celebrate than they had had for years. Decked out in white tie and tails, they gathered for a banquet to celebrate the opening of their splendid new premises on Bay Street. The lieutenant-governor of Ontario and the president of the University of Toronto were on hand to propose the toasts. Then the main speaker of the evening, Charles R. Gay, president of the New York Stock Exchange, expatiated upon the vital role of stock exchanges in the modern economy and lauded the TSE's new set-up as the 'last word in efficiency.' As the cigar smoke curled upward in the hotel banquet room, members of the audience, like their counterparts at other Canadian exchanges, anticipated a bright future with rising share prices and buoyant trading. When the brokers headed out into the night, all that remained to be done before they moved into their fine new home was to hook up the elaborate telephone system over the upcoming Easter weekend.[1]

The TSE's quarters were intended to speak directly to the vitality and significance of this institution. Architectural historian William Dendy writes, 'The formality of the building evokes the traditions of bankers' architecture; and its smoothed surfaces, fine materials, and a decorative programme that dramatically combines both the Art Deco and streamlined Moderne styles, expresses the astonishingly optimistic spirit of renewed industry and prosperity towards the end of the Depression.' Above the main doors stretched a carved frieze of gold-coloured stone showing workers in various Canadian occupations. Charles Comfort's design presents, in Dendy's words, 'flat, linear, mechanistic figures united with their machines by a dynamic zigzag pattern. This is the most striking piece of sculpture from the period in Toronto.' (Comfort indignantly rejected the flippant suggestion that the top-hatted businessman, representing finance, was deliberately shown with his hand in the pocket of a sturdy working man, an accurate symbolic reflection of what would shortly transpire inside the building.)[2]

Clad in pale Indiana limestone the façade rose flush from the street to a simple cornice-like moulding intended to telegraph the banklike solidity of the Classical style in an appropriately up-to-date fashion. Columnar panels separated the five three-storey-tall windows which gave on the impressive cork-floored trading room, seventy-two by one hundred and five feet with a ceiling thirty-nine feet high. Between these windows, overlooking the floor, Comfort painted eight tall murals in Cubist style depicting the major industries of Canada whose operations the TSE helped to finance: transport and communications, mining, smelting, pulp and paper, refining, agriculture, oil, engineering, and construction (see photos 21 and 22).[3] Architect S.H. Maw, responsible for much of the interior design, claimed to have been strongly influenced by 'modern motor car design' and to have aimed for 'the last word in modern achievement.' Yet he was careful to make sure that the executive suite on the third floor spoke to the 'sound tradition of British financial institutions,' with the president's office in the Queen Anne style and the managing committee's boardroom in Georgian. This impressive structure was intended to signal that at long last the exchange had achieved respectability as a key Canadian financial institution and had put behind it the sleazy reputation that had attracted so much criticism during the early 1930s.[4]

Surely, brokers told one another (and their long-suffering customers), the long-awaited surge of share prices above pre-Depression levels was finally at hand. The short-lived boom in mining stocks in 1933–4 had fizzled out, to everyone's disappointment, but now the future definitely looked brighter. The Dominion Bureau of Statistics index of common stock prices had inched steadily upward in almost every recent month, from 113 in May 1936 to 142 in February 1937 (or nearly to the level attained in early 1928). The weighted index of Canadian mining stocks, which had stood at 133 at the end of 1935, had now reached 177. (See appendix, figures A.1 and A.2.)

True, it had to be admitted that the revival in stock prices had already brought about a recurrence of some of the shady activities which had created such bad publicity for the brokerage community in the past. Now, however, provincial regulators across Canada seemed to have the authority and the experience to contain the problems. In Ontario John Godfrey at the OSC had been very active in 1936 and early 1937 in trying to stamp out abuses, while in British Columbia a major investigation into the affairs of Hedley Amalgamated Gold Mines had been announced just a few weeks earlier. Even more comforting, the regulators apppeared at long last to have accepted the stock exchanges as collaborators rather than antagonists in the business of cleaning up problems such as short selling and wash trading. The headline in the *Globe and Mail* on the day before the banquet accurately captured this feeling of cautious optimism: 'New Exchange May Be Symbol of Prosperity.'[5] Certainly, the TSE's members devoutly hoped that the worst was over and that when the gong sounded to start trading on 30 March, an era of prosperity would dawn.

I

As they gathered for the first time in their Georgian-style boardroom, the members of the TSE managing committee must have felt that they had grounds to congratulate themselves. The new building had been a considerable time in the planning. After the Standard Stock and Mining Exchange merged with the TSE early in 1934, the two separate trading floors for mines and industrials had continued to function because neither was large enough to accommodate everybody. In 1935 trading volume still hovered around 5 million shares for the industrial section on Bay Street, but mines and oils collapsed from over 333 million shares in 1934 to under 165 million on the old Standard floor on Temperance Street as the boom played itself out. A special committee of the board concluded that the only way of significantly reducing costs was to combine the two trading floors. Now was the time to build on the Bay Street site because interest rates and costs were extremely low; this proposal was unanimously approved at a general meeting of members in November 1935. A number of architects were asked to tender, and in the spring of 1936 a design costing $540,000 was approved, to be financed by an issue of first-mortgage bonds. The cornerstone was laid in August. With seat prices having now rebounded from a low of $20,000 in 1932 to $67,000 in the fall of 1936, the future seemed set fair by the time the grand opening took place.[6]

During the three years following the merger with the Standard the TSE board, under pressure from the Ontario Securities Commission, had worked hard to burnish the image of the exchange. Efforts had continued to improve the quality of the issues listed on the exchange and to compel companies to release more information to shareholders and investors. In the fall of 1935 the exchange began to require that listed companies disclose the existence of all option agreements to purchase treasury stock. Critics had long argued that these companies would be hurt if the public learned that sale of these shares would net only a proportion of the full price for corporate purposes. Yet investors apparently accepted that there were costs involved in raising capital, and mining promotions (where option agreements were almost universal) continued to be floated on the TSE.[7]

Early in 1936 a number of companies were abruptly delisted by the TSE without any explanation, and complaints appeared in the press about arbitrary and high-handed treatment. News was quickly leaked to the *Financial Post* that in one case there had been dubious financial arrangements made with the directors and in another that the company was conniving in disreputable share-selling tactics. The exchange had decided not to publicize these facts in order to protect the interests of the other shareholders, but had called company officials on the carpet before suspending trading, so that their pleas of ignorance were unjustified.[8]

By the time the new building opened the TSE normally required that before a listing was granted, there should be at least one hundred shareholders and that 10 per cent of the stock be in the hands of the public to guarantee a genuine market.[9] Once listed, companies were required to disclose any changes in the nature of their business operations, any issues of additional securities, the passing of dividends, and the preparation of annual reports. Since Ontario law required only that a financial report be tabled at the annual meeting, which could be held in an out-of-the-way place to discourage shareholders from attending, the exchange eventually insisted that a balance sheet and an income statement be sent to every shareholder within four months of the end of each fiscal year if the company wished to retain its TSE listing or its place on the Toronto Curb.[10]

The board also made considerable efforts to ensure that its rules and regulations were similar to those at the Montreal Stock Exchange and the Montreal Curb Market in order to prevent promoters from shifting listings to more advantageous locations. In July 1935 the MSE and the Montreal Curb joined in an agreement with the TSE to have uniform listing fees and to forbid the listing of companies that had not applied or paid the required sum. In addition, it was decided to allow members of the three exchanges to split commissions on a 50–50 basis. Arbitrage trading in mines and oils in an attempt to profit from price differentials between Toronto and Montreal was banned on the grounds that it simply drew away business from one exchange to the other to their overall detriment. Applications from the Vancouver and Winnipeg exchanges for similar commission-splitting arrangements were firmly rejected.[11] Careful attention continued to be paid to cooperation with the Montreal exchanges. In January 1936 a committee of TSE members recommended that commissions on trades be increased, but nothing was done until the MSE agreed to raise the rates on industrials in March. A few weeks later a large delegation from Montreal representing both the MSE and the Curb arrived in Toronto for a weekend to discuss issues of mutual interest.[12]

Arbitrage was permitted on industrial stocks, but members detected violating the ban on arbitrage in interlisted mines and oils were punished. In February 1937 C.C. Fields and Company and Flood, Potter and Company were each fined $2,000 and ordered to cease such activities. The only resource stocks in which arbitrage was permitted were Inco, Cominco, International Petroleum, and British American and Imperial Oil, which had traditionally been treated as industrials because they were not just explorers and developers but also production and refining companies.[13]

The scale of commissions remained a major concern for brokers. By 1938 the pressure of rising costs led members to begin agitating for higher rates despite the risk of driving away business. The MSE and the Montreal Curb moved first to introduce minimum commissions on small transactions. Though charges could be waived on trades worth less than $15 (itself a sign of how bad times were), orders valued between $15 and $50 would now cost customers at least $1 to execute, and over $50 not less than $2. The Montrealers also approached the TSE about an across-the-board increase in commission rates, but the Torontonians refused to go along, although the exchanges did agree upon increased listing fees for industrials in an effort to raise their revenues.[14]

Overseeing the enforcement of the rules at the TSE was an important part of the work of A.J. Trebilcock, who had come over at the time of the merger with the Standard. In January 1936 he was given the title of assistant secretary and executive manager at an increased salary of $10,000.[15] His responsibilities were wide-ranging. For instance, the exchange had procured approval from the Canadian Radio Broadcasting Commission to send out daily quotations on CKNC in the spring of 1935. Exchange members quickly recognized the potential of radio as a means of advertising their activities, but the board was determined to control the content of these broadcasts. Complaints about a program put on by Colling and Colling eventually led in December 1935 to the passage of formal rules limiting such broadcasts to providing price quotations and comment on the market as revealed by the quotations. Banned were predictions about the probable future course of the market as a whole or of any given security and quotations for unlisted shares. News items were not to include rumours but to be limited to company announcements about dividends, earnings, production levels, and plant construction. Trebilcock was directed to warn Colling and Colling that failure to comply would lead to cancellation of permission to broadcast.[16]

Although the exchanges tried to exert more control over their members, John Godfrey at the Ontario Securities Commission once again found himself still having to cope with antics by over-the-counter promoters similar to those that had surfaced during the brief boom in mining shares a couple of years earlier. As before, he sought to use his inquiries and well-publicized hearings to warn the investing public. For instance, in the spring of 1936 the OSC launched an investigation into Bidgood Kirkland Gold Mines, which had been on the verge of bankruptcy near the end of the previous year before rumours of a new ore strike sent share prices sharply upward. The president, A.L. Herbert, and the secretary-treasurer, Norman W. Byrne, had decided to reward themselves by procuring an option to purchase 100,000 treasury shares at 5 cents apiece, when the stock was trading between 20 and 25 cents. Approval was rushed through a board meeting in December 1935; director R.J. Neelands, who arrived late, was told nothing and kept in ignorance by Herbert and Byrne, who conspired to avoid sending him the minutes for fear that he would turn them in to the OSC.

Eventually, however, Neelands found out what was going on and reported the matter to Godfrey. During the OSC investigation Byrne defended himself by claiming that he had telephoned the commissioner and discussed with him the possibility that he and Herbert might be granted an option on 10,000 shares in recognition of their work in averting bankruptcy. Godfrey had made clear that he could only give unofficial advice, but that he saw no reason for the OSC to intervene provided that a shareholders' meeting approved the option. Byrne and Herbert had immediately procured an option ten times as large, which it was clear Godfrey would never have endorsed. Even after the formal inquiry began, Herbert hastened to the offices of the company's share transfer agent with a certified copy of the board minutes and procured a certificate for 100,000 shares. The OSC was forced to put out a stop order banning the issue of any further shares prior to a shareholders' meeting. The OSC inquiry led to cancellation of the options and the removal of the two men from the board.[17]

In 1937 Godfrey appointed lawyer J.J. Robinette to investigate the affairs of Red Lake Shore Gold Mines, whose shares had fallen from $2.40 in September 1936 to 80 cents by the following February. Robinette identified a number of possible causes including the circulation of unfounded rumours that a company official had absconded with its funds and the fact that the first gold brick produced had been worth only $24,000 rather than the anticipated $30,000. The major cause of the decline, however, appeared to have been pessimistic statements by President Robert W. Breuls about the size and value of the mine's ore reserves, which were merely personal calculations arrived at without a firm basis. Despite this conclusion Robinette reported that there did not appear to be grounds for prosecution of Breuls under section 444 of the Criminal Code for conspiring to manipulate share prices, though he was forced out as president of Red Lake Shore.[18]

And then there were the straight-out swindles: Godfrey's investigation into L.B. United Mines near the end of 1936 uncovered a comically tangled tale. The mining brokers Lancaster Brothers (hence the L.B. United) had acquired a block of stock in the company for 25 cents a share and commenced marketing it at about 65 cents in the fall of 1935. The brokerage's tipsheet, *Gold Mining Today*, had reported in February 1936 that the first gold brick would be shipped at the end of the month. Soon the firm leaked the news that the mint had returned the brick because analysis had shown a high platinum content mixed in with the gold. This story helped to push the price of the shares as high as 85 cents, and during the summer of 1936 T.P. Pinner of Lancaster Brothers told the *Financial Post* that had he been permitted by the OSC regulations to publish the assay results, he might have risked arrest for fraud, so high were they in precious metals.[19]

L.B. United therefore took the decision to spend $34,000 to build a mill at the mine to concentrate the ore, using a new process devised by metallurgist James Kelleher which he declared could produce highly concentrated (though not completely pure) platinum and gross up to $9,000 per day. At that point there also appeared a mysterious character called Hans Oberhauser, who claimed that *he* had a process which could turn the concentrate into pure metal. In the summer of 1936 Oberhauser set up a 'laboratory' at a disused brickworks beside Toronto's Don River, to which broker M.L. Lancaster invited a gathering of newsmen and scientists to witness a demonstration. When University of Toronto chemistry professor Fred Beamish analysed the small buttonlike objects produced by Oberhauser, however, he found them to be composed mainly of silver with no detectable platinum content. The angry Lancaster and the mine's general manager, W.S. Pratt, thereupon confronted Oberhauser at the brickworks. In keeping with the role of the cinematic mad scientist, Oberhauser seized a flask of sulphuric acid that was boiling on a gas jet and made to drink it. They wrestled the acid out of his hands and carted him off to see a doctor, from whence he departed to New York still insisting that he would prove his claim to have produced pure 'platinum sponge.' This circus abruptly ended the marketing campaign for the stock of L.B. United Mines: the OSC stepped in, closed down the mine, and appointed an engineer to sample the ore. When Colin A. Campbell reported that he could find no detectable traces of platinum, John Godfrey ordered a full-scale investigation.[20]

Two days of hearings before Godfrey in December 1936 produced high comedy as well as a flurry of finger pointing among the insiders at L.B. United. After hearing M.L. Lancaster's account of 'the amazing demonstration in Don valley last August,' the commissioner complained that he felt slighted at not having been invited, to which the broker urbanely replied that he believed Godfrey had been away fishing at the time. Loud laughter broke out when company president Dr W.E. Tindale announced that he had not invested a single cent in L.B. United but had attended every board meeting and retained full confidence in its future success. More sniggers were heard when general manager W.S. Pratt testified that he still believed there was platinum in the ore and that the failure to refine it was a mystery to him. Pratt said that Oberhauser was either crazy or crooked, but he admitted that he was ignorant of mining matters and had relied for all technical advice upon company engineer A. Carr-Harris. Carr-Harris, in turn, revealed that the decision to build the concentrating mill had been taken on the basis of just two ore samples, while Kelleher insisted that the mill had not been built on his recommendation since he was a metallurgist rather than an engineer.

OSC counsel J.J. Robinette dampened much of the good humour by pointing out that as early as February 1936 a respected assayer in the United States had reported finding no platinum in L.B. United's ore samples, and at the same time the Canadian mint had returned the company's gold brick because it contained too little gold along with some silver rather than platinum. T.P. Pinner of Lancaster Brothers admitted that despite these two reports the brokers had continued to push L.B. United shares. His feeble claim that the literature about the company had been designed to inform its shareholders rather than market stock was smartly squelched by Robinette's observation that nearly every circular contained advice to purchase these shares.

Had any platinum ever been found? Ontario provincial assayer William McNeill testified that the element was perfectly simple to detect, despite Kelleher's continuing insistence that he had found platinum in the ore only by using the secret process which he intended to patent and license to L.B. United for use in its mill. University of Toronto chemistry professor E.G.H. Ardagh reported that he had been unable to find any traces of platinum, but he suggested that some of the ore samples could have been salted. Before concluding the proceedings Commissioner Godfrey asked if any L.B. United Mines shareholders wished to be heard. One person defended the conduct of the management, but two women were highly critical of what had occurred; one of them claimed that the shares had been illegally sold to her by a door-to-door salesman, while another complained, 'I was told the wildest fairy tales. I'd like to see the public get a fair deal. I'd like to see something done to prevent men like this preying on widows.' With that advice ringing in his ears, Godfrey retired to consider his report.[21]

Within a fortnight came the findings on L.B. United. Most of the company's problems were blamed upon mining engineer A. Carr-Harris and metallurgist James Kelleher. In view of general manager W.S. Pratt's admitted ignorance of mining, he and the board could hardly be faulted for placing a good deal of confidence in trained professionals. No decision to build a concentrating mill should have been taken on the evidence of just a couple of ore samples when normally thousands would have been analysed before such an investment. Kelleher's platinum extraction process was dismissed with a backhanded slap, the commissioner noting that his evidence was not really credible and that he had already been the object of an investigation in another mining promotion. Lancaster Brothers was also criticized for failure to disclose to the shareholders and purchasers the negative results of the platinum assay and the return of the gold brick by the mint because of its contamination with silver. As a result the

OSC ordered that the brokers should not be entitled to recover the $64,000 that had been leant to L.B. United Mines unless a producing mine was developed or another significant find was made by the company in the Porcupine district of Ontario.[22]

Godfrey's report did not deal explicitly with whether the L.B. United ore samples had been salted with platinum, though University of Toronto chemistry professor J.T. King had testified that to do so would have been 'as easy as putting sugar in tea.' In fact, salting proved to be a very difficult problem for securities regulators to deal with. At that very time rumours were circulating throughout the brokerage community in Toronto of alleged contamination of the drill cores from Rubec Mines in the Cadillac area of Quebec. Since Rubec shares were being marketed in Ontario, Godfrey again chose mining engineer Colin A. Campbell to study the situtation. The drilling company and the management and promoters of Rubec proved cooperative, and Campbell eventually concluded that any salting had probably occurred in Quebec, so that the Ontario authorities were not directly involved. A further investigation by Quebec's securities regulator, William Amyot, confirmed the salting and even identified the guilty party, though Amyot refused to name the culprit because he was not persuaded that the act of salting a mine sample in itself was criminal conduct (though knowingly using such falsified results to sell shares would be fraud). When rumours of the salting had begun to circulate widely in November 1936, many speculators might have tried to profit by going short on Rubec stock in anticipation of a sharp fall in share prices, but that, said Amyot, was not punishable conduct.[23]

Even before the revelations about Rubec and L.B. United Mines, John Godfrey had already taken a number of steps to try to tighten up control over mining promoters in the spring of 1936 by specifying what was permitted in their sales literature. An OSC circular declared that maps were not to be designed to mislead about the location of ore bodies. Tipsheets had to disclose when promotional fees had been paid and could not masquerade as disinterested professional journals. At the same time the OSC decided to require all brokers, investment dealers, and securities issuers in Ontario (numbering at least a thousand in total) to file annual statements of assets and liabilities in order to retain registration. More important still, they had to submit to two surprise audits a year, since it was clear that some companies had raised sizeable sums from the public but done nothing to develop their properties. Taken together, Godfrey told an official of the Securities and Exchange Commission, these rules had brought about a 'general cleanup of irresponsible brokers.'[24]

He proved mistaken. By June 1936 the *Financial Post* was reporting a renewed influx of 'J. Rufus Wallingfords' from the U.S. financial underworld into Canada (see chapter 4). During the late summer the OSC had uncovered a number of large boiler-rooms that were skirting the law by selling only in the United States, though Godfrey managed to have several of them put out of business by getting Bell Telephone to cut off their service. Meanwhile, commission investigator Colonel D.F. Pidgeon, who had been brought in by Godfrey from the army's audit staff, was put to work touring Toronto's downtown hotels and apartment buildings, where shady operators were known to congregate. Pidgeon was given authority to examine people under oath and in one case had an arrest warrant issued on a charge of perjury, which led a man to take flight. Complaints were coming in from as far away as Nova Scotia, where the Halifax Board of Trade reported that people in rural districts were being telephoned from Toronto and Montreal by salesmen touting mining and oil shares. No doubt to its pleasure, even the board of the Vancouver Stock Exchange was able to register a complaint with the OSC in the autumn concerning telephone selling from Ontario in British Columbia.[25]

Despite Godfrey's efforts, the OSC proved unable to contain a wave of fly-by-night promotions as the mining-share price index rose from around 150 in February 1936 to over 175 a year later, while its base metal component shot from 230 to 340 during the same period.[26] Brokers exploited a number of loopholes in the Securities Act. Anybody unwise enough to sign and return a 'client card' to a brokerage expressing interest in receiving information about stocks could expect to be bombarded with tipsheets. Residents of Ontario who had made at least three transactions with a broker were considered 'regular' customers who could be solicited by its salesmen at will. Fearful that shady promoters were using certain brokerages as 'fronts,' Godfrey changed the regulations so that only individuals rather than firms could be registered with the OSC, and registrants were required to name their financial backers.[27]

At the start of 1937 the *Financial Post* launched a strong campaign reminiscent of its attacks upon the old Standard Stock and Mining Exchange and its leading brokers after the crash of 1929, complaining that crooked deals were as prevalent as they had been three years earlier near the end of George Drew's tenure at the OSC. Indeed, editor Floyd Chalmers claimed that the current situation might even be worse because the people of Ontario had now been deluded into thinking that they were being well protected. Why had John Godfrey suddenly gone soft on the crooks and their front men even though the newspaper had supplied him with the names of the worst offenders? Why were men with criminal records still being licensed by the OSC? Chalmers later claimed, 'Godfrey was not a good enforcer. I always felt he had too much sympathy for people who were continuing to make artificial markets, particularly for mining securities on the Toronto Stock Exchange.'[28]

Godfrey, who was just recuperating from a fairly serious illness, eventually decided that he must act. To deal with the increasing number of complaints about telephone selling in the United States, the OSC's regulations were modified in January 1937 to make clear that any registrants found to be peddling unqualified securities in the United States would lose their licences. This rule change elicited a letter of praise from the chair of the SEC, James M. Landis, and earned the OSC favourable publicity in the American press. Behind the scenes Godfrey began working closely with SEC staff member J.J. Callahan, even granting him authority under the Ontario Securities Act to come to the province and investigate certain boiler-room operations. On the basis of the information gathered by Callahan and OSC investigators, four Toronto brokerages were closed down for selling in the United States and a number of salesmen prosecuted for making fraudulent misrepresentations. As a result, the optimistic Godfrey wrote to Landis, 'I think we have very effectually closed practically all the boiler-rooms operating in Ontario which were selling into the United States.'[29]

These inquiries revealed that the boiler rooms were being run by thoroughly shady types with long records of brushes with the authorities. In one instance a 'Mr X' had surfaced in Ontario in late 1933 and during the brief boom of 1934 had created a brokerage that employed over a hundred salesmen as well as a tame radio broadcaster. When the OSC became suspicious and seized the firm's books, it was discovered that X was a principal of the company being promoted, which claimed to have a producing mine when in fact the property bore a sheriff's notice offering it for sale with no takers. Less than 15 per cent of the funds raised from the public had ended up in the company treasury, and nothing had been spent upon development. Those who had endorsed the man for registration with the OSC proved to know little about his background, which included previous legal problems in Australia and an outstanding warrant in Britain. The British offence was not deemed serious enough to justify the expense of deportation, so the offender was simply stripped of his OSC registration and allowed to remain in Canada. After lying low for a year or so, he had applied for and been granted a new licence.[30]

Another brokerage was headed by 'Mr Y,' an Irishman who had once worked with the notorious American stock swindler 'Jake the Barber' Factor. Y had been banned from re-entering Britain a couple of years earlier following a widely publicized scam and had retreated to Toronto, where he had operated for the previous year or so through a front man. This firm preserved a façade of respectability by sandwiching glowing accounts of its current mining promotion between sober reports on legitimate prospects in its tipsheet, which was mailed out by the hundreds across North America. Meanwhile, salesmen were telephoning as far afield as the southern United States to sell shares, being careful to avoid fraudulent misrepresentations that might attract the unwelcome attention of the OSC or the SEC. Any investors who complained were quickly repaid so that they would not approach the authorities. After his arrest this man was speedily deported to his native Ireland despite a personal plea to the federal minister of immigration.[31]

This effort to crack down seems to have convinced Godfrey that the OSC required wider powers to penetrate behind the front men. The *Financial Post* claimed, for instance, that the name of neither Y nor any other official of his firm was ever used when contracts or option agreements were signed, but rather that of another investment company with a vague and shadowy relationship to the first.[32] Godfrey therefore set about drafting a number of amendments to the Securities Act to give the OSC the necessary powers to cope with the problems that had recently arisen. When these changes were introduced into the Ontario legislature, however, they became the focus of intense debate.

Long before his election victory in 1934 Mitchell Hepburn had alleged that the prominent Conservative (and former prime minister) Arthur Meighen had been guilty of improper conduct because, as a member of the Ontario Hydro-Electric Power Commission under the previous government, he had voted to acquire the bonds of the Ontario Power Service Corporation from Abitibi Pulp and Paper in 1931 at a price of $90 at a time when they were trading around $30. Later it was revealed that personally and as a corporate officer Meighen was interested in $215,000 of these bonds, and Hepburn had been using this fact over the years as part of his effort to discredit Meighen and his fellow Tories. Never one to pass up a chance to score some partisan points, the premier announced at the opening of the legislature in February 1937 that there would be changes to the Securities Act, and he claimed that these revisions would finally permit a full investigation of the affair. He charged, 'The nefarious Abitibi deal was for the purpose of recouping Meighen's losses. It was a cold and calculated scheme to defraud the people for Meighen's benefit. He violated his trust for his own personal gain.'

Hepburn went on to claim that the attorney general of the day, William Price, had simply handed over any complaints to the newly appointed securities commissioner, George Drew, knowing full well that he lacked the authority to investigate the Abitibi case. Why, said the premier, he even had Drew's letter to Price admitting that there was nothing he could do in this case. The furious Price, still a leading member of the Conservative opposition, demanded to know if *his* side of the correspondence was extant; Hepburn retorted, 'No, you were too cute. You passed the buck to a man you knew could do nothing about this matter. Your letters, indeed! Catching you would be like trying to nail jelly to a wall. You wouldn't dare touch Meighen: he stood too well in the Conservative party, but we are going to touch him.' Price protested bitterly at being described as 'jelly' and spluttered about his probity while attorney general.[33]

This heated exchange naturally focused a great deal of attention upon the amendments to the Securities Act when they were introduced by Attorney General Arthur Roebuck a few weeks later. Some of the changes were mere housekeeping: for instance, the word 'commission' now formally replaced the term 'board' used in the legislation to describe the regulatory tribunal. There was also an amendment that seemed to confirm the government's commitment to the non-partisan administration of securities regulation by removing the authority to order investigations from the attorney general and turning it over to the OSC itself. Despite all the hue and cry, however, the real purpose of the amendments seems to have been to grant Godfrey powers to deal with problems that had arisen recently; the OSC could now investigate not only suspected frauds or crimes, but 'any act which may be unfair, oppressive, injurious, inequitable or improper to or discriminate against any holder, prospective holder, purchaser, prospective purchaser of any shares ... or any act whereby any unfair advantage may be secured by any person or company.' In addition, it was specifically provided that the commission might 'inquire into and examine ... the relationship which may at any time exist or have existed between any person or company and any other person or company by reason of investments, commissions promised, secured or paid, interests held or acquired, the loaning or borrowing of money, stock or other property, the transfer, negotiation or holding of stock, interlocking directorates, common control, undue influence or control, or any other relationship whatsoever.' Roebuck declared that this authority would provide the OSC with a 'much-needed searchlight.'[34]

Placed on the defensive, the provincial Conservatives tried to take the high ground of principle in opposing the amendments. In the legislature Leopold Macauley maundered on about 'star-chamber court methods.' George Drew, who was now vying for the leadership of the provincial Tory party, upped the ante even further: 'It is no longer a Securities Act. It becomes a law establishing personal insecurity by Act of Parliament and formally establishing the rigours of the Inquisition. It establishes effectively the Russian OGPU methods which have been employed so successfully by Stalin in removing all his political opponents ... Nothing like it has ever been seen in any Anglo-Saxon country before.' Hepburn brushed this rhetoric aside by saying, 'I'm not surprised that my honourable friends are trying to cover up a lot of crooks.'[35]

Surprisingly, the *Financial Post*, which had so recently been demanding that Godfrey crack down on swindlers in the securities business, changed its tune and denounced the new legislation, quoting a lawyer who had condemned the bill for permiting 'an unlimited inquisition into the affairs of any person or corporation whatever, with relation to any matter whatever, occurring or to occur at any time whatever in the past or in the future.' It seems likely that this shift reflected the financial community's strong antipathy to Arthur Roebuck following his legislation to repudiate the power-supply contracts between Ontario Hydro and the Quebec generating companies in 1935. The *Post* tried to insist that the amendments had little to do with the sale of securities and claimed that they had not been requested by Godfrey, who already felt that he had adequate powers to deal with offenders. The villain must, therefore, be Roebuck, 'Canada's No. 1 legislative Red,' not content with destroying the sanctity of contract but now bent upon undermining personal liberty and perhaps opening the way for a communist dictatorship.[36]

A more balanced assessment came from a leading Canadian businessman, Clifford Sifton, who suggested there was 'a considerable necessity for clear thinking and for keeping straight upon the question of devising necessary steps for the legal protection of citizens against unfair pressure of business and financial racketeering ..., the attacks appearing to me to be either deliberate special pleading or the result of muddle-headed thinking.' Investigation was not the same thing as punishment, and public inquiries provided protection, while those who had done nothing wrong had nothing to fear. The claim of personal privacy could not be used to cloak wrongdoing. Whatever disciplinary powers the OSC might be granted, only the courts could fine or imprison offenders.[37]

John Godfrey supplied his own defence in a speech to an American audience at the convention of the National Association of Securities Administrators at French Lick, Indiana, in the autumn of 1937. He noted that in 1916 Elihu Root had pointed out to the American Bar Association that administrative tribunals to which broad discretion was granted occupied a position theoretically at odds with the principle of the sovereignty of legislative bodies. Yet Root had predicted that such tribunals would come to exercise steadily expanding authority because of their utility and flexibility. Those who still called for the abolition of all regulatory controls over securities markets were simply turning their backs upon Root's insight.[38]

As it turned out, that speech was John Godfrey's swansong as Ontario securities commissioner; early in 1938 the Liberal government in Ottawa appointed him to the Ontario Court of Appeal. Despite all the to-do surrounding the revisions to the Securities Act in 1937, Godfrey seems to have relaxed his enforcement from that point onward, apparently satisfied that the situation was again under control. In the spring he sought to encourage mining exploration by permitting prospectors and promoters to form syndicates to raise up to $35,000 with only minimal regulation so long as 75 per cent of the money went into the treasury. Just before he retired, the requirements about the escrowing of vendor shares were relaxed somewhat in response to criticisms that prospectors and other insiders were unable to get their money out unless a mine was brought into production.[39]

Godfrey's successor at the OSC was Roy B. Whitehead, who had previously chaired the government's Industry and Labour Board. As though to emphasize that non-partisan administration was to continue to be the order of the day, Whitehead told the *Financial Post* that he had no party affiliations and his summons to the cabinet to discuss his appointment had come out of the blue. To reassure the financial community that it could expect business as usual, he said, 'I have no preconceived theories. I realize the job is a big one, and I would prefer to wait until after I have been in the swim for a year or two before I start theorizing.'[40]

Under Whitehead the OSC undertook relatively few new initiatives. After discussions with the Ontario Prospectors and Developers Association and the local branch of the Canadian Institute of Mining and Metallurgy, it was agreed that the commission would start publishing the details of all underwriting and option agreements for unlisted companies (as the TSE did for listed ones). But there were to be no regulations concerning the minimum prices for option shares or the size of underwriting commissions. Companies would simply be required to file their option agreements and financial statements and submit to twice-yearly surprise audits to ensure disclosure. In the autumn of 1938 the *Financial Post* noted that criticims of the OSC had declined markedly over recent months.[41]

Whitehead also did his best to maintain friendly relations with the Toronto Stock Exchange. When a case arose in which J.H. Crang and Company was charged with misconduct for misleading the exchange about the nature of its relationship with a non-member broker in London, Ontario, the commissioner met privately with the board to outline his views about what should be done and then retired to allow them to discipline Crang with a $2,000 fine. Near the end of 1938 Whitehead reached an agreement by which all complaints against exchange members would be referred to the new business conduct committee, with the OSC's registrar sitting in when such cases were considered.[42]

Despite these diplomatic efforts, mining men continued to lay the blame for the depressed condition of their industry upon over-strict regulation. The secretary of McIntyre Porcupine Mines, Balmer Neilly, received thunderous applause at the 1939 meeting of the Ontario Prospectors and Developers Association when he declared, 'With the best intentions in the world we have got the prospector all tied up in red tape. With our legislation we have lost track of the fundamental aim – making mines ... Fear is congealing prospecting.' Neilly went on, 'Let the government recognize prospecting for what it is: an outright gamble. Let us have no strings on the prize, an adventure without any restrictions ... Surely it is infinitely better that a man should gamble on a prospect than on a race horse or an Irish Sweepstake. On those, if you lose, you lose. When money is gambled on prospects, if you lose the money stays in Canada and more is known about the mining country.'[43]

In an effort to disarm such critics Whitehead announced a relaxation of regulations on 1 April 1939. Previously the OSC had required that vendor stock paid for properties be escrowed and only one share be released for every four sold to the public, so that prospectors, grubstakers, and promoters protested loudly that they could usually realize little cash for their holdings. Now the OSC would permit the release of 10 per cent of the vendor shares immediately and the remainder on a two-for-one basis. Thus in a typical 3-million-share mining company with 1 million vendor shares the insiders could dispose of up to 100,000 shares immediately, while the rest would be released as treasury stock was sold to the public. At the same time, however, Whitehead did tighten slightly the rules announced a year earlier by requiring that options on shares should net the company treasury a minimum of 5 cents each to avoid promoters obtaining 1-cent shares to sell for whatever the market would bear. The mining fraternity proved hard to please, however, and at a meeting near the end of the year the Ontario Prospectors and Developers Association passed another resolution demanding that almost all regulations be abolished, since the 'search for new mines to replace old ones is suffering from the most serious decline in experience because of the rules and regulations of the Ontario Securities Commission. The [Securities] Act ... had [sic] placed shackles around mining that are without limitation.'[44]

Despite the recurrence of frauds and scandals, when the market for mining shares revived slightly in 1936, many prospectors, promoters, and brokers remained hostile to the idea of regulation. Spurred on by adverse publicity, however, John Godfrey cracked down on some of the worst offenders and closed up a number of boiler rooms, and in 1937 the Securities Act was amended to give the OSC wider investigatory powers to expose front men and other shady operators. Nevertheless, when Roy Whitehead took over at the commission early in 1938, he loosened the reins slightly in order to encourage exploration. When a large number of new prospects still failed to develop, he again found himself subject to criticism that red tape was unduly hampering the mining industry.

II

Trading in mining shares in British Columbia rose sharply in 1936 and 1937. Volume on the VSE more than doubled to over 99 million shares in the first year and reached 120.7 million in the second (see appendix, table A.8). The weighted index price for Canadian base metal stocks (which were particularly important in the province) went from 200 at the end of 1935 to 340 by the spring of 1937. Moreover, in mid-1936 there were a number of significant gas discoveries in Alberta's Turner valley which further helped to revive the securities business in western Canada since many oil companies traded heavily in Vancouver. On 23 January 1937 the VSE's afternoon session was actually extended because there were so many unfilled buy orders on hand.[45]

Despite the well-publicized findings of fraud and other dishonest practices by the inquiries into Wayside Consolidated and Nicola Mines and Metals, released in the summer of 1935, the return of good times soon led to new criticism that regulation was impeding mineral exploration and mine development. Allegations continued that the superintendent of brokers, H.G. Garrett, had far too much discretionary power to limit the number of vendor shares granted for properties and to require them to be held in escrow to protect other investors. The Vancouver *Province* once again floated the suggestion that the single superintendent should be replaced by a three-person board including a financial expert and an official of the Mines Department. Garrett was thoroughly opposed to the idea, which he was convinced would only create a more cumbersome system. He pointed out to the attorney general that all the criticisms were phrased in generalities and that while lip service was paid to the public's protection, no safeguards were ever specified. Greedy promoters were simply discontented because they were unable to get hold of big blocks of low-cost vendor shares and feed them out to the public at inflated prices.[46]

Revived markets soon brought signs that shady dealing was back too. Early in 1937 Mines Minister G.S. Pearson became nervous because the shares of a number of mines, such as Whitewater, Reeves-McDonald, and Lucky Jim, which had been defunct since the crash, were once more trading actively on the VSE Curb. Garrett admitted the abuses, since many of these companies were never likely to be sound investments unless they were drastically reorganized to reduce the number of outstanding shares. Yet in light of the criticisms he was being subjected to, the superintendent was reluctant to intervene and spark renewed complaints that he was blocking exploration and development. He pointed out to Pearson that the government had no direct authority over the VSE to impose cease-trading orders, while forcing trading off the exchange floor might open the way to worse abuses in the over-the-counter market. All that Garrett could do was to warn the VSE board about the government's concern over this issue; if the exchange failed to act, unpleasant consequences would certainly follow.[47]

As though fated, the VSE immediately found itself with a major scandal on its hands. Hedley Amalgamated Gold Mines had traded for pennies over several years on the Vancouver Curb. As share markets heated up at the start of 1937, the company released highly favourable assay results. More than 2.5 million shares were traded during the next month and a half, with prices rising as high as $1.10, until the morning of 23 February, when the stock suddenly plummeted from 69 to 22 cents before the exchange ordered trading suspended at 11:15 a.m. Rumours flew that ore samples had been salted and that insiders had seized the opportunity to escape by dumping their stock before this information became public knowledge. The VSE board felt sufficiently alarmed that Attorney General Gordon Sloan was immediately asked to order an investigation under the Security Frauds Prevention Act. G.L. Fraser, who had handled the Wayside Consolidated inquiry, was appointed to examine all trading in the company's shares since the start of 1937.[48]

Before long a sorry tale of incompetence and dishonesty emerged. The government had had concerns about the company for some time. After it announced the discovery of gold in commercial quantities, checks had been made on some ore samples early in 1935 by A.M. Richmond, the resident engineer of the provincial Mines Department in Penticton; he suspected that there might have been salting, though conclusive proof was lacking. Moreover, the department was convinced that the company was exaggerating the size of its discovery, yet took no action because the stock price fell from 25 cents to 17 cents by mid-1935. Only then was the president ordered to make public a revised estimate of reserves or else the government would do so. As a result, the stock price continued to drop, and the department took no further action about the suspected fraud. After the new assay results were released in January 1937, more rumours of salting reached Superintendent Garrett, and the Department of Mines investigated once again. Assayer J.R. Williams discovered that one-half of the drill core that had been deposited with the province was much richer than the other half and informed the company that he too suspected salting. Company officials arranged a meeting with the deputy minister of mines, who suggested that the VSE board suspend trading at once; the exchange had refused to act on account of a flood of sell orders on hand until the collapse of the share prices forced its hand.[49]

Fraser's inquiry soon uncovered that Hedley's president, Russell E. Barker, owned options on 98,400 shares along with additional stock released from escrow. Taking advantage of the favourable news in early 1937, he had set about disposing of these through his brokerage firm, Burrard Stock and Bond, earning a profit of $50,000 in the process. In order to increase trading volume and sustain public interest in the stock, Barker also entered into an agreement with another broker, D.A. Hamilton and Company, to buy and sell Hedley through its house accounts. Enthusiasm was maintained by false progress reports from the alcoholic who served as mine superintendent.

When the assayer informed Barker about his suspicisions of salting, the president immediately passed on the news to other insiders so that they could dump their shares before prices collapsed completely. Director Hugh Davis, who also worked at Burrard Stock and Bond, not only sold all 72,000 shares he owned using a brokerage account in the fictitious name of 'Mrs Borrie' but even went 15,000 shares short, supposedly by mistake. Corporate secretary Frank Parsons passed on the news to another director, Gwynn Burrell; he was an official of another Vancouver brokerage, Western City Company, which disposed of 65,000 shares, while another insider got rid of 10,000 shares. Altogether 369,150 Hedley shares were sold on the morning of 23 February just before the cease-trading order was issued.[50]

Fraser commissioned mining engineer H.H. Stewart to re-examine the drill cores from Hedley for evidence of salting. Stewart reported early in May that the samples had been handled so much that he could come to no firm conclusions, but that when he had redrilled certain of the holes, he discovered that in at least two cases there was no gold at all. The evidence of salting seemed conclusive. Premier T.D. Pattullo quickly announced that warrants alleging a conspiracy to defraud had been issued for the mine superintendent and the president, Barker, who had reportedly left town some weeks earlier.[51]

Despite the laying of charges the Hedley Amalgamated affair proved an embarrassment for the government. Russell Barker might have had a serious conflict of interest as Hedley president and the leading broker handling its shares, but he had not violated the SFPA. Fraser's report made clear that share prices had been run up partly by vigorous trading between VSE members and the house accounts at D.A. Hamilton, the insiders taking small profits on dips and rises that also helped to draw the wider public into the stock. Yet there was no evidence of a conspiracy to manipulate prices by wash trading which might justify criminal charges, as own-account trading was not illegal. The VSE board protested angrily that there was nothing that it could have done in the absence of violations of exchange rules; after all, the share options had been approved by the superintendent of brokers. Fraser's suggestion that all the trades in Hedley on 23 February be cancelled was dismissed as impractical.[52]

The release of Fraser's two reports (one on the share trading, the other on the salting) in April and May of 1937 set off an unseemly bout of finger pointing inside the government. Superintendent Garrett was blamed for approving the options and the release of the escrowed shares which had provided Barker with low-priced stock to sell. The *British Columbia Financial News* got hold of the fact that Richmond's 1935 report to the Mines Department on suspected salting at Hedley had been suppressed and declared that the whole affair was 'a damning indictment' of government incompetence. Garrett, for one, agreed that the deputy minister of mines, John F. Walker, and his minister, George S. Pearson, were mostly to blame.[53]

In the circumstances the superintendent was even able to summon up a bit of sympathy for the VSE; he pointed out that successive attorneys general had always preferred that the government should stay at arm's length from this private institution, which, after all, was far from above suspicion. The members of the VSE board and its listing committee might have conflicts of interest, yet at the same time Garrett admitted that they were in a position to pass on snippets of information that he would never otherwise hear about. Better to seek the exchange's cooperation and be in a position to deal with new problems as they came to light.[54]

Facing a general election on 1 June 1937, the government decided to protect itself by shifting as much of the blame as possible onto Garrett. Even before Fraser's investigation was complete, the superintendent had been pressured into declaring that he was too overburdened to continue regulating the brokers in addition to his duties as registrar of companies and superintendent of insurance. When Fraser's final report was issued, Premier Pattullo announced that Garrett would continue to handle insurance but step down for a new appointee with sole responsibility as superintendent of brokers.[55]

Within the financial community the Hedley Amalgamated affair was treated with the usual boys-will-be-boys attitude. The *Financial Post*, for instance, observed that undoubtedly British Columbia mining promotion had received something of a black eye, just as was the case with Rubec in Quebec or Red Lake Shore in Ontario, but 'Perhaps such events are unavoidable in a venturesome industry where good fortune plays an important part.' More worrisome was the fact that the market began to slump again as the overall index of Canadian mining shares declined from 177 in February 1937 to 121 by October. British Columbia was hit particularly hard by falling base metal prices, which drove down the sub-index for such mining shares from 345 to just 192 in the same period. Many people were convinced that investor confidence had been severely damaged by the Hedley affair and the subsequent slide in stock prices.[56]

Premier Pattullo was eager to damp down any criticism of his government during the election campaign; he preferred to talk about the gold discoveries at Bridge River and Barkerville as heralds of the revival of prosperity. Once the election was safely over, however, and the Liberals had won another strong mandate, the government did begin to consider amendments to the provincial Security Frauds Prevention Act to prevent a recurrence of the Hedley scandal. The mining fraternity quickly launched a new effort to convince Premier Pattullo that over-strict rules were the root of the problem. Journalist Sidney Norman sent along the text of an article that rehashed all the old claims about securities regulation as a hindrance to development, forcing prospectors to hang onto escrowed stock, while only a few shady promoters profited by using regulation to persuade unwary investors to part with their money. Norman complained that Canadians had been duped into adopting American blue-sky laws, which had almost killed individualism and adventurousness there and had then laid waste the mining industry in Ontario. The ineffectiveness of blue-sky laws was notorious, said Norman, citing the well-publicized Julian Petroleum scandal in California during the 1920s, and he called upon the government to 'eliminate a foreign-born travesty upon justice.'[57]

The Joint Mining Council of British Columbia[58] responded to a call for consultation from Pattullo by admitting that recently there had been some 'unfortunate incidents in mining finance,' but it reiterated many of Norman's criticisms. The defects of blue-sky laws were again rehearsed: this legislation had been rushed through in the aftermath of the crisis in 1929–30 without adequate consideration; the result was that shady operators, aware that the public accepted registration of persons and companies as tantamount to government endorsement, could fleece unwary investors with little fear of punishment. In particular, the JMC complained about the amount of 'discretionary authority over mine financing' which the superintendent of brokers had come to exercise under the SFPA and called for the removal of these 'arbitrary powers.'[59]

Though endorsing the JMC's position about the powers of the superintendent, the Vancouver Stock Exchange tried to take a less-confrontational position. The VSE was particularly concerned to fend off changes to the SFPA that would give the government direct authority to intervene in the internal affairs of the VSE by issuing stop-trading or delisting orders. The president, Frank Hall, who put himself forward as a mild reformist, met with the premier along with exchange counsel Max Grossman to lobby for the preservation of autonomy in exchange for closer cooperation with the superintendent of brokers. Subsequently, another meeting was arranged with the new attorney general, Gordon Wismer. Something of a crimp was put in Hall's posture as a statesman when word of these discussions got back to the floor of the VSE, and a 'large and representative' gathering of stockbrokers voted to protest the proposals that Grossman and the president had put forward and demanded that the status quo be maintained.[60]

One person who would have no truck with the idea that excessive regulation was the cause of the current slump was Superintendent Garrett. On the eve of his replacement by E.K. DeBeck he wrote to the premier to explain that it was the Hedley scandal together with the lack of new mineral discoveries in British Columbia that was causing the problem. 'I make no mention of the charge that the "Securities Act" has killed mining in the province,' he told Pattullo, 'because in my view it is ridiculous.' What the act had done was to prevent investors from frittering away a great deal of money on dubious prospects and left the industry in fundamentally sound condition. Deputy Minister of Mines John F. Walker (who had survived the Hedley affair unscathed) heartily agreed that Garrett had 'hit the nail fairly on the head.' At the beginning of the year 'everything was set for what might have been one of the wildest mining booms in the history of this province.' Despite the slump the mining industry remained in prosperous condition, which 'shows clearly,' wrote Walker, 'that there is little or no relation between the mining industry and the stock market.' Now was the time to iron out any weak spots in the regulatory legislation before another bull market started.[61]

Across the border in the United States there were also regulators interested in seeing British Columbia's law beefed up. The SEC's regional administrator in Seattle wrote to DeBeck to suggest that they ought to work together to prevent illegal share pushing on both sides of the line. British Columbia, he observed frankly, 'has become in the nature of a sanctuary for those who desire with impunity to ignore the nature of the Federal Securities Act while distributing securities within the United States.' Vancouver's Old Colony Trading Company, for instance, was busy selling shares in Lightning Creek Gold Mines, and DeBeck agreed to have SEC staff members attend a meeting with him and Old Colony officials to explain that they were violating American law. The SEC hoped that British Columbia would go further and amend its Security Frauds Prevention Act to make it illegal for any resident to market shares in any other jurisdiction which had not been approved for sale there; the American official even helpfully enclosed a new draft section to be included in the legislation which he believed would accomplish this.[62]

Because of doubts about its constitutionality, that section was not included among the amendments to the SFPA presented by the government in the fall of 1937, but Attorney General Wismer announced that many other significant changes were proposed because scandals such as Hedley Amalgamated had demonstrated that the government needed wider powers. Henceforth companies would be required to make prompt disclosure to the superintendent of brokers about any significant changes in their physical or financial situation, and this information might be released to the public by the government if the company failed to do so. Not just making false statements but the failure to make disclosures would become an offence in itself, and the superintendent would now be permitted to issue corrections when he considered that misleading information had been released. For the first time the regulator would be given direct authority over the operations of the Vancouver Stock Exchange, including the power to demand full access to all its records and to issue cease-trading orders (which he could also use for over-the-counter stocks). Audits of brokers' books might be ordered at any time and lists published of those whose registration as brokers was currently under suspension. In addition, British Columbia would adopt Ontario's ban on door-to-door selling of securities and on using the telephone to sell shares to anyone except business associates and regular clients.[63]

Just in case the government showed signs of losing its resolve to push through the changes, CCF leader Lyle Telford charged that the 'Triple-S crowd' (which had promoted Wayside Consolidated) was back with another dubious offering. The syndicate owned 4.25 million of the 6 million shares of BC Nickel, and the prospectus promised that $2 million would be spent on exploration even though only $687,000 was to be raised by selling shares. Company lawyer Wendell B. Farris could only make the lame defence that the use of this figure in the prospectus was 'unauthorized,' though he insisted that the promotion was a fair one in which the insiders had put sizeable sums of their own money.[64]

Several of the proposed amendments to the SFPA attracted particular criticism from the financial community. Wismer had intended to require newspapers to publish the sources of all their information about company promotions and even to grant them privileged status so that the press could not be sued for libel. Brokers argued, however, that confidential information about mining and oil properties was sometimes highly reliable, and the flow might be cut off if the sources were bound to be named. In addition, it was claimed that a ban on brokerage clients giving blanket authority to pledge securities with the banks for loans would make it unduly difficult for brokers to finance their margin business. The government decided to drop these clauses but pressed ahead with the other changes.[65]

However reluctantly, VSE members had to come to terms with the new rules. Addressing the annual meeting in January 1938, President Frank Hall felt forced to admit that the Hedley Amalgamated 'fiasco' had undermined investor confidence (though he tried to blame the harm done to the exchange's reputation in central Canada upon 'irresponsible' remarks by some government officials). Small investors had dumped penny mining stocks as a result of losses in depressed markets. He pointed out that the board had expended a great deal of effort in the past year to restore the VSE's credibility, even going so far as to delist twenty-eight issues and tighten its listing rules. Despite these actions, said Hall, Attorney General Wismer had made clear that he was determined to introduce 'drastic' changes to the SFPA to bring it into line with regulations in other provinces and to ensure control over the exchange. Still, the president claimed that he had arrived at an understanding with the government that the board would be left to manage day-to-day affairs provided that it cooperated with the new superintendent of brokers. Hall added a pointed warning that members must be extremely careful in handling clients' securities, especially in the case of short sales or house accounts, and that if any violations of the rules were detected, there would have to be severe punishment meted out to avoid DeBeck's intervention.[66]

Having secured much wider authority over the VSE, the new superintendent also turned his attention to non-member brokers. DeBeck lamented the fact that the regulations required that an applicant put up only $1,000 worth of capital and secure a bond for the same amount in order to apply for registration. Many small firms were of doubtful financial stability, and to earn a decent living in an overcrowded business, people were tempted to engage in unethical practices or to demand unwarranted commissions. Even the well-established firms claimed that they had to charge mining promoters 20 to 25 per cent commission to sell their shares, while many brokers doubled as promoters and might profit from selling large blocks of low-priced option or vendor shares. No other occupation that entailed such financial responsibilities was as little regulated as these brokers, and DeBeck wanted to impose a code of professional conduct and force all applicants to pass an examination to demonstrate their competence.[67]

Because of his fears about the financial stability of some non-member brokers, DeBeck wanted the same powers to order surprise audits of their books as the VSE had over its members. With share prices depressed many firms were having a 'pretty thin time of it.' The superintendent's investigators uncovered falsified records, including securities reported to clients as purchased which had not been bought, securities recorded as delivered to clients which had never been sent, forged receipts for payments to clients, and even the payment of dividends on shares which had not been acquired for customers, a practice that had once been notorious among mining brokers such as Solloway, Mills and Company. In a distant echo of the crash of 1929 S.W. Miller was arrested in the spring of 1939 on charges of conspiracy to defraud the shareholders of two oil companies. As founder of Miller, Court and Company he had been a leading dealer in mining shares in the 1920s and a four-term president of the VSE, and after leaving his brokerage firm in the mid-1930s, he continued to promote mining and oil companies in the city. Miller's arrest seemed to symbolize the dark side of the history of securities markets on the west coast during the 1930s.[68]

III

The other stock exchanges in western Canada created fewer problems for regulators during the 1930s. Business was so scarce that the very survival of the

Winnipeg and Calgary exchanges was in question in this period. That they stayed open reflected the fact that both of them cooperated fairly closely with provincial authorities in regulating securities and brokers, and this quasi-official status helped to tide them over until somewhat better times returned towards the end of the decade.

The Calgary Stock Exchange took a terrific buffeting from the liquidation of Solloway, Mills and Company in 1930 since that firm had accounted for a very large percentage of trading. As the Depression worsened, local brokers struggled, and by the fall of 1932 a number of members had defaulted on their dues. A general meeting was held to consider closing the exchange altogether, but the idea was rejected. The number of seats was reduced from two hundred to one hundred in mid-1933, and before long there was a modest increase in volume and afternoon trading sessions were restored. Times continued to be hard, however, until dealing in oil stocks really took off after the Turner valley gas discoveries in 1936 helped to revive the CSE from its near-moribund state. By February 1937 the idea of closing the exchange entirely for a day to catch up with back-office business was even being discussed.[69]

Despite this new prosperity CSE members seemed more willing to cooperate closely with the regulators at the Alberta Public Utilities Board than their counterparts in Vancouver. Consideration was even given to inviting a PUB official to sit on the listing committee. In the end it was agreed that listing and delisting would be responsibilities of the exchange alone but would be carried out in close consultation with the PUB. For instance, in June 1937 the board's chartered accountant reported that Ranchmen's Oil and Gas was in bad financial shape and that the CSE ought to step in; Ranchmen's was told by the exchange to reorganize or else lose its listing. All listed companies were required to file financial statements by 1 September that year, and the eight that failed to comply were suspended from trading. A few weeks later the filing of notices of options, underwriting agreements, annual meetings, and dividend payments, as well as the completion of an annual questionnaire, was made mandatory.[70]

The Winnipeg Stock Exchange went even further in seeking to ensure its survival in the difficult times after the crash by making itself a part of the regulatory process. The Manitoba Security Frauds Prevention Act permitted the Public Utilities Commission to refuse registration to any broker who was not a member of a stock exchange. W.R. Cottingham of the PUC decided to grant the WSE wide powers over non-member brokers. The board hired D.L. Rossini as exchange manager, part of his task being to vet all applicants for approved status to ensure their solvency, examining all the issues they were offering, and dealing with complaints. Rejected applicants could appeal to the PUB, but they were normally granted a licence only if a large bond were deposited to cover business done in Manitoba. In the spring of 1931 Cottingham pronounced himself satisfied with these arrangements for eliminating 'chain store' dealers in mining and oil stocks and bringing about a general clean-up of the securities business in Manitoba.[71]

At the WSE's 1931 annual meeting President Jack Macdonald made clear the rationale for accepting these responsibilities, observing that at long last the exchange had become a significant institution rather than 'merely a trading floor.' Members should be proud that the government had delegated to the WSE 'the work of keeping the business of distributing securities in the hands of the right type of firms and individuals.' The importance of this role would be even more apparent when good times returned: 'In our Exchange we possess a very valuable franchise which has been made even more valuable by the confidence and responsibility placed upon us by the Public Utilities Board ... [W]e should take full advantage of the opportunity to establish ourselves in an impregnable position.'[72]

Hard times still lay ahead, however. Trading volumes declined further, and by 1933 the WSE board had decided to buy back three of its own seats for $600 apiece. Yet the PUC agreed to issue no new brokerage licences and to renew only those registered through the WSE so that in time all brokers would fall under its control. Securities issuers were directed to deal with exchange members or approved non-member brokers. As the market for mining shares heated up over the next year, some sixty companies were granted approval to distribute their shares in Manitoba once they had prepared a prospectus disclosing all material facts and agreed to the escrowing of vendor shares. Cottingham of the PUC expressed satisfaction with the system and the WSE's efforts to 'confine the business to legitimate and desirable individuals and firms.'[73]

Not that everything ran completely smoothly. In mid-1934 the member firm of MacKidd, Wither and Company was discovered to be selling shares in South Mackenzie Island Mines, which had been denied a place on the WSE Curb and was not registered for distribution in Manitoba. Despite an order from the WSE to desist, Alexander MacKidd permitted his salesmen to continue their high-pressure tactics, including long-distance telephoning, predicting large future price increases, and endeavouring to switch sounder stocks for South Mackenzie. When the press got wind of this activity, the WSE quickly called in MacKidd, though he was fined only $200 for his misconduct.[74]

To emphasize the close links between the WSE and the government regulators it was agreed near the end of 1936 that the listing committee should consist of the PUC's chair and his registrar, along with exchange manager Rossini and three members of the board.[75] Cottingham was very resentful when the Winnipeg *Tribune* ran a highly critical article about securities regulation in the province, comparing it unfavourably to the OSC. Ontario had only started to crack down on wrongdoers about 1934, he claimed, whereas Manitoba had been dealing with these problems since 1928. Cottingham reminded Attorney General W.J. Major how cooperative the WSE had been. For instance, the exchange had recently been ordered to secure certificates of solvency from all brokers. Ontario had quite different problems from Manitoba, which 'could not and should not afford anything like the machinery provided in that province.'[76]

Perhaps it was just as well that Cottingham resisted the temptation to give 'a very good trouncing' to the *Tribune* for criticizing his efforts. The brokers Anderson, Greene and Company went into liquidation in November 1936. Sorting through its chaotic records, the accountants discovered that the firm had been insolvent since 1931 but the WSE had permitted it to continue in business. Even when a certificate of solvency was not filed, the exchange had done nothing to enforce its by-laws. After an investigation former WSE president T.C. Anderson was charged with six counts of conspiracy and theft. The accountants concluded that while a self-regulatory system might work for the Toronto Stock Exchange, 'the smaller exchanges should not be the sole supervisory authority insofar as the financial standing of brokers is concerned.' Alberta already had the power to order surprise audits, and British Columbia required certificates to be filed with the government. The SFPA ought to be amended to create a superintendent of brokers with wide investigatory powers who should audit brokers periodically to ensure that they had at least $10,000 in working capital.[77]

In an effort to restore its previous cozy relationship with the PUB, the WSE board hastened to inform Attorney General Major that it was quite prepared to see audit requirements for brokers tightened up. Under amendments to the SFPA an official exchange auditor was appointed to analyse all members' financial statements. But the collapse of Anderson, Greene made it difficult to restore the status quo. In the autumn of 1938 there were further talks between the exchange board and the attorney general about changes to the act to avert future brokerage failures. Reluctantly, the WSE endorsed a proposal from the local branch of the Investment Dealers Association of Canada calling for wider government regulation of brokers to ensure their financial stability. When the Public Utilities Commission and the exchange auditor criticized broker Ernest W. Jackson for violating the escrow agreement for Star Lake Gold Mine shares early in 1939, the WSE felt compelled to demand his resignation as a member.[78]

The Winnipeg Stock Exchange survived the Depression crisis by becoming a part of the provincial regulatory process. The hard-pressed government of Manitoba proved willing to allow the PUB to delegate important responsibilities to the brokers themselves and to act mainly as a passive overseer of securities markets. Although this system experienced some problems, especially when Anderson, Greene and Company went into liquidation, it did help the exchange to endure the terrible blows of the 1930s. In Calgary the relationship between the stock exchange and the provincial regulator was not as close, but there too a more cooperative association between the two was worked out during this period.

In Ontario and British Columbia a more complex relationship evolved during the revival of securities markets in 1936 and 1937. The return of better times aroused the temptation to revert to the old ways of high-pressure share selling, insider dealing, and price manipulation as well as out-and-out frauds such as salting ore samples. Whether the promotion was Bidgood Kirkland, L.B. United Mines, or Hedley Amalgamated, a new roll of dishonour began to unfold. As a result, provincial regulators were compelled to resume the aggressive enforcement activities that had been allowed to lapse after the short-lived mining boom of 1933–4 ended. Investigations were conducted, reports published, charges laid, and eventually both provinces adopted revisions to their securities legislation in 1937 to give the regulators wider powers to expose and punish offenders. At the same time the stock exchanges were compelled by the threat of direct regulatory intervention to take a more active role in policing themselves. However grudgingly and reluctantly, the Toronto and Vancouver Stock Exchanges began to clean up their listings and trading practices to prevent the worst abuses.

Unfortunately for the brokerage community, however, the return of good times which they had so optimistically expected when the TSE opened its grand new building failed to materialize. In fact, the spring of 1937 proved not to be the start of a new take-off but the high point of the decade. Between March and October the Canadian share-price index fell by almost one-third from 147 to 106. Even as the brokers of Toronto left their grand celebratory banquet on 20 March, the fizz was going out of the toasts and tough times still lay ahead.

14

Uncertainty

Share prices and trading volume on Canada's stock exchanges did not revive during the late 1930s. This failure stemmed partly from the conviction that another general European war was becoming increasingly likely and partly from the impact of fiscal policy. Believing that a balanced budget was the best stimulus for economic growth, Ottawa curtailed spending in 1937 to reduce the federal deficit, which had ballooned during the Depression, and in doing so it dampened recovery. After the Munich crisis in 1938 the conviction that war with Germany was unavoidable became increasingly widespread. Many investors preferred to stay on the sidelines until the future became clearer for fear that the outbreak of hostilities would lead to the closure of stock exchanges and a rush to liquidate stocks and bonds like that which had occurred in 1914. The combination of these factors helped to create uncertainty in securities markets, which hampered any strong recovery.

Mackenzie King's government was a very late and reluctant convert to the notion of stimulating the economy through expansionary fiscal policies, preferring to wait for the recovery to take its own course. In his 1937 budget address Finance Minister Charles Dunning looked back upon the modest recovery that had begun a year or so earlier and actually warned against over-optimism and the dangers of a recurrence of the speculative excesses of 1920s.[1] The previous year he had predicted a deficit of $100 million (which actually totalled under $90 million), but now he announced his intention to cut spending a further $20 million, which with an anticipated rise in revenues of over $30 million should reduce the 1937 deficit to less than $40 million. Dunning succeeded in holding federal spending at just over $530 million in 1937 while revenues rose from $454 million to $517 million. Canada's GNP remained virtually stable at $5.2 billion in both 1937 and 1938 as federal policy helped to take the steam out of the nascent recovery. A similar policy of retrenchment in Washington helped to bring on the 'Roosevelt recession' which further dampened growth in North America.[2] Not until 1939 did Canada get its first purposefully Keynesian budget.[3]

The impact of these deflationary policies was all too evident in sharp declines on the stock markets. Rather than the dawn of the new era that the members of the Toronto Stock Exchange had expected when they celebrated the opening of their new building in March 1937, that event proved to be the high point of the decade. By the end of the year the index of Canadian share prices had fallen back to 1926 levels again, and in the spring of 1938 it dropped below 100 for the first time since the autumn of 1935. Thereafter it hovered around that level until war broke out two and a half years later. Mining stocks experienced a similar (though less-pronounced) decline, the weighted index falling from 172 in March 1937 to 121 by October and never rising above 160 again over the next couple of years. (See appendix, figures A.1 and A.2.)

Pessimism about the future was greatly increased by the conviction that another European war was becoming more and more likely. In September 1938 came the Munich crisis. Though British concessions averted a confrontation, the directors of the TSE began making contingency plans for war.[4] Hitler's troops marched into Prague in the spring of 1939 and took control of what remained of Czechoslovakia before the British government was roused to guarantee the independence of Poland. By that time many Canadians believed that war was inevitable and most anglophones were determined to fight at Britain's side; the German invasion of Poland in September 1939 simply confirmed their worst fears.

The establishment of the Bank of Canada in the mid-1930s had created for the first time a national agency responsible for the management of interest rates and the money supply, which were of crucial importance to financial markets. The bank's concerns included limits on margin trading in shares in order to control undue speculation like that which had prevailed in 1929. Some people also considered tighter federal regulation a desirable development since scandals such as Hedley Amalgamated in British Columbia had cast doubt upon the capacity of provincial regulators to clean up persistent problems even when armed with broader powers under securities legislation. Debate therefore continued about the respective roles to be played by the federal and provincial governments in the regulation of securities markets.

I

The 1932 decision of the Judicial Committee of the Privy Council in *Lymburn v. Mayland* handed constitutional jurisdiction over most aspects of the business of selling securities in Canada to the provincial governments (see chapter 11).

Nevertheless, in some quarters there persisted the belief that regulation by the federal government was essential, and the American example seemed to confirm this view. After its creation in 1934 the Securities and Exchange Commission in the United States gradually assumed wider responsibilities; the shocking revelations in 1938 that sent Richard Whitney, former president of the New York Stock Exchange and a leading opponent of government intervention, to the penitentiary for a serious fraud only seemed to reaffirm the necessity of such controls.[5]

The idea of national regulation of securities markets naturally appealed to bureaucrats in the office of the secretary of state in Ottawa. Some prominent Conservative politicians were also known to believe that Canada now required a national body equivalent to the SEC to supervise markets. For instance, George Drew endorsed this idea following his dismissal as Ontario securities commissioner in the autumn of 1934, arguing that it would ensure uniformity and prevent duplication of effort by provincial agencies. The board of the Toronto Stock Exchange was strongly in favour of such a plan, though discreetly so in order to avoid antagonizing the Ontario Securities Commission.[6]

In the spring of 1935 the federal Royal Commission on Price Spreads and Mass Buying, set up by the Conservative government of R.B. Bennett to examine the impact of the Depression upon small businesses, entered the debate. Commission investigators had undertaken a study of the role of promoters and investment dealers in the refinancing of several large Canadian firms during the late 1920s. Beginning in 1925 Wood, Gundy had arranged the buyout of the shareholders of the Robert Simpson Company for cash and shares financed by the flotation of collateral trust bonds in a holding company, followed by a large issue of preferred shares in 1928–9. Further reorganization had increased total capitalization from $14 million to $32 million through the writing up of asset values. Though the investment dealer had earned large fees and commissions, the Depression left the department store unable to meet the heavy burden of increased bond interest.

Another brokerage, Dominion Securities, had floated a big issue of common and preferred shares for Burns and Company in 1928 to raise the money to acquire the assets of the western food producer. Loaded with debt, the company was soon overwhelmed by the downturn and had to suspend its preferred dividend and default on its bond interest, ultimately necessitating a further reorganization. The royal commission report charged that the only reason for the creation of the holding company seemed to be the sale of additional securities, which had been facilitated through the investment house misstating income figures by manipulating depreciation allowances in a way that was culpable and verged on the fraudulent. The conclusion in both instances was that investment dealers could not be relied upon to protect the interests of investors since their main interest lay in marketing securities and collecting underwriting fees and commissions.[7]

The report also pointed out that the reluctance of the courts in Canada to inquire into non-cash compensation paid to insiders by companies was an invitation to stock watering. As a result, tighter control over corporate financing should be required to protect shareholders' rights and compel wider disclosure of financial information. For instance, companies ought to be made legally responsible for claims made by brokers marketing their securities. Though recognizing that the division of jurisdiction over companies between Ottawa and the provinces could not be ignored, the commission therefore recommended changes to prevent the recurrence of the abuses that had occurred during the boom of the 1920s. Most important was the creation of a Trade and Industry Commission which would include an Investor Securities Board with the power to review the capital structure of all federally chartered companies and approve all proposed issues of securities, taking account of capitalization in relation to asset values. The board would be given the power to fix levels of bonded indebtedness for industrial undertakings and could require them to disclose the collateral backing their securities (though it was admitted that mining ventures would probably require special treatment because of their speculative character and the difficulty of valuing properties).

This new board would pass upon all advertising material to be issued in connection with new flotations to ensure full disclosure and could block any non-approved issue. To counter the anticipated criticism that the review process would render the federal government responsible for the worth of the investments which it sanctioned, the report returned two answers. First of all, Ottawa already exercised close supervision and regulation over banks and life insurers but did not admit responsibility for losses that they incurred. Secondly, issuers could be banned from advertising the fact of federal approval to prevent this being used as a marketing tool. The underlying assumption was that this system would make it easier for federally chartered companies to market their securities and might ultimately lead more and more undertakings to shift their place of incorporation to Ottawa.[8]

As part of the attempt to recapture some of its rapidly waning support, the government of R.B. Bennett embarked upon its ambitious program of 'new deal' legislation in 1935, including a Trade and Industry Commission Act based upon the recommendations of the royal commission. The secretary of state was to have the authority to order the commission to examine and report upon any company proposing a new issue of securities. Though the bill received unanimous support in the House of Commons, Arthur Meighen, the government leader in the Senate, argued that such vetting lay beyond the authority of Parliament in the case of provincial companies and, in any event, would simply duplicate the work of provincial securities regulators. As a result these sections were deleted from the legislation.[9]

The only significant change in federal securities legislation at this time, therefore, came in amendments to the Companies Act passed in 1935. Ottawa's 1934 legislation had required all issuers to provide share buyers with a prospectus at least twenty-four hours prior to the acceptance of any application to purchase being finalized. This rule did not, however, apply to underwriters selling an issue purchased outright; that omission was now rectified despite doubts expressed by Meighen that such controls could constitutionally be applied to the owners of an issue of shares. The obligation of federal companies to disclose financial and other corporate information in their prospectuses and annual reports was extended and a provision inserted that directors must refrain from speculating in the shares of their companies and make annual disclosure of their transactions in such securities when requested by any shareholder. Stock was to be allotted for acquisitions only when 'adequate consideration' was received, and shares with special rights exclusive to management were prohibited. These changes made the federal Companies Act as strict in its disclosure requirements as any provincial legislation in the country.[10]

Institutions such as the Toronto Stock Exchange which already fell under provincial control were careful not to take any public stance on the issue of extending federal regulatory control over securities markets, even though they privately favoured a uniform national regimen. The TSE board had closely reviewed the Price Spreads report but had decided to take no action, merely directing administrator A.J. Trebilcock to maintain a watching brief. When the Investment Dealers Association of Canada established a committee to consider the potential impact of the royal commission recommendations, the TSE maintained its passive stance.[11]

The failure of efforts to extend federal regulation over securities markets gratified provincial regulators. The main mover behind the royal commission had, of course, been the renegade Vancouver Conservative MP H.H. Stevens, which must have given John Godfrey of the OSC wry pleasure in light of the results of his investigation into the affairs of the Manufacturers Finance Corporation in the summer of 1935. This undertaking was controlled by Nova Scotia senator J.A. McDonald as a vehicle to acquire liens on the products of his Amherst Piano Company. Piano dealers sold the liens to Manufacturers Finance, which assumed the obligation to collect money owing on the instruments from numerous instalment purchasers. The lien notes were supposedly insured against loss, but from the very beginning in 1923 McDonald had never tried to collect from any piano owner who defaulted. To avoid any investigation by the loss insurers he simply renewed the liens, so that some pianos carried as many as five separate liens. Meanwhile, he continued to pay heavy premiums to the insurers as an aid in selling preferred shares in Manufacturers Finance to the public. Since the company was losing money, the preferred dividends were paid from newly raised capital in a classic Ponzi scheme. And the irony of it was that the board of Manufacturers Finance was liberally stocked with other prominent Conservative politicians such as Gideon D. Robertson, P.E. Blondin, and none other than H.H. Stevens.

When the company collapsed into bankruptcy, it was further revealed that Stevens had signed an underwriting agreement with Manufacturers in 1925 which gave him exclusive rights to sell its shares in British Columbia and Alberta for a 3 per cent commission. Even though he knew that defaulted liens were not being covered by the insurers, he continued to employ salesmen to peddle the shares using misleading representations about the safety of this investment. Not only that, but Stevens had apparently sat on the company's board illegally for as long as a year since he had not bothered to purchase the necessary qualifying shares. Godfrey sternly condemned the directors for acting as mere 'rubber stamps' for Senator McDonald and his dishonest auditor, and flatly rejected the claim that board members were entitled to rely solely on information about the affairs of a company supplied by its management. In Britain, noted Godfrey, the likes of Stevens were contemptuously referred to as 'guinea pig' directors because they got paid in guineas for attending each board meeting and devoted no further attention to corporate affairs. The commissioner concluded his report on Manufacturers Finance by observing scathingly that Stevens had refused to attend the OSC's hearings and had defended his actions in ways that were simply not credible.[12]

H.H. Stevens defected from the Conservative party in the summer of 1935 to form his own Reconstruction movement, which helped to bring about the overwhelming rejection of R.B. Bennett's government and the return to office of the Liberals under Mackenzie King in the federal election. With his fellow Liberals in control of seven of the nine provincial governments, the prime minister summoned a dominion-provincial conference soon after the election to deal with a number of outstanding intergovernmental issues. One of these, though by no means a high priority, was the uniformity of company law. At the 1935 conference a committee on constitutional questions composed of provincial attorneys general together with the premiers of Quebec and Alberta met with Justice Minister Ernest Lapointe. There proved little difficulty in agreeing to a resolution that the federal secretary of state should convene a meeting of provincial officials in order to draft uniform company legislation to be submitted to the ten legislatures.[13]

None of the governments felt much urgency about the matter, however, and some provincial officials remained decidedly wary about any federal proposals. Almost a year passed before Ottawa finally got around to suggesting a meeting in November 1936. British Columbia's superintendent of brokers advised his premier to tread warily: in 1934 Ottawa had simply presented the provinces with a draft of the new Companies Act as a fait accompli. H.G. Garrett wanted the federal government to send out a set of proposals beforehand and recommended that if they were not acceptable, the province should decline to attend.[14]

When the meeting convened in early November, no BC representative was present, though this appears to have been because Premier Pattullo was considering a snap provincial election. The other eight provinces were represented by senior officials (or in the case of Prince Edward Island by its premier and attorney general, T.A. Campbell), and the under-secretary of state, E.H. Coleman, took the chair. After formal statements from various participants, the delegates turned their attention to the first order of business, a suggestion that a 'Dominion Securities Board' should be created. Though some representatives spoke in favour of the idea, it was coolly received by most of the provinces. All the end of the first day the conference had passed a resolution declaring that cooperation between governments was the appropriate solution, 'and it does not appear to be necessary to recommend the constituting of a Dominion Board to regulate the sale to the public of securities of Dominion companies.' The meeting therefore devoted its efforts instead to seeking agreement concerning the principles that should govern the regulation of securities markets across Canada, such as uniform prospectus requirements.[15]

The meeting of November 1936 effectively marked the end of Ottawa's efforts to create its own regulatory tribunal, an idea that stemmed mainly from the 1935 report of the Price Spreads commission. Provincial regulators had never evinced much enthusiasm for this concept, particularly in provinces such as Ontario, British Columbia, and Manitoba. Officials like Godfrey could point out that they already possessed wide experience and that the courts had granted the provinces extensive jurisdiction over the business of dealing in securities in the *Lymburn v. Mayland* decision. Federal interference in this area was unnecessary and unwelcome, particularly since the revisions of the Companies Act in 1934 and 1935 now imposed fairly stringent controls over promoters who chose to incorporate their undertakings in Ottawa. Better to seek uniformity of standards across the country and leave it to the provinces to oversee enforcement.

As share markets heated up near the end of 1936, Godfrey concluded that the most effective means of dealing with abuses such as telephone selling from one province to another and into the United States was to call his own intergovernmental conference. He invited SEC chair James M. Landis to bring along his staff and address this gathering in January 1937. Because of Godfrey's illness the meeting was postponed until early March, when officials of all nine provinces, the federal government, and the SEC (though not Landis himself, who had retired) gathered in Toronto. Agreement in principle was quickly reached that the disclosure requirements under the prospectus clauses of the federal Companies Act should serve as a minimum standard, though it was noted that additional information would be required for mining and oil promotions. Otherwise the rules developed under provincial regulatory legislation since 1930 would be left fundamentally unaltered. Ottawa's only responsibility would be the establishment of a clearing house for information to which each province and the SEC would report on rules, violations, offenders, and the like.[16]

A further meeting of provincial and federal officials was held in Winnipeg in the spring of 1938 to discuss matters that had not been settled a year earlier. Information was exchanged on a number of issues, but no more was heard of the idea of creating a federal tribunal like the SEC to regulate securities markets. Even the impetus to agree upon a uniform Companies Act seemed to have dissipated, and the provinces were left to go their separate ways.[17]

II

Federal bureaucrats could still exercise influence over securities markets in ways other than the creation of a formal regulatory body. By the autumn of 1936 concerns were reviving over the possible reappearance of excessive stock-market speculation, a fear raised by Finance Minister Charles Dunning in his budget address the following February. One means of control was the imposition of minimum margin requirements on share purchasers. The Securities Exchange Act of 1934 had granted the U.S. Federal Reserve Board authority to fix margins as part of its general responsibility for controlling the supply of money and credit.[18] In Canada margins continued to be governed informally by the willingness of the members of the Canadian Bankers Association to grant loans to brokers on the collateral of securities. Dealers could, of course, allow prize customers to borrow on highly favourable terms if they wished since the willingness to extend credit was an important competitive tool. The case of F.H. Deacon and Company demonstrated that there were still plenty of 'under-margined' accounts left over from the 1920s because of the inability or refusal of customers to put up additional funds and the reluctance of brokers to alienate them by selling out at a loss (see chapter 10).

Only in 1933 did the Montreal Stock Exchange finally establish the first formal rules binding its members regarding the margins permitted on new share purchases.[19] By June 1935 the MSE rules placed listed stocks trading under $3 on a cash basis (no margin), while those between $3 and $12 could be carried on a sliding scale of $3 per share (or as low as 33.3 per cent margin), and above $12 margins were 25 per cent, so that customers could borrow three-quarters of the cost of their purchases, though they were required to put up additional funds if prices declined.[20]

The establishment of the Bank of Canada in 1934 created an agency with responsibilities for the management of the supply of money and credit similar to the Federal Reserve Board in the United States. Beginning in 1936 the bank began to take an interest in margin requirements as a means of controlling speculation. Even though he lacked statutory authority to regulate margins, bank governor Graham Towers could rely upon his influence with the CBA to control the level of brokers' loans and try to nudge the exchanges in the desired direction. A report to the deputy governor in early 1936 noted that most Canadian brokers then had margin requirements like those of the Montreal Stock Exchange, shares under $3 being on a cash basis, with a 33.3 per cent margin on shares between $3 and $50 and 25 per cent above that level. In the United States, by contrast, the Federal Reserve had fixed margins at the much higher level of 55 per cent. A few weeks later the MSE raised its margin requirements for shares over $3 from 25 per cent to 30 per cent. The Toronto Stock Exchange, however, imposed no such formal controls over the lending practices of its members. That, in turn, created pressure in Montreal to reduce margins to 25 per cent to avoid a competitive disadvantage. In July MSE president H.J. Child advised Towers that some of his members felt 'that with the improvement of European conditions and the continuing low level of brokers loans our rate of 30% is too high. They point out that the Toronto Stock Exchange did not follow our lead in this respect which more or less compelled the Montreal Curb Market here to remain on the 25% basis, and have been told that banks are carrying securities for private clients on the 25% basis.'[21]

Towers's reply reminded Child that when they had discussed this matter at the beginning of the year, he had not felt 'that an increase in marginal requirements was essential at that time, but that it might become so if [trading] activity and rising prices continued.' The governor applauded the MSE's wise decision 'to start the ball rolling by a change to 30 per cent.' Since then, however, volumes and prices on the exchanges had declined somewhat, so that the TSE was reluctant to follow suit. A reduction of 5 per cent might not lead to any significant increase in trading, 'since the new demand would come from customers who are already holding all – or almost all – they can afford on the basis of present requirements.' Nobody could blame the MSE for making such a cut at present, but Towers was convinced that higher margins would probably be advisable within the next twelve months and standing pat now would avoid the disruption of another change before too long. In any event, the governor promised that he would 'talk to the banks and trust companies in regard to the desirability of following stock exchange minimum margins now and in future.' Towers therefore started to apply pressure on the TSE board to impose rules on its members for new share purchases. In September 1936 the board finally agreed to fix rates at 30 per cent on shares worth over $10, but it got cold feet and deferred the decision until after the semi-annual audit of members at the end of the month, fearing that the accountants would find a large number of brokers hard-pressed to meet the higher standard for many customers.[22]

Resistance to the imposition of formal margin rules remained strong in Toronto. In October 1936, with the level of brokers' loans rising sharply, Towers sent the Bank of Canada's auditor to sound out the president of the TSE. H.B. Housser advised that as a result of the merger bringing in the members of the Standard exchange, 'the mining members of the present T.S.E. are gradually becoming more conservative than formerly, including their attitude towards margin.' Nevertheless, he pointed out 'that there were no rules of the exchange whereby any member could be compelled to observe any minimum margin basis. As he stated [it], he would greatly prefer to accept an order for 1,000 shares of Int[ernational] Nickel on a 20% margin from a good client he knew than a smaller order on a 50% basis in some stock which enjoyed a limited market and other undesirable features.' Housser also expressed scepticism about the effectiveness of formal regulations such as those imposed by the Federal Reserve Board; having visited New York, he had concluded that '"those in the business" were much cleverer than "those not in it," and ways would be found whereby such margin requirements would be got around and "not too generally lived up to."' He also claimed that the Canadian Bankers Association was being hypocritical about tightening up credit; the TSE had approached its president, S.H. Logan, about an agreement on margin rates so that the banks would refrain from 'soliciting stock business,' but his 'reply was firmly negative on the grounds that the bankers were anxious to get loans out on a 20% margin for revenue purposes.'[23]

Ultimately, however, pressure from the Bank of Canada persuaded both brokers and bankers to change their tune. Logan called in the TSE's vice-president near the end of October and convinced him that the exchange ought to fix the margin on shares over $10 at 35 per cent. Stocks under $1 would remain on a cash basis, those from $1 to $3 on 50 per cent margin and from $3 to $10 on 40 per cent margin. The TSE's agreement, however, was contingent upon an understanding with the banks not to canvass brokerage clients or to try to take over their loans by offering lower rates; brokers would receive funds for half a per cent less than other borrowers provided that the collateral was listed stocks. Graham Towers made it clear that from now on he wanted the two major exchanges to obey firm rules about minimum margins on new purchases, rules that would be changed only after full consultations which the Bank of Canada would oversee. 'The new scale was introduced after having been agreed with the Chartered Banks and with the Trust Companies Association of Ontario and has since been adopted by the Land Mortgage Companies Association. In any further revisions the Stock Exchanges will doubtless follow the same procedure.'[24]

From that time forward the central bank effectively dominated the fixing of margin rates. In June 1937 TSE president N.C. Urquhart consulted Towers about what brokers ought to do about shares purchased at over $1 which subsequently fell below that. Should customers be required to put up additional sums to place these shares on a 100 per cent cash basis or else be sold out? The MSE, where much less low-priced stock was traded, favoured that idea since its members were also 'convinced that Toronto does not *maintain* margins at the regular figure as effectively as they do in Montreal.' The Torontonians proposed that in future shares priced between $1 and $3 should be carried on on a 50 per cent margin if the price fell below $1, provided that customers had paid at least 65 cents per share. Towers wanted that minimum to be 75 cents because of concern about a possible 'runaway market,' but eventually allowed himself to be persuaded to accept the TSE proposal. The members of the Canadian Bankers Association also consented to this arrangement, though taking care to note 'the general reservation, which applies to all these understandings, that the banks will be entitled to make certain necessary exceptions.' These new rules took effect on 1 September 1937.[25]

From its springtime high of 147 the index of Canadian share prices slumped to just over 100 by the autumn, and the exchanges began agitating for a cut in margin requirements to try to revive business. A delegation of brokers visited the Bank of Canada to put their case. President Urquhart of the TSE claimed that most client accounts were in good shape, judging by the recent surprise audit. Towers was not sympathetic, explaining that his goal was

that margins should be maintained at a figure which could be considered prudent and would provide ample protection against the wide swings in security values which had been, and no doubt would again be, experienced. I mentioned that our interest in this matter could be of two kinds;–

(1) that felt at a time when extravagant speculation was underway accompanied by rising loans, and

(2) that felt when other factors were not present, but nevertheless all concerned wished to keep the business on a sound financial basis.

The situation at present was as described in (2).

But the brokers argued that some relaxation of the rules was justified for psychological reasons, or as Towers put it, 'On previous occasions when margins have been raised, their members have naturally not all been pleased. But the members are now unanimous in their belief that the Committees' actions have been wise. If the Committees now yielded moderately to the demand for lower rates, they would strengthen their hands at a later date in enforcing higher ones when the need arose. I think that this probably applies not only between the Committees and their members, but also between ourselves and the Committees.'[26]

Towers therefore consented to a proposal for across-the-board cuts: shares under $1 would remain on a cash basis, but those between $1 and $4 would require 40 per cent margin with a minimum payment of 65 cents per share, those between $4 and $40 would carry 33.3 per cent margins, and over $40 the margin would be 30 per cent. These cuts were, in the governor's words, 'not very substantial' yet sufficient to demonstrate that the bank's rules were not 'too rigid.' The exchanges also persuaded him that shares purchased for $1 or more which sank below that minimum might continue to be carried provided clients maintained a 50 per cent margin. At the annual meeting of the Bank of Canada in February 1938 Towers reminded his audience of the continuing need to keep an eye on borrowing to finance speculative share purchases, but defended the current rules by noting that while bank loans to members of the Montreal and Toronto exchanges secured by Canadian stocks and bonds had hovered around $80 million through the first three quarters of 1937, they had declined to just $45 million by year's end.[27]

After the Munich crisis in the fall of 1938, with the Canadian share-price index still lingering near the 1926 level of 100, the Montreal Stock Exchange applied pressure for further cuts in margin rates, calling for 33.3 per cent on all stocks over $2 and 50 per cent on lower-priced shares with a minimum 65-cent payment. The MSE's chair argued that the changes would make only a slight difference but be 'easier to figure, and give ample protection to our brokers, providing they maintain a 65 cent minimum – if they don't they get a good stiff fine.' This time it fell to the TSE to take a more conservative line and oppose the reductions. After consultations with the Bank of Canada it was agreed that the exchanges would maintain the scale of margins established a year earlier with only a minor amendment to raise the margin on shares over $40 from 30 to 33.3 per cent for simplicity's sake. These rules remained in force when war broke out in September 1939.[28]

In the aftermath of Munich, officials of all Canadian stock exchanges began to fret about the deeply worrisome possibility of another general European war. The TSE board formulated a plan to remain open for business, if necessary by imposing minimum prices should London and New York suspend trading. Exchange members would be banned from trading listed issues over the counter. The MSE was consulted and agreed to impose similar rules, and the Bank of Canada was advised of these intentions.[29]

British appeasement restored an uneasy calm to the European situtation, but many people believed that it was only a matter of time before there was another crisis. Hitler's seizure of Czechoslovakia in the spring of 1939, therefore, found the financial community braced for the worst. The Bank of Canada asked all the exchanges to file contingency plans and made sure that the chartered banks were fully briefed. By then a general consensus had emerged that closure should be considered only as a last resort to avert a general panic. Even the imposition of minimum prices was unpopular in many quarters, as brokers were convinced that it would simply lead trading to shift to unofficial 'street' markets as had occurred during the First World War. The intention was therefore to impose highly flexible minimums for a temporary transition period in hopes that share prices would soon stabilize, particularly if the military news were favourable.[30]

As international tension mounted during August 1939 representatives of the MSE and TSE were summoned to Ottawa for consultation with the Bank of Canada. The Montrealers now had a change of heart and sought to impose minimum prices based upon the last sale of a board lot, with a ban on short selling, though with provision for subsequent reductions of the minimums in steps of up to 10 per cent to reflect current values. The TSE agreed to go along provided that off-floor trading of listed issues was banned. When German troops rolled into Poland on 1 September, the TSE immediately got in touch with Montreal and New York and learned that both intended to carry on business as usual. Nevertheless, some TSE directors got cold feet and at an early-morning board meeting proposed to impose minimums on all issues except those interlisted with the NYSE; this suggestion was voted down. Short selling was banned, however, and the directors adjourned to see how trading developed. Since the morning session was relatively uneventful, the board met again once the exchange had closed for the day and confirmed the decision not to impose any other controls. Keeping in close touch with each other and the banks over the next few days, the MSE and TSE boards stuck to their plans, particularly after the NYSE dropped any restrictions on 5 September. Two days later the Canadian exchanges also lifted their ban on short selling. The wisdom of this response seemed confirmed by a modest rush to buy 'war' stocks in industries expected to profit from mobilization.[31]

Canada's declaration of war on Germany in September 1939 produced no general upward surge in securities markets. Using its sweeping powers under the War Measures Act, the federal government quickly created a Foreign Exchange Control Board, which clamped tight restrictions on the purchase of other currencies, particularly the American dollar. Brokers who dealt heavily in U.S. securities faced an especially bleak future.[32] Germany's speedy triumph in Poland and the 'phony war' stalemate with Britain and France that followed created more uncertainty about the future. By the end of the year the index of Canadian stock prices remained becalmed around the 1926 level of 100. About the only comfort that stock exchange members could draw was that at least they were not compelled to watch helplessly as what trading there was shifted off the floor and onto the street, as had happened in 1914.

By late September the board of the Toronto Stock Exchange had struck a committee to consider means of cutting expenses; a week later eight employees were let go and others had their wages reduced in hopes of saving $12,500 annually. Many brokers were already having a hard time making ends meet, and in November the Montreal Stock Exchange proposed an agreement to raise commission rates. Around Christmas a special general meeting of the TSE approved increases to take effect on 2 January 1940. Stocks selling between $15 and $75 were not affected, but rates for higher- and lower-priced industrials would rise in anticipation of increasing revenues. As the 'low, dishonest decade' of the thirties dragged to its dismal conclusion, the members of the financial community in Canada could hardly look to the future with great optimism.[33]

The years just prior to the Second World War were a period of drift and uncertainty for securities markets in Canada. Share prices failed to recover much beyond 1926 levels except for the brief boom in 1936–7. In part this was because the federal government helped to choke off recovery in 1937 by reducing expenditures and increasing tax revenues. Not until 1939 would the country have a truly Keynesian budget that aimed at promoting growth.

The uncertainty also extended to precisely what role Ottawa was to play in regulation and control of securities markets. Some people were convinced that Canada ought to follow the model of the United States in the Securities Exchange Act of 1934 and set up a national tribunal in the interests of uniformity and efficiency. Needless to say, provincial officials did not share this point of view because they believed that they had succeeded in creating a fairly effective administrative structure which could withstand constitutional challenges in the courts while curtailing the activities of promoters of the shadier sort. The impetus for a federal securities board which came from the Royal Commission on Price Spreads faded away in 1935 and 1936, and the regulators instead emphasized increased intergovernmental cooperation.

In certain ways, however, the federal government did assume a more interventionist role in securities markets. After the creation of the Bank of Canada, Governor Graham Towers became determined to use his influence to control minimum margin requirements for share purchases to contain speculative forces. By exerting pressure upon the banks and stock exchanges, he eventually succeeded in persuading them to adopt firm rules with regard to new share purchases and to change them only after consultation with him. In addition, the growing concern about the possibility of a European war compelled the stock exchanges to consider how they would respond. Here, too, Towers played an important role in helping to shape and coordinate their plans. Thus until war was declared, the federal government chose to use its influence rather than imposing direct controls upon securities markets. Once the fighting began, however, Ottawa did intervene immediately through the imposition of foreign-exchange controls, which were soon followed by a myriad of other rules and regulations relating to the war effort.

The latter years of the 1930s had produced a mixed legacy so far as the regulation of securities markets was concerned. Canada did not follow the American model, by which the national Securities and Exchange Commission came to play a central regulatory role, yet at the same time Ottawa did begin to exert influence over certain important areas such as brokers' loans and margin requirements. Meanwhile the provinces, Ontario and British Columbia in particular, continued to police the business of selling securities. While they still relied heavily upon self-regulation by the stock exchanges, provincial officials were given wider powers to intervene to prevent unacceptable practices. Overhanging all these developments were persistent concerns about the depressed condition of share markets, concerns that were by no means dispelled after the outbreak of war. Some people began to wonder if the palmy days before 1929 would ever return.

Conclusion

Canadians like to think of themselves as cautious and conservative. Yet for all their churchgoing and insurance buying many of them have proved quite ready to take a flyer on the stock market. Beginning in the 1890s the appearance of low-priced shares in speculative mining companies offered an easy way to gamble when there were few other legal alternatives. Penny stock could be purchased on the basis of the latest rumours from the mines or simply as an outright speculation in hopes of a quick profit. If a mining property proved barren, investors could only curse their ill luck and hope for better the next time around.

This readiness to speculate sprang from more than just a desire to gamble, however. Canada's prosperity depends heavily upon resource exploitation, and national mythology holds that independent prospectors have been responsible for the most valuable mineral finds. Therefore putting money into junior mining shares could seem almost a patriotic duty: time and again industry propagandists contended that it was better to support grubstaking and diamond drilling than to bet on horse racing. Even if no valuable finds were made, geological structures became more clearly understood as a result. Though the system of mine financing meant that a great deal of money found its way into the hands of promoters and share pushers rather than into genuine exploration, this fact was obscured by the magnitude of some of the more spectacular discoveries. Canadians were always ready to line up to buy shares in the next 'sure thing.'

The development of the stock exchanges in Montreal and Toronto and later in Vancouver, Winnipeg, and Calgary made all kinds of share buying easier and more attractive, since the existence of a continuous market enabled purchasers to dispose of their holdings promptly or switch to more promising prospects. The liquidity created by the exchanges permitted stockbrokers to lend their clients a sizeable proportion of the price of the shares, which themselves served

as collateral for the loans. Margin trading, of course, offered tremendous opportunities for profits when as little as one-tenth of the cost of the stock had to be
put up in cash. Optimistic buyers usually ignored the fact that this same leverage
could operate just as swiftly in the opposite direction in a falling market, leaving
them faced with calls to advance more margin or see their shares sold out along
with the possibility of heavy losses. Meanwhile, short sellers who anticipated
declines could borrow shares and sell them in hopes of profiting by repurchas-
ing them later at lower cost.

The exchanges offered investors a certain assurance, at least in theory. Brokerage firms were required to live up to their obligations to deliver securities in
timely fashion or face the loss of their seats on the exchange. During the 1920s
greater protection was extended to customers by requiring members to submit to
periodic audits to ensure that they did not become financially overextended.
While not unknown, brokerage failures were fairly infrequent even during the
1930s, though many houses then found themselves at the mercy of their bankers
and other creditors and survived only with difficulty. Meanwhile, a good many
of their customers decided (or were forced) to liquidate their holdings.

Confidence might dissipate so swiftly and completely in a crisis that investors
could be faced with the evaporation of their holdings within the space of a few
days or even a few hours. The instinctive response of brokers in such times was
to close down markets altogether, in the hope that cooler heads might prevail if
given an opportunity to reflect at greater leisure. At the outbreak of war in 1914
and again upon Britain's sudden and shocking abandonment of the gold standard in 1931, Canada's stock exchanges did impose minimum prices; both times
the restrictions on trading dragged on for months before brokers and bankers
summoned up the courage to resume dealing freely. By that point, of course,
these stocks had often been sold outside the exchanges altogether.

Many shares, in fact, traded that way all the time. The more adventuresome
(or gullible) investors plunged into over-the-counter markets run through the
brokerages or the offices of company promoters. Those who shunned safer but
duller blue-chip shares for speculative mining stock often paid little attention to
the likelihood of a property evolving into a commercial mining operation; they
hoped merely that stock purchased for pennies might take off and go to $1.50,
$2.00, and beyond, allowing them to take quick capital gains which were tax-
free in Canada. The use of the telephone and the falling cost of long-distance
service after the First World War enabled salesmen in boiler rooms using high-
pressure selling methods to reach potential customers all across the continent.

A promoter might provide support for a speculative issue as long as it was in
primary distribution from the company treasury, buying back just enough stock
to keep it from slipping too much while pushing out as many shares as possible.

When a valuable mineral discovery was not made, the insiders sooner or later dumped their stock and allowed the price to slide downward. Even on the exchanges, price-support operations were not uncommon and were, in the main, legal provided that there was no conspiracy to manipulate share values. As a result of lax enforcement of exchange rules, wash trades, in which the same party was both buyer and seller, were often used to push up prices and draw in unsuspecting outsiders. If the stock took off, the support operations could be terminated as unnecessary, but more often bad news and rumours dragged prices down until stockholders had nothing to show for their pains but some finely engraved wallpaper.

When a venture went well, all could be sweetness and light, as happy investors contemplated a healthy flow of dividends and capital gains. If an investment did not pan out, however, questions were frequently raised. Angry shareholders might allege fraud or misrepresentation. This undoubtedly did occur on occasion, and by the time of the First World War calls were being heard for intervention by government to protect investors. However, the Hearst Music scandal in Manitoba seemed to show that even blue-sky laws could not always offer protection against a determined swindler.

The largest market for speculative shares, especially mining stocks, was located in Ontario, but the provincial government dithered about how to regulate securities markets even as they boomed during the 1920s. Blue-sky laws were twice passed there, but never proclaimed into law. Eventually Ontario did bring in a Security Frauds Prevention Act in 1928, which defined illegal conduct by brokers and their salesmen more precisely and at the same time required that these people be registered. Nevertheless, the crash of 1929 was widely blamed upon misconduct by brokers, some of whom were discovered simply to have bucketed many orders from their customers. By failing to execute instructions, brokers were able to conserve their scarce capital, confident that if margin clients paid the remainder of the purchase price and demanded delivery of their shares, they could always go into the market and acquire the necessary stock.

The arrest and conviction of a number of leading brokers for such offences in 1930 seemed to confirm the need for even tighter regulation. Ontario again took the lead in persuading the other provinces to pass a uniform Security Frauds Prevention Act. By 1931 the province had decided to beef up enforcement by creating a specialized agency to handle these matters rather than simply relying upon the hard-pressed staff of the attorney general; thus was born the Ontario Securities Commission. Share prices and trading volume remained stubbornly depressed throughout the decade as the uncertainty created by fear of another European war helped to sap the confidence of investors. When war came in 1939, the federal government quickly imposed controls on foreign exchange to preserve the value of the Canadian dollar against the American, which, in turn, reduced the appeal of securities to outsiders. The idea of minimum prices was once more considered by the stock exchanges, but eventually they decided to soldier on without them.

As the Allies staggered from one military disaster to another in 1940 and 1941, most people in the securities industry turned their energies to selling government bonds to finance the war effort. Had that opportunity not been available, the carnage in the brokerage business in the early 1940s might have been as severe as it had been a decade earlier. By 1943, however, with the tide of war turning and the probability of an Allied victory steadily increasing, Canadian investors began to shake off some of the apathy that had enveloped them since the crash. Mining promoters quickly swung into action again, their new prospects now including not just gold and silver but uranium and other exotic metals that might provide the sinews of war and peace in the coming atomic age. By the time peace returned in 1945 the gambling spirit of many Canadian investors had largely been restored, and they looked forward with keen anticipation to another boom. Speculative share buyers were once again ready to roll the dice in hopes of a valuable score.

Appendix:

Volume of Securities Traded on Canadian Stock Exchanges, 1901–1936

TABLE A.1 Listed trading on Montreal Stock Exchange, 1901–36

Stocks	1901	1902	1903	1904	1905
Banks	12,948	11,525	16,526	12,910	15,103
Railways	277,823	492,753	246,197	115,173	127,955
Electric railways	405,364	372,048	339,067	206,655	365,734
Utilities	335,505	–	–	67,048	73,748
Industrials	112,548	821,003	294,082	134,847	262,242
Mines	103,714	180,182	94,282	46,885	33,667
Junior mines[a]	1,508,163	523,536	193,875	60,200	34,816
Miscellaneous	78,104	224,516	206,137	100,264	133,457
Rights[b]	–	359,704	3,695	49,753	29,231
Total	2,834,169	2,985,267	1,393,861	793,735	1,075,953
Bonds (p.v. $000)	1,889.4	7,834.2	3,048.3	5,249.0	5,689.5

Stocks	1906	1907	1908	1909	1910
Banks	22,757	16,404	14,556	18,408	22,881
Railways	95,826	33,470	119,085	119,150	115,456
Electric railways	485,886	257,714	177,782	311,634	501,498
Utilities	60,406	37,863	270,599	279,398	14,728
Industrials	284,241	197,166	212,195	1,290,340	760,703
Mines	88,535	22,885	17,070	96,836	73,486
Junior mines[a]	–	1,500	651,880	1,161,232	391,938
Miscellaneous	224,531	120,053	206,708	43,044	20,656
Rights[b]	12,324	12,808	42,701	30,493	17,819
Total	1,274,506	699,863	1,475,104	3,339,747	2,147,426
Bonds (p.v. $000)	6,292.5	3,956.2	4,500.2	5,791.4	6,124.5

(continued)

TABLE A.1   (*continued*)

Stocks	1911	1912	1913	1914 (Jan.–July)	1915
Banks	32,568	49,510	25,459	14,750	3,913
Railways	158,727	205,211	177,622	78,456	6,904
Electric railways	493,747	263,308	260,293	199,962	104,098
Utilities	306,636	451,471	191,027	115,919	96,387
Industrials	705,290	894,250	541,381	324,956	1,106,877
Mines	10,141	1,902	7,672	4,312	445
Junior mines[a]	301,398	250,455	485,705	274,140	167,111
Miscellaneous	188,287	150,328	82,802	79,196	44,257
Rights[b]	58,360	83,195	267,807	170,317	40,356
Total	2,225,158	2,349,630	2,039,769	1,261,738	1,570,258
Bonds (p.v. $000)	5,968.8	6,319.5	5,147.7	2,770.7	1,838.4

Stocks	1916	1917	1918	1919	1920
Banks	7,110	9,745	7,934	26,185	33,756
Railways	5,520	1,042	223	410	266
Electric railways	395,926	145,207	88,800	270,573	257,401
Utilities	171,882	76,570	104,482	278,902	215,709
Industrials	2,356,290	707,248	736,384	2,995,605	3,529,676
Mines	125,367	41,805	6,350	146,803	62,288
Junior mines[a]	89,212	31,349	22,459	117,087	3,725
Miscellaneous	151,997	68,834	68,834	163,670	89,200
Rights[b]	92,764	39,843	41,998	61,129	16,954
Total	3,396,069	1,130,799	1,077,464	4,060,344	4,208,975
Bonds (p.v. $000)	13,329.4	11,837.8	6,716.4	71,550.9	27,278.1

TABLE A.1   (*continued*)

Stocks	1921	1922	1923	1924	1925
Banks	26,681	25,783	30,739	29,024	31,584
Railways	309	1,062	80	70	122
Electric railways	153,122	591,194	218,571	444,761	922,314
Utilities	199,433	249,415	455,410	427,354	413,763
Industrials	1,575,701	1,726,749	1,279,641	1,458,310	2,256,346
Mines	28,931	84,774	60,270	226,859	483,172
Junior mines[a]	3,950	120,665	450,138	272,072	193,13
Miscellaneous	85,578	111,671	47,465	97,955	127,382
Rights[b]	33,720	86,213	–	115,960	104,039
Total	2,107,426	2,997,527	2,539,910	3,072,366	4,601,857
Bonds (p.v. $000)	66,323.7	48,186.9	43,054.8	22,013.4	21,698.7

Stocks	1926	1927	1928	1929	1930
Banks	19,226	57,061	61,148	64,521	46,473
Railways	3,209	2,661	400	50	113,046
Electric railways	2,058,416	156,267	480,091	5,499,169	2,886,414
Utilities	835,948	3,929,471[c]	6,473,073[c]	1,471,413	2,007,656
Industrials	2,792,045	4,932,192	7,259,490	6,894,973	2,902,081
Mines	808,464	717,545	4,363,315	8,686,373	59,091
Junior mines[a]	176,739	139,047	231,670	49,165	3,071,734
Miscellaneous	309,180	171,263	328,294	453,692	1,972
Rights[b]	78,825	601,077	1,292,522	2,619,905	4,475,022
Total	7,081,150	10,706,614	20,490,003	25,739,261	15,563,489
Bonds (p.v. $000)	21,928.4	17,283.1	20,150.0	12,840.5	10,932.2

(*continued*)

TABLE A.1 (concluded)

Stocks	1931	1932	1933
Banks	37,844	16,618	30,053
Railways	246,190	400,384	378,086
Electric railways[d]	1,100,153	520,338	1,174,643
Utilities	1,348,693	617,298	928,694
Industrials	1,507,938	704,590	3,183,443
Mines	179,173	111,374	354,935
Junior mines[a]	723,384	438,046	1,330,700
Miscellaneous	161,417	92,906	218,660
Rights[b]	–	–	18,294
Total	5,309,270	2,904,879	7,671,782
Bonds (p.v. $000)	6,623.1	2,156.2	1,103.2

Stocks	1934	1935	1936
Banks	37,542	33,728	42,489
Railways	232,918	214,204	339,784
Electric railways[d]	401,021	–	–
Utilities	790,963	1,102,938	2,009,061
Industrials	1,866,969	1,606,640	4,128,662
Mines	772,686	258,696	659,798
Junior mines[a]	801,191	766,694	1,215,807
Miscellaneous	186,132	348,054	556,303
Fractions	190	66	260
Rights[b]	–	327,877	7,241
Total	4,610,196	4,703,907	8,959,405
Bonds (p.v. $000)	553.2	332.5	265.9

SOURCE: *Annual Financial Review (Canadian)*, vols. 1–37 (Toronto, 1901–37), comp. W.R. Houston

[a] Par value under $1 in 1901–8; under $5 after 1909

[b] Rights or warrants to acquire shares at preset prices

[c] Brazilian Traction was shifted from electric railways to utilities in 1927–8, trading 2,615,634 and 3,820,371 shares in those years respectively, before it was switched back to electric railways in 1929.

[d] Electric railways disappear as a separate category in 1935, when they were combined with utilities.

TABLE A.2   Montreal Curb Market: trading volume, 1930–36

Year	Total mines	Total general	Total volume	Bonds (p.v.)
1930	3,061,133	2,508,278	5,594,411	$213,300
1931	5,289,341	1,480,256	6,769,597	232,500
1932	4,269,470	1,090,842	5,387,312	157,400
1933	18,871,879	4,812,207	23,684,086	238,380
1934	21,400,591	2,864,651	24,265,242	341,685
1935	16,292,789	2,263,844	18,556,633	446,255
1936	69,182,453	6,117,764	75,300,217	202,110

SOURCE: *Annual Financial Review (Canadian)*, vols. 31–7 (Toronto, 1931–7), comp. W.R. Houston

TABLE A.3   Listed trading on Toronto Stock Exchange, 1901–36

Stocks	1901	1902	1903	1904	1905
Banks	50,474	62,797	38,635	35,047	50,510
Financial services	59,261	73,126	47,793	36,639	30,457
Navigation	12,924	36,682	31,243	8,957	19,214
Railways	145,811	579,852	414,315	103,414	75,543
Electric railways	176,053	325,793	196,345	109,250	183,057
Utilities	36,021	33,318	20,968	83,739	142,705
Industrials	42,821	338,916	135,336	113,666	100,113
Mines	39,126	169,543	96,650	45,496	56,341
Junior mines[a]	1,348,945	543,250	97,150	24,650	95,876
Rights[b]	–	8,859	4,987	14,939	12,617
Total	1,911,436	2,172,136	1,083,742	575,797	766,433
Bonds (p.v. $000)	468.2	2,601.0	1,050.6	1,165.9	1,347.4

Stocks	1906	1907	1908	1909	1910
Banks	55,779	28,929	21,065	21,083	20,271
Financial services	28,354	35,543	64,146	40,520	25,678
Navigation	26,197	4,044	6,515	13,156	3,418
Railways	15,071	5,216	17,880	19,376	14,101
Electric railways	144,833	162,307	174,586	234,078	297,985
Utilities	214,376	105,857	123,462	92,611	59,226
Industrials	70,770	33,239	33,731	252,492	122,167
Mines	156,612	35,386	7,290	44,174	48,991
Junior mines[a]	–	12,800	158,591	708,729	348,158
Rights[b]	30,024	13,126	2,794	16,154	547
Total	742,016	436,448	610,060	1,443,346	940,544
Bonds (p.v. $000)	3,214.0	2,937.2	3,578.0	3,659.7	2,829.2

TABLE A.3   *(continued)*

Stocks	1911	1912	1913	1914 (Jan.–July)	1915
Banks	24,544	34,597	25,572	16,900	3,710
Financial services	34,499	30,064	29,502	17,637	7,432
Navigation	20,302	10,115	9,827	9,010	36,248
Railways	14,067	10,770	13,344	16,453	1,569
Electric railways	40,903	500,858	370,914	255,133	47,777
Utilities	49,085	50,624	28,821	29,170	20,961
Industrials	174,233	306,519	190,119	47,457	232,464
Mines	5,012	1,541	1,284	1,085	10,610
Junior mines[a]	205,625	191,156	252,093	160,329	224,069
Rights[b]	46,283	46,264	12,486	55,987	7,184
Total	914,553	1,176,509	935,963	709,162	592,024
Bonds (p.v. $000)	1,998.2	1,715.3	1,001.7	572.0	160.3

Stocks	1916	1917	1918	1919	1920
Banks	5,107	7,123	5,941	21,343	20,196
Financial services	9,002	9,755	13,619	19,736	20,166
Navigation	187,850	72,542	42,424	66,717	33,471
Railways	1,256	1,715	648	14	5,924
Electric railways	119,054	87,529	68,825	14,013	149,542
Utilities	34,509	22,859	9,346	100,143	27,345
Industrials	702,498	213,207	110,441	362,966	256,901
Mines	89,953	32,953	62,130	29,430	17,870
Junior mines[a]	132,046	64,387	28,409	149,744	134,442
Rights[b]	18,523	820	–	15,042	4,207
Total	1,289,798	512,890	341,783	779,148	670,064
Bonds (p.v. $000)	746.0	5,246.1	3,345.6	60,468.5	27,835.5

(continued)

TABLE A.3   *(continued)*

Stocks	1921	1922	1923	1924	1925
Banks	17,526	21,627	37,660	24,162	32,363
Financial services	20,532	9,690	5,285	4,781	6,883
Navigation	46,599	37,550	7,698	12,197	21,090
Railways	16,081	18,464	13,783	11,134	13,726
Electric railways	153,642	443,061	94,086	231,665	397,824
Utilities	26,152	66,177	197,423	126,302	42,957
Industrials	171,505	216,907	177,861	179,409	573,902
Mines	34,353	62,843	59,658	98,669	276,908
Junior mines[a]	53,933	320,684	428,378	295,041	639,864
Rights[b]	7,694	17,539	3,310	18,123	2,701
Total	548,017	1,214,543	1,025,142	907,871	1,999,218
Bonds (p.v. $000)	58,933.1	28,418.1	4,663.2	1,558.5	939.9

Stocks	1926	1927	1928	1929
Banks	21,066	49,310	56,327	40,745
Financial services	5,750	6,839	13,372	22,099
Navigation	33,520	6,588	3,911	13,391
Railways	12,908	19,250	7,083	82,276
Electric railways	435,993	64,425	507,364	679,186
Utilities	31,975	88,215	194,804	64,337
Industrials	764,299	3,897,682	3,385,268	3,939,239
Mines	283,755	160,970	1,532,900	5,228,136
Junior mines[a]	860,399	301,809	136,376	66,075
Rights[b]	22,502	57,954	183,682	593,881
Total	2,472,167	4,663,042	6,021,087	10,729,365
Bonds (p.v. $000)	688.0	279.1	122.9	66.5

TABLE A. 3 *(concluded)*

Stocks	1930	1931	1932	1933
Banks	28,915	25,386	10,275	25,947
Financial services	7,326	6,594	1,647	5,409
Navigation	1,392	1,434	1,632	2,509
Railways	64,981	138.182	34,099	364,691
Electric railways	681,029	4,521	1,029	1,860
Utilities	25,439	407,434	301,108	980,021
Industrials	1,930,454	1,270,914	1,245,157	6,028,827
Mines	12,0058	34,135	58,581	111,153
Junior mines[a]	2,096,424	1,084,788	641,790	1,669,260
Oils	–	–	–	–
Rights[b]	1,790,576	–	–	
Total	6,638,94	2,973,358	2,297,418	9,189,667
Bonds (p.v. $000)	20.6	15.7	9.8	–

Stocks	1934	1935	1936
Banks	36,834	31,726	37,226
Financial services	5,218	10,120	12,809
Navigation	3,262	4,729	22,928
Railways	236,747	256,491	469,229
Electric railways	308,096	–[c]	–[c]
Utilities	31,133	418,902	1,234,827
Industrials	3,600,606	3,469,350	5,637,758
Mines	36,886[d]	93,006	299,668
Junior mines[a]	912,664[d]	1,094,367	1,332,434
Oils	–	283,052	1,877,019
Miscellaneous	–	153,635	27,499
Rights[b]	–	78	22,507
Total	5,171,621	5,815,588	10,973,976
Bonds (p.v. $000)	–	–	–

SOURCE: *Annual Financial Review (Canadian)*, 1–37 (Toronto, 1901–37), comp. W.R. Houston

[a] Par value under $1 in 1901–8; under $5 after 1909

[b] Rights or warrants to acquire shares at present prices

[c] Electric railways were combined with other utilities in 1935

[d] After the merger of the Standard Stock and Mining Exchange with the TSE in February 1934, Consolidated Mining and Smelting and Crow's Nest Pass Coal continued to be traded on the 'industrial section' of the TSE on Bay Street as mining stocks, while International Nickel was handled there, too, as a 'junior' mine. All other mining stocks were traded on the 'mining section,' the old SSME floor on Temperance Street (for which see table A.5 below).

TABLE A.4   Toronto Stock Exchange, unlisted section, 1908–13

Year	Number of issues	Trading volume	Unlisted bonds (par value)
1908	28	7,623,158	–
1909	32	7,840,745	–
1910	57	4,697,096	–
1911	108	8,085,727	$376,030
1912	109	3,389,217	228,965
1913	90	2,035,486	33,700

SOURCE: Annual Financial Review (Canadian), vols. 9–15 (1909–15)

TABLE A.5   Toronto Stock Exchange Curb (unlisted section), 1930–6

Year	Total general	Total mines
1930	2,272,571	751,422
1931	1,209,558	1,492,289
1932	744,401	196,659[a]
1933	3,064,210	–
1934	3,237,752	–
1935	2,574,589	–
1936	1,737,310	–

SOURCE: Annual Financial Review (Canadian), vols. 31–7, (Toronto, 1931–7), comp. W.R. Houston
[a] TSE Curb ceased trading mining shares on 1 May 1932 by agreement with Standard Stock and Mining Exchange.

TABLE A.6   Toronto Stock Exchange, mining section, 1934–6: listed issues[a]

Year	Volume
1934	333,014,464
1935	164,883,308
1936	438,131,865

SOURCE: Annual Financial Review (Canadian), vols. 35–7 (Toronto, 1935–7), comp. W.R. Houston
[a] These figures do not include the small Curb for unlisted mining stocks.

TABLE A.7   Standard Stock and Mining Exchange, 1909–33

Year	Seat prices High	Seat prices Low	Total volume	Total value	Average share price
1909	–	–	36,675,802	$ 17,110,722	$0.47
1910	–	–	28,126,200	10,797,767	0.38
1911	–	–	44,019,638	19,875,144	0.45
1912	–	–	20,841,088	8,499,507	0.41
1913	–	–	20,793,644	5,804,777	0.28
1913	–	–	12,724,687	4,199,223	0.33
1915	–	–	26,093,489	8,870,435	0.34
1916	–	–	35,911,413	17,088,642	0.48
1917	–	–	29,170,509	11,586,905	0.40
1918	–	–	20,868,541	6,575,038	0.32
1919	$ 1,250	$ 1,000	39,636,135	12,551,112	0.32
1920	1,200	1,100	17,358,156	6,412,346	0.37
1921	1,100	1,100	17,241,352	6,457,427	0.37
1922	3,000	1,500	71,124,824	29,074,198	0.41
1923	3,500	2,200	76,491,566	36,051,890	0.47
1924	5,000	2,000	69,257,918	29,853,687	0.43
1925	5,000	2,000	87,847,676	43,369,007	0.49
1926	12,000	4,350	129,753,966	125,175,876	0.96
1927	60,000	11,000	320,490,141	250,897,081	0.78
1928	100,000	65,000	330,407,100	614,808,561	1.86
1929	96,000	95,000	300,330,413	710,308,184	2.36
1930	30,000	12,000	90,493,311	139,870.964	1.54
1931	20,000	14,500	121,252,065	85,730,713	0.71
1932	15,000	10,000	79,731,119	54,746,214	0.69
1933	40,000	16,000	254,494,576	314,897,143	1.23

SOURCE: TSE, Historical Files, S-2, 'Standard Stock and Mining Exchange'

TABLE A.8   Vancouver Stock Exchange, 1925–39

Year	Volume	Value	Average share price
1925	24,309,208	$ 890,304	$0.04
1926	17,335,987	1,883,107	0.11
1927	21,317,577	5,176,895	0.24
1928	87,228,965	28,563,543	0.33
1929	143,023,643	133,525,733	0.93
1930	9,926,050	3,240,964	0.33
1931	16,653,912	2,753,266	0.17
1932	16,643,358	2,490,758	0.15
1933	88,258,610	28,915,200	0.33
1934	92,136,287	32,434,025	0.35
1935	47,208,890	14,567,081	0.31
1936	99,168,178	26,702,524	0.27
1937	120,699,523	33,497,284	0.28
1938	29,646,047	10,147,392	0.34
1939	21,134,233	8,879,484	0.42
1940	9,026,025	3,136,250	0.35

SOURCE: David Cruse and Alison Griffiths, *Fleecing the Lamb: The Inside Story of the Vancouver Stock Exchange* (Vancouver, 1987), appendix 1

FIGURE A.1   Common-stock index, 1919–39   (1926 = 100)

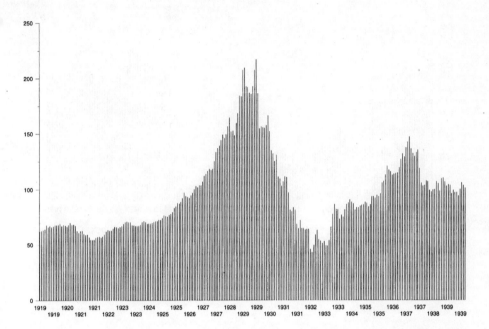

SOURCE: Dominion Bureau of Statistics, Monthly Index of Common Stocks, *Canada Year Book*, 1927–40

318   Appendix

FIGURE A.2 Mining-stock index, 1927–39 (1926 = 100)

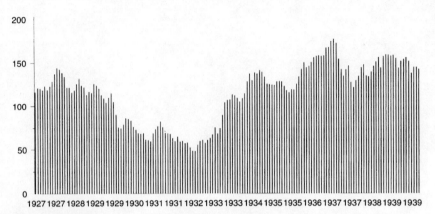

SOURCE: Dominion Bureau of Statistics, *Monthly Weighted Index of Mining Stocks,*
Canada Year Book, 1927–40

Notes

Abbreviations

AG	Attorney General (including records)
ASE	Alberta Stock Exchange
BCA	Bank of Canada Archives
BDAC	Bond Dealers Association of Canada
Corr.	Correspondence
CSE	Calgary Stock Exchange
EA	External Affairs Records
FP	*Financial Post* (Toronto)
HLRO	House of Lords Record Office
LB	Letter Book
MB	Minute Book
MCM	Montreal Curb Market
MSE	Montreal Stock Exchange
MT	*Monetary Times* (Toronto)
MUA	McGill University Archives
NAC	National Archives of Canada
PAA	Provincial Archives of Alberta
PABC	Provincial Archives of British Columbia
PAM	Provincial Archives of Manitoba
PAO	Provincial Archives of Ontario
PP	Premiers' Papers
PUB	Public Utilities Board
PUC	Public Utilities Commission
SEC, FOIA, #90–1128	United States, Securities and Exchange Commission, Freedom of Information Act release (to author), #1990-1128

SSME	Standard Stock and Mining Exchange (Toronto)
TSE	Toronto Stock Exchange (pre-1914 records are held at the exchange)
Unpub. SP	Unpublished Sessional Paper
VSE	Vancouver Stock Exchange
WSE	Winnipeg Stock Exchange

Chapter 1: Beginnings

1 The Amsterdam exchange dates from 1611; for a brief popular account of its origins, see John Brooks, 'The Amsterdam Cradle, the Town Where Stock Trading Was Born,' *The Games Players: Tales of Men and Money* (New York, 1980), 77–92.

2 E.P. Neufeld, *The Financial System of Canada, Its Growth and Development* (Toronto, 1972), 459–72, describes pre-Confederation securities markets.

3 On the transformation of business organization in the United States during the nineteenth century, see Alfred D. Chandler, *The Visible Hand: The Managerial Revolution in American Business* (Cambridge, Mass., 1977), 89–94. In a partnership or sole proprietorship the participants bore unlimited liablity for debts incurred by the undertaking, and in the event of business failure they might lose their entire fortunes, including real estate and family possessions. In a limited liability company each investor's losses were restricted to the amount of equity acquired in the corporation through the ownership of common shares.

4 Unfortunately, none of the nineteenth-century records of the Montreal Stock Exchange appear to have survived, and Edgar A. Collard's centennial history, *Chalk to Computers: The Story of the Montreal Stock Exchange* (Montreal, 1974), is so sketchy as to be little more than a chronology. See *Annual Financial Review (Canadian)* 1 (1901), comp. W.R. Houston, 2 (quoted).

5 Few nineteenth-century records of the TSE have survived; much of the the informa-tion about its early history presented here is drawn from John F. Whiteside's valuable study 'The Toronto Stock Exchange to 1900: Its Membership and the Development of the Share Market' (unpub. MA thesis, Trent University, 1979).

6 Ibid., 1–49; *Annual Financial Review* 1 (1901), 4 (quoted).

7 *MT*, 8 September 1871, 187; quoted in Neufeld, *Financial System*, 477. In fact, Whiteside, 'Toronto Stock Exchange to 1900,' 46, claims that it was only in 1875 that individual members of the TSE ceased to publish their own listings, a practice that was obviously an invitation to manipulation.

8 See Whiteside, 'Toronto Stock Exchange to 1900,' appendix 5, 'Communications: Stock Brokers and the Telegraph, Telephone and "Stock Ticker." '

9 The TSE began to meet twice daily in 1881; morning sessions only were held on Saturdays at noon, though they were often suspended in summer or around major holidays; on the Sabbath everyone rested.

10 Whiteside, 'Toronto Stock Exchange to 1900,' 50, 60–3; TSE Records, L-33, Board MB, 1876–1900, 3 August 1897

11 TSE Records, L-33, Board MB, 1876–1900, 21 September 1882; 25 June 1889

12 E. Gordon Wills, 'The Stock Exchange and the Street,' *Canadian Banker* 58 (spring 1951), 120

13 Wills, 'Stock Exchange,' 124; Whiteside, 'Toronto Stock Exchange to 1900,' appendix 5

14 TSE Records, L-38, Committee MB, 1900–11, 24 March 1905. Some witnesses thought that Webb had only used the word 'bung-hole.'

15 Ibid., 1900–11, 2 February 1906

16 Collard, *Chalk to Computers*, 14, 18; Whiteside, 'Toronto Stock Exchange to 1900,' 166–7

17 TSE Records, L-33, Board MB, 1876–1900, 15 October 1892

18 Whiteside, 'Toronto Stock Exchange to 1900,' 54–6, and table V-1 (163–4) for trading volumes.

19 Ibid., 59–60. Listing fees had originally been set at $100 in 1882, but were halved three years later.

20 Neufeld, *Financial System*, 477; Whiteside, 'Toronto Stock Exchange to 1900,' 65; TSE Records, L-33, Committee MB, 1876–1900, 12 April 1887

21 TSE Records, L-33, Board MB, 1876–1900, 26 June 1895

22 Whiteside, 'Toronto Stock Exchange to 1900,' 74–124

23 Borrowing by the Canadian federal and provincial governments was done in Britain, since the local capital market was deemed too small to absorb any large issues.

24 Neufeld, *Financial System*, 486–7; Whiteside, 'Toronto Stock Exchange to 1900,' 100

25 Whiteside, 'Toronto Exchange to 1900,' 237

26 Bulls are optimists who expect share prices to rise, while bears believe declines are imminent. Of obscure origins, these terms appeared in London in the early eighteenth century and gained currency everywhere; see E.V. Morgan and W.A. Thomas, *The Stock Exchange, Its History and Functions* (London, 1969 ed.), 60–1.

27 See Robert Sobel, *Panic on Wall Street: A History of America's Financial Disasters* (Toronto, 1969), 122–272.

28 Robert Sobel, *The Big Board: A History of the New York Stock Exchange* (Toronto, 1965), 132–3

29 Robert Sobel. *The Curbstone Brokers: The Origins of the American Stock Exchange* (New York, 1970), 83–164

30 Carl Bergithon, *The Stock Exchange, with Special Reference to the Montreal Stock Exchange and the Montreal Curb Market* (Montreal, 1940), 41, gives the following example of a transaction on the 33.3 per cent margin common at that time. A client orders 100 shares at $9, putting up $300 and borrowing $600 from the broker; should share prices fall to $8 the value of the block is only $800, but the client still

owes the broker $600, and the fall in value has reduced the client's equity from $300 to $200. To restore the margin to 33.3 per cent of $800 ($266.66) the client must put up $66.66. If he meets this call but the stock then falls to $7, the client's equity again declines by $100 to $166.66, and to restore it to 33.3 per cent of $700 ($233.33) he must put up another $66.66. If he fails to meet the margin call, the broker sells the block for $700, of which he takes $600 plus interest and commission, leaving the client with a loss of about $300.

31 *MT*, 27 October 1882, 459, and *Journal of Commerce*, 26 October 1883, 308; quoted in Michael Bliss, *A Living Profit: Studies in the Social History of Canadian Business, 1883–1911* (Toronto, 1974), 24

32 *MT*, 21 November 1902, 637

33 Whiteside, 'Toronto Stock Exchange to 1900,' 97; *MT*, 2 February 1900, 1012; 7 August 1903, 178 (quoted). Michael Bliss notes that in 1894 Bank of Commerce president George A. Cox denounced speculation in U.S. markets, and he observes that 'Cox differed from these speculators only in doing most of his stock manipulating in Canada. This example of the pot calling the kettle black demonstrated the near impossibility of distinguishing between "legitimate" and illegitimate speculation.' See Bliss, *Living Profit*, 25.

34 In 1892–3 the U.S. Congress debated the Hatch bill to impose a prohibitive tax upon trading in grain and cotton futures and provide for the licensing of brokers and the inspection of their books. With strong support from farm organizations, bills passed both the House of Representatives and the Senate, but failed to become law when the House refused to concur with amendments made in the Senate. See Cedric B. Cowing, *Populists, Plungers and Progressives: A Social History of Stock and Commodity Speculation, 1890–1936* (Princeton, NJ, 1965), 5–23.

35 Short sellers could face rapidly mounting losses if the stock that they were shorting began to rise. Bergithon, *Stock Exchange*, 43–4, gives the following example of shorts operating on a 33.3 per cent margin. To go short on 100 shares at $9 required $300, but if the stock went to $10 it would cost $1,000 to buy it in and the client's equity fell to $200. To restore the equity to 33.3 per cent of $1,000.00 ($333.33) would require an additional $133.33. If the shares went up to $11 and were then sold out, the short would lose about $225.

36 A highly entertaining account of the corner in the shares of the grocery chain Piggly Wiggly Stores on the New York Stock Exchange in 1922–3 may be found in John Brooks, 'The Last Great Corner: A Company Called Piggly Wiggly,' in *Business Adventures* (New York, 1969), 24–48. The NYSE's governing committee broke the corner in Piggly Wiggly and allowed the beleaguered shorts to escape by suspending trading in the shares along with the rules requiring prompt delivery of the stock.

37 By 1900, 250 different exchanges had existed in the United States alone, though most of them were short-lived. See R.C. Michie, *The London and New York Stock Exchanges, 1850–1914* (London, 1987), 167.

38 Michie, *London and New York Stock Exchanges*, 19, 87, points out that London was unique in that a separate company owned its building and earned fees from members, so that over 5,000 had been admitted by 1900. Other exchanges were much more restrictive about membership, which naturally sparked competition on occasion. See Alan Jenkins, *The Stock Exchange* (London, 1973), 113, for an account of an unsuccessful attempt to suppress after-hours street trading in American shares in 1895.

Chapter 2: Selling Stuff

1 O.J. Firestone, *Canada's Economic Development, 1870–1953* (London, 1958), table 11, 68

2 Ian M. Drummond, 'Capital Markets in Canada and Australia, 1895–1914: A Study in Colonial Economic History,' (unpub. PhD thesis, Yale University, 1959), 172, 184, appendix

3 On this change in the United States, see Thomas R. Navin and Marian V. Sears, 'The Rise of a Market for Industrial Securities, 1887–1902,' *Business History Review* 39 (1955), 105–38

4 E.P. Neufeld, *The Financial System of Canada, Its Growth and Development* (Toronto, 1972), 487–8. By the 1990s A.E. Ames and Company had disappeared in a merger with Dominion Securities, itself now a subsidiary of the Royal Bank of Canada, while Wood, Gundy became part of the Canadian Imperial Bank of Commerce.

5 On Deacon see J.T. Saywell, 'F.H. Deacon and Co., Investment Dealers: A Case Study of the Securities Industry, 1897–1945,' *Ontario History* 85 (1993), 167–70. Deacon's firm would eventually be folded into Midland Walwyn.

6 On Aitken's Canadian career, see Christopher Armstrong and H.V. Nelles, *Southern Exposure: Canadian Promoters in Latin America and the Caribbean, 1896–1930* (Toronto, 1988), 109–47. Royal Securities would eventually become part of Merrill, Lynch Canada, Inc.

7 See Christopher Armstrong, '"Making a Market": Selling Securities in Atlantic Canada before World War I,' *Canadian Journal of Economics* 13 (1980), 438–54, which draws upon HLRO, Beaverbrook, series A, in the House of Lords Record Office, London.

8 These reports are in HLRO, Beaverbrook, series A, vols. 11, 17, 19. Precise citations for the reports quoted below may be found in the article cited in n. 7.

9 Ibid., vol. 24, Aitken to R.C. Matthews, 14 July 1908

10 Ibid., vol. 19, Aitken to Ames, 17 January 1908; vol. 30, Ames to Aitken, 12 May 1909

11 Ibid., vol. 11, Ames to Aitken, 25 November, 13 December 1907; vol. 18, Aitken to J.G. White, 10 December 1907; vol. 17, Aitken to D.E. Thomson, 4 December 1907

12 Ibid., vol. 22, Aitken to R.E. Harris, 24 January 1908

13 Douglas How, *A Very Private Person: The Story of Izaak Walton Killam and His Wife Dorothy*, (n.p., 1976), 21

14 Lord Beaverbrook, *My Early Life* (Fredericton, NB, 1965), 128

15 Saywell, 'F.H. Deacon and Co.,' n. 9, 187

16 Ibid., 169

17 Philip Smith, *Harvest from the Rock: A History of Mining in Ontario* (Toronto, 1986), 139–40

18 The federal government had general powers of incorporation, and the provinces had authority to incorporate companies with 'Provincial objects,' a provision interpreted very liberally by the courts.

19 Brief accounts of the Rossland rush may be found in B.F. Townsley, *Mine-Finders: The History and Romance of Canadian Mineral Discoveries* (Toronto, 1935), 199–205, and D.M. LeBourdais, *Metals and Men: The Story of Canadian Mining* (Toronto, 1957), 38–45.

20 The Toronto *Globe*, for example, began to run a daily column of mining news; *MT*, 14 August 1896, 213, has a typical advertisement for the Big Three Gold Mining Company of Trail, BC; *MT*, 18 September 1896, 387, shows Toronto broker A.W. Ross and Company (who was handling distribution of Big Three) listing quotations for sixteen Rossland and Trail Creek stocks altogether. On the brokerage community, see John F. Whiteside, 'The Toronto Stock Exchange to 1900: Its Membership and the Development of the Share Market' (unpub. MA thesis, Trent University, 1979), 79–80, 210–7

21 *MT*, 23 October 1896, 554–5

22 Ibid., 4 June 1897, 1598. In an effort to appeal to more prudent investors some prominent Toronto businessmen announced in the same issue of the paper (1607) the creation of the 'Canadian Mining Trust [*sic*] Company' to raise money to invest in mining properties carefully and honestly, 'the names of the directors being esteemed a guarantee to this effect.' The incorporators included President Frederic Nicholls, Ontario's Lieutenant-Governor George Kirkpatrick, Senator George Cox, A.E. Ames, William Mackenzie, George Gooderham, Henry Mill Pellatt, W.R. Brock, and Joseph Flavelle. Prospectuses were available from the Ames and Pellatt brokerage houses.

23 Ibid., 22 January 1897, 976; 5 February 1897, 1045

24 Ibid., 14 July 1899, 47

25 Unlike banks, utilities, and industrials, whose promoters normally assigned par values of $50 or $100 to their shares, speculative mining ventures usually had par values of $1 or later $5.

26 *MT*, 12 February 1897, 1079

27 Ibid., 14 July 1899, 47; 4 August 1899, 143

28 Ibid., 14 October 1898, 504
29 Ibid., 21 November 1902, 637
30 PABC, AG, GR 429, Corr., A.F.H. Jones to J. Kirkup, 2, 15, 29 August (quoted) 1899; Kirkup to Jones, 9, 23 August 1899
31 See Townsley, *Mine-Finders*, 91, 204–5, and LeBourdais, *Men and Metals*, 41–5
32 Toronto *Saturday Night*, 25 July 1896
33 For a concise summary of British and Canadian company law and its relationship to securities regulation, see J. Peter Williamson, *Securities Regulation in Canada* (Toronto, 1960), 3–10.
34 An example of this kind of abuse was that in 1900 the promoter of the Canadian Inland Transportation Company granted himself $1.5 million of the $4 million par value worth of shares for his activities; see *MT*, 27 April 1900, 1414.
35 Shares in industrial undertakings (but not penny mining stocks) were normally sold on the instalment plan with 'calls' upon purchasers to subscribe sums up to the par value of the stock.
36 See *MT*, 8 July 1904, 36; Michael Bliss, *A Canadian Millionaire: The Life and Business Times of Sir Joseph Flavelle, Bart., 1858–1939* (Toronto, 1978), 72–4
37 Note the difference in spelling between the officially authorized name of the lake and that of the railway (now the Ontario Northland).
38 Albert Tucker, *Steam into Wilderness: Ontario Northland Railway* (Toronto, 1978), 1–17; Smith, *Harvest from the Rock*, 115–60
39 *Canadian Annual Review*, 1908, 270; *MT*, 15, 22 September 1905, 331, 363; 10 August 1906, 192
40 *Canadian Annual Review*, 1908, 270
41 Only hotelman Josh Smith, who had moved south from mining country, resisted the rush to buy mining shares and instead shipped fifteen carloads of potatoes to Cobalt, making a profit of $5 on each bag; see Leacock, *Sunshine Sketches of a Little Town* (Toronto, 1970 ed.), 26–7.
42 Floyd S. Chalmers, *A Gentleman of the Press* (Toronto, 1969), 159–63
43 *FP*, 12, 26 January, 9 February 1907 (all quoted).
44 Smith, *Harvest from the Rock*, 161–203
45 *MT*, 4 March 1904, 1178
46 Williamson, *Securities Regulation*, 9–10; *MT*, 12 January, 9 February 1907, 1031, 1224
47 The list began in *FP*, 5 October 1907, and continued weekly until 23 November 1907, excepting only 26 October, when the editor observed that the panic in New York had knocked stock prices down so low that only the insane and the penniless were not buying. The list reappeared on 16 May 1908, and the *FP* continued to provide extensive coverage to such promotions, whether under the title 'Black List' or not, for the next several years.

48 *FP*, 5, 12 October, 2, 23 November, 21 December 1907; Toronto *Globe*, 20, 31 December 1907; *Canadian Annual Review*, 1908, 272

49 *FP*, 11 April 1908. Eventually another broker was called in to market the remainder of the stock and place the company on a sound footing.

50 Ibid., 24 October, 21 November 1908

51 Ibid., 28 November 1908

52 *Canadian Annual Review*, 1908, 270–1; *FP* 13 March, 17 April 1909

53 *FP*, 3 April, 1 May (quoted), 1909

54 *FP*, 20 July, 10, 17 August 1907; 18 April 1908; *MT*, 13 April 1907, 1604

55 *FP*, 18 September 1909; *FP* responded defensively, arguing that Ontario had already amended its Companies Act along British lines in 1907 and that the other provinces and the federal government would soon follow suit; in any case, there were no more bad hats in Canada than in Britain.

56 Smith, *Harvest from the Rock*, 143–4

57 *FP*, 27 February, 13 March 1909

58 An Englishman, Horne Payne had a large interest in the British-controlled British Columbia Electric Railway and was involved with many of the ventures of Canadian William Mackenzie.

59 *FP*, 28 September, 12 October 1907

60 Ibid., 12 October 1907

61 Smith, *Harvest from the Rock*, 165–7, 171–3, 197–8

62 The Canadian Criminal Code, of course, already contained general sanctions against fraud and misrepresentation, which could be applied to security dealings but were rarely used for this purpose.

63 Canada, Senate, *Debates*, 4 April 1888, 252–9; House of Commons, *Debates*, 14 May 1888, 1404–12; Canada, *Statutes*, 1888, c. 42, 'An Act respecting Gaming in Stocks and Merchandise'

64 *R. v. Harkness*, 10 *Ontario Law Reports* (1905), 555

65 PAO, AG, series 4-32, 1906, #167, S.F. Washington to J.R. Cartwright, 26 January, 28, 31 March, 2 May 1906; Cartwright to Washington, 15, 30 March 1906. Deputy Attorney General Cartwright agreed that the proceedings could be stayed provided that the offenders gave a public undertaking not to resume such business anywhere in Canada, on the understanding that the cases could be resumed if necessary.

66 PAO, AG, series 4-32, 1906, #853, J.S. Corley to attorney general, 16 May 1906. Ibid., #1109, J.B. McKillop to J.R. Cartwright, 5 July 1906, stated that there were also one or two such operations in London, Ontario.

67 Salting involved mixing precious metals obtained elsewhere with ore samples in order to falsify assay results.

68 PABC, AG, Corr., file 6295–14–11, R.S. Lennie to W.J. Bowser, 11 July, 26 September, 10 October 1911; Bowser to Lennie, 18 October 1911

69 Hector Charlesworth, *More Candid Chronicles: Further Leaves from the Note Book of a Canadian Journalist* (Toronto, 1928), 184

70 Ibid., 185

71 *FP*, 22 January, 15 October 1911; *Saturday Night*, 22 October 1911. Another Montreal firm, Ashby and Lockwood, offered a return of 5 per cent per month on capital invested in multiples of $100, withdrawable only on thirty days' notice; see *FP*, 12 November 1910.

72 W.H.P. Jarvis, *Don Quixote in Finance* (n.p., 1920) 7–12; *FP*, 23 April, 17 September 1910. Jarvis himself personified some of the ethical problems of the era, however, since he often sold short the shares of companies that he was attacking in anticipation of falling prices.

73 *Saturday Night*, 10 June 1911 (quoted); the issue of 24 February 1912 contained a long story on Stoneham's activities.

74 *FP*, 26 March 1910; *Saturday Night*, 2, 9 April 1910

75 *FP*, 15 April 1911; *Saturday Night*, 29 April 1911

76 *MT*, 1 December 1906, 779, however, endorsed criticisms by Governor General Lord Grey of this proposal: 'It is impossible to put restrictions upon financial advertising ... [Y]ou cannot stop roguery by definitions and prohibitions of certain forms of words.'

77 *Saturday Night*, 2 April 1910; *FP* 18 March, 3 June 1911

78 *FP*, 26 November 1910; 15 April, 3 June 1911

Chapter 3: The Development of the Exchanges

1 *Annual Financial Review (Canadian)* 10 (1910), comp. W.R. Houston

2 Ibid. 1–15 (1901–15)

3 Montreal *Financial Times*, 18 October 1913; Edgar A. Collard, *Chalk to Computers: The Story of the Montreal Stock Exchange* (Montreal, 1974), 14, 18–19. The building was modelled upon the temple of Vesta in Rivoli.

4 MUA, MSE Records, box 418, Legal Opinions, 1895–1910, Campbell, Miller, Allan and Hague to W.R. Miller, 22 February 1900

5 TSE Records, L-33, Board MB, 1876–1900, 21 April 1897

6 Ibid., 27 May 1898; ibid., L-29, Mining Section of Toronto Board of Trade MB, 1899–1902, 16 May 1899, 13 February 1900; John F. Whiteside, 'The Toronto Stock Exchange to 1900: Its Membership and the Development of the Share Market' (unpub. MA thesis, Trent University, 1979), 218–19.

7 TSE Records, L-29, Mining Section of Toronto Board of Trade MB, 1899–1902, 21 February, 22, 29 May, 12 June, 23 November 1900; 24 September, 22 October, 5 November, 6 December 1901; ibid., L-38, Committee MB, 1900–11, 9, 30 December 1901; ibid., Historical Files, T-4–a(1), 'TSE History, 1852–1900,' copies of Ontario orders-in-council, 28 November 1900, 31 December 1901

8 TSE Records, L-30, SSME MB, 1905–9, 9, 30 November 1906; ibid., Historical
   Files, S-2, 'Standard Stock and Mining Exchange,' Memorandum re Yearly Sales and
   Values, 1909–1933, n.d.
9 Ibid., L-30, SSME MB, 1905–9, 13 July 1906; ibid., L-24, SSME LB, 1911–15, A.G.
   Robertson to Osler and Co., 15 June 1911
10 Ibid., L-24, SSME LB, 1911–15, A.G. Robertson to D.F. Maguire, Preston East Dome
   Mines, 28 December 1911; Robertson to Col. Carson, Porcupine-Crown Mines,
   12 May 1914. Carson was told that he must pay the listing fee, raised to $50 in July
   1911, or have the stock taken off the daily sheets.
11 Ibid., A.G. Robertson to George Robinson, 18 January 1912. Robertson complained
   that some of the information supplied about Achilles was 'a little vague.' The listing
   committee wanted to know exactly how many shares remained in the company
   treasury and asked why the report of a mining engineer had not been included.
12 Ibid., A.G. Robertson to William Laidlaw, 5 February 1913, asking what legal
   liability the exchange assumed in such a case.
13 Ibid., A.G. Robertson to Edward Brady and Co., Boston, 17 September 1913
14 Ibid., L-30, SSME MB, 1905–9, 26 October, 14 December 1906; 20 November 1908
15 Ibid., 2 November 1906; 6, 17 January (both quoted), 1 December 1908
16 Ibid., 3 August 1906; 8 January 1909
17 FP, 9, 23 April 1910; TSE Records, L-24, SSME LB, 1911–15, A.G. Robertson to
   William Laidlaw, 31 May 1911; Robertson to J.A. McIlwain, 26 December 1911;
   Saturday Night, 27 May 1911
18 TSE Records, Historical Files, S-2, SSME, Yearly Sales and Values, 1909–33, n.d.;
   ibid., L-24, SSME LB, 1911–15, A.G. Robertson to G.W. Clawson, 12 August 1913;
   Robertson to Miller, Ferguson and Hunter, 17 September 1913 (quoted). When the
   seat was finally sold, the board kept the proceeds to repay debts owned to the
   exchange; see ibid., Robertson to William Laidlaw, 23 February, 8 April 1914.
19 TSE Records, L-33, Board MB, 1876–1900, 21 June 1898; ibid., L-38, Committee
   MB, 1900–11, 6 April 1903, where it was resolved unanimously not to hold continuous sessions.
20 Whiteside, 'Toronto Stock Exchange to 1900,' 220–4. The board did enquire of
   Gooderham why he had not advised it of the shutdown in advance, but simply
   accepted his assurances that neither he nor his family had done any trading in War
   Eagle shares at the time. When the company issued its annual report a year later, the
   board decided that it would be inopportune to pursue an investigation and allowed the
   matter to drop. See TSE Records, L-33, Board MB, 1876–1900, 12 February 1900;
   ibid., L-38, Committee MB, 1900–11, 1 March 1901.
21 E.P. Neufeld, The Financial System of Canada, Its Growth and Development
   (Toronto, 1972), 476. Preferred shares gave their owners a legal claim prior to the

common shareholders upon the equity of the company and paid a fixed rate of interest, which made them attractive to more-conservative investors.

22 Whiteside, 'Toronto Stock Exchange to 1900,' 68–72, 132–40. TSE Records, L-34, Board MB, 1900–15, 5, 6 June 1900. In 1899 the rise in trading volume had led to the creation of the TSE clearing house to facilitate settlements among members; it was run by the National Trust under contract.

23 TSE Records, L-38, Committee MB, 1900–11, 3, 10 December 1900

24 Ibid., L-30, SSME MB, 1905–9, 30 November 1906; ibid., L-34, Board MB, 1900–15, 7 June 1907; ibid., L-38, Committee MB, 1900–11, 11 May 1908. A proposal to charge a $25 fee for unlisteds was voted down.

25 *Annual Financial Review* 11, 12 (1911–12)

26 TSE Records, L-38, Committee MB, 1900–11, 21 March 1901; 11 September 1906

27 Ibid., MB, 1900–11, 4 May 1909, 25 November 1910

28 Whiteside, 'Toronto Stock Exchange to 1900,' 72, 140, 239 (quoted); *Financial Times*, 29 November 1913

29 TSE Records, L-38, Committee MB, 1900–11, 14 June, 21–2 August 1911; ibid., L-39, Committee MB, 1912–14, 1 October 1912; 17 March, 5 May, 13 June, 18 and 23 July (adjourned meeting), 29 December 1913, 13 January, 6 February 1914

30 Stephen Leacock, *Sunshine Sketches of a Little Town* (Toronto, 1970 ed.), 26

31 *MT*, 29 May 1896, 1527. By 1901 Vancouver had 29,000 residents, and Victoria 21,000. David Cruise and Alison Griffiths in *Fleecing the Lamb: The Inside Story of the Vancouver Stock Exchange* (Vancouver, 1987), appendix 2, 'Stock Exchanges in British Columbia,' briefly describe some of the fifteen exchanges that came and went between 1877 and 1910 in Rossland, Stewart, and Prince Rupert as well as in the two major cities.

32 Cruise and Griffiths, *Fleecing the Lamb*, 3–16

33 PABC, VSE Records, Miscellaneous Corr., vol. 1, file 1, Harvey to John Kendall, 20 July 1908

34 Ibid., Committee MB, 1907–11, 16 July 1908 (quoted); 15 April, 5 May 1910. Cruise and Griffiths, *Fleecing the Lamb*, appendix 1, 'VSE Annual Trading Volume, Value and Financing,' 1908–86

35 Cruise and Griffiths, *Fleecing the Lamb*, 17–30

36 PABC, VSE Records, Committee MB, 1907–11, 6, 7, 9 April 1910

37 Ibid., Committee MB, 1911–17, 13 March 1914

38 Allan Levine, *The Exchange: 100 Years of Trading Grain in Winnipeg* (Winnipeg, 1987), 31–86.

39 PAM, WSE Records, Committee MB, 1907–22; *FP*, 11 January 1913

40 Ed Gould, *Oil: The History of Canada's Oil and Gas Industry* (n.p., 1976), 73–7

41 *FP*, 6 June 1914; Glenbow-Alberta Archives, ASE Records, CSE MB, 1914–15, 25,

28 May, 8 June 1914. The CSE had received a provincial charter of incorporation the previous year.

42 Glenbow-Alberta Archives, ASE Records, CSE MB, 1914–15, 25 May, 7, 13 July 1914; PABC, VSE Records, Board MB, 1911–17, 18, 22 May 1914

43 *FP*, 27 June, 4, 11, 18 July, 5 September 1914; Glenbow-Alberta Archives, ASE Records, CSE MB, 1914–15, 31 July, 17, 21 August, 19 October 1914. The Public, People's, Dominion, Consolidated, and Majestic exchanges formed the CGSE, leaving the Oil and Stock, Standard, King George, and Calgary exchanges also in existence.

44 Glenbow-Alberta Archives, ASE Records, CSE Corr., box 4, file 35, Carlile to CSE assistant secretary A.E. Graves, 16 June 1955

45 Ibid., CSE MB, 1914–15, 9, 10 June, 1915

46 Photograph reproduced in Gould, *Oil*, 73

47 Glenbow-Alberta Archives, ASE Records, CSE MB, 1915–26, 7, 22 July, 28 October, 4, 6 November, 27 December 1915; 6 January 1916; 3 February 1917

48 R.C. Michie, *The London and New York Stock Exchanges, 1850–1914* (London, 1987), 230, 238

49 United States Congress, House of Representatives, *Report of the Committee Appointed to Investigate the Concentration of Control of Money and Credit* (Washington, 8 February 1913), 116; quoted in Michie, *London and New York Stock Exchanges*, 232–3

50 *MT*, 14 March 1902, 1199 (quoted); 23 May 1902, 1518

51 On the persistence of such attitudes, see Christopher Armstrong and H.V. Nelles, *Southern Exposure: Canadian Promoters in Latin America and the Caribbean, 1896–1930* (Toronto, 1988), 19–20. Neufeld, *Financial System of Canada*, 88, notes of Canadian banks, 'The rule of thumb of confining lending to short-term, self-liquidating loans was probably necessary to ensure survival of the banks in the first fifty years of their existence. All "responsible" bankers favoured it, as they continued to do until after the Second World War.'

52 Michie, *London and New York Stock Exchanges*, 229–39

53 Call loans were funds lent by banks to brokerage houses to finance (margin and other) share purchases secured by notes that were callable by the lender at will. Canadian banks usually sent their call money to New York, where the markets were broader and more liquid.

54 *FP*, 6 May 1911

55 *Saturday Night*, 29 July 1911; W.H.P. Jarvis, *Don Quixote in Finance* (n.p., 1920), 7–10; *FP*, 16, 23 December 1911

56 Leacock, *Sunshine Sketches*, 28–9

57 Whiteside, 'Toronto Stock Exchange to 1900,' 126

58 Primary distribution refers to the sale of securities by issuers, underwriters, investment dealers, or brokers directly to outside investors.

59 See Armstrong and Nelles, *Southern Exposure*, 108–13.

60 HLRO, Beaverbrook Papers, series A, vol. 2, Aitken to D.W. Robb, 23 December 1903

61 For an account of the Porto Rico promotion, see Armstrong and Nelles, *Southern Exposure*, 129–37; HLRO, Beaverbrook Papers, series A, vol. 19, Ames to Max Aitken, 21 May 1908 is quoted.

62 TSE Records, L-34, Board MB, 1900–15, 2 June 1903; ibid., L-38, Committee MB, 1900–11, 16 July 1903, 13 April 1904; Michael Bliss, *A Canadian Millionaire: The Life and Business Times of Sir Joseph Flavelle, Bart., 1858–1939* (Toronto, 1978), 74–6, explains that Ames's father-in-law, the wealthy Senator George Cox, engineered the recovery.

63 *Canadian Annual Review*, 1903, 495, 501

64 Canada, House of Commons, *Debates*, 21 July 1903, 7005–53

65 *FP*, 15 June 1907; *MT*, 15, 22 June 1907, 1988, 2032

66 Robert Sobel, *Panic on Wall Street: A History of America's Financial Disasters* (Toronto, 1969), 297–321; *FP*, 16 March, 19, 26 October 1907. The Toronto *World*, 14 October 1907, reported the rumours re Pellatt and Pellatt.

67 *FP*, 2 November 1907

68 *Ames v. Conmee*, 38 *Supreme Court Reports* (1907), 601

69 Ibid.

70 *FP*, 16 February 1907

71 Ibid., 9, 16 March 1907

72 Robert Sobel, *The Curbstone Brokers: The Origins of the American Stock Exchange* (New York, 1970), 112. In 1909 the NYSE lost a long-running legal battle to deny Consolidated members its ticker service and finally moved to ban all dealing between NYSE and Consolidated members, which led the latter to decline in importance. But in 1913 New York state prohibited the exchange from imposing such bans on tickers, and the Consolidated gained a new lease on life. From time to time the NYSE also considered banning dealings with the Curb but did not do so because of wide opposition from NYSE members, whose orders accounted for 85 per cent of Curb trading.

73 *FP*, 19, 26 June (quoted) 1909

74 Ibid., 8, 15 January, 2 April 1910; Robert Sobel, *The Big Board: A History of the New York Stock Exchange* (Toronto, 1965), 198–9

75 Playfair and Martens quoted in *FP*, 8 January 1910

Chapter 4: Blue Skies

1 *FP*, 28 January 1911

2 George Randolph Chester, *Get-Rich-Quick Wallingford: A Cheerful Account of the Rise and Fall of an American Business Buccaneer* (Philadelphia, 1908), 9–110

3 George Randolph Chester, *Young Wallingford* (Indianapolis, 1910), 16

4 See both George Randolph Chester, *Wallingford in His Prime* (Indianapolis, 1913) and *Wallingford and Blackie Daw* (Indianapolis, 1913).

5 David Pringle, *Imaginary People: A Who's Who of Modern Fictional Characters* (London, 1987), 483

6 *FP*, 21 April 1922, recorded the arrival in Listowel, Ontario, of three Americans of the 'Wallingford clan,' who got a $25,000 loan from the town and sold $30,000 worth of stock locally to finance a plant to manufacture the 'Perfect Wheel' under patents which proved worthless, using machines that their manufacturers soon repossessed. On 7 July 1922 the paper noted that Toronto's booming Danforth district was full of 'Wallingford understudies in mahogany premises,' while as late as 13 June 1936 it reported on the 'Wallingfords' drawn to Toronto and Montreal from the U.S. financial underworld by the booming market for mining shares.

7 Stephen Leacock, *Arcadian Adventures with the Idle Rich* (Toronto, 1959 ed.), 22–56

8 See *Adventure* vol. 1, nos. 6, 7 (April, May 1911).

9 This biographical information comes from a pamphlet by Guy L. Stebbing entitled *A Personal Sketch of A.F.A. Coyne*, which may be found attached to Coyne (of Coyne Consolidated Oilfields Ltd., Montreal) to the Alberta PUB, 5 April 1927, in PAA, Acc. 65.74, PUB, file 780a.

10 PAA, Acc. 65.74, PUB, file 744, Coyne to PUB, 20 June 1917; James E. Reilly to Coyne, 25 June 1917; B.G. Ferguson, *Athabasca Oil Sands: Northern Resources Exploration, 1875–1921* (Edmonton, 1985), 11–30

11 Bulyea was alerted to Coyne's return to Canada by a federal government official, who remembered him in Alberta as a 'first class humbug.' See PAA, Acc. 65.74, PUB, file 744. O.S. Finnie, director NWT and Yukon Branch, Department of Interior, to G.H. Bulyea, 25 September 1922; Bulyea to Finnie, 30 September 1922, Personal.

12 Ibid., undated clipping from Toronto *Telegram*; ibid., file 780a, A.F.A. Coyne to PUB, 5 April 1927, enclosing various pamphlets.

13 *Saturday Night*, 6 January 1912. The issue of 3 February 1912 described a typical 'squeeze' and showed a map of Saskatoon indicating that the lots offered for sale lay much too far from downtown ever to be valuable.

14 *FP*, 2 March 1912

15 L. Frank Baum, *The Wizard of Oz* (Chicago, 1900).

16 Michael Parrish, *Securities Regulation and the New Deal* (New Haven, Conn., 1970), 5–6, points out that local businessmen eager to exclude out-of-staters from competing to raise capital also supported the laws. See also *FP*, 29 July 1911.

17 Manitoba, *Statutes*, 1912, c. 75. On the origins of the Manitoba PUC, see Christopher Armstrong and H.V. Nelles, *Monopoly's Moment: The Organization and Regulation of Canadian Utilities, 1830–1930* (Philadelphia, 1986), 193–6.

18 PAM, WSE MB, 1 May, 31 July 1912; ibid., Unpub. SP, Manitoba, 1926, box 161, item 1 (3 parts), 'Typescript of evidence to Select Standing Committee [of the

Legislative Assembly] to enquire into all matters relating to the promotion and operation of the Hearst Music Company Limited and the Farmers' Packing Company Limited' (hereafter Hearst Music Committee), testimony of H.A. Robson, 30 December 1925, 389–90

19 *FP*, 3 August 1912

20 PAM, Unpub. SP, 1926, box 161, Hearst Music Committee, testimony of Robson, 30 December 1925, 371

21 Ibid., 371–2; Manitoba, *Statutes*, 1914, c. 105; 1914–15, c. 69

22 PAM, Unpub. SP, 1926, box 161, Hearst Music Committee, testimony of Robson, 30 December 1925, 372–6

23 Ibid., 374 (quoted), 380, 394

24 Ibid., 376–8; *Financial Times*, 16 May 1914; Manitoba, *Statutes*, 1916, c. 88

25 PAM, Unpub. SP, 1926, Box 161, Hearst Music Committee, testimony of Robson, 30 December 1925, 376–8

26 Ibid., 372–3, 378, 401. *Saturday Night*, 7 November 1914, did contain some excerpts from Robson's rejection letters to applicants.

27 PAM, Unpub. SP, 1926, box 161, Hearst Music Committee, testimony of Robson, 30 December 1925, 376, 401–2

28 Saskatchewan, *Statutes*, 1914, c. 18; *FP*, 20 June 1914; *Saturday Night*, 25 April 1914; *Financial Times*, 4 July 1914

29 *FP*, 11 April, 11 July 1914; *Financial Times*, 4 April 1914. On 27 June 1914 the *Times* reported that one of the fur companies was advertising that its directors were 'men of probity,' though the corporate secretary had served three years in the pentitentiary for obtaining money by false pretences.

30 *Saturday Night*, 4, 18, 25 April, 10 October 1914

31 PAO, AG, series 4-32, 1915, #2282(2), memorandum from W.B. Wilkinson to AG, 12 October 1915

32 Alberta, *Statutes*, 1916, c. 8

33 PAA, PUB, Acc. 65.74, file 744, A.F.A. Coyne to PUB, 20 June 1917; J.E. Reilly to Coyne, 25 June 1917

34 Ibid., Byers and Heffernan to Deputy AG A.G. Browning, 26 June 1917; clippings from Edmonton *Bulletin*, 5, 12 October 1918; Coyne to PUB, 18 October 1918. The delegation was abandoned because of the influenza epidemic.

35 Ibid., Coyne to PUB, May 1919

36 Ibid., file 737, C.T. Pinfold to A.A. Carpenter, 15, 19, 26 May 1916; Carpenter to Pinfold, 18 May 1916; Carpenter to Skeena Copper Company, 23, 26 May 1916

37 PABC, AG, Corr., file 7162–12–14, J.J. Miller to Bowser, 30 June 1914; *FP*, 1 August 1914; *Financial Times*, 25 July 1914

38 PABC, AG, Corr., file 7162–12–14, F.M. Pratt to M.A. Macdonald, 30 January 1917; Macdonald to Pratt, 9 February 1917

39 *Financial Times*, 10 March 1917

40 Thomas Mulvey, *Company Capitalization Control: Report upon Existing Legislation in Canada and Elsewhere by the Under Secretary of State* (Ottawa, 1913), lxvii–lxviii.

Chapter 5: War Clouds

1 Sir Robert Borden was visiting in Ontario's Muskoka district and had to be hastily summoned back to Ottawa by telegram; he arrived on 1 August. See R.C. Brown, *Robert Laird Borden: A Biography*, vol. 1, *1854–1914* (Toronto, 1975), 258–63.
2 Carl Bergithon, *The Stock Exchange, with Special Reference to the Montreal Stock Exchange and the Montreal Curb Market* (Montreal, 1940), 13 (quoted); Toronto *Globe*, 30 July 1914, which quotes McDougall.
3 *Globe*, 30, 31 July, 1 August 1914; PAM, WSE MB, 31 July 1914; Glenbow-Alberta Archives, ASE Records, CSE MB, 31 July 1914; PABC, VSE MB, 31 July 1914
4 *Globe*, 31 July, 4, 5, 19 August, 1914; NAC, TSE Records, Committee MB, 1914–19, 5, 8 August 1914; *FP*, 8 August 1914
5 *FP*, 20 April 1918, which noted that the interest rates on brokers' loans had remained unchanged since 1908 despite the closure of the exchanges in 1914.
6 *Globe*, 30 July 1914; *Financial Times*, 8 August 1914
7 W.T. White, *The Story of Canada's War Finance* (Montreal, 1921), 5–10. Barry Eichengreen, *Golden Fetters: The Gold Standard and the Great Depression, 1919–1939* (New York, 1992), 68, n. 3, notes that it has usually been argued that governments permitted stock exchanges to suspend operations so that banks could protect their solvency by valuing securities at pre-crisis levels. He adds that in 1914 J.M. Keynes argued the reverse, that the banks were used to protect stock markets since suspending trading prevented banks from forcing customers to put up additional margin or selling shares, thus further depressing share prices; Keynes's argument seems correct in the Canadian case.
8 NAC, TSE Records, General Meeting MB, 1915–27, 18 August 1915
9 *Financial Times*, 8 August 1914; *FP*, 15 August 1914; NAC, TSE Records, Committee MB, 1914–19, 11 September 1914
10 NAC, TSE Records, Committee MB, 1914–19, 17 September 1914; *FP*, 12 September 1914; *Globe*, 15 September, 2 October 1914
11 TSE Records, L-24, SSME LB, 1911–15, A.G. Robertson to Dr R.H. Brown, 21 August 1914; *Globe*, 20, 25 August 1914; *FP*, 22 August, 19 (quoted), 26 September 1914
12 NAC, TSE Records, Committee MB, 1914–19, 26 August, 14 October 1914; *Financial Times*, 29 August, 10, 17 October 1914. Some brokers instituted general pay cuts, others called in only half their staff in a given week.
13 NAC, TSE Records, Committee MB, 1914–19, 7, 9, 13 October 1914; *Globe*, 15,

19, 22, 24, 27 October, 5 December 1914; *FP*, 10, 17 (quoted) October 1914; *Financial Times*, 17 October 1914

14 *Financial Times*, 31 October 1914; *Globe*, 7 (quoted), 13 November 1914

15 *Globe*, 17 November 1914; *FP*, 21 November 1914; NAC, TSE Records, Committee MB, 1914–19, 8 December 1914

16 *Globe*, 15, 21 December 1914; *Financial Times*, 19 December 1914

17 *Financial Times*, 23 January, 3 April 1915; *FP*, 27 February, 13 March 1915

18 *FP*, 3, 10 April; *Financial Times*, 10 April, 1915; NAC, TSE Records, Committee MB, 1914–19, 30 March, 1, 14, 16 April 1915

19 *FP*, 8 May 1915; *Financial Times*, 15 May 1915

20 NAC, TSE Records, Committee MB, 1914–19, 22 June, 7 July 1915; ibid., General Meeting MB, 1915–27, 18 August 1915

21 Ibid., Committee MB, 1914–19, 13, 27 September, 4 November 1915; *FP*, 4 December 1915

22 Quoted in Brent, Tovell and Co. to TSE president G. Tower Fergusson, in ibid., 8 December 1915

23 *FP*, 6 May, 1 July 1916

24 NAC, TSE Records, Commitee MB, 1914–19, 24 February, 6, 24 March, 19 April, 4 May, 14 June 1916; *FP*, 13, 20 May, 1 July 1916; 20 April 1918

25 *Financial Times*, 19 December 1914; White, *Canada's War Finance*, 12–3, 18

26 White, *Canada's War Finance*, 19–20

27 Ibid., 23–8 (quoted); *FP*, 20 (quoted), 27 November, 4 December 1915, 10 March 1917. *Financial Times*, 27 November 1915, listed the top twenty subscribers: J.K.L. Ross, $500,000; E.C. Whitney, $130,000; R.B. Angus, $100,000; Herbert Holt, $100,000; James O'Brien, $100,000; James Redmond, $100,000; Thomas Shaughnessy, $100,000; Mark Workman, $100,000; R.D. Martin, $60,000; J.W. Flavelle, $50,000; George G. Foster, $50,000; E.T. Gault, $50,000; H. Vincent Meredith, $50,000; John C. Newman, $50,000; Farquhar Robertson, $50,000; W.G. Ross, $50,000; E.S. Jacques, $40,000; A.J. Dawes, $25,000; Hugh Parton, $25,000; Beaumont Sheppard, $23,000.

28 *Financial Times*, 27 November 1915; *FP*, 27 November (quoted), 4, 25 December 1915

29 R.C. Brown, *Robert Laird Borden: A Biography*, vol. 2, *1914–1937* (Toronto, 1980), 43–4, notes White's inherent conservatism and pessimism about the country's financial capacity in this period.

30 White, *Canada's War Finance*, 31–2; *FP*, 25 March 1916; *Financial Times*, 25 March, 1 April 1916. The five-year bonds paid 5.10 per cent and were issued at 99.56 per cent, the tens paid 5.36 per cent at 97.13 per cent and the fifteens paid 5.5 per cent at 94.94 per cent. Only subscriptions under $2,000 were allotted in full for the latter series, under 20 per cent of larger subscriptions being filled.

31 White, *Canada's War Finance*, 28, 59
32 E.P. Neufeld, *The Financial System of Canada, Its Growth and Development* (Toronto, 1972), 503–4
33 Neufeld, *Financial System of Canada*, 504–5; *FP*, 17 June 1916. In 1925 the BDAC was renamed the Investment Bankers Association of Canada, which was affiliated to the U.S. organization of the same name. But in 1934 the Bank Act prohibited anyone but the chartered banks from using the term 'banker,' and the organization became (and remains) the Investment Dealers Association of Canada.
34 White, *Canada's War Finance*, 28; *FP*, 26 August, 9, 16, 23, 30 September 1916; 10 March 1917. Subscriptions between $25,000 and $100,000 were allotted $25,000 plus 30 per cent of the balance, those between $100,000 and $1 million got $100,000 plus 40 per cent of the balance, and those over $1 million got that amount plus 26 per cent of the balance.
35 *FP*, 13 January 1917; *Financial Times*, 13 January 1917
36 *FP*, 24 February 1917
37 Ibid., 3, 10, 17, 24, 31 March, 7 April 1917. Those who subscribed for $25,000 to $100,000 got $25,000 plus 80 per cent of the balance, those between $100,000 and $1 million got $25,000 plus 70 per cent of the remainder, and those over $1 million got that sum plus 45 per cent of the remainder.
38 Ibid., 10 November 1917
39 White, *Canada's War Finance*, 62; Neufeld, *Financial System of Canada*, 505; *FP*, 6 October 1917
40 *FP*, 8, 15 December 1917
41 *FP*, 3, 10, 17 November 1917; NAC, TSE Records, General Meeting MB, 1915–27, 30 October 1917; ibid., Committee MB, 1914–19, 16 January 1918
42 *FP*, 15, 22, 29 December 1917; NAC, TSE Records, Committee MB, 1914–19, 2, 15, 16 January 1918
43 *FP*, 23 March 1918; NAC, TSE Records, Committee MB, 1914–19, 11 March, 28 May 1918
44 NAC, TSE Records, Committee MB, 1914–19, 31 December 1918; *FP*, 4, 18 January, 31 May 1919. Minimum bond prices were lifted on the MSE on 8 February 1918; see Bergithon, *Stock Exchange*, 14.
45 *FP*, 5, 19 August 1916, *Financial Times*, 5 August 1916
46 NAC, Justice Department Records, RG 13 A2, vol. 218, file 1918/74, Memorandum, unsigned, 30 June 1917; draft order-in-council, 3 July 1918. At the same time White told the Ontario provincial treasurer confidentially that he intended to go to the New York market again when the Canadian market was 'pretty full.' See NAC, W.T. White Papers, vol. 4, folder 16, White to T.W. McGarry, 21 June 1917, 2562.
47 NAC, Justice Department Records, RG 13 A2, vol. 218, file 1918/74, White to E.L. Newcombe, 5 July 1917; Ontario attorney general I.B. Lucas to Justice Minister C.J. Doherty, 15 February 1918; ibid., White Papers, vol. 5, folder 17, E.R. Wood to

White, 3 January 1918, Personal, 2757–8; ibid., R.L. Borden Papers, RLB 2186, Alberta premier Charles Stewart to Borden, 17 January 1918, 130596; White to Borden, 22 January 1918, 130601–2. The matter was also discussed in Parliament; see Canada, House of Commons, *Debates*, 25 March 1918, 115–27. In an attempt to placate the provinces the regulations were amended to permit provincial issues to be approved *after* they were placed on the market, and Ottawa agreed to make advances to provincial governments to meet issues maturing abroad so that they would not need to borrow domestically. See *Canadian Annual Review*, 1918, 478.

48 *FP*, 12 January, 27 July, 17 August 1918

49 *FP*, 29 December 1917; 8 February 1919; *Financial Times* 26 January 1918; Neufeld, *Financial System of Canada*, 506. The committee was composed of G.H. Wood, Edwin Hanson, Purvis McDougall, R.A. Stephenson, A.M. Nanton, H.R. Tudhope, J.A. Mitchell, and W.A. Mackenzie.

50 Neufeld, *Financial System of Canada*, 506; *FP*, 12 October 1918; PABC, VSE MB, 27 September 1918, 7 January 1919

51 Neufeld, *Financial System of Canada*, 506; *FP*, 30 November, 28 December 1918; 25 January, 8 February 1919

52 *FP*, 1 February 1919. The BDAC created committees to deal with (1) federal legislation, (2) provincial legislation in each locality, (3) municipal credit, (4) public utility and industrial financing, (5) membership, (6) the annual program, and (7) the constitution. Thirty-one members came from the Maritimes and Quebec, twenty-eight from Ontario, and seventeen from western Canada.

53 Neufeld, *Financial System of Canada*, 506; *FP* 13 December 1919

54 Neufeld, *Financial System of Canada*, 506–7; NAC, TSE Records, General Meeting MB, 1915–27, 25 February 1920; *FP*, 28 February, 6 March, 1920

55 *FP*, 19, 26 June 1920

56 Ibid., 3, 10, 17 September 1920. The government threatened to compile a list of those who demanded U.S. funds even though it lacked authority to punish them.

57 *FP*, 29 October, 3 December 1920. Gordon Wills was present at the meetings as president of the TSE, though he wrongly gives the date as 1921; see E. Gordon Wills, 'The Stock Exchange and the Street,' *Canadian Banker*, 58 (spring 1951), 122–3

58 *FP*, 24 September 1920. Wood, Gundy, R.A. Daly, W.A. Mackenzie and Company, and Turner, Spragge and Company purchased seats.

Chapter 6: Highbinders and Re-loaders

1 Winnipeg *Free Press*, 19 December 1924; PAM, Unpub. SP, Manitoba, 1926, box 161, Report of the Select Standing Committee of the Legislature on Certain Companies which have gone into liquidation, February, 1926

2 *FP*, 19 February 1926

3 PAM, Unpub. SP, Manitoba, 1926, box 161, Item 1 (3 parts), 'Evidence to Select Standing Committee [of the Legislative Assembly] to enquire into all matters relating to the promotion and operation of the Hearst Music Corporation and the Farmers' Packing Company Limited' (hereafter Hearst Music Committee), testimony of Snider, 21 July 1925, 1–5

4 *FP*, 4 December 1925

5 PAM, Unpub. SP, 1926, box 161, Hearst Music Committee, testimony of Fink, 21 July 1925, 8–9; *FP*, 4 December 1925; 2 April 1926

6 PAM, Unpub. SP, Manitoba, 1925, no. 37, Macdonald to Deputy Attorney General John Allen, 9 January 1923

7 Ibid., F.H. Gates to Hearst, 25 October 1923

8 Ibid., J.W. Wilton to Attorney General R.W. Craig, 19 December 1925, 2 January 1926

9 Manitoba, *Statutes*, 1919–20, c. 88; 1920, c. 117

10 PAM, Unpub. SP, 1925, no. 37, Wilton to Craig, 1 February 1923; Deputy Attorney General Allen to Macdonald, 13 February 1923

11 PAM, Unpub. SP, 1926, box 161, Report of the Select Standing Committee of the Legislature on Certain Companies which have gone into liquidation, February, 1926

12 *Saturday Night*, 29 November 1924

13 PAM, Unpub. SP, 1926, box 161, Report of the Select Standing Committee of the Legislature on Certain Companies which have gone into liquidation, Feburary, 1926

14 PAM, Unpub. SP, 1925, no. 37, Arrest warrant for Hearst from Winnipeg police magistrate G.F. Richards, 17 December 1924; Printed circular from Winnipeg Police Department, 31 December 1924; Chase National cashier William P. Holly to J.B. Nicholson, 6 January 1925; *FP*, 1 January 1926

15 *FP*, 2 January, 6 March, 4 December 1925; Winnipeg *Free Press*, 24 June 1926

16 PAM, Unpub. SP, 1926, box 161, Hearst Music Committee, testimony of Carl B. Fink, 21 July 1925, 11–12; testimony of T. Harry Webb, 7–11; testimony of John Anderson, 23 July 1925, 192–3, where the remarks of Major Taylor, MLA, are found.

17 See Winnipeg *Free Press*, 19 December 1925; 24, 25, 31 March; 1, 2, 7, 8, 9, 10, 13 April 1926.

18 Ibid.

19 The *Oxford English Dictionary* defines 'high-binder' as an early-nineteenth-century American term for 'one of a gang which commits outrages on persons or property,' which came to be used 'abusively to denote a swindler.'

20 On Sheldon see chapter 4 above; on Ponzi see *Saturday Night*, 7, 28 August 1920, and *FP*, 13 August 1920, reporting Ponzi's address to the Montreal Kiwanis.

21 On Ponzi see, for instance, Robert Sobel, *The Great Bull Market: Wall Street in the 1920s* (New York, 1968), 17–19, and Joseph Bulgatz, *Ponzi Schemes: Invaders from*

Mars and More Extraordinary Popular Delusions and the Madness of Crowds (New York, 1992), 11–27.

22 *FP*, 10 December 1926; 29 April, 21 October 1927; 27 January, 15 June, 24 August 1928; 5 June 1930. One of the few cars that Brooks actually manufactured is preserved in the Canadian Automotive Museum in Oshawa, Ontario.

23 Patrick Boyer, *A Passion for Justice: The Legacy of James Chalmers McRuer* (Toronto 1994), 62. As a young Crown attorney McRuer prosecuted this and a number of other stock fraud cases described in ibid., 60–2. I am indebted to Professor Martin Friedland for bringing this reference to my attention.

24 *Saturday Night*, 11 January, 8, 15 February 1919

25 PAO, AG, series 4-32, 1915, file #2282 (2), Memorandum from W.B. Wilkinson to AG, 12 October 1915

26 Ibid., 1920, file #3866, Memorandum from W.B. Wilkinson to AG, 14 January 1919 [i.e., 1920]; see also *FP*, 29 March 1919; *Financial Times*, 29 March 1919.

27 PAO, AG, 4-32, 1919, file #1872, Deputy AG Edward Bayly to T.J. Agar, 30 July 1919; Press release, n.d. [August 1919]; Memorandum from Bayly to J.G. Schiller, Provincial Secretary's Department, 4 September 1919; *FP*, 23 August 1919

28 PAO, AG, 4-32, 1919, file #1872, W.C. Fox to Lucas, 21 August 1919

29 Ibid., 1920, file #3866, Masten to Raney, 28 January 1920; Memorandum from W.B. Wilkinson to Raney, 5 February 1920; *FP*, 31 January 1920

30 PAO, AG, 4-32, 1920, file #3866, Raney to F.W. Hay, 12 February 1921

31 *FP*, 22, 29 July, 5, 19, 26 August 1921; *Saturday Night*, 1 October 1921

32 O'Brien to Raney, 1 February 1922; reprinted in A.H. O'Brien, *Report on Blue Sky Legislation* (Toronto, 1922), which records that he was recruited on 12 September 1921.

33 O'Brien, *Report on Blue Sky Legislation*.

34 NAC, TSE, Committee MB, 21 November 1921; *FP*, 23 June, 7, 28 July 1922

35 PAO, AG, 4-32, 1928, file #1726, T.F. Sutherland to A.W. Rogers, 18 January 1928, enclosing memorandum from Sutherland to Mines Minister Henry Mills, 11 April 1923

36 *FP*, 1 December 1922; NAC, TSE, Committee MB, 2 March 1923

37 Ontario, *Statutes*, 1923, c. 38; PAO, G.H. Ferguson Papers, General Corr., box 46, copy of Bill no. 66, 1923, 'An Act Respecting the Sale of Securities'; *FP*, 12 May 1923

38 New Brunswick, *Statutes*, 1923, c. 19; *FP*, 30 March, 26 May, 8, 22 June 1923

39 PABC, AG Corr., file C–39–2, Memorandum from H.G. Garrett to AG J.W. Farris, 2 December 1919. The premier, John Oliver, agreed with Garrett's position; see ibid., memorandum from Oliver to Farris, 12 December 1919

40 Ibid., W.E. Payne, Vancouver Board of Trade, to AG Farris, 4 March 1921; memorandum from Garrett to AG, 10, 23 March, 8 November 1921; 27 November

1922; D.B. Martyn, Department of Industry, to AG, 19 March 1921; T.H. Wilson, Penticton Board of Trade to AG, 28 October 1921; ibid., file L-323–39, Archie Johnson to Charles Maloy, 15 March 1921; *Saturday Night*, 19 March 1921

41 *Saturday Night*, 15 July 1922; PABC, AG Corr., file C-39-2, Memorandum from J.W. Dixie to AG A.M. Manson, 30 April 1923; *Canadian Annual Review of Public Affairs*, 1923 (Toronto, 1924), 300 (quoted).

42 *Ruthenian Farmers Elevator Company v. Lukey* (1922), 3 *Western Weekly Reports*, 396

43 *Ruthenian Farmers Elevator Company v. Lukey* (1923), 3 *Western Weekly Reports*, 138, quoting Turgeon, J. at 149; *FP*, 4 May, 27 July 1923

44 *R. v. Henderson; ex parte Queen* (1924), 51 *New Brunswick Reports*, 346; *FP*, 17 August, 30 November 1923

45 PAO, G.H. Ferguson Papers, General Corr., box 46, Johns to Ferguson, 18 August 1923 enclosing 'Memorandum re Ontario Companies Act and Sale of Securities Bill.'

46 *FP*, 17 August 1923; *Financial Times*, 22 September 1923; PAO, G.H. Ferguson Papers, General Corr., box 46, Kingsmill to Ferguson, 1 September 1923; Ferguson to Kingsmill, 5 September 1923

47 *Lukey v. Ruthenian Farmers Elevator Company* (1924), *Supreme Court Reports*, 56. Davies is quoted at 58–9, Idington at 65.

48 *R. v. Henderson; ex parte Queen* (1924), 51 *New Brunswick Reports*, 346

49 PAA, PP, file 367, J.A. Cross to J.E. Brownlee, 24 April 1926. On earlier cases which had extended provincial powers to incorporate companies, see Christopher Armstrong, *The Politics of Federalism: Ontario's Relations with the Federal Government, 1867–1942* (Toronto, 1981), 100–7.

50 PAO, AG, 4-32, 1926, #1455, Bayly to AG, 5 July 1926, Confidential.

51 PAO, G.H. Ferguson Papers, General Corr., box 50, Gordon Philip to Ferguson, 3 January 1924; Post to MLAs, 31 March 1924

52 PAO, G.H. Ferguson Papers, General Corr., box 50, O'Brien to Ferguson, 28 March 1924; *Financial Times*, 27 June 1924; PAM, Unpub. SP, 1926, box 161, Hearst Music Committee, testimony of A.H. Williamson, 30 December 1925, 405–7

53 Ontario, *Statutes*, 1924, c. 48. On the impact of the *Lukey* decision, see PAO, AG, 4-32, 1927, #2544, Memorandum from F.V. Johns to W.H. Price, 20 July 1927.

54 Sixty years later J.C. McRuer recalled that when he was a young Crown attorney, Nickle had invited him to address the Conservative caucus on the prevalence of fraudulent share pushing and to defend the proposed bill; many MPPs were unsympathetic, and one Bay Streeter complained, 'I'm not going to have any Crown Attorney snooping around in the companies I'm concerned with'; see Boyer, *Passion*, 70–1, where this meeting is wrongly dated (following McRuer) to 1923.

55 *Saturday Night*, 19 April 1924; *Financial Times*, 1 August 1924; *FP*, 15 August 1924;

PAO, G.H. Ferguson Papers, General Corr., box 57, J.J. Kerr to Ferguson, 26 November 1925; Ferguson to Kerr, 17 December 1925

56 Quebec, *Statutes*, 1924, c. 61; *Financial Times*, 23 February, 14, 21, 28 March 1924; *FP*, 28 March 1924

57 PAA, Acc. 65.74, PUB, file 778, J.H. Woods to Brownlee, 16 March 1925

58 Ibid., Carpenter to James Fisher Co., 7 April; Carpenter to Joseph T. Shaw, MP, 11 April 1925

59 Ibid., Brownlee to Carpenter, 21 January 1925; PAM, John Bracken Papers, box G531, file 4, R.W. Craig to Bracken, 27 April 1925; PAM, Unpub. SP, 1926, box 161, Hearst Music Committee, testimony of R.W. Craig, 31 December 1925, 461–4

60 The Farmers' Packing Company had gone bankrupt after paying heavy commissions to high-pressure salesmen brought in from the United States to sell its shares; there was also brief consideration of the Northwestern Life Assurance Company, which had sold large amounts of stock despite twice being refused a certificate. See PAM, Unpub. SP, 1926, box 161, Report of the Select Standing Committee of the Legislature on Certain Companies which have gone into liquidation, February, 1926.

61 Robson's views on blue-sky legislation presented to this committee are cited extensively in chapter 4.

62 PAM, Unpub. SP, 1926, box 161, Hearst Music Committee, testimony of H.A. Robson, 30 December 1925, 381–8

63 Ibid., testimony of Williamson, 30 December 1925, 404–9

64 Ibid., Report of the Select Standing Committee of the Legislature on Certain Companies which have gone into liquidation, February, 1926

65 Ed Gould, *Oil, The History of Canada's Oil and Gas Industry* (n.p., 1976), 77–80

66 PAA, Acc. 65.74, PUB, file 779a, Memorandum re Sale of Shares Act, n.d. [December 1926].

67 Ibid., file 779b, PUB to L.W. Brockington, 24 April 1926

68 Ibid., file 779a, Memorandum re Sale of Shares Act, n.d. [December 1926].

69 Ibid., file 779b, PUB to Millican and Millican, 11 March 1926; ibid., file 779a, Memorandum re Sale of Shares Act, n.d. [December 1926], quoted.

70 Ibid., file 779a, PUB to California commissioner of corporations, 8 June 1926, and reply, and letters to regulators in Oklahoma, Texas, Kansas, Montana, Minnesota, and Wisconsin, who all replied in similar terms.

71 PAA, PP, file 367, J.E. Brownlee to H.S. Spencer, MP, 21 April 1926; ibid., Acc. 65.74, PUB, file 780a, PUB to C.S. Klingman, 21 March 1927, and reply, 29 March 1927 (quoted); Memorandum from PUB re Sale of Shares Act, 25 October 1927; ibid., file 779b, W.C. Benner, St. Marys, Ontario, to PUB, 18 May 1926; PUB to Benner, 2 June 1926. Of the eighteen companies applying to the PUB three federal ones were approved and one dropped its application, while one Montana company was refused; of the Alberta companies two dropped their applications (one refusing

even to file a geologist's report), and one only wanted authority to sell additional shares.

72 PAA, PP, file 367, Brownlee to King, 22 March 1926; Brownlee to H.S. Spencer, MP, 7 April 1926; *FP*, 14 May 1926; PAA, Acc. 65.74, file 779b, S.P. Grosch, Saskatchewan Local Government Board, to PUB, 3 April 1926; PUB to Grosch, 8 April 1926

73 PAM, John Bracken Papers, box G531, file 4, R.W. Craig to Bracken, 27 April 1925; *Dominion Provincial and Interprovincial Conferences from 1887 to 1926 / Conferences fédérales-provinciales et conférences interprovinciales de 1887 à 1926* (Ottawa, 1951), 111–2; PAO, G.H. Ferguson Papers, General Corr., box 87, Ferguson to King, 15 June 1926; King to Ferguson, 17 June 1926. Federally incorporated loan and trust companies and any others designated by federal order-in-council would also be covered, but other companies whose activities fell under exclusively federal jurisdiction, such as banks, would be exempt unless so designated.

74 PAO, AG, 4-32, 1926, #1455, Mulvey to Ferguson, 21 June 1926

75 A full account of this political manoeuvring may be found in H. Blair Neatby, *William Lyon Mackenzie King, 1924–1932: The Lonely Heights* (Toronto, 1963), 130–75.

76 PAO, AG, 4-32, 1927, #2544, W.H. Price to T.C. Davis, 28 December 1928

Chapter 7: Fighting Fraud

1 Carl Bergithon, *The Stock Exchange, with Special Reference to the Montreal Stock Exchange and the Montreal Curb Market* (Montreal, 1940), 12–15, 34–6

2 Ibid., 15, 33

3 *Annual Financial Review (Canadian)* 25–30 (Toronto, 1925–30), comp. W.R. Houston.

4 Bergithon, *Stock Exchange*, 31–2

5 Ibid., 15–16. Listing fees on the MSE started at $1,000 for 200,000 shares and rose to $3,500 for 1 million shares, while mines began at $500 with a maximum of $15,000 for both categories; Curb fees started at $500 for industrials and $100 for mines. The MSE normally required 25 per cent of a listed issue to be in the hands of the public. The Curb would settle for 20 per cent for industrials and 10 per cent for mines, and did not require as much disclosure of financial information, while issues could be traded on the Curb's unlisted department without disclosing such information at all. See ibid., 20–5.

6 *Financial Times*, 25 March 1922; 13 August 1926; 15 July 1927; *FP*, 9 March 1923; 28 May 1926; 7 October 1927

7 *Annual Financial Review* 25–30

8 NAC, TSE Records, Committee MB, 4 December 1920; 14 March 1923; 7 November 1924; 15 June 1925; 25 January 1926; Toronto *Daily Star*, 19 March 1937

9 *FP*, 21 July 1919; NAC, TSE Records, Committee MB, 11 November 1919: *Saturday Night*, 21 August 1920

10 *FP*, 2 March, 20 May (quoted), 4 August 1922; 7 March 1924; *Canadian Annual Review of Public Affairs*, 1924–5, 598; Bergithon, *Stock Exchange*, 49

11 NAC, TSE Records, Committee MB, 26 October 1920; 26 November 1925

12 Ibid., 16 October 1922; 25 April 1923

13 Ibid., 18 December 1923; 17 June 1925

14 Ibid., SSME, Member Corr., file 324.5, Homer L. Gibson to SSME secretary Philip G. Kiely, 8 December 1922

15 *FP*, 19, 26, September, 3, 10 October 1924; 5 June 1925

16 PAO, AG, 4-32, 1925, #3079, Memorandum from AG's legal secretary A.W. Rogers to Leroy L. Hunter, 8 December 1925. Hunter was complaining that an order of his had been bucketed, but that he could not get any satisfaction from the SSME and wanted a prosecution launched; see ibid., Hunter to Premier G.H. Ferguson, 3 November 1925.

17 *FP*, 15, 29 May, 5 June, 14 August 1925

18 Ibid., 8 January, 19 February, 5 March, 2 April 1926

19 NAC, TSE Records, SSME MB, 29 December 1925; 2 February, 22 July, 18 November 1926

20 Glenbow-Alberta Archives, ASE Records, CSE MB, 23 February, 13 March, 6 November, 1 December 1926; 29 March, 27, 30 June, 8 November, 12 December 1927; *Financial Times*, 22 April 1927

21 Glenbow-Alberta Archives, ASE Records, CSE MB, 29 February, 23 April, 5 June, 17 December 1928; 16 April, 4 June 1929; *FP*, 16 March 1928; Ed Gould, *Oil, The History of Canada's Oil and Gas Industry* (n.p., 1976), 81

22 PAM, WSE MB, 2 April, 12 June 1928; *FP*, 2 March 1928; *Financial Times*, 16 March, 13 April 1928; PAO, AG, 4-32, 1928, #892, Manitoba PU commissioner W.R. Cottingham to A.W. Rogers, 13 March 1928

23 PABC, VSE MB, 14 May, 22 July 1924; 18 May 1926; ibid., Miscellaneous Corr., vol. 1, file 1, Report of the president, 11 May 1926

24 PABC, VSE MB, 9, 18, 21 (quoted), 24 November, 8 December 1927; 30 January, 13 February, 5 March, 26 April, 1928; 12 February, 12, 25 March, 22 July 1929; *FP*, 2 December 1927; 27 January 1928

25 PAO, AG, 4-32, 1925, #3079, W.F. Nickle to Dr J.J. Kerr, 12 October 1926; NAC, TSE Records, SSME MB, 9, 17 December 1926

26 Toronto *Telegram*, 19 March 1927; Toronto *Daily Star*, 22 March 1927; *FP*, 25 March 1927; *Financial Times*, 25 March 1927; NAC, TSE Records, SSME MB,

18 March 1927; PAO, AG, 4-32, 1927, #741, Frank Leslie to AG W.H. Price, 19 March 1927

27 For complaints re Kiely and Smith, see NAC, TSE Records, SSME Member Corr., file 324.14; e.g., C.G. Bell to SSME, 19 March 1927. On Kemerer see ibid., file 324.12; e.g., W. Garfield Case to SSME, 24 March 1927, and especially John Forrest to F.J. Crawford, 23 March 1927.

28 Ibid., SSME MB, 24 March 1927; PAO, AG, 4-32, 1927, #741, A.J. Trebilcock to Price, 25 March 1927

29 *FP*, 25 March 1927; *Financial Times*, 25 March 1927. At the annual meeting of South Keora Mines in April 1927, it was reported that Kiely had paid $88,000 into the company treasury and taken down 120,000 shares at 5 cents under his option agreement; see *FP*, 22 April 1927

30 PAO, AG, 4-32, 1927, #741, draft letter from AG to SSME, 21 March 1927; Trebilcock to Price, 25 March 1927; NAC, TSE Records, SSME MB, 18, 24 March 1927

31 PAO, AG, 4-32, 1927, #741, Memorandum from Price to Bayly, 24 March 1927; Bayly to Armour, 24 March 1927; Armour to Bayly, 24, 25 (quoted) March, 1927; Armour to Price, 25 March 1927

32 *FP*, 22 April 1927; PAO, AG, 4-32, 1927, #741, Memorandum from Price to Bayly, 2 (quoted), 19 April 1927; Memorandum from Bayly to Price, 20 April 1927; NAC, TSE Records, SSME MB, 31 March 1927

33 PAO, AG, 4-32, 1927, #741, decision in *Kemerer v. Standard Stock and Mining Exchange*, 21 May 1927; NAC, TSE Records, SSME MB, 17 June 1927; ibid., SSME Member Corr., file 324.12, SSME assistant secretary J.J. Kingsmill to Kemerer, 4 July 1927

34 PAO, AG, 4-32, 1927, #741, Memorandum from Price to Bayly, 2 April 1927; Bayly to secretaries of NYSE, MSE, and TSE, 5 April 1927; Bayly to Draper Dobie, 30 May 1927

35 NAC, TSE Records, SSME MB, 27 June 1927; PAO, AG, 4-32, 1927, #741, Memorandum from Rogers to Price, 29 June 1927; Rogers to A.J. Trebilcock, 4 July 1927; Memorandum from Price to Rogers, 14 July 1927

36 PAO, AG, 4-32, 1927, #741, Memorandum from A.W. Rogers to W.H. Price, 29 June 1927; NAC, TSE Records, SSME Member Corr., file 324.12, Gibson to N.C. Urquhart, 15 June 1927

37 See *FP*, 11 March, 8, 22 April, 28 May, 23 September 1927; *Financial Times*, 10 June, 22 July 1927.

38 *FP*, 16 December 1927; PAO, AG, 4-32, 1927, #2944, Rogers to Munday, 1 March 1928

39 *Saturday Night*, 11 February 1928; *Financial Times*, 17 February 1928; *FP*, 24 February 1928

40 PAO, AG, 4-32, 1927, #741, Memorandum from Rogers to Price, 29 June 1927; memorandum from Price to Rogers, 14 July 1927

41 *FP*, 30 September, 28 October 1927; *Saturday Night*, 15 October 1927; PAO, AG, 4-32, 1927, #2648, Report of Wilton C. Eddis and Sons, CAs, on Toronto Securities, Milton Janis, et al., 14 October 1927; Ontario AG to British Consul, New York, 15 October 1927; E.H. Lockwood to Sir Harry Armstrong, 14 March 1928; Memorandum from Edward Bayly to AG, 25 October 1929. The New York attorney general's office worked closely with Ontario authorities on such matters at this time; see ibid., 1927, #2259, John J. Tobin to A.W. Rogers, 4 October 1928, addressed to 'Dear Arthur'

42 Toronto *Daily Star*, 8, 23 November 1927; *Financial Times*, 2 September, 18 November 1927; *FP*, 18 November 1927; PAO, AG, 4-32, #2259, Hiram E. Stone to Toronto police chief, 17 August 1927; Stone to E. Bayly, 28 September 1927; Memorandum from A.W. Rogers to Price, 21 August 1927; Cotnam to Price, 26 October 1927; Price to Solicitor General Lucien Cannon, 17 May 1928

43 PAM, John Bracken Papers, box G660, file 1453, Memorandum from R.W. Craig, 11 April 1927; Manitoba, *Statutes*, 1924 (Consolidated Amendments), c. 175; ibid., 1926, c. 33; *In re Sale of Shares Act and Municipal and Public Utility Board Act* (1927), 36 *Manitoba Law Reports*, 583

44 PAO, AG, 4-32, 1927, #741, Memorandum from Price to Rogers, 14 July 1927; Armour to Rogers, 11 August 1927

45 *FP*, 2 September 1927; NAC, TSE Records, SSME MB, 20 September 1927

46 NAC, TSE Records, Committee MB, 26 May, 6 June, 22 September, 4 October 1927

47 *FP*, 28 May 1926; 2 September, 7, 14, 28 October 1927; *Financial Times*, 13 August 1926

48 NAC, TSE Records, SSME MB, 27 October 1927; PAO, AG, 4-32, 1927, #741, A.J. Trebilcock to A.W. Rogers, 28 October 1927; Memorandum from Rogers to W.H. Price, 29 October 1927

49 PAO, AG, 4-32, 1927, #741, Memorandum from Price to Rogers, 21 November 1927; Rogers to Trebilcock, 23 November 1927

50 Ibid., Trebilcock to Rogers, 25 November, 2 December 1927

51 Ibid., Rogers to Trebilcock, 26 November 1927; *FP*, 25 November 1927

52 PAO, AG, 4-32, 1927, #741, R.E. Kemerer to Rogers, 21 November 1927

53 Ibid., Trebilcock to Rogers, 8 December 1927; NAC, TSE Records, SSME MB, 7 December 1927; ibid., TSE Committee MB, 9, 30 November; *FP*, 18 November 1927

54 *Financial Times*, 18, 25 November 1927; PAO, AG, 4-32, 1927, #3091, Memorandum from Price to Assistant Provincial Secretary W.W. Dennison, 29 November 1927; Dennison to Edward Bayly, 20 December 1927, Confidential; CID inspector

C.D. Hammond to assistant OPP commissioner Alfred Cuddy, 29 December 1927; *Financial Times*, 20 January, 4, 11 May 1928; *FP*, 11 May, 1 June 1928

55 *FP*, 6 January 1928; PAO, AG, 4-32, 1927, #2936, Price to SSME secretary Draper Dobie, 12 December 1927; Memorandum from A.W. Rogers to Price, 8 May 1928

56 PAO, AG, 4-32, 1927, #3408, CID inspector E.W. Hammond to Assistant OPP Commissioner Alfred Cuddy, 18 December 1927; Memorandum from Rogers to Price, 20 December 1927

57 Ibid., 1927, #741, Rogers to assistant NY AG Timothy J. Shea, 28 December 1927; John J. Tobin to Rogers, 10 January 1928; Rogers to W.H. Price, 12 January 1928

58 NAC, TSE Records, General Corr., Pre-1950, file 329.25, Draper Dobie to A.W. Rogers, 26 January 1928; Price to Dobie, 8 February 1928; Dobie to Price, 15 February 1928; ibid., SSME MB, 14 February 1928

59 *Clarke v. Baillie* (1912), 45 *Supreme Court Reports*, 50

60 NAC, TSE Records, General Corr., Pre-1950, file 329.25, Price to Draper Dobie, 17 February 1928; J.J. Kingsmill to Price, 7 March 1928; ibid., SSME MB, 22 February 1928

61 Ibid., SSME MB, 6, 19 March, 10, 18 April, 10, 16 July 1928; *FP*, 30 March 1928

62 *Dominion-Provincial Conferences, November 3–10, 1927, December 9–13, 1935, January 14–15, 1941 / Conférences fédérales-provinciales, du 3 au 10 novembre 1927, du 9 au 13 décembre 1935, les 14 et 15 janvier 1941* (Ottawa, 1951), 'Precis of Discussions, Dominion-Provincial Conference, November 3 to 10, 1927,' 13–4

63 The ever-vigilant under-secretary of state, Thomas Mulvey, enquired on what legal grounds Price was intervening in the internal affairs of the SSME (which was after all provincially incorporated) in rewriting its by-laws; Price's deputy replied that the exchange had asked for assistance. See PAO, AG, 4-32, 1927, #3091, Mulvey to Edward Bayly, 4 January 1928; Bayly to Mulvey, 5 January 1928.

64 *Financial Times*, 25 November 1927; PAO, AG, 4-32, 1928, #892, Rogers to Manitoba deputy AG John Allen, 22 February 1928; ibid., 1927, #2544, Memorandum from Bayly to Price, 20 February 1928; ibid., Legislative Assembly Records, RG 49, series I-7-E, box 2, E.G. Long to Price, 24 November 1927

65 Ontario, *Statutes*, 1928, c. 34; PAO, AG, 4-32, 1928, #3033, notes for speech by Price on Security Frauds Prevention Act, n.d. [March 1928] (quoted).

66 PAM, Unpub. SP, 1926, box 161, Hearst Music Committee, testimony of A.H. Williamson, 30 December 1925, 405–7

67 PAO, AG, 4-32, 1927, #741, Memorandum from Rogers to Price, 29 June 1927; NAC, TSE Records, SSME MB, 8, 19 March 1928; ibid., TSE General Corr., Pre-1950, file 330.7, Draper Dobie to W.H. Price, 22 March 1928; Rogers to Dobie, 26 March 1928

68 *FP*, 18 May, 27 July 1928; *Saturday Night*, 19 May 1928

69 PAO, AG, 4-32, 1928, #790, Price to Justice Minister Ernest Lapointe, 14 April

1928; Postmaster General P.J. Veniot to Lapointe, 21 April 1928; Albert Kohn to
Price, 14 August 1928; A.W. Rogers to Kohn, 17 August 1928; *FP*, 1 June 1928
70 *FP*, 25 November, 16, 23 December 1927, 13 April 1928; *Financial Times*, 8 June,
3 August 1928
71 *Financial Times*, 27 January, 23 March, 11, 18 May, 14 September 1928
72 *FP*, 23 November 1928; *Financial Times*, 1 March 1929. The Ontario authorities had
been keeping an eye on Larkin for some time too, and the Mines Department noted
that his claim that his Quartz Lake Mine was comparable to the Dome, Hollinger,
McIntyre, and Kirkland Lake camps because it lay south of a lake was 'nothing less
than silly.' Larkin then tried to butter up Arthur Rogers in the Attorney General's
Department by addressing him as 'Colonel.' Rogers replied, 'I am not and never was
a Colonel, and the war is over anyway. My rank was Lieutenant, but we prefer that
ranks be dropped in this country.' He added a warning that Larkin had better register
his salesmen under the Security Frauds Prevention Act if they were operating in
Ontario. See PAO, AG, 4-32, 1927, #3117, T.F. Sutherland, Mines Department, to
Rogers, 18 January 1928; Larkin to Rogers, 26 April 1928, and reply, 16 May 1928.
73 NAC, TSE Records, SSME MB, 15 May 1928; ibid., TSE Committee MB, 28 May,
20 September 1928; ibid., TSE General Corr., Pre-1950, file 333.27, TSE president
C.E. Abbs to members, 25 July 1928; *Financial Times*, 19 October 1928
74 *AG for Manitoba v. AG for Canada* (1929), *Appeal Cases*, 260
75 PAO, AG, 4-32, 1927, #2544, memorandum for the AG, 8 January 1928 [i.e., 1929].
76 Ibid., T.C. Davis to Price, 20 December 1928; Price to Davis, 26 December 1928
77 Ibid., Memoranda from Price to Bayly, 27 December 1928; 7 January 1928 [i.e.,
1929] (quoted).
78 The Manitoba act only required a licence where the sales were part of 'continued
and successive' acts, a form of wording imported from U.S. law to permit isolated,
unlicensed trades.
79 PAO, AG, 4-32, #2544, Bayly to Davis, 8 January 1929, with copies to Davis's
counterparts, W.J. Major of Manitoba and J.F. Lymburn of Alberta
80 Saskatchewan, *Statutes*, 1928–9, c. 68 ; Manitoba, *Statutes*, 1929, c. 48; Alberta,
Statutes, 1929, c. 10; Prince Edward Island, *Statutes*, 1929, c. 8
81 PABC, AG, Corr., file L-323–29, Davis to AG R.H. Pooley, 6 February 1929; Price
to Pooley, 13 February 1929
82 British Columbia, *Statutes*, 1929, c. 11 ; *FP*, 5 April, 20 June 1929
83 *FP*, 9 November 1928; NAC, TSE Records, Committee MB, 14 December 1928;
ibid., SSME MB, 18 December 1928
84 NAC, TSE Records, Committee MB, 14 November 1928; 5 February 1929
85 *FP*, 3 May 1929; *Financial Times*, 24 May 1929; NAC, TSE Records, General Corr.,
Pre-1950, file 329.15, Gordon H. Benson to SSME, 20 June 1929. Trading sheets in
this file show that the CMOE was still handling between 80,000 and 120,000 shares

daily in February 1930, though the SSME had refused its application for its ticker service.

86 NAC, TSE Records, SSME MB, 31 October 1928; 4 March, 12, 23 April 1929; ibid., SSME Member Corr., file 323.19, J.J. Kingsmill to T.U. Fairlie, 18 February, 1929; ibid., file 334.1, Kingsmill to D.C. Smith, 24 April 1929; *FP*, 27 June 1929; *FP*, 16, 26 April 1929. The Unlisted Stock Market later changed its name to the International Stock Exchange, but it does not seem to have done a great deal of business; see ibid., TSE General Corr., Pre-1950, file 331.26, E.A. Marks to J.M. Miller, 7 August 1929.

87 NAC, TSE Records, SSME MB, 4 January 1929; ibid., TSE Committee MB, 27 February 1929; *FP*, 15 March 1929

88 *FP*, 8, 22 March 1929; PAO, AG, 4-32, 1929, #3033, Memorandum from A.W. Rogers to Price, n.d. [March 1929]; Ontario, *Statutes*, 1929, c. 51

89 NAC, TSE Records, Committee MB, 7, 16, 20 May, 15, 24, 31 July 1929

90 Ibid., SSME MB, 1 October, 3 December 1929. See, e.g., ibid., TSE General Corr., Pre-1950, file 329.25, Rogers to SSME assistant secrtetary J.J. Kingsmill, 11 April 1929, which is one of a series of requests for information from the SSME throughout that year. PAO, AG, 4-32, 1928, #790, Rogers to John C. Martelon, Denver, Colo., 23 January 1929

91 *FP*, 27 June 1929. The SSME was sufficiently proud of its new-found reputation that a few days later its lawyer wrote to the Alberta attorney general's department to express concern that 'Standard Stock Exchanges' were operating in both Calgary and Edmonton and to suggest that these be induced to change their names so that the 'speculating public' would not be gulled into thinking that they were branches of the Toronto exchange; see NAC, TSE Records, General Corr., Pre-1950, file 334.1, A.J. Trebilcock to J.J. Frawley, 4 July 1929.

Chapter 8: Crash

1 I.W.C. Solloway, *Speculators and Politicians* (Westmount, Que., 1932), 91–2; NAC, TSE Records, SSME Member Corr., file 326.7, Solloway to SSME, 24 November 1928; *FP*, 3 April 1930; PAO, AG, 4-32, 1933, #2168, Memorandum on behalf of I.W.C. Solloway by Slaght and Cowan, n.d. [1934]. In his book Solloway claims to have had 1,500 employees, while his lawyers later gave a figure of 670 clerks (which might have excluded the sales force); Solloway said he belonged to fourteen exchanges; his lawyers noted eighteen seats on different exchanges, which seems much more plausible.

2 Solloway, *Speculators and Politicians*, 93–7; NAC, TSE Records, SSME MB, 2 February 1926

3 Solloway, *Speculators and Politicians*, 96 (quoted), 99–101

4 Ibid., 94, 98–9; NAC, TSE Records, SSME, MB, 7 December 1927; *FP*, 2 September 1927. The chronology of Solloway's SSME seat purchases is confused since the memorandum re *Rochester v. Solloway*, n.d. [October 1931] in NAC, TSE Records, SSME, Member Corr., file 326.10, claims that the second and third seats were bought in mid-1927 and that the third purchase was not recorded in the exchange's minute books, while the minutes of 7 December 1927 do record this purchase. The second seat was held in the name of A.E. Irvine, and the third in the name of F.E. Robinson.

5 See chapter 7 above.

6 Solloway, *Speculators and Politicians*, 103–8

7 NAC, TSE Records, General Corr., Pre-1950, file 332.6, Solloway to N.C. Urquhart, 22 October, 3, 7 (quoted) November 1928; J.J. Kingsmill to Solloway, 7, 14 November 1928

8 Ibid., SSME Member Corr., file 326.7, Solloway to SSME, 24 November 1928; ibid, file 326.8, Solloway to L.J. West, 12 January 1929; ibid., SSME MB, 5 December 1928

9 Solloway, *Speculators and Politicians*, 112–6; NAC, TSE Records, SSME Member Corr., file 326.8, Solloway to SSME, 17 June 1929; J.J. Kingsmill to Solloway, 3 July 1929; *FP*, 8 March, 29 August 1929

10 See John Brooks, *Once in Golconda: A True Drama of Wall Street, 1920–38* (New York, 1969), 113–26

11 See Fetherling, *Gold Diggers of 1929*, 108–26; the quotations are from 117, 122, 124.

12 Brooks, *Once in Golconda*, 126–8

13 NAC, TSE Records, Committee MB, 4, 6, 9, 15 November 1929; ibid., SSME MB, 7, 8, 12 November 1929

14 Brooks, *Once in Golconda*, quotations are from 22, 29; the story of the Stutz corner is told at 24–40.

15 Brooks, *Once in Golconda*, 69–72

16 See chapter 7 above.

17 *FP*, 22 August, 31 October 1929

18 See NAC, TSE Records, General Corr., Pre-1950, file 329.25, which contains a series of letters from Rogers; ibid., file 327.9, Felix Allard to assistant secretary J.J. Kingsmill, 11 May 1929, and Kingsmill to Allard, 16 May 1929, deals with a typical complaint that shares had been sold far below the market price reported on that day.

19 NAC, TSE Records, SSME Member Corr., file 323.19, J.J. Kingsmill to T.U. Fairlie, 18 February 1929; ibid., General Corr., Pre-1950, file 334.1, Kingsmill to D.C. Smith, 24 April 1929; file 334.19, A.J. Trebilcock to VSE, 28 January 1932; *FP*, 12 December 1929

20 NAC, TSE Records, SSME MB, 8, 9, 10, 31 July, 13 August, 23 October, 18, 21 November 1929; 21 January 1930

21 Ibid., 10 October (quoted); 18, 25, 26 November, 3, 17 December 1929

22 FP, 26 February 1926; PAO, AG, 4-32, 1928, #945, Memorandum from W.W. Dennison to W.H. Price, 31 August 1928

23 FP, 14, 21 November, 5 December 1929. At the banquet opening the new Standard exchange in June 1929, Attorney General Price had suggested that the public needed to be educated about short selling, and one member later admitted that most people believed it to be banned by exchange rules; see FP, 18 July 1929

24 Ibid., 7, 14 November, 5 December 1929

25 NAC, TSE Records, SSME Member Corr., file 326.9, Solloway to SSME, 16 November 1929; ibid., SSME MB, 19 November 1929

26 PAA, PP, file 117, Brownlee to Ferguson, 21 November 1929

27 Price to Ellison Young, 13 January 1931; quoted in J.T. Saywell, 'F.H. Deacon and Co., Investment Dealers: A Case Study of the Securities Industry, 1897–1945,' Ontario History 85 (1993), 175

28 W.H. Price interview with Larry Zolf, c. 1960, 7; I am indebted to J.T. Sawywell for a copy of this material.

29 PAA, PP, file 117, Price to Brownlee, 4 December 1929, Private and Confidential.

30 FP, 19, 26 December 1929; 16 January 1930

31 NAC, TSE Records, SSME MB, 5, 10 December 1929; FP, 5 December 1929

32 NAC, TSE Records, Committee MB, 20 November 1929; ibid., SSME Member Corr., file 324.16, Frank S. Leslie to SSME, 29 November 1929. The four interlisted stocks were International Nickel, British American Oil, Imperial Oil, and International Petroleum, which the TSE argued were really industrials, while the SSME claimed them as resource issues.

33 Ibid., SSME Member Corr., file 326.9, F.J. Shaughnessy, Solloway, Mills, to SSME, 3 January 1930; FP, 16 January 1930

34 Solloway, Speculators and Politicians, 131–51,: PAA, PP, file 217, J.E. Brownlee to R.J. Cromie, Vancouver Sun, 14 January 1930, Confidential; Price interview, 7 (quoted); Glenbow-Alberta Archives, ASE Records, CSE MB, 13, 31 January, 1 February 1930; NAC, TSE Records, General Corr., Pre-1950, file 327.24, CSE secretary to SSME president, 14 January 1930

35 NAC, TSE Records, SSME MB, 21, 22, 24 January 1930; FP, 16 January 1930

36 FP, 23 January 1930

37 FP, 23, 30 January 1930; PAA, PP, file 117, Price to J.F. Lymburn, 25 January 1930, Private and Confidential.

38 FP, 23, 30 January 1930; NAC, TSE Records, SSME MB, 22, 24 January 1930; ibid., TSE, General Corr., Pre-1950, file 327.24, SSME to CSE, 14 January 1930;

file 329.26, L.J. West to Price, 23 January 1930; file 274.3, Statement by TSE president C.E. Abbs, 22 January 1930

39 NAC, TSE Records, SSME MB, 24, 27, 28 January 1930

40 *FP*, 6 February 1930; PAA, PP, file 117, W.H. Price to J.F. Lymburn, 30 January 1930. In addition to Solloway and Mills those charged were William J. Smart and Maurice Young of Gibson, D.S. Paterson, Austin Campbell, and Edgar E. Maclean of Paterson; James J. Hepplestone and John W. Wray of Moysey; and Malcolm Stobie and Charles J. Forlong of Stobie, Forlong.

41 Solloway, *Speculators and Potlicians*, 209

42 NAC, TSE Records, SSME MB, 30 January 1930; PAA, PP, file 117, Price to J.F. Lymburn, 18 February 1930, Private and Confidential.

43 NAC, TSE Records, SSME MB, 31 January 1930, 12:45 p.m. Draft agreement with the AG of Ontario, n.d. [31 January 1930], attached to Price to J.F. Lymburn, 24 February 1930, Private and Confidential, in PAA, PP, file 117

44 NAC, TSE Records, SSME MB, 31 January 1930, 8 p.m. At this meeting the board also began to keep a set of 'Confidential Supplemental Minutes,' which cover the period 31 January 1930 to 7 October 1931 and may be found tipped into the back of the SSME MB covering 3 January 1929 to 30 December 1930. These supplemental minutes deal with the financial problems of individual firms, which are not named in the regular minutes, and their efforts to reduce short positions, secure additional capital, etc.; this supplement (hereafter cited as SSME Supp. MB) is quoted here.

45 NAC, TSE Records, SSME Member Corr., file 324.5, Homer L. Gibson and Co. to Trust and Guarantee Company, 3 February 1930 (with similar letters from the three other firms); agreements of Gibson, Paterson, Moysey, and Solloway, Mills with SSME, 4 March 1930

46 Glenbow-Alberta Archives, ASE Records, CSE MB, 31 January, 1 February 1930; PABC, VSE MB, 13, 15, 30, 31 January, 1 February 1930

47 NAC, TSE Records, SSME MB, 31 January 1930, 12:45 p.m.; *FP*, 6, 13 February 1930

48 NAC, TSE Records, SSME MB and Supp. MB, 3, 5 February 1930

49 NAC, TSE Records, SSME MB, 5 February 1930; *FP*, 6 February 1930; PAA, PP, file 117, Brownlee to Price, 29 January 1930; Price to J.F. Lymburn, 1 February 1930

50 NAC, TSE Records, SSME MB and Supp. MB, 10 February 1930

51 *Report of the Inter-Provincial Conference, February 10th to 14th [1930]* (Toronto, 1930), 2–3 and appendix A.

52 Ibid., 4–5 and appendix C.

53 Ibid.

54 The assumption was that all the assets of an individual seat holder (or a partnership)

would be available in the case of a bankruptcy; for that reason the Montreal, New York, and London exchanges forbade companies holding seats, but doing so was permitted on the SSME and TSE (where twenty-two of sixty-two seats were company-owned) on the grounds that companies might have more capital than individuals. See *FP*, 29 May 1930.

55 *Report of the Inter-Provincial Conference, [1930]*, 3–5 and appendix B.
56 PAA, PP, file 117, Price to Lymburn, 18, 24 February 1930, both Private and Confidential.
57 NAC, TSE Records, SSME Member Corr., file 324.5, W.J. Boland to A.J. Trebilcock, 11 February 1930; ibid., General Corr., Pre-1950, file 274.3, Mackenzie Williams to C.E. Abbs, 4 February 1930; ibid., TSE Committee MB, 3 February 1930; *FP*, 27 February 1930
58 Ibid., SSME MB, 18, 22, 24, 25 February, 3, 5 March 1930; ibid, Supp. MB, 20 March 1930
59 Ibid., SSME MB, 13 March 1930; ibid., SSME Member Corr., file 326.9, L.L. Masson to SSME, 19 March 1930; file 329.17, A.J. Trebilcock to William A. Orr, 31 March 1930
60 *FP*, 3 April 1930
61 NAC, TSE Records, General Corr., Pre-1950, file 329.20, A.J. Trebilcock to G.T. Clarkson, 24, 30 April 1930; file 329.26, Trebilcock to A.W. Rogers, 28 May 1930; ibid., SSME MB, 4 June 1930. Only nineteen of the fifty members bothered to turn up for the meeting.
62 *FP*, 15 May 1930; NAC, TSE Records, SSME MB, 22, 23 April 1930; Supp. MB, 22 April, 7 May 1930; ibid., SSME Member Corr., file 326.10, Solloway to SSME, 23 April 1930
63 NAC, TSE Records, SSME MB, 30 April, 20 May, 9 September, 17 October, 5 November 1930; Supp. MB, 4 June, 18 August, 3 November 1930
64 Solloway, *Speculators and Politicians*, 152–3, 187–90
65 NAC, TSE Records, SSME MB, 24, 26 June, 2 July 1930; Glenbow-Alberta Archives, ASE Records, CSE MB, 27 June 1930; PABC, VSE MB, 25 June 1930
66 *FP*, 26 June (quoted), 3 July 1930; NAC, TSE Records, SSME MB, 27 July 1930. Solloway, Mills formally surrendered its last SSME seat in October; see ibid., 14 October 1930.
67 See NAC, TSE Records, General Corr., Pre-1950, file 329.20, Rogers to A.P. Croker, 26 June 1930, for an example of the form letter, of which there are many others.
68 PAA, PP, file 117, W.H. Price to J.F. Lymburn, 29 October 1930, Private and Confidential; Solloway, *Speculators and Politicans*, 211–3
69 Solloway, *Speculators and Politicians*, 214–5; PAA, PP, file 117, Price to J.F. Lymburn, 31 October 1930, Private and Confidential; *FP*, 13 November 1930

70 *FP*, 2, 23 October, 6 November 1930; 19, 26 February, 26 March, 24 October 1931

71 A successor firm, Stobie, Forlong Assets Ltd., was created to try to manage a work out by gradually selling securities to pay off creditors, who were given debentures in the new company; further stock-market declines hampered this attempt, and by late 1932 only about 25 cents on the dollar was available to pay claims of between $3.5 million and $4 million. See *FP*, 24 October 1931; 15 October 1932

72 NAC, TSE Records, SSME MB, 27 July, 30 September, 14, 21 October, 3, 14 November 1930; ibid., General Corr., Pre-1950, file 329.17, A.J. Trebilcock to Ontario comptroller of revenue, 20 October, 6, 18 November, 29 December 1930. At the same time Morgan U. Kemerer, who had created controversy for the SSME in 1927–8 and had done no exchange business for more than a year, was expelled, and he was soon after convicted of selling unregistered securities under the SFPA; see ibid., Trebilcock to comptroller, 26 November 1930.

73 PAO, AG, 4-32, 1933, #2168, Memorandum on behalf of I.W.C. Solloway by Slaght and Cowan, n.d. [1934].

74 *FP*, 26 February 1931; Solloway, *Speculators and Politicians*, 193

75 *FP*, 11 February 1933; 15 February 1936

76 Ibid., 10 June 1933; 29 February 1936; 17 April 1937

77 Ibid., 10 June 1933; 15 February 1936

78 Ibid., 23, 30 September 1933. The latter issue carried a front-page cartoon showing an ordinary taxpayer being thrust into a Roman amphitheatre full of angry lions while Justice Minister Hugh Guthrie was helping Solloway, his tunic only slightly torn, into the safety of the seats, over the caption, 'Thumbs Up and Thumbs Down: It is reported that the Government has settled a $700,000 income tax claim against I.W.C. Solloway, former mining promoter, for $100,000.'

79 *FP*, 15, 29 February (quoted), 6 June 1936

80 *FP*, 17 April, 10 July 1937; Toronto *Daily Star*, 7 January 1938; Solloway, *Speculators and Politicians*, 155 (quoted).

81 PABC, AG Corr., GR 1723, reel B7487, file S-338–3, Chief Justice J.W. Farris to AG Gordon Wismer, 8 October 1949. Solloway was relicensed, and he re-entered business as I.W.C. Solloway and Associates promoting oil and mineral exploration, information for which I indebted to his son, Alan J. Solloway.

82 NAC, TSE Records, SSME MB, 19 September 1930

83 Ibid., 19 September, 9, 23, 30 October, 27 November 1930. In fact, Solloway, Mills did not surrender its last seat until 14 October according to the SSME MB.

84 Ibid., 19, 30 December 1930; ibid., TSE, General Corr., Pre-1950, file 333.19, A.J. Trebilcock to H.G. Garrett, 9 December 1930

85 *FP*, 16 October 1930; Carl Bergithon, *The Stock Exchange, with Special Reference to the Montreal Stock Exchange and the Montreal Curb Market* (Montreal, 1940), 49–50. Truax, Carsley and Company was the other firm liquidated.

86 PAM, WSE MB, 9 June 1931

87 Glenbow-Alberta Archives, ASE Records, CSE MB, 10 June 1930; 9, 19 June 1931

88 *FP*, 12 January 1931; PABC, VSE MB, 22 July, 26 August, 11 September, 3 November, 2 December 1930; ibid., AG Corr., file S-309-1-B, Memorandum from Garrett to AG, 12 January 1931

89 *FP*, 22, 29 January, 19 February, 1931; *FP* noted that Stimson's advertised claims were not strictly true since the company had distributed a municipal issue for the town of Scott, Saskatchewan, before the First World War, which had gone into default.

90 *FP*, 30 April, 4 June 1931; *Financial Times*, 26 June 1931 (quoted).

91 PABC, AG Corr., file S-309-1-G, Report on the Security Frauds Prevention Act by H.G. Garrett, 18 February 1931

Chapter 9: Into the Depths

1 NAC, TSE Records, SSME MB, 6 February 1931; *FP*, 12, 26 February 1931

2 Charles P. Kindelberger, *The World in Depression, 1929–1939* (Berkeley, 1973), 157–70

3 NAC, TSE Records, SSME MB, 21 September 1931; MUA, MSE Records, MCM MB, 21 September 1931; PABC, VSE MB, 21 September 1931; PAM, WSE MB, 21 September 1931; *FP*, 26 September 1931

4 NAC, TSE Records, SSME MB, 22 September 1931; MUA, MSE Records, MCM MB, 22 September 1931; PABC, VSE MB, 22 September 1931; *FP*, 3 October 1931

5 NAC, TSE Records, SSME MB, 1 October 1931

6 Ibid., 5, 7, 9 October 1931

7 *FP*, 4, 11, 18, 25 June, 2 July 1931

8 The quotations are from NAC, Graham Spry Papers, Diary, 6 October 1931, and Bank of Nova Scotia Archives, Directors MB, 6 October 1931; both are cited in J.T. Saywell, 'F.H. Deacon and Co., Investment Dealers: A Case Study of the Securities Industry, 1897–1945,' *Ontario History*, 85 (1993), 176–7. Not until March 1933 did Bennett make a public reference to the risk of a run on the banks in answer to a parliamentary question; see *FP*, 1 April 1933. On the links between the Royal and McDougall and Cowans, see James L. Darroch, *Canadian Banks and Global Competitiveness* (Montreal, 1994), 128.

9 *FP*, 10, 24 October, 7 November 1931. The McDougall firm owed its secured creditors $16.1 million, Greenshields $2.1 million, and Watson $1.2 million while customers with unpaid balances numbered 2,298, 1,794, and 274 respectively. McDougall had borrowed $2.7 million in the United States including $710,000 from forty-nine different New England institutions; its largest loan from a Canadian bank was $750,000, though overall its loans in Canada totalled much more than in the

United States. Greenshields had also borrowed $710,000 from thirteen New England institutions versus $1.1 million in Canada, and Watson had four New England loans worth $140,000 as against Canadian debts of $660,000

10 *FP*, 10, 17 October 1931; MUA, MSE Records, MCM MB, 8, 15 October 1931; NAC, TSE Records, SSME 'Confidential Supplemental Minutes, 1930,' 5 October 1931 (tipped into SSME MB, 1929–30); Glenbow-Alberta Archives, ASE Records, CSE MB, 13, 21 October, 3, 9, 24 November, 22 December 1931

11 *FP*, 10, 17 October 1931; NAC, TSE Records, General Corr., Pre-1950, file 332.1, acting assistant secretary, MSE, to A.E. Marks, 13 Octobver 1931; ibid., SSME MB, 7, 9, 13, 23 October 1931

12 *FP*, 31 October, 14 November 1931, 9 January, 26 March 1932

13 Ibid., 7, 21, 28 November 1931, 9 January, 20 February, 30 April, 19 August 1932

14 NAC, TSE Records, General Corr., Pre-1950, file 332.1, Printed circular from secretary-treasurer Grant Johnston, MCM, 24 October 1931; Mitchell to W.E.J. Luther, 28 October 1931 (quoted); ibid., SSME MB, 18 November 1931

15 *FP*, 21, 28 November 1931; NAC, TSE Records, General Corr., Pre-1950, file 332.1, TSE acting assistant secretary A.E. Marks to MSE assistant secretary, 31 October, 2, 24 November 1931

16 *FP*, 19, 26 December 1931, 9, 16 January 1932

17 *FP*, 26 December 1931; NAC, TSE Records, General Corr., Pre-1950, file 327.33, CBA president J.A. McLeod to TSE president G.C. Mitchell, 19 December 1931

18 PABC, VSE MB, 20 December 1931; PAM, WSE MB, 21 December 1931; MUA, MSE Records, MCM MB, 21 December 1931; NAC, TSE Records, SSME MB, 21 December 1931; ibid., TSE, General Corr., Pre-1950, file 327.33, G.W. Nicholson to J.A. McLeod, 8 January 1932; McLeod to G.C. Mitchell, 9 January 1932

19 *FP*, 26 December 1931, 9 January 1932

20 *FP*, 23 January 1932; NAC, TSE Records, General Corr., Pre-1950, file 327.33, J.A. McLeod to G.C. Mitchell, 18 January 1932; CBA secretary Henry T. Ross to Mitchell, 20 January 1932; A.E. Marks to Ross, 8 March 1932. The last shows that for 19–29 February TSE clients sold $485,900 worth of U.S. securities and bought only $290,400, while British and European securities worth $43,100 were purchased as against sales of $27,300. The file contains similar statements for the spring of 1932 which show large surpluses of sales of U.S. securities as against purchases. See also MUA, MSE Records, MCM MB, 19, 26 January 1932.

21 MUA, MSE Records, box 418, Legal Opinions, 1917–33, Lafleur, MacDougall, Macfarlane and Barclay to E.M. Smith and Eric McCuaig, 8 January 1932; Smith, Fairbanks and Company to MSE chair, 11 January 1932, enclosing the opinion and urging that all minimums should be dropped and free trading resumed.

22 NAC, TSE Records, General Corr., Pre-1950, file 327.33, McLeod to G.C. Mitchell, 30 December 1931. The peg for the smaller Banque Canadienne Nationale was

reduced only $5, and after second thoughts the Bank of Commerce was given similar treatment. See ibid., Henry T. Ross to Mitchell, 2 January 1932; *FP*, 9 January 1932

23 *FP*, 9, 16 January 1932; NAC, TSE Records, General Corr., Pre-1950, file 332.1, Printed circulars from MSE secretary-treasurer A.S. Cassils to members, 8, 11 January, 2 February 1932

24 MUA, MSE Records, MCM MB, 9, 14, 15 January, 2, 6, 13, 18 February 1932; NAC, TSE Records, General Corr., Pre-1950, file 332.1, G.C. Mitchell to W.E.J. Luther, 15 February 1932, noting that Canada Wire and Cable had approached the TSE about dropping its peg; Printed circular from A.S. Cassils to MSE members, 17 February 1932; *FP*, 20, 27 February 1932

25 NAC, TSE Records, General Corr., Pre-1950, file 332.1, G.C. Mitchell to W.E.J. Luther, 10 March 1932; Luther to Mitchell, 11 March 1932

26 MUA, MSE, MCM MB, 9, 12 April 1932; NAC, TSE Records, General Corr., Pre-1950, file 327.33, G.C. Mitchell to J.A. McLeod, 25, 28 April 1932; McLeod to Mitchell, 27 April 1932

27 NAC, TSE Records, General Corr., Pre-1950, file 332.1, W.E.J. Luther to J.A. McLeod, 29 April 1932; ibid., file 327.33, Henry T. Ross to G.C. Mitchell, 17 May 1932; *FP*, 28 May 1932

28 *FP*, 28 May, 4 June 1932. At the same time, exchange audits revealed that two other Montreal firms, Johnston and Ward and Hanson Brothers, were in shaky condition, and the registrar of the Quebec SFPA discussed the matter with the premier, but it was decided to take no action against them at the time though both were warned to accept no new accounts; see MUA, MSE Records, MCM MB, 12 July 1932.

Chapter 10: The Ordeal of F.H. Deacon

1 J.W. Popkin, *The First Century: A History of the Investment Department, Sun Life Assurance Company of Canada, 1871–1973* (n.p., n.d.), 33. The Sun lost at least $125 million as a result of a decline in the market value of shares after 1929.

2 J.T. Saywell, 'F.H. Deacon and Co., Investment Dealers: A Case Study of the Securities Industry, 1897–1945,' *Ontario History* 85 (1993), 175, quotes the Bank of Nova Scotia's *Manual* dated 1929.

3 *FP*, 10 October 1931; *The Toronto Stock Exchange: Toward an Ideal Market* (Toronto, 1983), 12

4 PAO, F.H. Deacon and Company Records, box 2, State of the Company, Memorandum re TSE membership between August 1929 and November 1932, n.d.

5 E.P. Neufeld, *The Financial System of Canada: Its Growth and Development* (Toronto, 1972), 509 (quoted). Neufeld adds that, paradoxically, it was Wood, Gundy's expansion in the 1920s that 'laid the foundation for its emerging as the

dominant underwriting firm in the period following the near disastrous years of the Great Depression.'

6 In addition to the Deacon records in the PAO (hereafter PAO, F.H. Deacon) I have also been fortunate to make use of an unpublished manuscript by J.T. Saywell entitled 'F.H. Deacon, Hodgson Inc.: A Biography ' (1986) (hereafter Saywell, Deacon ms.), which also relied upon some interviews and other private collections, as well as the same author's 'F.H. Deacon and Co.' in *Ontario History*, 85 (1993), 167–91

7 Saywell, Deacon ms., 12–3, 26, 36–7; PAO, F.H. Deacon, box 2, State of the Company, Memorandum re interview with Mr. Paterson and Col. Edmonds re Dominion Tax, 4 December 1934 (quoted).

8 PAO, F.H. Deacon, box 2, State of the Company, Memorandum re interview with Mr Paterson and Col. Edmonds re Dominion Tax, 4 December 1934; ibid., box 4, Personnel, 1933–55, Memorandum re T.G. Drew-Brook, 4 December 1933, Confidential.

9 On Drew-Brook and his exotic activities in the Second World War helping to recruit for and run a clandestine unit to train British spies which was located just east of Toronto, see David Stafford, *Camp X: Canada's School for Secret Agents, 1941–45* (Toronto, 1986).

10 PAO, F.H. Deacon, box 4, Personnel, 1933–55, Memorandum re T.G. Drew-Brook, 4 December 1933, Confidential.

11 Deacon's TSE audit, 30 September 1929, cited in Saywell, Deacon ms., 49; PAO, F.H. Deacon, box 4, Personnel, 1933–55, Memorandum re T.G. Drew-Brook, 4 December 1933, Confidential; ibid., box 2, State of the Company, Memorandum re interview with Mr Paterson and Col. Edmonds re Dominion Tax, 4 December 1934

12 Certificate by Brokers' Auditor, 15 November 1929, quoted in Saywell, 'Deacon and Co.,' 176; brochure quoted in Saywell, Deacon ms., 50–1

13 PAO, F.H. Deacon, box 2, State of the Company, Memorandum for Mr E.G. Long, 23 October 1937

14 Ibid., box 3, Bank of Commerce, 1933–4, Deacon to Logan, 17 December 1934, Personal.

15 These events are recounted in great detail in ibid., box 2, State of the Company, Memorandum re Colonel Gordon and Clarkson, Gordon and Dilworth, Our Auditors, 28 November 1932. Note the resentment evident in the title of this memorandum: 'Our Auditors.'

16 Saywell, Deacon ms., 54

17 PAO, F.H. Deacon, box 2, State of the Company, Memorandum re conversation with Col. Gordon, 5 January 1931 [i.e., 1932]; Memorandum re Colonel Gordon and Clarkson, Gordon and Dilworth, Our Auditors, 28 November 1932. Ironically, the

same week *FP*, 9 January 1932, reported proudly that the TSE had not had a single case of insolvency since Gordon started his audits.

18 PAO, F.H. Deacon, box 2, State of the Company, Memorandum re Colonel Gordon and Clarkson, Gordon and Dilworth, Our Auditors, 28 November 1932

19 Ibid., Deacon to directors of Mutual Life, n.d. [3 May 1932], Confidential; Memorandum re Colonel Gordon and Clarkson, Gordon and Dilworth, Our Auditors, 28 November 1932

20 Ibid., Minutes of meeting in board room at Bank of Nova Scotia re F.H. Deacon and Co., 20 May 1932; Memorandum re Stock Exchange Committee, 22 June 1934, stating that another $150,000 worth of life insurance was pledged to Morrow Screw and Nut.

21 Ibid., Continuation of memorandum re meeting with Col. Gordon, Mr Franks, Col. Mitchell, 19 June 1933; ibid., box 3, Bank of Commerce, 1933–4, Deacon to S.J. Logan, 17 December 1934, Personal; Royal Bank, 1932–46, Memorandum of interview with Mr Rea and Mr Dobson, assistant general manager, Wednesday, at 10.30 a.m., 17 May 1932

22 Ibid., Bank of Montreal, 1932–3, Deacon to Clark, 6, 10 May 1932, Personal.

23 Ibid., Deacon to F.W.C.C. Clark, 14 September 1932; Deacon to S.C. Norsworthy, 20 September 1932, Personal; Norsworthy to Deacon, 22 September 1932, Personal; memorandum re F.H. Deacon and Co. account and Bank of Montreal, 8 February 1935, Personal (quoted).

24 Ibid., box 2, State of the Company, Memorandum re [meeting with] J.A. McLeod, 2 November 1932; ibid., box 3, Bank of Montreal, 1932–3, Memorandum of interview with Mr MacFadyen, supervisor, Bank of Montreal, 19 December 1932; Deacon to Mewburn, 21 December 1932

25 Ibid., Deacon to Mewburn, 3 January 1933; Deacon to Clark, 31 July 1933, Personal (quoted); Memorandum re Bank of Montreal loan, 14 August 1933; Memorandum re Bank of Montreal loan, 15 August 1933

26 Ibid., Memorandum of interview with Mr Clark, Bank of Montreal, 22 May 1933; Deacon to M.W. Wilson, 20 February 1934; Memorandum re F.H. Deacon and Co. account and Bank of Montreal, 8 February 1935, Personal; contains Deacon's angry recollection of the remark by the AGM of the Royal, quoted above, that the 'damned Bank of Montreal ... wouldn't live up to their agreement.'

27 Deacon family legend has it that antagonism between Deacon and Gordon existed from before the First World War, when they were militia officers at the Niagara camp and Deacon declined to hold up a troop train for more than half an hour to await the arrival of Gordon's tardy regiment; see Saywell, Deacon ms., 54.

28 Philip Creighton, *A Sum of Yesterdays* (Toronto, 1984), 115, says that three Toronto firms dominated public accounting in Ontario in the 1920s and 1930s. Clarkson,

Gordon had the largest practice, though Edwards Morgan had a better client list; Thorne, Mulholland, Howson and McPherson trailed behind.

29 Deacon was particularly annoyed because someone from A.E. Ames and Company had telephoned Drew-Brook to describe what had occurred at the auditors even before he had returned to his own office; he later complained about this leak to the senior Gordon, who huffily replied that his firm had a thirty-five-year record of keeping things confidential. On his way back to the office Deacon had spoken to T.A. Bradshaw on Bay Street, who could have passed on the information to his former partners at Ames, but Deacon continued to blame the auditors; see PAO, F.H. Deacon, box 2, State of the Company, Memorandum of interview with Col. Gordon, Mr Franks, and Col. Mitchell, 19 June 1933.

30 Ibid., box 3, Bank of Montreal, 1932–3, Deacon to S.C. Mewburn, 21 December 1933, reporting comments of E.J. Davis, another large Deacon creditor.

31 Ibid., box 2, State of the Company, Gordon to banks and loan companies, 15 September 1932; ibid., box 3, Bank of Montreal, 1932–3, Memorandum of interview with Mr MacFadyen, Supervisor, Bank of Montreal, 19 December 1932

32 Ibid., box 2, State of the Company, Memorandum re meeting on 21 October 1932; Memorandum re Colonel Gordon and Clarkson, Gordon and Dilworth, Our Auditors, 28 November 1932

33 Ibid., Memorandum re Colonel Gordon, 2 November 1933; Memorandum re Clarkson, Gordon and Dilworth, Our Auditors, 28 November 1933 (both quoted).

34 Ibid., Memorandum for the Hon. N.W. Rowell, 2 November 1932 (quoted); Memorandum for the Hon. Mr Rowell, K.C., 9 November 1932

35 Ibid., Rowell to Deacon, 11 November 1932, Personal; Memorandum of interview with Col. Gordon, Mr Franks, and Col. Mitchell, 19 June 1933. If this latter claim was true, no evidence of such advice survives in the Deacon collection; it seems more likely that he was trying to keep Gordon and the others off balance.

36 Ibid., Memorandum of interview with J.A. McLeod, president [of the Canadian] Bankers Association, 2 November 1932; Memorandum re [meeting with] J.A. McLeod, 2 November 1932 (quoted).

37 Ibid., Minutes of meeting in the board room at Bank of Nova Scotia re F.H. Deacon and Co., 20 May 1932; Memorandum re Colonel Gordon and Clarkson, Gordon and Dilworth, Our Auditors, 28 November 1932

38 Toronto *Mail and Empire*, 21 April 1933; PAO, F.H. Deacon, box 2, State of the Company, Continuation of memorandum re meeting with Col. Gordon, Mr Franks, Col. Mitchell, 19 June 1933

39 PAO, F.H. Deacon, box 2, State of the Company, Memorandum of interview with Col. Gordon, Mr Franks, and Col. Mitchell, 19 June 1933. It was at this point that Deacon rehearsed his grievance that somebody had leaked the news of what had

happened at Clarkson, Gordon's offices a year earlier when he had refused point-blank to resign from the exchange. Since Clarkson denied talking to anyone, Deacon claimed that one of the Gordons, father or son, must have been the source of the information; Gordon was not amused.

40 Ibid., Memorandum of interview with Col. Gordon, Mr Franks, and Col. Mitchell, 19 June 1933; Continuation of memorandum re meeting with Col. Gordon, Mr Franks, Col. Mitchell, 19 June 1933 (both quoted).

41 Ibid., box 3, Bank of Montreal, 1932–3, Deacon to Mitchell, 19 June 1933, Personal.

42 Ibid., box 2, State of the Company, Memorandum re F.H. Deacon and Co., 12 June 1936, which shows clients' debit balances levelling off at just over $1 million for September, October, and November 1933 before starting a steady decline; ibid., box 3, Bank of Montreal, 1932–3, Deacon to B.L. Mitchell, Royal Bank, Toronto, 24 August 1936

43 Ibid., Royal Bank, 1932–46, Memorandum of interview with Mr Rea and Mr Dobson, assistant general manager, Wednesday, May 17 at 10.30 a.m., 1932; ibid., box 2, State of the Company, Minutes of meeting in board room at Bank of Nova Scotia re F.H. Deacon and Co., 20 May 1932

44 Ibid., box 3, Bank of Montreal, 1932–3, Deacon to F.W.C.C. Clark, 14 September 1932; Memorandum of interview with Mr D.C. Rea, Royal Bank, 21 February 1933; Memorandum re Bank of Montreal loan, 14 August 1933

45 Ibid., box 4, Personnel, 1933–55, Drew-Brook to Deacon, 2 December 1933; Memorandum re T.G. Drew-Brook, 4 December 1933, Confidential; Jennison to Deacon, 12 December 1933; ibid., box 2, Administrative, Memorandum re Stewart Robertson, 8 December 1933

46 Ibid., box 4, Personnel, 1933–55, Memorandum re T.G. Drew-Brook, 4 December 1933, Confidential.

47 Ibid., box 2, State of the Company, Memorandum re meeting on 21 October 1932; Memorandum re Colonel Gordon, 2 November 1932

48 Ibid., box 4, Personnel, 1933–55, Memorandum re T.G. Drew-Brook, 4 December 1933, Confidential.

49 Ibid., box 2, State of the Company, Memorandum re statement of F.H. Deacon and Co. prepared by Campbell, Lawless, Parker and Black for period ending 31 October 1934

50 Ibid., Memorandum re Stock Exchange Committee, 22 June 1934; Memorandum re Statement of F.H. Deacon and Co. prepared by Campbell, Parker, Lawless and Black for the period ending 31 October 1934 (both quoted).

51 Ibid., Deacon to TSE president Harold Franks, 9 March 1934, Confidential. The other members of the 'small committee' were now George Blaikie and G.W. Nicholson and N.C. Urquhart (formerly from the SSME following the merger of the two exchanges).

52 Ibid., Memorandum re interview with Colonel Drew, 19 February 1934; as further evidence of Gordon's malign influence, Deacon pointed out that the auditors had altered the amount of capital required to cover the debits in partly secured accounts from 25 to 33.3 per cent at the start of 1934, thus reducing the firm's capital account from $15,200 to $8,400.

53 NAC, TSE Records, MB, 16 February 1934; PAO, F.H. Deacon, box 2, State of the Company, Deacon to Franks, 9 March 1934, Confidential.

54 PAO, F.H. Deacon, box 2, State of the Company, Memorandum re Stock Exchange Committee, 22 June 1934

55 Ibid., Memorandum [from Edmonds] re discussion with Mr Pettit re Clients' Debit Balances, 25 June 1934

56 Ibid., Memorandum re Stock Exchange Committee, 22 June 1934

57 Ibid., Memorandum re meeting at Col. Gordon's office, 25 July 1934

58 NAC, TSE Records, MB, 24 July 1934

59 PAO, F.H. Deacon, box 2, State of the Company, Memorandum re meeting at Col. Gordon's office, 25 July 1934; Memorandum re instructions from the [TSE] Committee to F.H. Deacon, 25 July 1934

60 FP, 16 October 1934; NAC, TSE Records, MB, 16 October 1934

61 PAO, F.H. Deacon, box 2, clipping from Hush, 1 September 1934; State of the Company, Memorandum re statement of F.H. Deacon and Co. prepared by Campbell, Lawless, Parker and Black for period ending 31 October 1934

62 Ibid., Memorandum re interview with Colonel Drew, 19 February 1934; Memorandum re statement of F.H. Deacon and Company prepared by Campbell, Lawless, Parker and Black for the period ending 31 October 1934

63 Ibid., box 3, Bank of Montreal, 1932–3, Deacon to M.W. Wilson, 20 February 1934; Memorandum re F.H. Deacon and Co. account and Bank of Montreal, 8 February 1935; Bank of Commerce, 1933–4, Deacon to S.H. Logan, 17 December 1934, Personal; ibid., box 2, State of the Company, Memorandum re statement of F.H. Deacon and Co. prepared by Campbell, Lawless, Parker and Black for period ending 31 October 1934

64 Ibid., box 3, Bank of Montreal, 1932–3, Memorandum re Royal Bank and My Personal Loan of $300,000, 22 March 1935

65 Ibid., box 2, Company History, 1938, Memorandum re Commissions and Operating Expenses of F.H. Deacon and Co., 1929–37, n.d.; State of the Company, Memorandum re F.H. Deacon finances, 12 June 1936; NAC, TSE Records, MB, 16, 30 December 1935

66 NAC, TSE Records, MB, 29 January 1937. The Montreal Stock Exchange had no fixed provisions, though its panel of auditors was supposed to watch carefully to see that members' capital was not unduly depleted or that too much money had been loaned on one security or group of securities. Members were required to report funds

borrowed on collateral of Canadian securities, and the monthly figures were published; see Carl Bergithon, *The Stock Exchange, with Special Reference to the Montreal Stock Exchange and the Montreal Curb Market* (Montreal, 1940), 50–1.

67 PAO, F.H. Deacon, box 3, Bank of Nova Scotia, 1933–7, Memorandum of interview with Mr Fraser, Bank of Nova Scotia, 8 February 1937; Memorandum re Bank of Nova Scotia interview with J.A. McLeod, 9 January 1937

68 *FP*, 25 September 1937; Saywell, Deacon ms., 86–7. At the same time Williams, McLean and Bell was forced by the TSE to close; see NAC, TSE Records, MB, 7, 8, 13 October 1937

69 Saywell, Deacon ms., 88

70 NAC, TSE Records, MB, 1 March 1938

71 In 1937 the free-capital requirement had been fixed at 7.5 per cent on balances over $250,000 (see n. 65 above), and it is not clear when the limit was raised to $500,000.

72 At the same time S.R. MacKellar and Company was petitioned into bankruptcy after the TSE auditors discovered they had been misled; the firm eventually secured additional capital and was readmitted to membership; see NAC, TSE Records, MB, 9 March, 6 April 1938.

73 PAO, F.H. Deacon, box 3, Bank of Montreal, 1932–3, Memorandum re interview with Mr Dobson, general manager of Royal Bank, Montreal, 16 March 1939; Deacon to Dobson, 17 March 1939, Personal; Deacon to Wilson, 31 March 1939, Personal.

74 Ibid., box 2, State of the Company, Memorandum of interview with Col. Gordon, Mr Franks, and Col. Mitchell, 19 June 1933

75 Under the Quebec Security Frauds Prevention Act of 1930 the MSE and the Montreal Curb were empowered to appoint an exchange auditor to oversee the auditing panel and fix dates for surprise audits; the boards also had power to order full or partial audits of members at any time; see Bergithon, *Stock Exchange*, 49–50.

76 PAO, F.H. Deacon, box 2, State of the Company, Memorandum for the Hon. N.W. Rowell, 2 November 1932

Chapter 11: Reform

1 PAO, AG, 4-32, 1931, #338, Rogers to Lapointe, 27 February 1930, enclosing *Report of the Inter-Provincial Conference, February 10th to 14th [1930]*, of which appendix C reiterated the recommendations of the 1926 interprovincial conference, where the premiers had agreed that they should regulate share sales by all but companies such as banks and railways which fell under exclusive federal jurisdiction, as well as any other undertakings specifically exempted by the federal government by order-in-council. For an account of the conference, see chapter 8.

2 Ibid., Rogers to Mulvey, 28 May 1930; Price to R.H. Pooley, 26 January 1931

3 See chapter 7; *AG for Manitoba v. AG for Canada* (1929), *Appeal Cases*, 260; PAO, AG, 4-32, 1931, #338, Memorandum from Rogers, n.d. [1930]. Ontario meanwhile continued to investigate share sales by federal companies, citing the 1931 decision in *R. v. Hazzard et al.*, where it was held that a bartender selling liquor without a provincial licence could not escape regulation by arguing that the hotel was owned by a federal company; see *FP*, 27 February 1932.

4 PAA, AG, 'Mayland v. Lymburn,' item 3540, J.L. Johnston to Lymburn, 2 January 1931; Lymburn to Frawley, 4 February 1931; Frawley to Lymburn, 11 February 1931; A.A. McGillivray to Frawley, 27 February 1931

5 *Mayland and Mercury Oils v. Lymburn and Frawley* (1931), 25 *Alberta Law Reports*, 310; Harvey is quoted at 313, 314, 316.

6 PAO, AG, 4-32, 1931, #338, Pooley to Price, 12 January 1931; Price to Pooley, 26 January 1931; Price to provincial AGs (except PEI), 7 February 1931

7 *Report of Inter-Provincial Conference, [1930]*, appendix C; Canada, *Statutes*, 1930, c. 11, s. 5, which added s. 231a to the Criminal Code in the words proposed by the conference; PAO, AG, 4-32, 1931, #338, Price to Guthrie, 7 February 1931; Cahan to Price, 14 February 1931; PAA, AG, 'Mayland v. Lymburn,' item 3540, Lymburn to Cahan, 14 May 1931; ibid., item 3541, Cahan to Lymburn, 24 May 1931

8 PAO, AG, 4-32, 1931, #961, Brownlee to Price, 17 April 1931; Price to Tilley, 12 May 1931; Price to Guthrie, 29 May 1931; PAA, AG, 'Mayland v. Lymburn,' item 3541, Price to Brownlee, 22 April 1931

9 *Lymburn v. Mayland* (1932), *Appeal Cases*, 320–1

10 PAA, AG, 'Mayland v. Lymburn,' item 3544, J.J. Frawley to H.G. Garrett, 28 November 1931; *Lymburn v. Mayland* (1932), *Appeal Cases*, 319–20

11 *Lymburn v. Mayland* (1932), *Appeal Cases*, 318. Atkin is quoted at 324, 326.

12 PAA, AG, 'Mayland v. Lymburn,' item 3544, Garrett to Frawley, 24 February 1932; Frawley to Rogers, 20 February 1932; Tilley to Frawley, 6 February 1932

13 PAO, AG, 4-32, 1933, #31, Memorandum to AG from Edward Bayly, 9 January 1933

14 NAC, R.B. Bennett Papers, vol. 173, 116163, 116260–3, Agenda for Interprovincial Conference, 17 January 1933; Resolutions of the Dominion-Provincial Conference, Ottawa, January 17–9, 1933

15 *Report of the Dominion Provincial Conference, 1934* (Ottawa, 1934), 3–4; Canada, *Statutes*, 1934, c. 33; *FP*, 5 May, 16 June 1934

16 Joel Seligman, *The Transformation of Wall Street: A History of the Securities and Exchange Commission and Modern Corporate Finance* (Boston, 1982), 1–121

17 Ontario, *Statutes*, 1931, c. 48; *FP*, 2 April 1931; PAO, AG, 4-32, 1931, #1234, copy of Order in Council, 6 May 1931, appointing Drew at a salary of $10,000 from

1 May. At the end of the year A.W. Rogers, who had mainly been responsible for enforcing the SFPA for the AG since 1928, left the civil service and joined the staff of the Canadian Bankers Association in Montreal.

18 Ontario, *Statutes*, 1932, c. 53, s. 36; 1933, c. 59, s. 33

19 British American Oil, Imperial Oil, and International Petroleum were interlisted, along with International Nickel and Consolidated Mining and Smelting, being claimed as industrials by the TSE and as resource stocks by the SSME.

20 NAC, TSE Records, SSME MB, 1, 10, 17 April, 8 May, 14 June, 7 July, 20 August 1931; *FP*, 5, 12 March 1931

21 NAC, TSE Records, SSME MB, 4 June, 14, 15, 17 July, 20, 26 August, 9 September 1931; see also 'Confidential Supplemental Minutes, 1930' tipped into SSME MB for January 1929–December 1930, for record of meetings of 10 March, 15 July 1931.

22 NAC, TSE Records, SSME MB, 20 August 1931; *FP*, 18, 25 July 1931

23 *FP*, 9 January 1932; NAC, TSE Records, SSME MB, 4, 19 December 1931; 25 January, 23 February 1932; ibid., TSE General Meeting MB, 28, 30 December 1931

24 NAC, TSE Records, SSME MB, 21, 22 March 1932 (both quoted).

25 NAC, TSE Records, General Corr., Pre-1950, file 333.32, G.W. Nicholson to G.C. Mitchell, 23, 29 March, 9 April 1932; Mitchell to Nicholson, 24 March, 26 April 1932; ibid., file 334.8, Memorandum of agreement, 26 April 1932; ibid., TSE General Meeting MB, 22 April 1932 ibid., SSME MB, 5, 11, 25 April 1932;

26 Ontario, *Statutes*, 1931, c. 48; NAC, TSE Records, SSME MB, 13 May 1931. On 1 September 1931 the Quebec SFPA also required exchange members to have an annual audit followed by a surprise inspection four to eight months later; see NAC, TSE Records, General Corr. Pre-1950, file 332.1, H.J. Child, Montreal Curb Market, to TSE president, 3 September 1931.

27 NAC, TSE Records, General Corr., Pre-1950, file 333.3, Drew to Nicholson, 11 January 1933, A.J. Trebilcock to Drew, 6 February 1932. The issue arose because the exchange was claiming repayment of the advance made to the bankrupt firm out of the proceeds of the sale of its seat.

28 Ibid., Drew to Nicholson, 1 March 1932; Drew to SSME secretary, 29 February 1932 (both quoted); A.J. Trebilcock to Drew, 5 March 1932. Eventually the complaints about this case reached the *FP*, which reported in May that Masterson and Co. had gone into liquidation as a result of the unfavourable publicity; see *FP*, 9 April, 21 May 1932.

29 NAC, TSE Records, General Corr., Pre-1950, file 333.3, Drew to SSME secretary, 10 March 1932 (two letters); A.J. Trebilcock to Drew, 11 March, 6 April 1932; Drew to Trebilcock, 14 March 1932; ibid., SSME MB, 9 February, 5 April, 4, 10 May 1932

30 Ibid., General Corr. Pre-1950, file 333.3, Trebilcock to registrar, Ontario Securities

Commission, 25 June 1932; Palen to Trebilcock, 30 June 1932; Trebilcock to Palen, 5 July 1932

31 PABC, AG, Corr., file S-309-1-G, Report on the SFPA by H.G. Garrett, 18 February 1931

32 *Financial Times*, 22 April 1932 (quoted); *FP*, 30 April 1932; NAC, TSE Records, General Corr., Pre-1950, file 333.2, W.E. Segsworth to G.W. Nicholson, 28 May 1932; A.J. Trebilcock to Segsworth, 2 June 1932; *FP*, 2 July, 29 October 1932. The exchange representatives were N.C. Urquhart, Manning Doherty, and J.T. Cannon.

33 *FP*, 24 September, 8, 15 October 1932; NAC, TSE Records, General Meeting MB, 20 September 1932; ibid., General Corr. Pre-1950, file 333.32, G.C. Mitchell to G.W. Nicholson, 21 September 1932; A.J. Trebilcock to Mitchell, 5 October 1932; ibid., SSME MB, 14 September, 5 October 1932

34 *FP*, 28 January, 4, 11 February 1933

35 NAC, TSE Records, General Meeting MB, 23 January, 27 April, 1 May 1933; *FP*, 25 February, 4 March 1933

36 *FP*, 25 November, 9, 16 December 1933, 3 February 1934; NAC, TSE Records, General Meeting MB, 5 December 1933; ibid., TSE MB, 3 February 1934

37 *FP*, 23 December 1933, 10 February 1934

38 NAC, TSE Records, MB, 26 April 1934

39 Ibid., 16, 20, 22, 27 February 1934; *FP*, 17 March 1934

40 NAC, TSE Records, MB, 9, 10, 13 April 1934; *FP*, 14 April 1934 (quoted).

41 NAC, TSE Records, MB, 11 April 1934

42 *FP*, 19 May 1934

43 *FP*, 15 April, 20 May 1933

44 *FP*, 31 March (quoted), 7, 14 April 1934; interview with Chalmers by J.T. Saywell, 12 October 1972, 22–3, courtesy of the interviewer.

45 *FP*, 14 April 1934

46 *FP*, 7 July 1934

47 *FP*, 14 April, 21 July 1934

48 NAC, TSE Records, MB, 14, 28 August, 11, 18, 20 September 1934; *FP*, 20 October 1934

49 On the Hepburn government's dismissal of Conservative appointees, see J.T. Saywell, *'Just Call Me Mitch': The Life of Mitchell F. Hepburn* (Toronto, 1991), 170–3.

50 *Who's Who in Canada*, 1945–6 (Toronto, 1946). Later, of course, Drew would become leader of the Ontario Conservatives and premier in 1943, before going to Ottawa as federal Opposition leader in 1948.

51 *Who's Who in Canada*, 1945–6 (Toronto, 1946). Roebuck was later appointed to the Senate, where he served for many years.

52 PAO, M.F. Hepburn, Corr., box 177, Roebuck to Drew, 15 September 1934. Drew to Roebuck, 18 September 1934; Drew to Hepburn, 18 September 1934
53 PAO, M.F. Hepburn, Corr., box 177, Drew to Hepburn, 28 September 1934
54 Toronto *Daily Star*, 27, 29 September 1934. Drew carefully collected press clippings from all across the province concerning the controversy, which may be found in PAO, George Drew Papers, Scrapbook, 1934
55 PAO, M.F. Hepburn, Corr., box 177, Roebuck to Hepburn, 29 September 1934
56 Toronto *Daily Star* and *Telegram*, 1 October 1934
57 PAO, M.F. Hepburn, Corr., box 177, Drew to Hepburn, 2 October 1934
58 Toronto *Globe*, 2, 6 (quoted) October 1934
59 Toronto *Daily Star* and *Telegram*, 3 October 1934. Drew's salary had been cut by 20 per cent in 1933 as part of the government's across-the-board economy program; the other person rumoured to have been considered as commissioner was another 'Liberal stalwart,' Lewis Duncan; see Toronto *Mail and Empire*, 3 October 1934.
60 Toronto *Daily Star*, 3 October 1934; PAO, M.F. Hepburn, Corr., box 177, Press release re OSC, n.d. [10 October 1934]
61 Toronto *Globe*, 5 October 1934
62 *FP*, 20 October 1934
63 *Border Cities Star*, 16, 17 October 1934. The superintendent of insurance said that Walkinshaw's suspension was only routine and not for cause.
64 Toronto *Globe*, 12 October 1934; *FP*, 10, 17 November, 1 December 1934
65 PAO, M.F. Hepburn, Corr., box 190, McCullagh to Hepburn, 11 January 1935; NAC, TSE Records, MB, 24 October 1934; 23 April, 23 July 1935 (quoted).
66 Saywell, '*Just Call Me Mitch*,' 240–7
67 *FP*, 25 July 1936
68 PAO, Hepburn Papers, Private, 1937 Budget Address, Godfrey to Hepburn, 17 March 1937. I am indebted to J.T. Saywell for bringing this letter to my attention.

Chapter 12: Challenges

1 David Cruise and Alison Griffiths, *Fleecing the Lamb: The Inside Story of the Vancouver Stock Exchange* (Vancouver, 1987), 50
2 PABC, AG Corr., file S-309-1-G, Garrett to VSE, 27 May 1933; *FP*, 8 July 1933
3 PABC, AG Corr., file S-309-1-G, Memorandum from Garrett to AG [also sent to the premier], 14 June 1933; *FP*, 8 July 1933
4 PABC, AG Corr., file S-309-1-V, Jukes to Pooley, 25 July 1933
5 Ibid., Cosgrove to Garrett, 7 July 1933, Personal; Memorandum from H.E. Landman to AG, 19 July 1933; Pooley to Cosgrove, 20 July 1933; Pooley to Jukes, 28 July 1933
6 Ibid., Cosgrove to AG, 2 August, 16 December 1933

7 Ibid., Cosgrove to AG, 10 November, 16 December 1933 (with Garrett's minute); Memorandum from Garrett to AG, 8 December 1933

8 Ibid., file S-309-2, Memorandum from Garrett to AG, 11 December 1933

9 Ibid., Memorandum from Garrett to AG, 11 December 1933 (quoted); ibid., file S-309-1-G, Memorandum from Garrett to AG, 13 February 1934; Sloan to Ontario AG W.H. Price, 21 February 1934

10 *FP*, 7, 21 July, 4, 11, 25 August 1934; PABC, PP, 1934, file A-36–D, A.W. Ryder to Pattullo, 29 June 1934; Pattullo to Ryder, 30 June 1934; ibid., AG Corr., file S-309-1-W, Memorandum from Garrett to AG, 12 July, 22 August 1934

11 British Columbia, *Statutes*, 1930, c. 64; *St. John v. Fraser; Bartley and Co. et al. v. Russell*, 49 *British Columbia Reports* (1934–5), 302, 274

12 PABC, VSE MB, 8 January 1935; ibid., AG Corr., file SA-309-1-R, Memorandum from Garrett re Bill to Amend the Securities Act, 20 March 1935; *FP*, 6 April 1935

13 *Bartley and Company, Inc., Erdofy and Benson v. Russell; St. John and the Vancouver Stock and Bond Company Limited v. Fraser and the Attorney-General of British Columbia*, 49 *British Columbia Reports* (1934–5), 502, quoting G.W. Craig, KC (for Bartley) at 503–4 and Farris, KC at 505

14 Ibid., quoting McCrossan, KC (for Fraser) at 506–7

15 Ibid., quoting Martin at 520, 515, 517 and Macdonald at 526

16 Ibid., quoting Macdonald (quoting Fraser) at 531 and at 530, 531, 536

17 Ibid., quoting McPhillips at 520; *FP*, 2 February 1935, quoting McPhillips.

18 *Local Government Board v. Arlidge* (1915), *Appeal Cases*, 138

19 *George St. John and the Vancouver Stock and Bond Company Limited v. George L. Fraser, Supreme Court Reports* (1935), 441; quoting Davis (quoting Dunfermline) at 451 and 453–4, 452

20 Ibid.; Davis is quoted at 445, 447, 446

21 PABC, AG Corr., file S-309-1-W, M.E. Salt to Deputy AG E. Pepler, 11 July 1935; clipping from *Western Canada Mining News*, 24 July 1935; ibid., VSE MB, 16, 17 July, 4, 20 September 1935

22 PABC, AG Corr., file S-309-1-N, Memorandum from G.L. Fraser to AG re Investigation of Nicola Mines and Metals Co., 4 September 1935

23 Ibid.; *FP*, 20 July 1935

24 PABC, AG Corr., file S-309-1-R, Memorandum from Garrett to AG, 26 August 1935; Memorandum from Sloan to Garrett, 29 August 1935

25 Ibid., PP, 1935–6, file A-36–D, Text of address to Mining Institute, University of Washington, Seattle, 22 January 1936, and reply by Norman.

26 Ibid., AG Corr., file S-309-1-G, Memorandum from Garrett to AG, 9 April 1936

27 Ibid., Farris, Farris, Stultz, Bull and Farris to AG, 19 May, 9 June 1936 (both quoted); Memorandum from Garrett to AG, 21 May 1936

28 *FP*, 17 October 1936

29 Ibid., 30 January 1937, quoting Godfrey's speech of 18 March 1935
30 PAO, George Drew Papers, scrapbook, 1934, clippings from Toronto *Globe*,
    18 October 1934, Toronto *Mail and Empire*, 20 October 1934, Ottawa *Evening
    Journal*, 23 October 1934; SEC, FOIA #90-1128, Godfrey to J.J. Burns, 17
    December 1934 (Burns replied that this was 'a most ingenious method of coping
    with an insidious social evil' but noted that the U.S. constitution and the authority of
    the SEC rendered such a remedy impossible there); ibid. Burns to Godfrey, 30
    January 1935
31 *FP*, 3 (quoted), 24 November 1934; 18 January 1936
32 Ibid., 20, 27 October, 1 December 1934
33 PAO, M.F. Hepburn, Corr., box 229, James E. Day to Hepburn, 24 October 1934,
    Personal and Confidential; R.H. Elmhirst to Day, 14 November 1934
34 *Report of the Ontario Securities Commission in the Matter of an Investigation into
    the Gunnar Gold Mines Limited*, by John M. Godfrey (Toronto, 12 February 1935).
35 *FP*, 15, 22 December 1934; 2 February (quoted), 30 March 1935
36 MUA, MSE Records, MCM MB, 14 February, 20 March 1928; 21 January 1930;
    10 March 1931 (quoted); 15 August, 1 September, 27 October, 7 December 1932;
    4 July 1933
37 Ibid., 31 January 1933; 10 February 1934
38 Ibid., 10 March 1931 (quoted); 27 October 1932; 31 January (quoted), 19 December
    1933; 8 January 1934 (quoted).
39 Ibid., 2 January, 20 March, 22 May, 5 June, 15, 27 November 1934
40 *FP*, 5 January, 2 February 1935; MUA, MSE Records, MCM MB, 3 January 1935,
    including Amyot to MCM, 17 December 1934; NAC, TSE Records, MB, 8 January
    1935
41 MUA, MSE Records, MCM MB, 14, 21 March, 5, 11 April 1935; NAC, TSE
    Records, MB, 11, 12 March, 9, 30 July, 8 October, 18 December 1935
42 *FP*, 5, 19 January, 23 March 1935; NAC, TSE Records, MB, 15 January 1935
43 *FP*, 3 August 1935; 28 March 1936; NAC, TSE Records, MB, 5 September 1935;
    6 January 1936

Chapter 13: Revival Stalled

1 Toronto *Globe and Mail*, 22 March 1937
2 William Dendy and William Kilbourn, *Toronto Observed: Its Architecture, Patrons
   and History* (Toronto, 1986), 226–8; and see also Tim Morawetz, 'Art Deco
   Becomes Moderne,' in *Designing the Exchange: Essays Commemorating the
   Opening of the Design Exchange* (n.p., 1994), 35–49, where the frieze is also
   discussed by Rosemary Donegan in 'Legitimate Modernism,' 51–7, with the source
   of the joke pictured at 57.

3 The trading room and the murals are discussed in both Morawetz, 'Art Deco Becomes Moderne,' and in Donegan, 'Legitimate Modernism,' 57–67.

4 *Globe and Mail*, 19 March 1937 (quoted); Toronto *Daily Star*, 19 March 1937; the two papers respectively devoted ten and seven pages of articles and advertising to the TSE and its new building the day before the banquet.

5 *Globe and Mail*, 19 March 1937

6 NAC, TSE Records, MB, 24 September, 12, 13, 27 November 1935; 27 March, 29 September 1936; 16 March 1937; *FP*, 15 August 1936; 6 February, 20 March 1937

7 *FP*, 8 August 1936

8 Ibid., 1 February 1936

9 The more staid Montreal Stock Exchange normally required 25 per cent of shares to be in the hands of the public, and the Montreal Curb Market 20 per cent for industrials and 10 per cent for mines; see Carl Bergithon, *The Stock Exchange, with Special Reference to the Montreal Stock Exchange and the Montreal Curb Market* (Montreal, 1940), 23–4.

10 *FP*, 20 March, 27 November 1937

11 NAC, TSE Records, MB, 8 October, 18 December 1935

12 Ibid., 15 January, 20 March, 12 May 1936

13 NAC, TSE Records, MB, 2 February, 19 April 1937; *FP*, 1 May 1937

14 NAC, TSE Records, MB, 28 November, 6 December 1938; Bank of Canada Archives, file SD, series N, vol. 3, TSE president Frank G. Lawson to Graham Towers, 28 November, 9 December 1938; MSE chair Grant Johnston to Lawson, 29 November 1938. These records were drawn to my attention by J.T. Saywell.

15 NAC, TSE Records, MB, 15 January 1936

16 *FP*, 4 May 1935; NAC, TSE Records, MB, 30 April, 10, 18 December 1935. A few days later Trebilcock reported to the board that Colling had started predicting the future course of the grain market, and the broker had to be warned that commodity news must be treated the same way as securities markets; see ibid., 18 December 1935.

17 *FP*, 4 April, 16 May 1936. Herbert and Byrne did not give up easily, and at the annual meeting they sought an option on 30,000 shares, which was granted after the proxy votes cast by the Neelands faction were disqualified on the technicality that the proxy form used was for a federal rather than an Ontario company. Herbert and Byrne also got themselves re-elected to the board, but the resulting outcry led to the holding of another meeting, which reversed these decisions; see ibid., 25 April 1936

18 Ibid., 17 April, 8, 15 May 1937

19 Ibid., 1 August, 5 December 1936

20 Ibid., 1 August, 14 November, 5 December 1936

21 Ibid., 5 December 1936

22 Ibid., 19 December 1936

23 Ibid., 5 (quoted), 26 December 1936; 24 April 1937

24 Ibid., 28 March, 4 April 1936; SEC, FOIA #90–1128, Godfrey to J.F. Healey, 6 April 1936

25 Ibid., 13 June, 8, 22, 29 August 1936; PABC, VSE MB, 27 October, 17, 24 November 1936

26 Dominion Bureau of Statistics, *Canada Year Book, 1937* (Ottawa, 1937), 804

27 *FP*, 5, 12 December 1936

28 *FP*, 9, 16, 23, 30 January, 6 February 1937; interview with Chalmers by J.T. Saywell, October, 1972, 14, courtesy of the interviewer.

29 SEC, FOIA #90–1128, Godfrey to Landis, 15 December 1936; 17 February 1937 (quoted); Landis to Godfrey, 11 February 1937; Godfrey to SEC general counsel Allen E. Throop, 11 February 1937, attaching notice from OSC registrar W.A. Brant, 14 January 1937 banning sales of issues not qualified in the United States.

30 *FP*, 30 January, 13 February 1937

31 *FP*, 13 February 1937. In the summer of 1936 it was noted that some boiler room operators had discovered that more sobersided sales literature actually worked better than traditional high-pressure pitches, and some promoters had even felt compelled to invest some of the money which they raised from the public in developing properties in order to avoid trouble with the OSC; see ibid., 8 August 1936.

32 Ibid., 30 January 1937

33 *Globe and Mail*, 24 February 1937; on the Abitibi deal and the controversy see J.T. Saywell, *'Just Call Me Mitch': The Life of Mitchell F. Hepburn* (Toronto, 1991), 98–9, 117–9, 295–6. I am indebted to Professor Saywell for bringing to my attention material on the 1937 revision of the Securities Act.

34 Ontario, *Statutes*, 1937, 1st session, c. 69, s. 2, 3, 6; *Globe and Mail*, 20 March 1937, quoting Roebuck.

35 *Globe and Mail*, 20 March 1937 (quoting Macauley), 24 March 1937 (quoting Hepburn); *Manitoba Miner*, 1 April 1937 (quoting Drew).

36 *FP* denounced the rest of the press for failing to join in its condemnation, presumably a veiled reference to the fact that the *Globe and Mail* was now controlled by Hepburn's close friend George McCullagh, who as a former broker might have been expected to criticize the amendments, while Joseph E. Atkinson's Toronto *Daily Star* was, as always, staunchly pro-Liberal; see *FP*, 3 April 1937.

37 NAC, J.W. Dafoe Papers, General Corr., 1937–8, vol. 10, Sifton to Victor Sifton, 8 April 1937

38 *FP*, 6 November 1937

39 Ibid., 13 November 1937; 29 January 1938

40 Ibid., 18 February 1938. Whitehead had graduated from Osgoode Hall in 1915 and then served in the Canadian Expeditionary Force for three years, before joining the law firm of Tilley, Johnston, which he left in 1923 to become the legal secretary of the church union committee overseeing the creation of the United Church of Canada.

With that task completed in 1927, he joined Massey-Harris, where he served until entering the civil service.

41 NAC, TSE Records, MB, 12 April 1938; *FP*, 16 April, 29 October 1938
42 NAC, TSE Records, MB, 26, 27 April, 2 May, 28 November 1938
43 *FP*, 18 March 1939
44 Ibid., 8 April, 16 December 1939
45 Dominion Bureau of Statistics, *Canada Year Book*, 1938 (Ottawa, 1938), 827; David Cruise and Alison Griffiths, *Fleecing the Lamb: The Inside Story of the Vancouver Stock Exchange* (Vancouver, 1987), 53
46 PABC, AG Corr., file S-309-1-G, Memorandum from Garrett to AG, 6 November 1936; *FP*, 21 November 1936
47 Ibid., file S-309-1-V, Pearson to AG Gordon Sloan, 20 January, 4 February 1937; Memorandum from Garrett to Sloan, 29 January 1937; Garrett to VSE secretary, 5 February 1937
48 Ibid., file S-309-1-H, VSE to AG, 23 February 1937; Deputy AG Eric Pepler to Fraser, 24 February 1937; ibid., VSE MB, 23 April 1937; *FP*, 6 March 1937
49 PABC, PP, 1937–8, file A-20a-D, Deputy Minister of Mines John F. Walker to Minister George S. Pearson, 19 April 1937
50 PABC, AG Corr., file S-390-1-H, Report upon Trading in the Shares of Hedley Amalgamated Gold Mines Limited from January 7, 1937, to February 23, 1937, by G.L. Fraser, 3 April 1937; *FP*, 17 April 1937
51 PABC, AG Corr., file S-309-1-H, H.H. Stewart to G.L. Fraser, 4 May 1937; Report on Hedley Amalgamated Gold Mines (N.P.L.) by G.L. Fraser, 5 May 1937; Press statement by Pattullo, 8 May 1937; *FP*, 15 May 1937. Both accused ultimately received prison sentences for their activities; see *FP*, 7 May 1938.
52 PABC, AG Corr., file S-309-1-H, Memorandum from Garrett to AG, 7 April 1937; ibid., VSE MB, 9 April, 10 May, 1937; *FP*, 17 April 1937
53 Cruise and Griffiths, *Fleecing the Lamb*, 54–5. PABC, PP, 1937–8, file A-20a-D, is filled with material designed to absolve the Department of Mines for failing to act sooner, which suggests that Garrett was right.
54 PABC, AG Corr., file S-309-1-V, Memorandum from Garrett to AG, 7 May 1937
55 PABC, PP, 1937–8, file A-36-D, Garrett to Sloan, 29 March 1937; ibid., AG Corr., file S-309-1-H, Press statement by Pattullo, 8 May 1937; *FP*, 8 May, 26 June 1937
56 *FP*, 22 May 1937; Dominion Bureau of Statistics, *Canada Year Book, 1938*, 827; PABC, PP, 1937–8, file A-36-D, Memorandum from H.G. Garrett to Premier T.D. Pattullo, 30 June 1937
57 Margaret Ormsby, *British Columbia: A History* (Vancouver, 1958), 465; *FP*, 26 June 1937; PABC, PP, 1937–8, file A-32-D, Norman to Pattullo, 5 July 1937, enclosing text of article submitted to Vancouver *Sun*. Norman was the former mining editor of the paper who had recently moved to a similar post with the *Globe and Mail*. For an

account of the Julian affair, see Jules Tygiel, *The Great Los Angeles Swindle: Oil, Stocks and Scandal during the Roaring Twenties* (New York, 1994).

58 The JMC was created in the mid-1930s by the Mining Bureau of the Vancouver Board of Trade, the BC Chamber of Mines, the BC branch of the Canadian Institute of Mining and Metallurgy, and the VSE, each of which appointed three delegates to its board.

59 PABC, AG Corr., file S-309-4, F.M. Black, JMC, to Pattullo, 15 July 1937; ibid., VSE MB, 8, 21 June 1937 (all quoted).

60 PABC, AG Corr., file S-309-1-G, Grossman to Wismer, 8 July 1937, Wismer to Grossman, 9 July 1937; J. Edward Sears to Wismer, 7 October 1937

61 PABC, PP, 1937–8, file A-36-D, Memorandum from Garrett to Pattullo, 30 June 1937; Memorandum from Walker to Garrett, 8 July 1937

62 SEC, FOIA #90–1128, Day Karr to DeBeck, 5 August 1937

63 *FP*, 13 November 1937

64 Ibid., 11 December 1937. Victor Spencer, Ben Smith, and David Sloan were the original promoters; C.D. Keeding of Toronto replaced Sloan after his death.

65 *FP*, 13 November, 4 December 1937; British Columbia, *Statutes*, 1937, c. 69

66 PABC, VSE MB, 11 January 1938; *FP*, 26 February 1938

67 PABC, AG Corr., GR 1723, file S-338-3, Memorandum from DeBeck to AG, 5 April 1938; Memorandum from DeBeck, n.d. [1938].

68 PABC, AG Corr., GR 1723, file S-338-3, Memorandum from DeBeck to AG, 28 February 1938 (quoted); *FP*, 27 May 1938. Miller was charged along with J.W.R. McLeod, president of Hargal Oil and Freehold Oil, and at the same time David B. Manley, who had taken over Miller, Court and Manley, was accused of the theft of 330 shares of Bralorne Mines stock.

69 Glenbow-Alberta Archives, ASE Records, CSE MB, 1 November, 13, 28 December 1932; 11 June, 11 July 1933; 12 February 1937

70 Ibid., 12 February, 6, 13, 20, 27 April, 1, 25 June, 5 July, 31 August, 8, 15 September, 8 October 1937

71 PAM, WSE MB, 10 June 1930; 16 February, 9 June 1931; *FP*, 19 March 1931 (quoted).

72 PAM, WSE MB, 9 June 1931

73 Ibid., 16, 23 May, 6, 13 June 1933; 15 June, 26 September (quoted) 1934

74 Ibid., 22, 26 June, 22 November 1934; 10 January 1935

75 Ibid., 29 October 1936; this MB also contains the minutes of the listing committee.

76 PAM, AG, GR 950, file 138, Cottingham to Major, 4 January 1937 (quoted); same to same, 9 January 1937; ibid., WSE MB, 7 January 1937

77 PAM, AG, GR 950, file 138, Cottingham to Major, 4 January 1937 (quoted); Dunwoody, Nicholl and Saul and Co., accountants, to AG W.J. Major, 13 February

1937, Confidential (quoted); Crown attorney Orville M. Kay to Major, 16 February 1937
78 PAM, WSE MB, 24 March, 26 April, 8 June 1937; 14 October, 23 November 1938; 4 January, 14 February, 4 April 1938

Chapter 14: Uncertainty

1 H. Blair Neatby, *William Lyon Mackenzie King, 1932–9: The Prism of Unity* (Toronto, 1976), 187–9
2 F.H. Leacy, ed., *Historical Statistics of Canada*, 2nd ed. (Ottawa, 1983), H1–18, H19–34; F1–13. In 1936 the GNP had grown by $600 million, and in 1939 it rose only $350 million. On the 1937 recession, see Charles P. Kindelberger, *The World in Depression, 1929–1939* (Berkeley, 1973), 271–6.
3 On the slow acceptance of Keynesian ideas in Canada, see Robert B. Bryce, *Maturing in Hard Times: Canada's Department of Finance through the Great Depression* (Kingston and Montreal, 1986), 115–21; Bryce, who had studied with Keynes at Cambridge, joined Finance in 1938 just after the National Employment Commission proposed a series of expansionary initiatives that were largely rejected by the cabinet.
4 NAC, TSE Records, MB, 13 September 1938; *FP*, 1 October 1938
5 John Brooks, *Once in Golconda: A True Drama of Wall Street, 1920–38* (New York, 1969), 241–87
6 PAO, Legislative Assembly records, series I-7–E, box 1, R. Leighton Foster to F.V. Johns, 31 October 1934; *FP*, 10 November 1934; NAC, TSE Records, MB, 14 November 1934
7 Canada, Royal Commission on Price Spreads and Mass Buying, *Report* (Ottawa, 1935), 27–38 and appendix 4: 349–63
8 Ibid., 39–45
9 *Canadian Annual Review*, 1935–6, 31–2; *FP*, 13 July 1935
10 E.P. Neufeld, *The Financial System of Canada, Its Growth and Development* (Toronto, 1927), 537; *FP*, 15 June, 13 July, 14 September 1935. The Ontario Companies Information Act, which became law in 1934, allowed the province to pass regulations to expand the disclosure requirements for prospectuses, and the regulations under the Securities Act already forbade trading in a newly-issued security until a prospectus was delivered to a purchaser, but the province did not require such a comprehensive annual report as Ottawa did.
11 NAC, TSE Records, MB, 9 April, 21 May 1936. The IDA was the new name for the Investment Bankers Association, which had to be rechristened following the 1934 revisions to the Bank Act.

12 *FP*, 27 July, 3 August 1935
13 Canada, *Dominion-Provincial Conferences, November 3–10, 1927, December 9–13, 1935, January 14–15, 1941 / Conférences fédérales-provinciales, du 3 au 10 novembre 1927, du 9 au 13 decembre 1935, les 14 et 15 janvier 1941* (Ottawa, 1951), 'Dominion-Provincial Conference 1935, Record of Proceedings, Ottawa, December 9–13, 1935,' 38, 72
14 PABC, PP, 1935–6, file A-36-d, Memorandum from Garrett to Premier Pattullo, 1 October 1936
15 Minutes of the first meeting of the Dominion-Provincial Committee on Company Law, 3–7 November 1936 (typescript in the author's possession).
16 *FP*, 12 December 1936; 20 March 1937; SEC, FOIA #90-1128, Godfrey to Landis, 15 December 1936; PAM, AG, GR 950, file 138, Report of the Conference on Securities Law Administration, 8–13 March 1937
17 Minutes of the 2nd Annual Conference of Administrators of the Provincial Securities Acts and Officials of the Dominion Government, 24–7 May 1938 (typescript in the author's possession); *FP*, 31 December 1938
18 Joel Seligman, *The Transformation of Wall Street: A History of the Securities and Exchange Commission and Modern Corporate Finance* (Boston, 1982), 93
19 Carl Bergithon, *The Stock Exchange, with Special Reference to the Montreal Stock Exchange and the Montreal Curb Market* (Montreal, 1940), 58, notes, 'In earlier years the amount of margin required had been left to the discretion of individual members, the rates often varying.'
20 BCA, file SD, series N, vol. 1, copy of MSE Committee ruling re by-law XXIV, section 10, 25 June 1935, Confidential; these valuable Bank of Canada records were brought to my attention by J.T. Saywell.
21 Ibid., Memorandum to the deputy governor re stock margins, 19 February 1936; Child to Towers, 10 March 1936, enclosing MSE committee ruling, 9 March 1936, Confidential; same to same, 13 July 1936
22 BCA, file SD, series N, vol. 1, Towers to Child, 17 July 1936; NAC, TSE Records, MB, 11 August, 9, 15 September 1936
23 BCA, file SD, series N, vol. 1, Memorandum from E. Dricker to deputy governor, 2 November 1936
24 NAC, TSE Records, MB, 27 October, 17, 25 November 1936; BCA, file SD, series N, vol. 1, N.C. Urquhart to Logan, 31 October 1936, H.B. Housser to deputy governor, 12 November 1936; Towers to H.C. Beatty, Trust Companies Section, Montreal Board of Trade, 22 December 1936 (quoted).
25 BCA, file SD, series N, vol. 3, Memorandum from Towers of conversation with Urquhart, 24 June 1937; ibid., vol. 2, CBA secretary A.W. Rogers to general managers, 28 July 1937 (quoted); Towers to Rogers, 13 August 1937; A.J. Trebilcock to Towers, 18 August 1937; Memorandum of conversation with Messrs.

Urquhart, Lawson, McKenna and Johnston of the Toronto and Montreal Stock
Exchanges, 29 October 1937 (quoted re MSE's views of TSE's laxity over rule
enforcement); NAC, TSE Records, MB, 22 June, 7, 13 (quoted), 20, 27 July, 10,
17 August 1937

26 BCA, file SD, series N, vol. 2, Memorandum from Towers of conversation with
Messrs. Urquhart, Lawson, McKenna and Johnston of the Toronto and Montreal
Stock Exchanges, 29 October 1937; Towers to Thomas Bradshaw, 29 October 1937,
Personal (both quoted).

27 BCA, file SD, series N, vol. 2, Towers to Bradshaw, 29 October 1937, Personal
(quoted); NAC TSE Records, MB, 26, 28 October, 2 November, 14 December 1937;
FP, 26 February 1938

28 NAC, TSE Records, MB, 28 November, 6 December 1938; BCA, file SD, series N,
vol. 3, TSE president Frank G. Lawson to Towers, 28 November, 9 December 1938;
MSE chair Grant Johnston to Towers, 29 November 1938

29 NAC, TSE Records, MB, 13, 27 September, 4 October 1938; *FP*, 2 October 1938

30 NAC, TSE Records, MB, 21, 25 April, 9, 16 May, 1939; *FP*, 22 May 1939, which
also reported that U.S. treasury secretary Henry Morgenthau and SEC Chair
Marriner Eccles had convened a meeting of exchange officials to consider the
American response in the event of war.

31 NAC, TSE Records, MB, 9, 22, 29 August, 1, 2, 4, 5, 6, 7 September 1939; *FP*,
9 September 1939

32 On the creation of the FECB, see Joseph Schull, *The Great Scot: A Biography of
Donald Gordon* (Montreal and Kingston, 1979), 34–41.

33 NAC, TSE Records, MB, 26 September, 3 October, 25 November, 22 December
1939. *FP*, 30 December 1939, reported that industrials between $1 and $5 had
previously paid a uniform commission, but now this would increase with each $1 of
the selling price, while shares selling from $50 to $125 had been split into three
groups at $25 intervals, the first bearing the current commission and stocks over $75
and $100 paying more.

Photo Credits

Index